Postcolonial Ecocriticism

D1610144

This second edition of the foundational work *Postcolonial Ecocriticism* has been fully updated to consider new developments since its original publication in 2010. Graham Huggan and Helen Tiffin examine relationships between humans, animals and the environment in postcolonial literary texts, newly addressing such key areas as climate change studies, disability studies and queer ecology. Considering the postcolonial first from an environmental then a zoocritical perspective, the book looks at:

- narratives of development in postcolonial writing
- entitlement and belonging in the pastoral genre
- colonialist 'asset stripping' and the Christian mission
- the politics of eating and representations of cannibalism
- animality and spirituality
- sentimentality and anthropomorphism
- the place of the human and the animal in a 'posthuman' world.

Re-visiting the work of authors as diverse as J.M. Coetzee, Joseph Conrad, Daniel Defoe, Jamaica Kincaid and V.S. Naipaul, this landmark text offers a comprehensive introduction to a dynamic subject area, usefully adding a select annotated bibliography at the end.

Graham Huggan is Chair of Commonwealth and Postcolonial Literatures at the University of Leeds, Yorkshire, UK.

Helen Tiffin was formerly Canada Research Chair in English and Post-Colonial Studies at Queen's University, Ontario, Canada, and is now Honorary Professor of Post-Colonial and Animal Studies at the University of Wollongong, NSW, Australia.

Postcolonial Ecocriticism
Literature, Animals, Environment

Second edition

Graham Huggan and Helen Tiffin

Routledge
Taylor & Francis Group

LONDON AND NEW YORK

First published 2010, this edition published 2015
by Routledge
2 Park Square, Milton Park, Abingdon, Oxon OX14 4RN

and by Routledge
711 Third Avenue, New York, NY 10017

*Routledge is an imprint of the Taylor & Francis Group, an informa
business*

British Library Cataloguing-in-Publication Data
A catalogue record for this book is available from the British Library

Library of Congress Cataloging-in-Publication Data
Huggan, Graham, 1958-
Postcolonial ecocriticism : literature, animals, environment / Graham
Huggan and Helen Tiffin. -- Second edition.
pages cm
Includes bibliographical references and index.
1. Ecocriticism. 2. Human ecology in literature. 3. Animals in
literature. 4. Human-animal relationships in literature.
5. Postcolonialism in literature. I. Tiffin, Helen. II. Title.
PN98.E36H85 2015
809'.9336--dc23
2014039647

ISBN: 978-1-138-78418-5 (hbk)
ISBN: 978-1-138-78419-2 (pbk)
ISBN: 978-1-315-76834-2 (ebk)

Typeset in Sabon
by Taylor & Francis Books

MIX
Paper from
responsible sources
FSC
www.fsc.org   FSC® C013604   Printed and bound by CPI Group (UK) Ltd, Croydon, CR0 4YY

Contents

Preface

The first edition of *Postcolonial Ecocriticism* came out in 2010. It was in good company. That year also saw the publication of Pablo Mukherjee's *Postcolonial Environments*, Laura Wright's *Wilderness into Civilized Shapes*, and Bonnie Roos and Alex Hunt's *Postcolonial Green*; while 2011 would see Rob Nixon's *Slow Violence and the Environmentalism of the Poor*, Byron Caminero-Santangelo and Garth Myers' *Environment at the Margins*, and Elizabeth DeLoughrey and George Handley's *Postcolonial Ecologies* – all accomplished additions to a list that has grown larger, and more internally differentiated, with each passing year. To be sure, not all of these books match the more restricted remit of postcolonial ecocriticism; but if anything they have broadened its horizons, taking both environmental and animal criticism (whose boundaries were already porous) in new and exciting directions that indicate that the field is in a boom phase – one which all the current evidence suggests will continue to flourish even as the by now all-too-familiar critical reservations surrounding both postcolonialism and ecocriticism have never seriously declined. Not so long ago, postcolonial ecocriticism was being described as 'nascent' (Wright 2010: 175). That is certainly no longer the case today; indeed, some practitioners in the field are now dismissively seen as mainstream, with the qualifier 'critical' serving to confirm this, and with more radical voices, e.g. those in critical animal studies, issuing dire warnings about scholastic indulgence and the anaesthetising logic of the academic 'corporate-bureaucratic machine' (Best 2009).[1]

If academic work will always run the risk of being institutionally co-opted, it is similarly vulnerable to accusations of inconsistency. *Postcolonial Ecocriticism* was seen by some, either as having failed to make good on its own provisional claims to critical interventionism, or as being bewilderingly torn between methods derived from the 'anthropocentric' legacies of eco-materialism and the more 'ecocentric' alternatives offered by deep green views of ecological interconnectedness that directly challenge human-centred perspectives on the world (Carrigan 2011; Nichols 2011; O'Brien 2009; Vadde 2011). The first criticism is fair only to the extent that postcolonial ecocriticism's spirited attempt to 'strike a balance between the study of literature, the application of science, and the role of social activism' (Wright 2010: 175) simultaneously recognises that that balance is never likely to be achieved. The second is not really a criticism at all: more the recognition of a constitutive tension that has marked postcolonial ecocriticism since its inception, and which continues to characterise it as a methodologically and philosophically eclectic research field. Similar tensions can be found after all in both postcolonial studies and environmental studies; and they loom larger still within the capacious field of animal studies, the various and sometimes warring strands within which demonstrate a dizzying plurality of sociological and psychological perspectives, posthumanist and ecofeminist approaches, and postmodern and postcolonial theoretical trends (Best 2009; Waldau 2013).

The so-called *animal turn* in humanities and social sciences has inevitably informed recent developments in postcolonial ecocriticism, one of whose tasks is to ask what makes us human in the first place – what elevates us above other animals, or rather what we arrogantly believe gives us the right to separate their lives from ours (Montgomery and Kalof 2012; Weil 2010). It is easy to see why the animal turn might attract postcolonial critics; for, as Kari Weil puts it, animal studies 'stretches to the limit questions of language, of epistemology, and of ethics that have [long since] been raised in [...] postcolonial studies: how to understand and give voice to others or to experiences that seem impervious to our understanding; how to attend to difference without appropriating it or distorting it; how to hear and acknowledge what it may not be possible to say' (2010: 4). And it is equally easy to understand why a second methodological and philosophical shift – let us call it the *ecological turn* – has lent a materialist edge to postcolonial ecocriticism, which is now more likely than it was to engage with the planetary dimensions of ecological crisis, and to recognise that this crisis requires urgent practical action rather than just a sophisticated critical re-articulation of theoretical concerns (DeLoughrey and Handley 2011; Heise 2008).

At the same time, the ecological turn requires that postcolonial ecocriticism operate as 'more than a simple extension of postcolonial methodologies into the realm of the human material world; it must [also] reckon with the ways in which ecology does not always work with the frames of human time and political interest' (DeLoughrey and Handley 2011: 4). One obvious frame is that of global climate change, which stresses the mutual entanglement of human and natural history, but also suggests at another level that the planet, far from being shaped and determined by human beings, is entirely indifferent to human interests and concerns (Chakrabarty 2009; Spivak 2003). Global warming, recently billed as 'the ecological trauma of our age' (Morton 2013: 9), posits a huge challenge to both postcolonial criticism, which has mainly been driven by (human) ontological considerations, and ecocriticism, which has tended to fall back on place-based notions of 'nature' and 'environment' that now find themselves confronted by a hyper-phenomenon that straddles vast expanses of geographical space and operates across multiple historical scales (Chakrabarty 2012; Clark 2010; Morton 2013).

However, *contra* excitable eco-philosophers like Timothy Morton and Timothy Clark, global warming neither marks the 'closure' of place-specific modes of ecocriticism (Clark 2010) nor spells an 'end' to conventional, environmentally coded understandings of 'world' and 'nature' (Morton 2007, 2013); rather, it requires a broader *ecological* conception of natural-cultural relations on several different levels – including the planetary level – than has tended to be the case in much ecocriticism until now. Postcolonial approaches remain helpful here in ensuring that the ongoing struggle for global environmental justice is pursued; that cultural differences are taken into account in building bioregional models of sustainability and resilience; and that new ways of thinking about the human – also thinking *beyond* the human – are developed that recognise the imbrication of social and ecological factors in what Rob Nixon calls today's 'high age of neoliberalism' (2011: 17): an age characterised by the conspicuously uneven distribution of natural resources, the forced displacement of animals and people, and routine abuses of transnational corporate power.

Much of this vocabulary – 'justice', 'sustainability', 'resilience', etc. – is drawn from the lexicon of *political ecology*, which looks (in Bryant's classic late 1990s definition) at the fraught 'political dynamics surrounding material and discursive struggles with the environment in the [contemporary] Third World' (1998: 89; see also Robbins 2011; Peet, Robbins and Watts 2010). But while political ecology covers a wide range of social science disciplines, it often excludes humanities subjects. These are included in another relatively recent formation, *environmental humanities*, which seeks to counteract technocratic approaches to environmental management by emphasising the historical depth and cultural specificity of current environmental problems, and by paying close attention to the moral and ethical relations that obtain between humans and non-humans in an ecologically threatened world (Robin 2008). Postcolonial ecocriticism might best be described today as a branch of environmental humanities that is heavily influenced by, but non-identical with, political ecology. To see postcolonial ecocriticism as a politically oriented branch of environmental humanities is – as with postcolonial and environmental studies as a whole – to open it up to a range of different disciplines, in which literature and history, the formative disciplines for environmental humanities, play a significant but by no means defining role.

That said, literature continues to play the dominant part in post-colonial ecocriticism, and it will continue to do so in the second edition of this book. This raises an issue that continues to influence the reception of postcolonial ecocriticism, namely its (for some) narrow focus on representation and the 'close reading' of literary and other cultural texts. An excellent recent response to this is in the coda to Jennifer Wenzel's essay in DeLoughrey and Handley's *Postcolonial Ecologies*. Here, Wenzel makes a plea for postcolonial ecocriticism as an interventionist discourse which requires that 'we distinguish and understand the relationship between [...] the interventions made by the literary texts we read [and] the interventions of our critical acts' (2011: 150). As Wenzel goes on to explain, 'the texts we read make their interventions not as empirical evidence of ecological crisis nor as ready-made blueprints for action [...] but rather through their particularly literary mediations' (2011: 151). Our task as critics is to pay close attention to such mediations, which involves cultivating a sense both of our own 'worldliness' as readers and of the larger, society- and history-embracing 'worldliness' of the literary text (Wenzel 2011: 151; see also Said 1983).

In this second edition of *Postcolonial Ecocriticism*, as we did in the first, we share Wenzel's Said-inspired view of the capacity of writing and reading as 'worldly' critical activities, as modes of engagement that may not necessarily lead to direct action but raise consciousness of its possibilities and draw attention to the urgency of the causes they seek, however obliquely or even ambivalently, to present. Perhaps postcolonial ecocriticism, like the diverse literature it explores, slides between 'advocacy' and 'activist' roles without ever fully identifying with either of these. Perhaps it needs, as Rob Nixon suggests, more capacious understandings of 'writing' and 'reading' in a digital age in which '"writer" has become a demotic designation: less grand, less glamorous, and more likely to involve a mongrel blend of word, image, and video' (2011: 279). And per-haps it requires a more pluriform conception of environmental conscious-ness and acting-in-the-world than that contained in works of imaginative literature, though one of the distinct benefits of reading literature is that it adds singularity to specificity, while another is that literature has an enduring capacity to combine multiple, often conflicting perspectives and to operate across numerous temporal and spatial scales (Attridge 2004b; Eco 2006). For Pope, the proper subject of mankind was Man; today's

'Age of Ecology' contests this (Worster 1977). Is the proper subject of postcolonial ecocriticism literature? The point is moot, but insofar as material transformation is predicated on imaginative understanding, literature and the variegated practices of writing and reading it engenders are a subject that postcolonial ecocriticism cannot do without.

Note

1 Critical animal studies (CAS) differentiates itself from mainstream animal studies (MAS), seeing the latter as being compromised by its narrow focus on the human-animal relationship and as underestimating the broad co-evolutionary principles by which nonhuman animals are 'inseparably embedded in human history and are dynamic agents in their own right' (Best 2009). Here as elsewhere (another example would be critical cosmopolitanism), the qualifying adjective 'critical' problematically suggests a morally superior view of its subject that claims the oppositional language of radical activism for its own.

Acknowledgements

Sincere thanks are due to friends and many former colleagues at Queen's University, Canada; to Steph Pfennigwerth for her dedicated and meticulous research and to Jane McGennisken for her speed, good humour and sage advice. Our grateful thanks to Ruth Blair and Kirsten Holst-Petersen for their astute comments; and to Victoria Burrows and Elle Leane for their support and encouragement. Thanks, finally, to the following: Anthony Carrigan, Liz DeLoughrey, Sabine Schlüter and Alan Ward. Short passages of Part 1, section 1 are taken from an essay originally published in *Modern Fiction Studies*: '"Greening" Postcolonialism: Ecocritical Perspectives'. Our thanks to the publisher and editors of the journal for allowing this material to be reprinted here.

Introduction

In April 2000, the American magazine *Time* published a commemorative Earth Day issue. Featuring a beaming Bill Clinton in Botswana and, more sinisterly, a series of double-page spreads advertising Ford Motor Company's commitment to the environment, the magazine duly joined the millennial rallying cry to save the planet, issued on behalf of a country that has done far less than one might reasonably expect to protect the global environment but far more than it could possibly have hoped to 'reinvent the imperial tradition for the twenty-first century' (Lazarus 2006: 20) – a country that has actively and aggressively contributed to what many now acknowledge to be the chronic endangerment of the contemporary late-capitalist world.

In a very different vein, the same year also saw a re-issue of *The Unquiet Woods*, the Indian historian Ramachandra Guha's classic account of the Chipko movement – a 1970s peasant revolt against commercial forestry practices in the Northern Indian Himalayan region which is often considered to be a paradigmatic example of those grassroots, often Third World-based, resistance movements that are sometimes bracketed under the capacious heading: the 'environmentalism of the poor' (Guha and Martinez-Alier 1997). Taking its cue from one of the movement's populist leaders, Sunderlal Bahuguna, Guha's book suggests that 'the ecological crisis in Himalaya is not an isolated event [but] has its roots in the [modern] materialistic civilization [that] makes man the butcher of Earth' (Bahuguna, quoted in Guha 2000: 179). For all that, Guha's aim is not to show how modernity *per se* has contributed to ecological destruction in twentieth-century India – still less to suggest that peasant movements like Chipko are doomed remnants of a superseded pre-modern era – but rather to outline some of the ways in which state-planned industrialisation in postcolonial India, even while it claims to practise one version or other of sustainable development, has only succeeded in 'pauperizing millions of people in the agrarian sector and diminishing the stock of plant, water and soil resources at a terrifying rate' (196).

Is there any way of reconciling the Northern environmentalisms of the rich (always potentially vainglorious and hypocritical) with the Southern environmentalisms of the poor (often genuinely heroic and authentic)? Is there any way of narrowing the ecological gap between coloniser and colonised, each of them locked into their seemingly incommensurable worlds? The opposing terms seem at once necessary and overblown, starkly distinct yet hopelessly entangled.[1] After all, in their different ways, *Time* magazine and Guha's book are *both* arguing the need to bring postcolonial and ecological issues together as a means of challenging continuing imperialist modes of social and environmental dominance; while both are suggesting, at the same time, that allegedly egalitarian terms like 'postcolonial' and 'ecological' are eminently co-optable for a variety of often far-from-egalitarian (national) state interests and (transnational) corporate-capitalist concerns.

How are we to read the burgeoning alliance between postcolonial and environmental studies, the increasing convergence of postcolonialism and ecocriticism, in such conflicted, even contradictory, contexts? In one sense, the case for 'green postcolonialism' (Huggan and Tiffin 2007) or 'postcolonial ecocriticism' (Cilano and DeLoughrey 2007) is painfully obvious.[2] As Pablo Mukherjee (2006) puts it:

> Surely, any field purporting to theorise the global conditions of colonialism and imperialism (let us call it postcolonial studies) cannot but consider the complex interplay of environmental categories such as water, land, energy, habitat, migration with political or cultural categories such as state, society, conflict, literature, theatre, visual arts. Equally, any field purporting to attach interpretative importance to environment (let us call it eco/environmental studies) must be able to trace the social, historical and material co-ordinates of categories such as forests, rivers, bio-regions and species.
>
> (144)

In another sense, however, the coming together of postcolonial and eco/environmental studies is hedged about with seemingly insurmountable problems. For one thing, the two fields are notoriously difficult to define, not least by their own practitioners; and they are not necessarily united even in their most basic interpretative methods or fundamental ideological concerns. Internal divisions – e.g. those between broadly Marxist and post-structuralist positions within postcolonial studies, or those between environmental and animal-rights activism within eco/environmental studies – are constitutive of both fields, but these may easily be glossed over in broad-based attempts to find similarities, e.g. the commitment to social and environmental justice, or differences, e.g. what Cilano and DeLoughrey (2007) call the 'unproblematized division between people (on the postcolonial side) and nature (on the ecocritical one)' (75). Large-scale distinctions based on the initially attractive view that postcolonial studies and eco/environmental studies offer mutual correctives to each other turn out on closer inspection to be perilous. The easy assertion, for instance, that the postcolonial field is inherently anthropocentric (human-centred) overlooks a long history of ecological concern in post-colonial criticism; while any number of examples could be mustered to fend off the counter-charge that eco/environmental studies privileges a white male western subject, or that it fails to factor cultural difference into supposedly universal environmental and bioethical debates. Even more subtle discriminations such as Nixon's or Lawrence Buell's may not hold up to closer critical scrutiny, while Murphy's well-intentioned calls for diversity and inclusivity are insufficiently grounded, disguising the Anglo-American biases that make their own critical pluralism possible – a common critique of ecocriticism (which is perhaps more inclusive than some of its detractors imagine) that holds, too, for postcolonial criticism (which is perhaps less inclusive than some of its advocates attest).

One way out of this morass is to insist that the proper subject of postcolonialism is colonialism, and to look accordingly for the colonial/imperial underpinnings of environmental practices in both 'colonising' and 'colonised' societies of the present and the past. Here, postcolonial ecocritics have frequently followed the lead of the influential environmental historians Alfred Crosby and Richard Grove, whose work reveals the historical embeddedness of ecology in the European imperial enterprise, without necessarily endorsing the Eurocentrism lurking behind these two authors' own critical attitudes (Tiffin 2007a). A further irony is that the flexibility of Crosby's term *ecological imperialism* – which ranges in implication and intensity from the violent appropriation of indigenous land to the ill-considered introduction of non-domestic live-stock and European agricultural practices – has tended to come at the cost of its historical specificity, either blurring the boundaries between very different forms of environmentalism or, in a move arguably character-istic of postcolonial criticism, collapsing imperialism into an all-purpose concept-metaphor that fails to distinguish between general ideologies of domination and specific socio-historical effects.

One characteristically broad understanding of ecological imperialism is that of the Australian ecofeminist Val Plumwood (2001), who links her philosophical attack on the dualistic thinking that continues to structure human attitudes to the environment to the masculinist, 'reason-centred culture' that once helped secure and sustain European imperial dominance, but now proves ruinous in the face of mass extinction and the fast-approaching 'biophysical limits of the planet' (5). Any *historical* analysis of practices and patterns of ecological imperialism, Plumwood insists, must return to this *philosophical* basis, acknowledging those forms of instrumental reason that view nature and the animal 'other' as being either external to human needs, and thus effectively dispensable, or as being in permanent service to them, and thus an endlessly replenishable resource (4–5).

Another form of ecological imperialism goes under the more contemporary-sounding term *biocolonisation*, used by a variety of environmental and bioscientific scholars to cover the broadly biopolitical implications of current western technological experiments and trends (Kimball 1996; Shiva 1997). Examples here range from biopiracy – e.g. the corporate raiding of indigenous natural-cultural property and embodied knowledge – to western-patented genetic modification (the 'Green Revolution') and other recent instances of biotechnological suprematism and 'planetary management' (Ross 1991) in which the allegedly world-saving potential of science is seconded for self-serving western needs and political ends.

A third form of ecological imperialism is *environmental racism*, defined by the American environmental philosopher Deane Curtin as 'the connection, in theory and practice, of race and the environment so that the oppression of one is connected to, and supported by, the oppression of the other' (2005: 145). Environmental racism has both positive and negative components, accruing just as easily to those considered romantically to be in harmony with nature, e.g. via the familiar trope of the 'ecological Indian' (Krech 2000), as to those accused of damaging their environment on the basis of cultural attributes directly or indirectly associated with their race. Environmental racism is perhaps best understood as a sociological phenomenon, exemplified in the environmentally discriminatory treatment of socially marginalised or economically disadvantaged peoples, and in the transference of ecological problems from their 'home' source to a 'foreign' outlet (whether *discursively*, e.g. through the more or less wholly imagined perception of other people's 'dirty habits', or *materially*, e.g. through the actual re-routing of First World commercial waste). Above all else, though, environmental racism is an extreme form of what Plumwood calls 'hegemonic centrism' – the self-privileging view that she sees as underlying racism, sexism and colonialism alike, all of which support and reconfirm each other, and all of which have historically been conscripted for the purposes of exploiting nature while 'minimising non-human claims to [a shared] earth'³ (2001: 4).

Racism and speciesism

For Plumwood, these claims extend both to environmental and animal actors, since what she calls 'our [collective] failure to situate dominant forms of human society ecologically [has been] matched by our failure to situate non-humans ethically, as the plight of non-human species continues to worsen' (2001: 2). 'Hegemonic centrism' thus accounts not only for environmental *racism*, but also for those forms of institutionalised *speciesism* that continue to be used to rationalise the exploitation of animal (and animalised human) 'others' in the name of a 'human- and reason-centred culture that is at least a couple of millennia old' (2001: 8). As Plumwood argues, the western definition of humanity depended – and still depends – on the presence of the 'not-human': the uncivilised, the animal and animalistic. European justification for invasion and colonisation proceeded from this basis, understanding non-European lands and the people and animals that inhabited them as 'spaces', 'unused, underused or empty' (2003: 53). The very ideology of colonisation is thus one where anthropocentrism and Eurocentrism are inseparable, with the anthropocentrism underlying Eurocentrism being used to justify those forms of European colonialism that see 'indigenous cultures as "primitive", less rational, and closer to children, animals and nature' (2003: 53).

Within many cultures – and not just western ones – anthropocentrism has long been naturalised. The absolute prioritisation of one's own species' interests over those of the silenced majority is still regarded as being 'only natural'. Ironically, it is precisely through such appeals to nature that other animals and the environment are often excluded from the privileged ranks of the human, rendering them available for exploitation. As Cary Wolfe, citing Jacques Derrida, puts it:

> [T]he humanist concept of subjectivity is inseparable from the discourse and institution of a speciesism which relies on the tacit acceptance that the full transcendence to the human requires the sacrifice of the animal and the animalistic, which in turn makes possible a symbolic economy in which we can engage in a 'non-criminal putting to death', as Derrida phrases it, not only of animals but of humans as well by marking them as animal.
>
> (1998: 39)

The effectiveness of this discourse of species is that 'when applied to social others of whatever sort', it relies upon 'the taking for granted of the institution of speciesism; that is, upon the ethical acceptability of the systematic, institutionalised killing of non-human others' (39). In other words, in assuming a natural prioritisation of humans and human interests over those of other species on earth, we are both generating and repeating the racist ideologies of imperialism on a planetary scale. In working towards a genuinely post-imperial, environmentally based conception of community, then, a re-imagining and reconfiguration of the human place in nature necessitates an interrogation of the category of the human itself and of the ways in which the construction of ourselves *against* nature – with the hierarchisation of life forms that construction implies – has been and remains complicit in colonialist and racist exploitation from the time of imperial conquest to the present day.

Postcolonial studies has come to understand environmental issues not only as central to the projects of European conquest and global domination, but also as inherent in the ideologies of imperialism and racism on which those projects historically – and persistently – depend. Not only were other people often regarded as part of nature – and thus treated instrumentally as animals – but also they were forced or co-opted over time into western views of the environment, thereby rendering cultural and environmental restitution difficult if not impossible to achieve. Once invasion and settlement had been accomplished, or at least once administrative structures had been set up, the environmental impacts of western attitudes to human being-in-the-world were facilitated or reinforced by the deliberate (or accidental) transport of animals, plants and peoples throughout the European empires, instigating widespread ecosystem change under conspicuously unequal power regimes.[4]

Despite the recent advances of eco/environmental criticism, English studies in general, and postcolonial studies more particularly, have yet to re-situate the species boundary and environmental concerns at the centre of their enquiries; yet the need to examine these interfaces between nature and culture, animal and human, is urgent and never more pertinent than it is today. After all, postcolonialism's concerns with conquest, colonisation, racism and sexism, along with its investments in theories of indigeneity and diaspora and the relations between native and invader societies and cultures, are also the central concerns of animal and environmental studies. Moreover, as the American environmental historian Donald Worster acknowledges, it is in the myriad relationships between material practices and ideas – especially in cross-cultural contexts – that day-to-day planetary life is lived and futures are governed: practices and ideas that are inseparable from issues of *representation* – as will be made clear throughout this book.

In his historical studies *The Columbian Exchange* (1973) and *Ecological Imperialism* (1986), Alfred Crosby considers the ways in which both materials and ideas were exchanged between Old World and New in a number of anything but even contexts. In the colonies of occupation, these radical inequalities or exchanges seemed most evident — or at least initially — in the military and political arenas, while in the settler colonies it was the results of *environmental* imperialism that were often most immediately clear. Different conceptions of being-in-the-world had indeed long been exchanged by individuals or groups under colonialist circumstances: eastern religions had intrigued Europeans for several centuries, while the oral cultures of the Pacific Islands and Africa had provoked interest and admiration in many westerners as well. But in Australia, North America, New Zealand and South Africa, genuine curiosity about and respect for indigenous cultures, philosophies and religions was rare, and even the most well-intentioned of missionaries, settlers and administrators tended to conceive of themselves as conferring (or imposing) the gifts of civilisation upon the benighted heathen with little or no interest in receiving his or her philosophical gifts in return.

Settlers arrived with crops, flocks and herds, and cleared land, exterminating local ecosystems, while human, animal and plant specimens taken to Europe from these 'new' worlds were, by contrast, few and often inert in form. (Interestingly enough, no human, animal or plant, whether wild or domesticated, transported from the colonies to Europe was in a position to wreak comparable havoc on European ecosystems.) Moreover, they did not arrive as part of traditional agricultural or pastoral practices or with the authority of the normative; instead, they were isolated exotics:

> Indians paraded before royal courts; like turkeys and parrots in cages were the innocent signifiers of an otherness that was [...] exotic, that is, non-systematic, carrying no meaning other than that imposed by the culture to which they were exhibited.
>
> (Wasserman 1984: 132)

European imports to the newly settled colonies — humans, animals, plants — were regarded on the other hand as necessary and 'natural' impositions on, or substitutes for, the local bush or wilderness; and even if these invading species were initially difficult to establish or acclimatise, they soon prospered in lands where their control predators were absent. The genuinely natural ways of indigenous ecosystems were irretrievably undone as 'wild' lands were cleared for farming or opened up to pastoralism.

Skewed as they were in favour of the colonising culture, such exchanges were nevertheless often more complex in practice than this apparently simple pattern of invasion, land-clearing and destruction might lead us to suppose. As Worster (1994) suggests, material and ideological impositions are often disturbed by the complexities of the local elements they seek to displace and by the inappropriate, contradictory ideas and practices they catalyse; and thus it was that European/western human and environmental relations, once transported to the colonies, underwent pressures that were sometimes transformative in their turn. Inefficacious as they might frequently have seemed, the indigenous peoples, as well as animals and plants, of the colonies also altered – albeit to a limited extent – European/western conceptions and practices. More usually, however, ideas of animal treatment and land use initially formed in Europe predisposed colonial administrators and settlers to a facile belief in the apparently limitless resources of the settler colonies. Such places, after all, were apparently untamed, unowned and, above all, *unused*; and, accordingly, settlers set about rendering them productive and profitable through imported methods rather than by accommodating them to local circumstances.

As Virginia Anderson shows in her scrupulously researched 2004 study *Creatures of Empire: How Domestic Animals Transformed Early America*, such invasions of animals and plants were by no means systematic; nor did the animals and plants themselves (or, for that matter, practices of animal husbandry and cultivation) in the new environments of the early North American colonies remain unchanged. Anderson focuses on three settlement areas from New England to the Chesapeake, and on the settler-invaders' importation of domestic cattle and their effects on the environment; on Native American (Indian) attitudes, practices and livelihoods; on relationships between the settlers and various Indian cultures; and to some extent on animals, both domestic and wild, themselves.

Although concerned exclusively with early settlement in America, Anderson's study necessarily raises the issue of the part played by animals in human histories. In its discussion of conflicts and, more rarely, co-operation between settlers and Indians over land and livestock, *Creatures of Empire* interrogates animal categories many westerners tend to take as givens: wild and tame; game and produce; animals and ownership; and, ultimately, relations between and definitions of humans and animals themselves. For example, as Anderson argues, cattle, horses, pigs and goats – all of which had been transported across the Atlantic with great difficulty – were generally seen by colonists as serving two vital purposes. The first was to provide food and labour, but the second was to provide a model of civilised living for the indigenous population. The domestication of animals – the discipline required by animal husbandry – was seen to exert civilising (Christianising) influences on the native populations. Meanwhile, as the colonists became increasingly familiar with Indian living conditions, they regarded such domesticating practices as a key to curing Indian 'laziness'.

In pre-invasion Australia, the nature of the environment had dictated nomadism as the only way of life for both people and animals, but native North American groups needed to be only partially nomadic. Indian cultural groups occupied particular territories, and there were semi-permanent settlements where the women cultivated corn, although hunting forest animals provided the Indians with their vital sustainable base. This general dependence on hunting allowed the American colonists to exaggerate 'the extent of native mobility in order to undermine Indians' territorial claims' (Anderson 2004: 191). And, as in Australia and South Africa, the growing numbers of colonists regarded the lands they occupied as theirs by right, while the alleged nomadism of the Indians suggested to them that there was no native interest in land ownership. The same attitudes were applied to animals. The transported stock 'naturally' belonged to the settlers, while native animals, the very basis of Indian existence, were 'naturally' considered fair game. Not surprisingly, then, livestock and game increasingly became the subjects of human conflict.

Anderson shows however that, as encroaching white settlement forced such issues, there were early attempts at compromise and adaptation on both sides. 'Nursing separate grievances, Indians and colonists struggled to resolve the seemingly intractable problems that livestock created' (191). Such attempts at resolution 'partook as much of diplomacy as of law' and proceeded in an 'unsystematic and ad hoc fashion', with both Indians and colonists 'groping their way towards expedients that helped to reduce friction, if not to eliminate its root cause' (191). But as settler numbers increased and more and more forest was cleared to pasture livestock, native animal habitats (and thus animal numbers) were drastically reduced. More and more cattle went semi-wild and strayed into Indian areas, and the informal agreements necessarily became less effective for both parties.

The English colonists had 'invariably judged the Indians' obvious "failure" to domesticate New World beasts as evidence of their backwardness' (32). But with 'ample protein readily available through hunting, [the] Indians [of New England and the Chesapeake] had no incentive to domesticate animals for food, even if likely candidates had been present' (33). Until the increasing disappearance of game forced them into stock husbandry in the service of the settlers, they had no reason to adopt this so-called 'civilised' mode. Moreover, the colonists' distinction between 'domesticated' and 'wild' was obviously quite unfamiliar to Native Americans. Various Indian groups had formed 'loose associations with wild dogs for purposes of hunting' (36), while Indian women often encouraged hawks to help protect their corn crops; but the absence of the European distinction in Indian culture formed much of the basis of the conflict and misunderstanding. Indians did not own living animals in the same way as the colonists, and to the Indians these were strange new wild creatures whose powers had yet to be assessed and understood (39).

Yet *both* cultures hunted (wild) animals and, as Anderson argues, this might have provided some commonality. Both tracked animals in order to kill them, and both had rituals associated with the practice; they shared an enthusiasm for the chase, for the male camaraderie that hunting afforded together with the peculiar male satisfaction of killing. Both regarded hunting as useful practice for warfare. But the rock on which potential similarities foundered was the very different views held by Indians and colonists about human relations with their animal prey:

> Aware of the power of animal spirits, native hunters treated their prey with respect and performed rituals defined by reciprocity. Although not quite a relationship of equals, the connection between Indians and prey was not essentially hierarchical. But notions of domination and subordination were central to the English, who believed that the act of hunting epitomized the divinely sanctioned ascendancy of humankind over animals.
>
> (58)

This was a fundamental difference, and English attitudes to the social and cultural roles of hunting also eroded potential commonality. Because Indian women were the agriculturalists, Indian men were perceived as lazy, energised only by the hunt. In English eyes, hunting was a pastime, an upper-class social ritual, not a survival necessity. And, ironically, it was this upper-class model that came most readily to mind:

> Had colonists perceived a parallel between native hunters and lower-ranking Englishmen who trapped game in order to put meat on the table, they might have acquired some understanding of a vital part of Indian culture. By likening Indian men to gentlemen of leisure, however, colonists indulged moral judgements that had little to do with social and economic conditions in native villages.
>
> (62)

Once such an assumption had been made, it became part of a persisting stereotype, encouraging the view that Indians 'who wasted time with hunting and also failed to domesticate animals obviously needed to learn how to exploit properly the abundant fauna the Lord had placed in the New World for the benefit of humans' (62).

If, as Crosby and, to a lesser degree, Anderson argue, the triumph of Anglo-European settlers over North American (and subsequently South African and Australian) indigenous populations was effected over the ensuing centuries through environmental – and hence cultural – derangement on a vast scale, such destructive changes were premised on *ontological* and *epistemological* differences between European and Indian ideas of human and animal being-in-the-world. The ultimate irony of this hegemonic triumph is that in the twenty-first century the west is increasingly attempting to re-think and re-capture practices generated through the very respect for animals and nature that the early settlers so righteously scorned.

Aesthetics, advocacy, activism

As Lawrence Buell has aptly remarked, 'criticism worthy of its name arises from commitments deeper than professionalism' (2005: 97), and in the genesis and subsequent practice of the relatively new fields of postcolonial and eco/environmental studies, such commitment has usually been both evident and energising. Postcolonial critiques of European imperialism and colonialism, as well as studies of their post-independence legacies, have from the outset been informed by ethical and political concerns, while the burgeoning area of environmental analysis and critique, particularly though by no means exclusively in the humanities, has in large part emerged out of genuine alarm at the future of the planetary environment and its inhabitants. Such concerns come in the wake of taken-for-granted human domination where anthropocentrism and western imperialism are intrinsically interwoven. Consequently, both postcolonial critique and eco/environmental studies have been, and remain, 'deeply polemical' (Buell 2005: 97) while maintaining their commitment to a rigorous scholarship – one which, however, finds itself increasingly compromised by a global capitalism that has not always been challenged to the same degree as the imperial behaviours it instantiates and inspires.

A similar caveat applies to the crossover field of postcolonial ecocriticism, which also involves an 'aesthetics committed to politics' (Cilano and DeLoughrey 2007: 84), with its historical understandings of the socio-political origins of environmental issues overriding the apolitical tendencies of earlier forms of ecocriticism that often seemed either to follow an escapist pastoral impulse or to favour an aesthetic appreciation of nature for its own sake (Heise 2006; Levin 2002). Not that ecocriticism required a sudden influx of postcolonialists to reform it, having long since gone through its own social-ecological – if not explicitly post-colonial – turn.[5] Indeed, it seems necessary to point out that the convergence of postcolonial and eco/environmental studies over the last decade or so is neither intellectually unbidden nor historically unanticipated; rather, it has given greater visibility, in the first case, to the ecological dimensions of earlier postcolonial analyses and, in the second, to the increasingly global outreach of a US-based ecocriticism that had always been aware of its own 'eco-parochialist' tendencies, and that had often shared postcolonialism's distrust for national self-congratulation and unmarked racial politics (as Robert Young among others points out, non-western ecofeminism significantly pre-dates the emergence of North American ecocriticism, showing the way for western practitioners' ongoing self-examination of their own motives and laying the basis for their own internal gendered/racialised critiques).

What the postcolonial/ecocritical alliance brings out, above all, is the need for a broadly materialist understanding of the changing relationship between people, animals and environment – one that requires attention, in turn, to the cultural politics of representation as well as to those more specific 'processes of mediation [...] that can be recuperated for anti-colonial critique' (Cilano and DeLoughrey 2007: 79). This suggests (1) the continuing centrality of the imagination and, more specifically, imaginative *literature* to the task of postcolonial ecocriticism and (2) the mediating function of social and environmental *advocacy*, which might turn imaginative literature into a catalyst for social action and exploratory literary analysis into a full-fledged form of engaged cultural critique.

While Cheryll Glotfelty's definition of ecocriticism as 'a study of the relationship between literature and the physical environment' (Glotfelty and Fromm 1996: xviii) remains influential, the primary role of literary analysis in ecocriticism is increasingly disputed; and, as Glotfelty herself admits, its mandate is now usually accepted as extending to the fields of environmental philosophy and bioethics, where, 'as a theoretical discourse, [it] negotiates between the human and the nonhuman worlds' (xix).[6] Equally disputed is ecocriticism's relationship with the biological and environmental sciences, especially ecology, which some ecocritics are legitimately accused of invoking more in hope than understanding, and from which leading concepts (holistic systems, interdependence, energy transfer, etc.) continue to be drawn – less literally than metaphorically – as wishful means of explaining 'the way in which literature functions in the world' (O'Brien 2007: 182). Ecology, it might be argued, tends to function more as *aesthetics* than as *methodology* in eco/environmental criticism, providing the literary-minded critic with a storehouse of individual and collective metaphors through which the socially transformative workings of the 'environmental imagination' (Buell 1995) can be mobilised and performed.

As the American ecocritic Lawrence Buell, from whose work the term is drawn, suggests, the environmental imagination engages a set of aesthetic preferences for ecocriticism which is not necessarily restricted to environmental realism or nature writing, but is especially attentive to those forms of fictional and non-fictional writing that highlight nature and natural elements (landscape, flora and fauna, etc.) as self-standing agents, rather than support structures for human action, in the world (Buell 1995; see also Armbruster and Wallace 2001). While it would be a mistake to see ecocriticism as being more concerned with inhabiting the world than with changing it – as being fundamentally more interested in phenomenological than political processes – it is clearly the case that *postcolonial* ecocriticism tips the balance towards the latter, and that its own aesthetic choices reflect this (although postcolonial criticism, like eco/environmental criticism, still needs to be understood as a particular *way of reading*, rather than a specific corpus of literary and other cultural texts). This way of reading is as much affective as analytical – not that the two terms are mutually exclusive – and morally attuned to the continuing abuses of authority that operate in humanity's name. Literary analysis, in this last sense, works towards confirming an environmental ethic that sees 'environmental justice, social justice, and economic justice [not as dissonant competitors] but as parts of the same whole' (Curtin 2005: 7).

What all of this suggests is that postcolonial ecocriticism – like several other modes of ecocriticism – performs an *advocacy* function both in relation to the real world(s) it inhabits and to the imaginary spaces it opens up for contemplation of how the real world might be transformed. The word 'advocacy' needs to be treated carefully here, for as Rebecca Raglon and Marian Scholtmeijer among others argue, it is by no means always the case that either postcolonial or environmental literature overtly (or even covertly) advocates for a particular human constituency, species, place or ecosystem (Raglon and Scholtmeijer 2007: 123). Nor, even when it does, are the forms of advocacy it promotes necessarily compatible; for example, *environmental* literature may well appeal to broader ecological systems and processes that *animal* literature rejects in favour of more specific human-animal interactions, while *postcolonial* literature is more likely to show the conflicts that arise when different forms of advocacy are brought together, e.g. by examining the social, cultural and political factors at play in the eviction of local (indigenous) people from nature reserves and wildlife parks (Elder, Wolch and Emel 1998; Raglon and Scholtmeijer 2007).

If postcolonial ecocriticism draws out the advocacy function that is often embedded within postcolonial, animal and environmental literature, it tends to do so with an eye on that literature's specific aesthetic properties, without succumbing to an instrumental view of literature as 'self-consciously directed and shaped by [a desired outcome] and a coherent set of ideas' (Raglon and Scholtmeijer 2007: 123). After all, postcolonial and eco/environmental writing, even if it is directed towards specific goals (e.g. the desire to protect wilderness, or to promote the rights of abused animals and/or peoples), is always likely to transcend its categorisation as 'protest literature', while not even in its most direct forms is it a transparent document of exploitation or a propagandistic blueprint for the liberation of the oppressed. Accordingly, postcolonial ecocriticism preserves the aesthetic function of the literary text while drawing attention to its social and political usefulness, its capacity to set out symbolic guidelines for the material transformation of the world (Huggan and Tiffin 2007). To that extent, it can be seen as an interventionist or even activist enterprise, along the lines of Robert Young's shorthand definition of postcolonialism as 'a politics and philosophy of activism that contests the disparity [between western and non-western cultures/peoples], and so continues in a new way the anti-colonial struggles of the past' (2003: 4).

For Young, activism has as much to do with the need for epistemic decolonisation – what the Kenyan writer Ngũgĩ wa Thiong'o calls the 'decolonisation of the mind' – as with more directly physical forms of social struggle, and with theorising the ideas of a political practice that is 'morally committed to transforming the conditions of exploitation and poverty in which large sections of the world's population live out their daily lives' (Young 2003: 6). This view, strongly inflected by Marxism, finds its equivalent in the eco-materialist stance of literary/cultural critics like Pablo Mukherjee, whose work looks at the ways in which contemporary postcolonial crises are inextricably connected with ecological crises, or environmental philosophers like Deane Curtin, whose self-given task is to sketch out the lineaments of a libertarian environmental ethic for a postcolonial world (Mukherjee 2006; Curtin 2005). For both Mukherjee and Curtin, as for Young, critical intervention can itself be considered to be a form of activism, and the critique of colonialism proves to be indistinguishable from an attack on the global-capitalist system that continues to support colonialism in the present, much as it sustained it in the past. This suggests, in turn, that postcolonial ecocriticism is broadly *eco-socialist* in inspiration, and is less likely to be sympathetic to positions like that of Jonathan Bate, who envisions the transference from a 'red' to a 'green' politics and who, while committed to social change, remains careful to distinguish between a phenomenological eco-poetics and an instrumental ecopolitics in a broad-based attempt to account for what it might mean to dwell authentically and responsibly on earth.[7]

However, to call all postcolonial ecocriticism 'eco-socialist' runs the risk of being both rhetorically inaccurate and politically programmatic, and it might be better to see it from a range of not necessarily compatible methodological, ideological and, not least, *cultural* perspectives – as will turn out to be the case in this book. Here, the recent work of scholars like Anthony Vital proves particularly useful. In his excellent 2008 essay 'Toward an African Ecocriticism', Vital suggests that the best way to reconcile postcolonial criticism and eco/environmental criticism might be to take into account 'the complex interplay of social history with the natural world, and how language both shapes and reveals such interactions' (90). It is not enough, however, to acknowledge that all understandings of the world are delivered through language, but necessary to qualify 'this assumption with the recognition that different languages [...] permit varieties of understanding' that are both historically determined and socially/culturally formed (90). The task of postcolonial criticism, in this context, is to explore 'how different cultural understandings of society and nature' – understandings necessarily inflected by ongoing experiences of colonialism, sexism and racism – 'have been deployed in specific historical moments by writers in the making of their art' (90). These sentiments are very much of a piece with the approach adopted in this book, which, also in the spirit of Vital's essay, perceives 'a new kind of concern for the environment emerging in the post-colonial era, one attuned to histories of unequal development and varieties of discrimination' (90); and, one might add, to the historical interaction between ideologies of empire and ideologies of genre. The book is interested, in this last sense, in how particular genres and modes – pastoral, for instance, or the beast fable – have been transformed in different cultural and historical contexts, and in how postcolonial writers from a variety of regions have adapted environmental discourses, which have often been shaped in western (European) interests, to their own immediate ends. The book is equally concerned with demonstrating the knowledge of *non*-western (non-European) societies and cultures, which has always been part of the postcolonial critical project (Young 2003: 4–7), and is a task to which ecocriticism – both in spite and because of its Euro-American origins – is increasingly committed at a time when 'the environmentalist ambition is to think globally, but doing so in terms of a single language is inconceivable – even and especially when that language is a hegemonic one' (Heise 2006: 513). In reaching out across languages and cultures, postcolonial ecocriticism is paradoxically driven – as is this book – by the impossibility of its own utopian ambitions: to make exploitation and discrimination of all kinds, both human and nonhuman, visible in the world; and, in so doing, to help make them obsolete.

Writing wrongs

Since the 1990s, ecological issues have engaged a number of humanities scholars who regard them as not marginal but foundational to their disciplines. For researchers in geography, anthropology, philosophy and politics, for instance, animal and environmental considerations are increasingly seen as the necessary *basis* for human studies. But whereas in previous decades, literary studies had often taken the lead in mapping major humanities field shifts – the turn to critical theory ushered in by English's marriage with philosophy in the late 1960s or the rise of postcolonial studies in the 1980s and 90s, for instance – the literary has lagged behind in this most recent of revolutions. One obvious reason has been that literature, with its traditional emphasis on plot, character and psychological states, has been seen perforce as being focused on individuals or groups of humans, or at least anthropomorphised animals, even in genres such as traditional pastoral or romantic elegy where human interaction with, and apparent concern for, the natural world come to the fore. The emphasis of pastoral has generally been on the impact of the environment on the human rather than the other way around. And while literature has certainly dealt with the fates and even the psychologies of animals, these have – at least until recently – been highly anthropomorphised, acting more often than not as a staple of fiction for children rather than adult readers. For western writers, at least, it has been more difficult to anthropomorphise the environment which, far from having its own providential fortunes and narrative trajectories, has been regarded as a mere backdrop against which human lives are played out. And even when writers have given some attention to the natural (extra-human) environment, critics have generally downplayed its significance in their own considerations of the work. Similarly, potential emphasis on the importance of animal subjects – the death of a pet, disease in a sheep flock – tends to focus attention on the *human* reactions to such loss or losses.

Since the 1990s, however, there has been evidence in both literature and literary criticism of the centralising of ecological issues in literary studies, leading to some radical experiments in genre practice, point of view/interpretative focus, and other potentially innovating aspects of literary form. Not that these about-turns are likely to strike us as being entirely unfamiliar. After all, during the latter half of the twentieth century apparently peripheral issues and marginal literatures had come to assume an increasingly important place in both public and scholarly reading practices while exercising significant – and persistent – re-interpretative pressure on European canonical works. Yet all such critical/stylistic revolutions, displacing as they do the earlier paradigms, are given to producing *aporias* in their turn; and among these, as we argue in this book, are the formative roles played by the environment and animals in shaping human lives. To understand why this lag has occurred in both English studies and postcolonial studies in particular, we need to consider the hegemonic role of English literature and literary studies in colonial education systems, together with the ways in which, through colonial institutions and practices, western ideologies suborned and supplanted other ways of (human) being-in-the-world (Ashcroft, Griffiths and Tiffin 1989; Viswanathan 1990). For colonialist interpretation necessarily resulted in the destruction or erosion of alternative apprehensions of animals and environment, blocking understanding of those crucial inter-actions between the human and the 'extra-human' (Plumwood 2001) that form the substance of this book.

If the conjunction of postcolonialism and ecocriticism has begun to prove mutually illuminating in terms of, say, colonial genesis and con-tinuing human inequalities and environmental abuses, the two areas have often been in conflict. While there are numerous instances of individual ecocritics questioning the promotion of conservationist ideals over those of human development where, as is often the case, the two are in com-petition, ecocriticism has tended as a whole to prioritise extra-human concerns over the interests of disadvantaged human groups, while post-colonialism has been routinely, and at times unthinkingly, anthropocentric (Huggan 2004; Nixon 2005). Meanwhile, whereas ecocriticism, at least in part, has developed out of literary studies in response to changes in per-ception of the extra-human and its place in literature, animal studies (except where it is regarded as a sub-branch of ecocriticism) has developed independently through disciplines such as philosophy, zoology and religion. Not surprisingly, then, zoocriticism – as we might term its practice in literary studies – is concerned not just with animal *representation* but also with animal *rights*, and this different genesis and trajectory from that of ecocriticism necessarily informs its intersection with the post-colonial. And just as ecocriticism and animal studies have developed rather differently, the two fields' conjunctions with postcolonialism to this point have also proceeded unevenly. Since Alfred Crosby's pioneering demonstration of the significance of environmental factors (under which he includes non-human animals) in imperial conquest and subsequent colonisation, a number of studies of the intersections between the fields of ecocriticism and postcolonialism have been produced (Cilano and DeLoughrey 2007; Huggan 2004; Nixon 2005; O'Brien 2001). By contrast, zoocriticism, understood here in the context of intersections between animal studies and postcolonialism, is still in its infancy (see, however, Armstrong 2008, an early but instantly seminal work). As it is emerging, postcolonial zoocriticism shares with postcolonial ecocriticism the exploration of conflicted areas and problems: wildlife protection and conservation on land needed for poor human communities; human communities evicted from their homeland to make way for game parks to benefit wealthy tourists; and, contained within these and other examples, a deep concern for rights (Raglon and Scholtmeijer 2007). Yet further conflicts and concerns inevitably arise within the field of zoocriticism, many of them attached to the philosophical limitations of rights discourses themselves. Should animals, for example, have equal rights with humans; and if so, under which circumstances? With whose rights should we begin, and with whose rights – with what possible philosophical understanding and/or legal notion of rights – can we end? (Mitchell, in Wolfe 2003: ix–xiv). In postcolonial texts, where vilification of designated 'others' was and is frequently metaphorised as a question of civilisation versus savagery, human versus animal, whose wrongs are eventually to be righted, and – given human/animal similarities or the inextricable link between racism and speciesism – whose equalities are to be acknowledged and inequalities fought against; and in whose *name*, not just what *form*?

It thus bears reminding that, in bringing these apparently independent fields together, we are concerned not just with competing interests in terms of rights, but also with those broader categories – including the category of 'rights' itself – that such interests necessarily call into question. One thing seems certain: if the wrongs of colonialism – its legacies of continuing human inequalities, for instance – are to be addressed, still less redressed, then the very category of the *human*, in relation to animals and environment, must also be brought under scrutiny. After all, traditional western constitutions of the human as the 'not-animal' (and, by implication, the 'not-savage') have had major, and often catastrophic, repercussions not just for animals themselves but for all those the West now considers human but were formerly designated, represented and treated as animal. The persistence of such openly discriminatory categorisations invites an endless repetition of the wrongs of the past (Wolfe 2003). This book seeks accordingly to raise questions of rights and wrongs – both in the past and in the present – through the focal area of *representation*, primarily though not exclusively literary representation, since it is representation in all its forms which produces 'that mental type of encounter in which perceptions, ideologies, ethics, laws and myths' have become part of our 'dialogue with nature' (Worster 1994). But at the same time, we recognise that the very idea of rights, especially the granting or extending of rights to others of all kinds, may itself be regarded as in essence anthropocentric, since it is only the dominant (human) group that is in the position to do so; we are thus interested in the philosophical possibility of the wrongness of rights while remaining committed to the moral imperative of righting wrongs as well.[8]

As might be expected, the book seeks neither to offer solutions to these complex questions nor to resolve the intellectual and moral challenges they raise, but rather to examine a pressing situation in which postcolonial writing, theory and practice finds itself increasingly confronted by a variety of broadly extra-human concerns. Given the relatively uneven development of ecocriticism and zoocriticism, differing approaches to their intersections with the postcolonial have necessarily been adopted here, and although we fully recognise that these fields frequently overlap, we have chosen nonetheless to divide the book into two largely self-sustaining parts.

The first part of the book, which is divided into two sections, focuses on the intersection of postcolonial and environmental issues as these have emerged across the historical faultlines of literary genre. In the first section, we argue that one of the central tasks of postcolonial ecocriticism to date has been to contest western ideologies of development, but without necessarily dismissing the idea of 'development' itself as a mere tool of the technocratic west. We duly enquire into the relative successes of postcolonial authors, at least some of whom self-consciously double as social and environmental activists, in pursuing anti- or counter-developmental methods in their literary work. Beginning with a consideration of probably the two most visible postcolonial writer-activists in the field, Arundhati Roy and Ken Saro-Wiwa, we then go on to look at a wide range of anti- and/or counter-developmental strategies in literary works by writers from the Caribbean and, especially, Pacific Islands regions, including Jamaica Kincaid, Epeli Hau'ofa, Witi Ihimaera and Patricia Grace. While we suggest that all of these writers are against the kind of developmentalism that panders to global-corporate interests, the works in question fall short of arguing that globalisation, and the potentially destructive forms of social/environmental development it fosters, can simply be bypassed. Rather, the battle is not so much against development itself as an intrinsically harmful activity or process as against the flagrant social and environmental abuses that continue to be perpetrated in its name. Hence the broadly *counter*-developmental, rather than explicitly *anti*-developmental, thrust of much of the material studied in the section, which is committed to recognising the existence of alternative social and environmental knowledges that are neither acknowledged nor necessarily understood by development experts in the west.

The first section then ends with an epilogue that focuses on the 'eco-catastrophes' to which unrestrained development has given rise, notably global warming, and argues that global warming requires not just new ways of thinking beyond the human, but also a renewed attention to the long histories of slavery and colonialism, which need to be re-thought in ecological terms. The first section emphasises postcolonised communities' sense of their own cultural identities and entitlements, which often represent the ontological basis for their territorial claims to belong. Claims and counter-claims of entitlement and belonging – which are often at heart ontological rather than specifically juridical questions – form the basis for the material we go on to study in the second section, which, like the first, shows both the political and aesthetic implications of postcolonial literature's continuing pursuit of social and environmental justice in an unevenly developed world. The literary mode on which this section focuses is *pastoral*, used by a variety of postcolonial writers, particularly from so-called 'settler societies' (here: Australia, Canada and South Africa), to explore the tensions between contradictory forms of social and political allegiance through which the juridical pressures of entitlement clash with the ontological insistence to belong. These tensions are historically – and necessarily – complex. Pastoral, we suggest, is about the legitimation of highly codified relations between socially differentiated people – relations mediated, but also mystified, by supposedly universal cultural attitudes to land. We seek to contribute to the demystification of these and other like-minded attitudes by charting the political implications and imperatives of pastoral across a range of work by the Australian poets Judith Wright and Oodgeroo Noonuccal and the South African novelists Nadine Gordimer and J.M. Coetzee. A further subsection looks at the rather different, if no less conflicted, history of pastoral representation in the Caribbean via the work of the Trinidad-born writer V.S. Naipaul, which – going against the grain of Naipaul criticism – is held to champion post-pastoral forms of communal existence that implicitly support the interconnectedness of land and labour in pursuit of a socially responsible life. We then end with an extended coda on the (literal) staging of conflicts of entitlement and belonging, mostly within a cross-cultural indigenous performance context in which the stage becomes a contested space where different spatial fantasies and histories are accumulated, and the land is revealed both as speaking subject and as disputed object of discursive management and material control.

The second part of the book shifts from a broadly *ecocritical* to a more narrowly *zoocritical* focus. It is divided into three sections, each of which adopts a slightly different emphasis, but all of which are effectively co-dependent, with primary texts floating from one section to another and a strongly anti-anthropocentric argument driving the whole. The first section considers the impact and legacies of colonialist asset stripping, colonial discourse, and Christian missionising. It initially uses Joseph Conrad's turn-of-the-century novella *Heart of Darkness* to consider what is omitted in his celebrated critique of Belgian colonialism, and to assess some of the ways in which a canonical colonial text has been influential in both Europe and its former colonies (including those of Africa) in disseminating an authoritative version of Africa to the west. Chinua Achebe's critique of Conrad's racism is discussed with reference to the ways in which African characters in Conrad's text are excised through their lack of speech and purely metaphoric function; Barbara Gowdy's novel *The White Bone* is then considered in response to both. We also discuss the benefits and dangers of anthropomorphic representation and language in humans and animals; some brief reflections on J.M. Coetzee's fictional treatise *The Lives of Animals* then bring the section to a close.

In the second section of Part II, we consider the role of Christianity – particularly the Bible – in colonisation, as well as responses to a Christian interpellation that marginalises women and animals. The symbolic Christian sacrament has links to pre-Christian cannibal rituals, and this leads us into a discussion of the role of cannibalism, both in practice and as metaphor, as foundational in the imperial 'othering' of animals and humans. Daniel Defoe's *Robinson Crusoe* is the canonical text that forms the basis of this discussion, and considerations of conquest and commerce are raised again here in different contexts. Carnivory (meat-eating) also comes under scrutiny in postcolonial re-writings of the wrongs embedded in imperial and/or anthropocentric attitudes to animals and humans. Texts to be considered include Timothy Findley's *Not Wanted on the Voyage*, Thomas King's *Green Grass, Running Water*, Yann Martel's *Life of Pi*, Samuel Selvon's *Moses Ascending*, and J.M. Coetzee's *Elizabeth Costello*.

The third and final section considers questions of animal and human agency, cross-species contact including sexuality, and clashes between human and animal interests in postcolonised contexts. Texts here include Amitav Ghosh's *The Hungry Tide*, Peter Goldsworthy's *Wish*, Marian Engel's *Bear*, and Zakes Mda's *The Whale Caller*. Drawing on the work of Jacques Derrida, we also consider a number of postcolonial texts that envision more equitable relations between animals and humans, and humans and other humans, including Robyn Williams' *2007* and J.M. Coetzee's *Elizabeth Costello*. As in other sections in Part II, the overall thrust of the argument is that the *righting* of imperialist wrongs necessarily involves our *writing* of the wrongs that have been done – and are still being done – to animals, and demands our critical engagement with the ways in which both continuing problems of abuse and their potential amelioration are represented in British colonial and Anglophone postcolonial texts.

The book then closes with a postscript that brings its central arguments fully up to date in the context of what is now increasingly asserted to be a 'post-natural' or even a 'posthuman' world. For some critics, the relentless manipulation of nature foreshadows the inevitable death of nature (Merchant 1980); for others, nature now extends to other, scientifically manufactured forms (Haraway 1997). Whether contemporary technoscience is to be seen as a neocolonialist enterprise is moot, as is the view that it has ushered in a new era of the posthuman. Meanwhile, critical attacks on humanism's continuing ideological insufficiencies point to its intellectual rationale for the imperial civilising mission and for other authoritarian regimes and systems which, both consciously and unconsciously, have abused humanity in humanity's name. Whether the human is to be renewed, even as humanism is discarded, must remain an open question in a postcolonial context: one which – for better or worse – has often expressly articulated both the centrality of human experience and a variety of humanist concerns. But as our brief concluding discussions of the work of Zadie Smith and Margaret Atwood suggest, human liberation will never be fully achieved without challenging the historical conditions under which human societies have constructed themselves in hierarchical relation to other societies, *both* human *and* non-human, and without imagining new ways in which these societies, understood as being ecologically connected, can be creatively transformed.

Notes

1 Binaries of this type continue to plague both postcolonial and environmental studies, prompting critics such as Guha (see above) to speak exasperatedly of a 'cowboys-and-Indians' approach to contemporary social-environmental conflicts. However, as Guha is also ready to acknowledge, there *is* a viable distinction to be made between what he and Joan Martinez-Alier (1997) call 'full-stomach' and 'empty-belly' environmentalisms – the latter sometimes being a matter of mere survival – under conditions of conspicuously uneven development in the global-capitalist world. Marxist critics like Neil Lazarus make a similar point about the 'new imperialism', which stifles conflict even as it repeatedly provokes it, and which requires concerted opposition from postcolonial critics who have paradoxically 'failed to recognise the

unremitting actuality and indeed [...] intensification of imperialist social relations in the times and spaces of the postcolonial world' (2006: 12). Lazarus overstates the case, but his point still stands that it is quite possible – indeed, vitally necessary – to speak *both* of entangled allegiances in the contemporary capitalist world order *and* of continuing struggles that pit obvious exploiters against the obviously exploited, the visible oppressor against the equally visible oppressed.

2 Although the terms 'green postcolonialism' or, more commonly used, 'postcolonial ecocriticism' are often used interchangeably, the different combination of noun and qualifying adjective implies that it is postcolonialism, in the first case, and ecocriticism, in the second, that is being rendered subject to revisionist critique. 'Postcolonial ecocriticism' will be used in this book from here on as a way not just of opening out the postcolonial dimensions of ecocriticism, but also of suggesting that the critical study of environmental literature may play its part in the undoing of the epistemological hierarchies and boundaries – nowhere more apparent than under historical and/or contemporary conditions of colonialism – that have set humans against other animals, and both against an externalised natural world. What actually counts as 'environmental literature' is moot, and is further complicated by the inclusion of animals, the formalised study of which has not always been in keeping with the tenets of ecocriticism as an analytical mode (for a more inclusive approach, see Garrard 2004; also Tiffin *et al.* 2007a). For a critique of the insufficiencies of ecocriticism *vis-à-vis* animals, see section two of this Introduction and, especially, Part II of this volume; for a further consideration of environmental modes and genres, see section three of the Introduction and Part I.

3 Another fundamental form of environmental racism is that attached to human over-population, particularly when the problem is associated primarily or even exclusively with so-called 'population explosions' in the Third World (Mount and O'Brien 2013; Shiva 1988). Since at least the 1960s, when Paul Ehrlich's best-seller *The Population Bomb* was published, the mantra of 'zero population growth' has frequently been considered a racist proposition, especially when it is linked – however tenuously – with the unpalatable history of eugenics earlier in the century (for a further discussion of eugenics, see the Postscript to this book). It is also a potentially *sexist* proposition in so far as anxieties around global over-population and the threat it poses to the world's carrying capacity are mapped onto the bodies of women from the global South (Mount and O'Brien 2013). A number of postcolonial critics – notably Gayatri Spivak – have spoken out against this, while fierce critiques of state-sanctioned birth control are woven into literary works such as the Ghanaian writer Ama Ata Aidoo's 2001 novel *Changes*, one of whose female characters likens government family planning measures to 'murderous programmes [with] beautiful names' (Aidoo 2001: 15, quoted in Mount and O'Brien 2013: 531; see also Spivak 1987).

However, while most postcolonial analysis focuses on over-*consumption* – and the social, economic and political inequalities at its heart – rather than over-*population* as the most pressing issue, the latter arguably remains too intractable a problem to be reduced to standard iterations of the anti-colonial politics of gender and race. This is not just due to mounting population pressure around the globe, but also to recent changes in the composition of national populations, which now make it increasingly difficult to identify these populations by race or to track their growth by birth rates alone. As a deadly combination of war and so-called 'natural disasters' – climate change, flood, famine, and so on – displaces ever-increasing numbers of people, it is arguable that most of the world will soon become genuinely multicultural, while even those with seemingly steady states will have their populations significantly increased by migration. These intensifying conditions have given rise to what might be described as a new wave of writing about over-population within a larger, planetary context that is currently witnessing the disappearance of entire ecosystems along with the accelerated losses of many different species of animals and plants.

Much of this new work is by westerners, thereby running the risk of reifying earlier north-south binaries, but some of it takes place in southern settings or consciously addresses a variety of colonial and imperial themes. Three briefly rendered examples will suffice here. In Dale Smith's maverick fable *What the Orangutan Told Alice* (2001), two American children are led into the Indonesian forest to be educated about the ways in which species and habitats are disappearing. Their twin mentors are a human scientist (Anne), and a speaking orangutan (the Old Man), and both show the children the urgency of redressing the ecological devastation brought about human greed. Part of that greed manifests itself in the desire for self-reproduction: 'As long as humans keep reproducing at their present rate, [the destruction is] not going to stop', says the Old Man; and Anne agrees, adding that 'the problem is that there are too many people and they are having way too many babies' (Smith 2001: 74).

A decade earlier, Lionel Shriver's *Game Control* (1994) features an apparently fanatical anti-population-growth philanthropist, Calvin Piper, who has established a research facility in the heart of Africa in order to develop a disease designed to cull all human populations (with the exception of Israel's, which he believes to have already suffered its share of culling during the Second World War). Piper's scheme collapses in the end, but this does not necessarily invalidate all his arguments; and as in another more recent American novel, Jonathan Franzen's *Freedom* (2010), the fiction allows controversial views to be put forward that many readers may find unpalatable – if still persuasive – while withdrawing from the more extreme positions it takes up. In *Game Control*, gung-ho Piper cannot bring himself to kill a single soul; while in *Freedom*, the novel's most fervent disciple of 'zero population growth', Walter Berglund, eventually sacrifices his ideals on the altar of big business (he also has children from his own failed marriage), though the novel still grants him its only speech in capital letters, as reproduced below:

WE ARE ADDING THIRTEEN MILLION HUMAN BEINGS TO THE POPULATION EVERY MONTH. THIRTEEN MILLION MORE PEOPLE TO KILL EACH OTHER IN COMPETITION OVER FINITE RESOURCES AND WIPE OUT EVERY OTHER LIVING THING ALONG THE WAY. IT IS A PERFECT FUCKING WORLD AS LONG AS YOU DON'T COUNT EVERY OTHER SPECIES IN IT. WE ARE A CANCER ON THE PLANET.

(Franzen 2010: 244)

Berglund's beliefs are supported at least in part by his assistant and temporary lover, Lalitha, who modifies his extremist view that bearing children should increasingly be seen as an 'embarrassment' by suggesting that reproduction remains a right but certainly doesn't require 'congratulations anymore' (2010: 221). However, by the end of the novel this hardline position has softened considerably, and Walter – who by this time has lost Lalitha – has become a family man once more. *Freedom* may not be a 'postcolonial' text in most accepted understandings of the term, but it shares the emphasis on internal dialogue and the kinds of confrontational position-taking that are familiar in postcolonial novels, which often deal head-on with controversial themes. Over-population is one such theme, and numerous positions can be taken up in the face of it; it would be inaccurate in this context to see only one post-colonial position, whether it is framed and phrased in terms of either an accusation or a threat.

4 Such primary transformations frequently laid the foundations for today's international trade patterns, whose inequalities in design and implementation are euphemised as a new, positive 'globalisation'. On the complex connections between imperialism and globalisation – and on globalisation as in effect a form of 'new imperialism' – see Brennan *et al.* (2004) and Harvey (2005); see also endnote 8 below.

5 See, for example, Buell (1995), who, while conceding that there is 'continuing stress and disputation within the [environmental] movement as well as resistance from opposing interests', argues that its primary task has increasingly become to raise public consciousness of interlinked social and environmental issues that require immediate action and change (97–98). For a useful thumbnail sketch of shifting emphases both within global environmental movements and the still largely academic, western-based discipline of ecocriticism, see also Heise 2006.

6 While the interdisciplinary remit of postcolonial ecocriticism is increasingly recognised (see, for example, Cilano and DeLoughrey 2007), the position of literature and literary studies within this disciplinary mix is uncertain – as in other branches of contemporary ecocriticism. To some extent, this book observes the conventional distinction between *ecocriticism* as a literature-centred, if not literature-exclusive, approach that highlights cultural representational strategies and *green cultural studies* as a cluster of more conspicuously cross-disciplinary critical initiatives in which the category of 'nature' is looked upon with suspicion and the category of 'culture' is treated inclusively, with a particular view to the analysis of popular forms (Head 1998; O'Brien 2007). According to these terms, the book is more an exercise in ecocriticism than green cultural studies, though – as subsequent sections illustrate – it is as committed to *animal* as to *environmental* issues, which is by no means always the case in ecocriticism, and which (among other reasons) leads it to adopt a methodologically hybrid, internally inconsistent approach.

7 For a more detailed analysis of Bate's distinction between ecopoetics and ecopolitics, articulated most clearly in his 2000 study *The Song of the Earth*, see Part 1, section 2. For useful summaries of ecocriticism's phenomenological legacy, see also Garrard 2004 (esp. Chapter 6), Heise, and Levin.

8 See, for example, the important work of the American critic Joseph Slaughter, whose 2008 book *Human Rights, Inc.* begins by pointing out the apparent paradox that we are currently living in an Age of Human Rights and an Age of Human Rights Abuse. Slaughter attributes this paradox to what he calls the 'discursive victory of human rights' in the contemporary era (2). Human rights,

he says, have 'triumph[ed] in their apparent banality', but this progress narrative tends to disregard the fact that human rights violations – like the international law designed to prevent them – have become 'increasingly systematic, corporate and institutional', with some violations being committed in the 'Orwellian name of human rights themselves' (2). Taking its cue from Slaughter, this book opens out three problem areas for the discourse of rights: universalism, anthropocentrism and globalisation. In the first category, we might say, following Slaughter, that just because (human) rights supposedly have universal application doesn't make them universally legible: there is a considerable gap between what people *should* know about rights – including their own rights – and what they *actually* know. In the second, the prosecution of human rights is contingent on the general acceptance of the category 'human', but as our book hopefully makes clear, this category can no longer be taken for granted in what is emerging increasingly (if by no means incontestably) as a 'posthuman' world. And finally, in the third, the contradictions built into (human) rights discourses tend to be confirmed by current conditions of globalisation: while it is true that the increasing interconnectedness of modern life allows for the possibility of global systems of adjudication and governance, even the utopian goal of global citizenship, it also provides a rationale for uneven development and the human rights abuses that stem from it. Similarly, the globalist mantra of interconnectedness isn't necessarily an ecological mantra, often being driven by neoliberal rather than egalitarian principles, or by neoliberal principles that use egalitarian principles to their own ends.

Part I

Postcolonialism and the environment

1 Development

Introduction

One of the central tasks of postcolonial ecocriticism as an emergent field has been to contest – also to provide viable alternatives to – western ideologies of development. These contestations have mostly been in alignment with radical Third-Worldist critiques that tend to see development as little more than a disguised form of neocolonialism, a vast technocratic apparatus designed primarily to serve the economic and political interests of the west. A more balanced, if no less trenchant, critique of development is urgently needed for both postcolonial and environmental criticism, and this is the far-from-easy task that the following section undertakes. Several fundamental questions can immediately be brought to the fore here: what *is* development? How should it be defined and measured, and whose interests does it serve? What is development's historical relationship to colonialism and imperialism; whither development in an increasingly globalised postcolonial world? Is development sustainable, and what is its connection to the environment? Last but not least, what can postcolonial ecocriticism add to current and/or historical debates on development? To what extent have postcolonial *writers*, in doubling as cultural and environmental *activists*, been successful in pursuing an anti- or counter-developmental approach?

These questions are complex, all the more so in that the word 'development' is taxed with considerable semantic difficulties of its own. Development is generally recognised to be a strategically ambiguous term, adapted to the different needs of those who use it, and shot through with self-congratulation and condescension, based as it all too often is on the enormous cultural assumptions and presumptions of the west (Black 1999: 3). As the German sociologist Wolfgang Sachs puts it, pulling no punches, the international development debate has tended to mimic 'the rise and fall of political sensibilities within the [affluent] Northern countries', particularly the US; thus, 'unfettered enthusiasm for economic growth in 1945 reflected the West's desire to restart the economic machine after a devastating war; the emphasis on manpower planning echoed American fears after the shock of Sputnik in 1957; the discovery of basic needs was stimulated by President Johnson's domestic war on poverty in the 1960s; and so, too, for [contemporary] concerns about worldwide inequality: what development means depends on how the rich nations feel' (Sachs 1997: 26).

Harsh though they are, Sachs's words echo widespread fears, particularly in the so-called 'beneficiary' countries of the Third World, that development is at best a form of strategic altruism, in which technical and financial assistance from the self-designated First World is geared to its own economic and political concerns. Perhaps the most extreme form of this view is that development is little more than a myth propagated by the west that, under the guise of assisted modernisation, re-establishes the very rift (social, political, economic) between First and Third Worlds that it claims to want to heal (De Rivero 2001). This myth of development, taking false support from ideas promiscuously linked to the Enlightenment ideology of progress and the Darwinian survival of the fittest, enjoins the less 'advanced' southern countries to close the gap on their wealthier northern counterparts, and in so doing to subscribe to a capitalist growth model that is both demonstrably unequal and carries a potentially devastating environmental cost (De Rivero 2001: 110). If development is a myth, it is also a 'historically produced discourse' (Escobar 1995: 6) which can arguably be seen along similar lines to those of Saidian Orientalism, and which, like latter-day versions of Orientalism, operates a regime of representation that is aimed at consolidating the social, cultural and political authority of the west in a postcolonial world (Escobar 1995). 'Developmentalism', as the Colombian anthropologist Arturo Escobar dubs this discourse, involves the 'developmentalization of the Third World, its progressive insertion into a regime of thought and practice in which certain interventions for the eradication of poverty became central to the [late-capitalist] world order' during the period immediately following the end of the Second World War (24).[1] Much like Sachs, Escobar attributes the post-war 'invention of development' to the historical confluence of several different factors: the demands of decolonisation; the pressures of the Cold War; the need to find new markets; and the faith in modern science and technology as a panacea for social and economic ills (32). Development, Escobar insists, is as much a mechanism of discursive control as an agency of economic management, based on the assumption that the western values it inculcates are indisputably the right ones, and characterised by a 'top-down, ethnocentric, and technocratic approach' in which people and cultures are treated as 'abstract concepts, statistical figures to be moved up and down [at will] in the charts of "progress"' (44).

This abstract view of development and the players within it is arguably backed up by economic agencies such as the International Monetary Fund and the World Bank which, also created as part of the US-led 'war on poverty' in the immediate post-war era, effectively turned poor people into 'objects of knowledge and management', and poor nations into targets for social and political intervention by the privileged countries against whose measures they were to be judged (Escobar 1995: 23). For radical critics of development, this financial apparatus merely increased the gap between rich and poor, helping to create what the Peruvian ex-diplomat Oswaldo de Rivero calls a modern form of 'socio-economic apartheid: a planet in whose northern hemisphere there is a small archipelago of wealthy nation-states, surrounded by the majority of mankind' (De Rivero 2001: 24). A more liberal view is the one taken by the Indian Nobel prize-winning economist Amartya Sen, who acknowledges the interference intrinsic to western development practices but still accepts development's basic premise: to address the persistence of poverty, environmental degradation and the violation of human freedom in the contemporary globalised world (Sen 2000: xii). For Sen, the primary objective of development is not economic growth (though this is certainly to be wished for) but the expansion of human freedom: 'The role of economic growth in expanding [social] opportunities has to be integrated into [a] more fundamental understanding of the process of development as the expansion of human capability to lead more worthwhile and more free lives' (295). Development is first and foremost *human* development, and can thus be measured in terms of an enlargement of human choices that actively requires 'the removal of [those] major sources of unfreedom' (3) – poverty, social unrest, political repression – that by definition limit the scope and quality of people's everyday lives. While Sen sees development in terms of both economic growth and the expansion of human capability, his theory is perhaps best seen as a humanisation of the abstract principles of economic productivity. Freedom, for Sen, consists at least in part in the freedom to participate in the global market system he supports. This is capitalism with a conscience, attuned to the contemporary realities of social inequality. The market, Sen insists, is not just a vehicle of self-interest but an instrument of social justice; and development, similarly, isn't just about 'growth' *per se*, but about the various mechanisms that promote and protect the quality of human life.

Definitions of development, then, are in part arguments about the social, as well as economic, benefits of a world market system that, depending on perspective, is (1) not necessarily antithetical to human equality or (2) rides roughshod over local human and environmental interests in the attempt to secure preferential conditions for international trade. Just how colonialist is this system? To some extent, it might be argued, modern theories and practices of development are part of a well-intentioned attempt to repair the damage caused by colonialism, helping to create the more advantageous economic and political conditions that might allow historically marginalised and/or exploited peoples to work towards building their own future while consolidating their own individual and collective human rights. However, in Gustavo Esteva's view, development and the progression it implies is better understood as a form of 'colonizing anti-colonialism' in which the poor countries of the world are simultaneously seen as socially and politically 'backward', and in which the 'positive meaning of the word "development" – profoundly rooted after [at least] two centuries of its social construction – is a reminder of what [these countries] are not' (Esteva 1997: 116–31). Development, understood this way, is a classic example of the self-privileging discourse of *neocolonialism*, as put into practice by people and governments primarily interested in exploiting others in the name of the noble cause (Black 1999: 268).[2] Far from putting an end to old-style imperialism – as Truman might have it – modern (post-war) development finds new ways of instantiating it, e.g. through the ongoing collaboration between national governments and gargantuan transnational companies whose economies exceed those of all but the largest 'developing' countries, and whose financial and technical assistance is provided in terms that continue to favour the west (Esteva 1997: 9–11; see also Spybey 1992). This contemporary transnational dispensation aligns development with a predatory socio-economic system – global capitalism – that effectively spreads inequality at the same time as it champions its own adherence to freedom, democracy and human rights (De Rivero 2001). While these global conditions are often touted as being new, they provide a reminder of the historical connection between colonial expansion and capitalist production, in which the export of capital and its concentration in monopolies inexorably led to a territorial division of the world (Larrain 1989). They also indicate the double truism that the current circumstances of globalisation, as well as those that had obtained under previous empires, cannot help but produce *uneven* development; and that development, indexed to the rise of global capitalism, has historically created the rationale for expansion and the 'pacification' of local peoples so as to make way for favourable conditions of international trade (Havinden and Meredith 1996: 87).

More recently, postcolonialism's troubled relationship to globalisation has brought with it a renewed attention to the possibilities of 'post-development', which may be loosely understood as a set of revisionist strategies through which development is re-articulated at grass-roots levels, and which emerges from the recognition that the non-homogeneity of the world system requires that the multiple modernities encapsulated within it be negotiated in local terms (Rahnema and Bawtree 1997; Saunders 2002). Post-development, in Kriemild Saunders's words, confronts 'the fundamental contradiction of global capitalism and economic growth with the goals of equity, empowerment and a sustainable environment' (Saunders 2002: 17). It doesn't imply an outright rejection of development, but rather emphasises the untenability of those dominant models of 'catch-up' development that are based on the twin principles of western cultural hegemony and economic growth. Such models are characterised, post-development theorists argue, by 'a colonial mentality stamped by [the] overvaluation of industrial societies and a [corresponding] devaluation of subsistence-based communities', which often work with different sets of social and ecological principles, and which tend – in very general terms – to formulate a view of the world that privileges simple living, and in which spiritual and socio-cultural well-being is accorded greater importance than material growth (19). To some extent, of course, this rose-tinted view of subsistence-based societies is a recipe for romanticism, but post-development theorists are no more unified in their philosophy than their neoliberal counterparts, and are not necessarily opposed to at least some of their alleged opponents' principles, e.g. the value of western science and technology, or the need to match 'efficiency' to 'sufficiency' models in the pursuit of a fulfilled life (Saunders 2002).

'Sustainability' is the watchword of these theorists, but at the same time many of them are suspicious of the coupling of sustainability and development, on the grounds that preserving the term 'development', in whatever shape or combination, implies a continuing attachment to the idea of development as economic growth. More suspicious still are those radical theorists, like Wolfgang Sachs, who see sustainable development as just the latest ruse deployed by the apostles of development ideology to ward off critiques of development's destructive tendencies: 'No development without sustainability; no sustainability without development [...] Development emerges rejuvenated from this liaison, the ailing concept gaining another lease on life' (Sachs 1997: 29). Sachs sees contemporary catchphrases such as the 'survival of the planet' in similar vein, as little more than a political alibi for the latest 'wave of state intervention in people's lives all over the world' (33). He links this wave to what he calls a 'global ecocracy', whose concerns for environmental management rely on forms of administrative control and technological one-upmanship that cannot help but suggest that 'calls for the survival of the planet are often, upon closer inspection, nothing [other] than calls for the survival of the industrial system [itself]' (35).

Sachs is joined here by Escobar, who sees sustainable development in terms of 'the resignification of nature as environment; [as] a reinscription of the Earth into capital via science; [as] the reinterpretation of poverty as [an] effect of destroyed environment; [and as] the new lease on management and planning as arbiters between people and nature' (Escobar 1995: 203). Taken together, these measures suggest that sustainable development, far from being an attempt to adjust development to social and environmental concerns, is rather the First World's latest initiative to 'colonize the last areas of Third World social life that are not yet completely ruled by the logic of the individual and the market, such as water rights, forests, and sacred groves' (198). Like Sachs, Escobar sees sustainable development in terms of the sustainability of the *market* as a primary regulating mechanism in the determination of people's everyday lives. For both, the term 'environment' itself implies the marketability of nature, providing an implicit rationalisation for the control and management of natural resources by the global urban-industrial system and its primary political ally, the nation-state. In this sense, sustainable development implies that it is economic growth, rather than the environment, that needs to be protected, and that environmental degradation is to be fought against principally because it impedes this growth:

> The epistemological and political reconciliation of economy and ecology proposed by sustainable development is intended to create the impression that only minor adjustments to the market system are needed to launch an era of economically sound development, hiding the fact that the economic framework itself cannot hope to accommodate environmental considerations without substantial reform.
>
> (197)

Sachs and Escobar probably go too far in dismissing the regenerative possibilities of sustainable development. (Still more caustic is Esteva, for whom all attempts at rebranding development – 'human-centred', 'participatory', 'integrated', 'sustainable', etc. – are doomed to failure as development continues to mean its opposite: 'from the unburied corpse of development, every kind of pest has started to spread' (6).) The ecological term 'sustainability', despite its flagrant abuses, seems worth sustaining – at least for the moment – not least because it can become a useful banner under which to fight for social as well as ecological justice in the postcolonial world. Still, sustainability needs to be uncoupled from what Escobar calls the 'developmentalization of the environment': a pet project of the global-capitalist development apparatus in which, under the aegis of 'planetary management', 'the Western scientist continues to speak for the [entire] Earth' (194; see also Ross 1991).[3] Similarly, sustainability needs to be recognised not just for what it is, but *where* it is, e.g. in the self-monitoring practices of indigenous (Fourth World) societies or in the non-commodified relations to nature that are often central to the function of subsistence-based economies, and that help to determine the livelihood of historically marginalised social groups (Saunders 2002). (Ironically, one of the tendencies of development discourse is to blame the southern poor for their lack of environmental consciousness, thus shifting blame away from the industrial polluters of the north.)

Postcolonial critics and, especially, postcolonial *writers* have made a valuable contribution to ongoing debates about social and economic development in many regions of the formerly colonised world. Their contributions have consisted for the most part of protest literature, sometimes in its most overt forms such as non-fictional reportage and political pamphletry, but also in more indirect forms such as novels, poetry and plays. The primary function of much of this literature has been that of global consciousness-raising in a wide variety of (post)colonial contexts in which the twin demands of social and environmental justice are conspicuously displayed. However, to label such writing as either 'advocacy' or 'activism' risks underestimating its aesthetic complexities – one of several points where postcolonial criticism meets ecocriticism, which is similarly attentive to the negotiations between political imperative and aesthetic play. As already argued in the Introduction to this book, postcolonial ecocriticism is that form of criticism which appreciates the enduring *non*-instrumentality of environmental writing, as well as gauging its continuing usefulness in mobilising individual and collective support. This insistence on the at least partial autonomy of the literary text, which is a feature of both postcolonial and environmental criticism, will be adhered to in this study, although literary choices are rarely without their political consequences, as postcolonial/environmental writers (and indeed all writers) know. Arundhati Roy, whose work forms one of the central planks of this chapter, puts it well in her characteristically combative discussion of the overused term 'writer-activist', which we will quote here at length:

> The term 'writer-activist' [...] is strategically positioned to diminish both writers and activists. It seeks to reduce the scope, the range, the sweep, of what a writer is and can be. It suggests, somehow,

that writers by definition are too effete to come up with the clarity, the explicitness, the reasoning, the passion, the grit, the audacity and, if necessary, the vulgarity, to publicly take up a political position. And conversely, it suggests that activists occupy the coarser, cruder end of the intellectual spectrum. That activists are by profession 'position-takers' and therefore lack complexity and intellectual sophistication, and are instead fuelled by a crude, simple-minded, one-sided understanding of things. But the more fundamental problem I have with the term is that this attempt to 'professionalize' protest has the effect of containing the problem and suggesting that it's up to the professionals – activists and writer-activists – to deal with it [...] The fact is that what's happening today is not a 'problem', and the issues that some of us are raising are not 'causes'. They are huge political and social upheavals that are convulsing the world. One is not involved by virtue of being a writer or activist. One is involved because one is a human being. Writing about it just happens to be the most effective thing a writer can do. It is vital to deprofessionalize the public debate on matters that vitally affect the lives of ordinary people. It's time to snatch futures back from the 'experts'. Time to ask, in ordinary language, the public question and to demand, in ordinary language, the public answer [...] Frankly, however trenchantly, angrily, persuasively or poetically the case is made out, at the end of the day a writer is a citizen, only one of many, who is demanding public information, asking for a public explanation.

(2002: 186–87)

Roy's insistence on the public accountability of the writer is one of the mantras of postcolonial ecocriticism. But so, too, is her insistence that writers aren't alone in seeking explanations for vital everyday issues, and that social responsibility (her main criterion for global citizenship) is a task that needs to be shared. Finally, Roy's view that writers have a valuable role to play in what she calls the 'deprofessionalization' of public debate strikes a chord with many of the writers whose work will be analysed in this chapter, as with much of the literature that is looked at in this study as a whole. Still, her conviction that writers must sometimes take sides in protesting against flagrant social and/or environmental injustices needs to be measured against the constitutive instabilities of her chosen (literary) form. It is this tension between content and form, this alertness to the mendacities of language, that is the stuff of literary criticism in general and postcolonial ecocriticism in particular, and examples will not be lacking in this chapter – not least within the body of Roy's own work.

Abuses of power

If one of the axioms of postcolonial ecocriticism is that there is no social justice without ecological justice, then that axiom is no more clearly illustrated than in the nightmarish events surrounding the death on 10 November 1995 of Nigerian writer-activist Ken Saro-Wiwa, who was tried and executed along with eight of his Ogoni kinsmen for a crime he did not commit. Saro-Wiwa's execution, which went ahead despite a public outcry, turned him into 'Africa's first environmental martyr' (Nixon 2005: 233) while creating international consciousness of the twin causes for which he died: the irreparable damage done to Ogoni farmland and fishing waters by the huge oil conglomerate, SPDC (Shell Petroleum Development Company), and the political oppression of his people, marginalised and exploited by a tyrannical Nigerian state. In his posthumously published detention diary, *A Month and a Day* (1995), Saro-Wiwa describes the struggle in terms of two simultaneous wars, one an 'ecological war' fought against Nigerian-based multinational oil companies, principally Shell and Chevron, and the other a 'political war' aimed at nothing less than an extermination of the Ogoni people by systematically dispossessing them of their fundamental human rights and locally generated wealth (97). Saro-Wiwa's death was widely seen as an instance of tragic heroism in which the life-long fight he took up on behalf of his impoverished people became emblematic of both local and global struggles against the depredations of international capitalism and for the right to a clean earth (Quayson 1998: 76–77). These struggles have since been mythicised, with Saro-Wiwa coming to be seen as a global symbol of the general struggle for human rights and social/ecological justice, and with the 'sanctity of his story' taking on an almost 'sacred weight' (Wiwa 2000: 161, 11). And, as we will see, they have also been allegorised in ethnic terms as the fight of minority societies to be recognised within the overarching context of the nation, and in ecopolitical terms as a critique of the ongoing exploitation of natural resources by oil-capitalism and a 'vampire' state (Apter 1998).

A further allegorical context revolves around the phrase 'growth without development', in terms of which the huge squandering of oil-generated revenue in Nigeria can be seen as symptomatic of both the fetish-value of international petrodollars and the social/ecological ruination brought about by oil-capitalism's predatory alliance with the nation-state (Apter 1998). Two faces of development emerge here: a 'false' face in which development supplies an alibi for the protection of strategic political and economic interests, and a 'true' face in which it provides a catalyst for the promotion of civil society and human rights. As we hope to demonstrate, these two faces are revealed in the 'Saro-Wiwa affair' across a variety of different *contexts* (social, political, economic) and the discourses that are attached to them, but are also articulated across a variety of different literary *genres* (tragedy, creation fable, the morality tale). A postcolonial-ecocritical understanding of the ongoing Ogoni struggle for compensation against social death and environmental degradation thus needs to be seen *both* in terms of these interwoven contexts *and* in terms of the different ways in which the struggle has been represented, not least in the writings of Saro-Wiwa himself.

The primary context against which the continuing narrative of Ogoni struggle needs to be read is that of colonialism or, perhaps better, neocolonialism, the long and at times elaborate process by which 'the multinational companies [came to] replace colonial power in Nigeria, and indeed in the Third World as a whole' (Na'Allah 1998: 26). The more particular history of Shell is largely illustrative of this process. As Andrew Rowell, James Marriott and Lorne Stockman explain in their study *The Next Gulf: London, Washington and Oil Conflict in Nigeria* (2005), the exploitation of oil and gas in the Niger Delta dates back to the early part of the twentieth century, when an extensive development scheme was launched by the colonial administration in Lagos and overseen by the Colonial Office in London (53). This scheme, initially tied to the lucrative palm-oil, rubber and timber industries, helped consolidate the colonial monopoly structure that would later become central to the oil business, which officially began with explorations north of Lagos by the German-owned Nigerian Bitumen Company, but would soon become exclusively associated with British interests following German defeat in the First World War (54). A second major initiative was the founding in 1936 of a joint venture company whose two main players, Royal Dutch Shell and British Petroleum (BP), claimed a monopoly over Nigerian oil, reminiscent of that previously held by the British-owned Royal Niger Company (56). While the Second World War brought a temporary halt, oil prospecting continued apace in the late 1940s and early 1950s, culminating in a major find in Olibiri (Ijawland) in 1956. As Rowell *et al.* observe, 'the find at Olibiri would not have been possible without colonial help. To Shell-BP, the colonial government was more than just a favourable government; [rather,] Shell-BP's interests in Nigeria and those of the British state were completely intertwined' (58–59). Oil prospecting in the Niger Delta, then, was a political process from the very beginning, and there was the clearest of mutual dependencies between colonial financial and legal backing and the geological search. Shell's continuing dominance in post-independence Nigeria – it produces over half of the country's oil – is very much part of this colonial legacy; and although the Nigerian oil industry has since been nationalised, Shell, now operating in tandem with the Nigerian National Petroleum Corporation (NNPC) as part of the giant joint-venture Shell Petroleum Development Company (SPDC), is generally considered to have maintained a distinct advantage over its closest competitors, holding what amounts in practice to a controlling stake (Rowell *et al.* 2005). The importance of oil revenue to Nigeria can hardly be overestimated: oil accounts for around 90 per cent of the country's export earnings, and more than 80 per cent of the Federal Government's total revenues (Rowell 1996: 289). Moreover, since the discovery of oil Nigeria has become a leading player in the global energy industry: it is currently the tenth largest oil producer in the world, and this status is all the more important given ongoing unrest in the Middle East, with important customers such as the United States of America looking increasingly to the Gulf of Guinea (comprising Nigeria and its significantly smaller oil-producing neighbours, Equatorial Guinea, Cameroon and Gabon) as a desirable, possibly even essential, alternative to the Persian Gulf (Rowell *et al.* 2005).

Oil, the life-blood of the nation, has enabled Nigeria to trumpet its independence in the postcolonial era, to finance a large number of state development projects, and to claim a leadership role in the so-called African Renaissance: the cultural revitalisation of the black and African world (Apter 1998: 135). However, Nigeria is arguably no more in control of its own resources than it was during the colonial period. Decisions about when and where to prospect are more likely to be made in London or Washington than Lagos, and, as Rowell *et al.* argue provocatively, a new Atlantic Triangle is emerging in which 'the US and Europe both finance and consume Africa's resources' – resources that need to be defended at all costs (202). What has resulted over time is a 'militarisation of commerce' (Ake, quoted in Rowell 1996: 315) in which vast oil reserves are placed under permanent – and often highly volatile – protection, and an appropriation of petroleum resources on a scale that amounts to the 'privatisation of the state' (Ake, quoted in Rowell 1996: 315). Andrew Apter calls this 'state vampirism' and charts the process by which the newly oil-rich Nigerian state 'expanded at its own expense, ostensibly pumping oil-money into the nation while secretly sucking it back into private fiefdoms and bank accounts' (143). State vampirism also describes the way in which the Nigerian state, and those corrupt bureaucrats who allegedly operated in its interests, preyed upon the people they claimed to serve, funnelling vast amounts of money and resources into the hands of a neocolonial elite (Apter 1998; see also Soyinka 1996).

Yet if this neocolonial context looms large in Saro-Wiwa's sustained critique of state power in contemporary Nigeria, so too does the *domestic* colonialism that underpins it. Thus, while Saro-Wiwa is unrelenting in his attacks on the self-consuming body of the African state, 'conceived in the European colonialist interest for imperial or commercial purposes' (1995: 123), he is equally scathing in his analysis of the 'indigenous colonialism' that has been practised against Nigeria's minorities in the name of crass ethnic preferentialism, the cultivated indifference of a centralised state system, and the arbitrary brutalities of three decades of self-serving military rule. As Saro-Wiwa makes clear in all his work, the history of oil in Nigeria has been synonymous with a history of colonial oppression that operates at several different levels, and whose most obvious victims are 'the Ogoni people and, by implication, the ethnic minorities and indigenous people' of Nigeria, specifically, and Africa as a whole (1995: 39). (The *indigeneity* of the Ogoni seems worth stressing here. As Saro-Wiwa argues in his trenchant analysis of the Nigerian civil war, *On a Darkling Plain* (1989), and in his pointedly entitled polemic, *Genocide in Nigeria: The Ogoni Tragedy* (1992), the Ogoni are an indigenous people whose traditional life-ways were established long before the creation of Nigeria, and whose livelihoods have effectively been usurped by the joint workings of transnational commerce and the state. This is presumably what Saro-Wiwa means when he sees the Ogoni as genocidal victims of 'domestic colonialism' in Nigeria, and when he lambastes the arrogance of successive military regimes that have subjected them to 'abject poverty, slavery, dehumanisation and [potential] extinction' (1995: 97). This presumably also lies behind his attempts to seek international recourse for the Ogoni via such consciousness-raising events as the International Year for the World's Indigenous People, directed by the United Nations General Assembly, and sponsored by – among others – the United Nations Development Programme, UNESCO, and the Centre for Human Rights (1995: 89).)

Despite the odds, Saro-Wiwa never lost faith in the possibility of re-establishing Ogoni culture, and of recreating a society that had been destroyed by 'European colonialism, neo-colonialism, or the newly inspired and even more destructive "black colonialism"' (1995: 130). 'Everything [has] happened to the Ogoni,' he admits ruefully: 'Colonisation, pacification, absorption into Nigeria, allocation into Eastern Nigeria [...] The experience of the Ogoni people in the twentieth century, briefly put, is a tale of administrative neglect, [and] of exploitation and slavery in which the British colonial administration, the newly emergent Nigerian nation-state, [and] the multi-national oil giant Shell have [all] had a role to play' (124–25). Exemplary of this desire to rebuild is a document that Saro-Wiwa was instrumental in drafting, the 1990 Ogoni Bill of Rights, which sets out the grounds for ethnic autonomy, economic reparation, and environmental control (1995: 48–49; see also Quayson 1998: 70–71). Included in the Bill are suggestions for (human) development, but on the Ogoni's terms, not those of their would-be benefactors. Shell has always maintained its commitment to the principle of community development in Ogoniland, citing its support for the building of schools and hospitals, and its willing provision of assistance in a variety of socially and economically beneficial forms. However, the fact remains that Shell has raked only a small percentage of its vast profits back into the communities on which its impact has often been devastating, whether through tacit support for the brutalities of the military, or through open disrespect for the social and environmental needs of a notably unstable, if historically profitable, region that lost all semblance of independence when it was placed at the mercy of the Nigerian state (Rowell *et al*. 2005: 126–27; see also Young 1999). Shell's far-from-impressive track record in Nigeria has drawn criticism from a number of different quarters, including some of the NGOs and 'fair trade' companies with which it actively competes in the global-ethical stakes. As Rowell *et al*. suggest, quite neutrally: 'The issue of Shell's sustainable development has become a battleground between the NGOs' (127); or, as Robert Young puts it, much more bluntly: 'Who [...] would ever have thought that companies would begin to take each other on [...] in this new imperialist era of global capitalism, in which ethics has become another commodity that sells products?' (1999: 446).[4]

This battle over the interpretation of development can also be seen in the competing discourses that crowd in on the Saro-Wiwa legacy, from the corporate statism of the Babangida and Abacha regimes to the survivalist ethno-nationalism of the Ogoni, to the 'responsible' environmentalisms which, propagated by virtually all parties, are often in direct contradiction to the facts. As usual, Saro-Wiwa, untiring in his self-conferred roles as human-rights activist and environmental campaigner, provides a valuable corrective, cutting through the corporate 'greenwash' to demand compensation for his people:

> In Ogoni[land], Shell locations lie pat in the middle of villages, in front and back gardens – and that should lay a particular responsibility on Shell to be absolutely cautious in its operations. The company, however, remains negligent and wilful. [...] If one spill from the *Exxon Valdez* could cost Exxon five billion dollars in punitive damages, Shell must pay more than the four billion dollars which the Ogoni have demanded in reparation for the ecological damage to the people and land over a 35-year period in which there have been spills, blow-outs and continual gas-flaring [...] in the Niger Delta – one of the richest areas on earth.
>
> (1995: 112–13)

Saro-Wiwa is by no means the only one to have drawn similar conclusions from the evidence. A fragile riverine ecosystem, the Niger Delta, has effectively been laid waste by several decades of oil and gas exploration and production, making it one of the most ecologically endangered regions in the world (Rowell 1996: 290). The crisis is exacerbated by the region's high population density – 1,250 people per square kilometre, as compared to the national Nigerian average of 300 (Rowell 1996: 290) – which means that a large number of people are trapped in an 'environmental nightmare' (Watts 1994): cancers and other serious medical conditions are prevalent in the area, and many farmlands and waterways have been polluted beyond repair. While Shell is right in asserting that at least some of this damage has been caused by 'bunkering' (illegal tapping) and industrial sabotage, the company has been – and remains – reluctant to accept the scale of environmental degradation of which it stands accused, or to offer compensation for its activities in the past (Mittee 1999; Young 1999). At the same time, particularly in the wake of Saro-Wiwa's death, it has devoted a great deal of time, money and energy to improving public relations, e.g. in a number of high-profile television advertisements, and in a series of self-monitoring environmental reports (Rowell *et al.* 2005). Despite the qualified success of these initiatives, Shell, which withdrew from Ogoniland in the mid-1990s, remains understandably distrusted by the vast majority of the people who live there, and has become a worldwide target for environmental activists, some of whom have turned the 'Saro-Wiwa affair' into valuable cultural capital in support of their own anti-development campaigns (Rowell *et al.* 2005). However, the canonised status of Saro-Wiwa among environmentally oriented activists and NGOs has not always been matched by their academic counterparts, with the result that his life and work, in both postcolonial and ecocritical circles, has not been given the attention it deserves. One reason for this is, as Rob Nixon points out, that ecocriticism has tended until recently to focus on American or American-based writers, so that 'someone like Saro-Wiwa, whose environmentalism was at once profoundly local and profoundly international, [is often] bracketed as an African, the kind of writer best left to the postcolonialists' (2005: 234). Another is that postcolonial criticism, in its turn, has concentrated on a handful of 'representative' African writers, leaving Saro-Wiwa, who is not generally included within this pantheon, once again out in the cold. Ironically, both 'schools' have had difficulties accommodating full diversity within their respective literary canons, even as 'diversity', and the social responsibilities it carries, has been one of their most insistent rallying calls (Huggan 2004).

Still, a writer like Saro-Wiwa, obvious though the choice is, presents further difficulties for postcolonial ecocriticism. The first difficulty is that of accounting for what might be called his metonymic function as a global spokesperson for social and environmental issues: a function that can easily lead to moralistic generalisations about endemic political corruption in Africa, or the nefarious role of transnational companies in robbing local people of their livelihoods, or the heroic part played by freedom fighters and resistance movements prepared to take on the assembled might of global commerce and the state. The second difficulty (which is linked to the first) is that of taking full account of the literary qualities of writing that is often assumed to be purely instrumental: as if transparent messages were all that were contained within even the most factual of non-fictional reports. This second difficulty is compounded in Saro-Wiwa's case by the sheer range of his published writing, which encompasses newspaper journalism (the genre for which he is probably best known in Nigeria), television drama, satire, poetry and fiction, as well as autobiographical non-fiction (the genre for which he is probably best known in the wider western world). This sub-section concludes by considering two dominant genres/modes in which the Saro-Wiwa story has been couched, in part but by no means exclusively by Saro-Wiwa himself, tragedy and allegory or, more specifically, fable: genres/modes which indicate that environmental polemic, like other forms of protest writing, often blurs the boundaries between fiction and non-fiction, cutting across a number of accepted literary forms.

The most concerted attempt to look at Saro-Wiwa's life and work within the context of tragedy has been Ato Quayson's, in a fine essay written for a commemorative volume of essays that appeared in 1998, three years after his death. As Quayson suggests, tragedy may provide 'tools by which to analyse political actions at the dual levels of structure and agency', particularly in contexts where academic and journalistic discourses intermingle, and the meaning of 'tragedy' is inflected both by the scholarly and the everyday. It is at this intersection of the scholarly and the everyday, Quayson suggests, that 'a re-reading of the events leading to Ken Saro-Wiwa's death may be productively located. This is to attempt a form of translation in which real life events are viewed through the prism of the emotionally and philosophically charged discourse of literary tragedy' (Quayson 1998: 59). Saro-Wiwa's life and death were tragic, Quayson contends, in so far as they exemplified ethical values 'pre-eminently expressed in a will to act in the face of forces that would negate them' (65). In other words, Saro-Wiwa's determination to confront a military regime that he full knew would probably respond by doing away with him conferred on him a tragic hero status 'because he committed himself to his people but could not possibly [have] controlled all the forces he unleashed' (77). Sacrificial commitment of this kind,

Quayson suggests, helped elevate Saro-Wiwa into a tragic figure, turning him at the same time into a spokesperson for all Nigeria, and enabling his struggle to transcend local riverine politics to 'capture the frustrations of a nation – in the now understated words of [fellow Nigerian writer] Chinua Achebe – no longer at ease' (73).

Quayson's interpretation of Saro-Wiwa's life seems unduly over-determined. But as he crucially points out, tragedy was also one of the registers in which Saro-Wiwa himself chose to articulate the struggle of the Ogoni, notably in his 1992 book *Genocide in Nigeria: The Ogoni Tragedy*, in which he made it clear that 'the terrible predicament of the Ogoni [...] could only be relieved by the total commitment of his own life' (65). This tragic register is echoed across the body of Saro-Wiwa's writings and, in particular, in those interviews in which he insists that his mission is to lay down his life for a people he fears might go extinct:

> There is a clear definition of genocide by the United Nations: any-thing done to destroy a group of people. Now, if you take the Ogoni case for instance, you pollute their air, you pollute their streams, you make it impossible for them to farm or fish, which is their main source of livelihood, and then what comes out of their soil you take entirely away and you say we will give you 1.5 percent or 3 percent, but we are not giving it to you [...] Now, if more people in Ogoni [land] are dying than are being born, if Ogoni boys and girls are not going to school, not primary not secondary, if those who manage to scale through [sic] cannot find jobs; if when they find jobs they don't get promotion because promotions don't even go by any standards at all, then surely you are leading the tribe to extinction. Ogoni people are going extinct.
>
> (Saro-Wiwa 1998: 351–52)

In the interview, Saro-Wiwa steers a fine line between activism and victim rhetoric, skilfully manipulating two registers he knows are discursively opposed but, at the same time, politically enmeshed. This rhetorical skill can also be seen in *Genocide*, which recounts the tragedy of the Ogoni as a political/ecological fable in which its various actors (Shell, the Ogoni, the Military Dictatorship, the Ethnic Majority) are called upon to 'highlight [...] mythic themes, and to prefigure those allegorical dimen-sions [that link] Ogoniland to the Nigerian nation' (Apter 1998: 124). Fables of this kind are often morally polarised, pitting the survival struggles of downtrodden indigenous peoples against the acquisitive ambitions of global capitalism and the state. They are also self-consciously romanti-cised, as in the opening paragraph of *Genocide*, where Saro-Wiwa depicts the pre-colonial Ogoni as living in a state of nature, inseparable from the territory (which Saro-Wiwa also significantly calls Ogoni) they inhabit:

> To the Ogoni, rivers and streams do not only provide water for life – for bathing, drinking, etc.; they do not only provide fish for food, they are also sacred and are bound up intricately with the life of the community, of the entire Ogoni nation.
>
> (1992: 12–13; also quoted in Apter 1998: 125)

As Andrew Apter suggests, this 'foundational account of an "original affluent society" [...] serves as a charter for Ogoni ownership' while setting the tone for the narrative of deprivation that follows, in which the Ogoni are both spiritually desecrated and materially dispossessed (1998: 125). Morality tales of this type draw no obvious conclusion, succumbing instead to a form of tragic inevitability that would be emotionally overwhelming were it not strategically exaggerated – just as the charge of genocide itself, though not without foundation, has a predominantly rhetorical force. The combination of fable and high moral drama that can be seen in Saro-Wiwa's autobiographical accounts of the Ogoni struggle also tends to be replicated in the critical discourse that is applied to them, indicating a general tendency in activist writing towards a theatricalisation of the issues it sets out. A further tendency (probably reproduced here) is to weave romantically between life and work, so that the former becomes exemplary and the latter becomes inseparable from the life to which it gives meaning: a characteristic of confessional autobiography and other ethically oriented literary forms. Certainly, it is tempting to see Saro-Wiwa's life and work as exemplary, though, as his son Ken points out in his moving memoir of his father, the view of Saro-Wiwa as a latter-day saint is inevitably misleading, investing his life with the status of a legend 'embellished and mystified with each retelling', and fusing it with the similarly sanctified struggle of the Ogoni as a story that is 'supposed to be told and retold' (Wiwa 2000: 11). To some extent, as the son recognises, the father *wanted* to be a legendary figure, actively conspiring in his own media creation as a 'global symbol of the struggle for human rights, social justice, the environment and just about everything else under the sun' (161). As the son also acknowledges, there is something almost comical about the way in which the father's name has subsequently been co-opted for a variety of causes he would not necessarily have supported:

> He would have laughed off the irony that NGOs that had politely turned him away two years before were now falling over themselves

to write proposals and to get funding for projects to ensure that
'Ken Saro-Wiwa's death was not in vain'. Streets were renamed,
scholarships announced and public holidays declared. His name was
used and abused. Refugees would apply for asylum, claiming to be
related to Ken Saro-Wiwa. I received calls from all over Europe
asking me to verify that so-and-so was a relative. Bogus foundations
were launched, such as the one set up in the Ivory Coast by Stephen
Wiwa and Janet Wiwa, who claimed to be the son and wife of someone called Dr. Kenneth Saro-Wiwa. They even received a donation
from a lawyer in Pakistan! And while these people were dining out
on my father's name, his critics were chipping away at his reputation
and character.

(161–62)

This is the stuff of satire, and Saro-Wiwa, a master of the form, would
doubtless have appreciated it. However, his legacy remains as one of
Africa's most famous prisoners of conscience, a deeply courageous if by
no means uncomplicated figure who, for many, has come to stand for the
political struggle for minority rights in Nigeria and the environmental
struggle for land and water rights across the western world.

Second in global visibility only to Saro-Wiwa is the Indian writer
Arundhati Roy, whose fulminating essays 'The Greater Common Good'
(1999) and 'The End of the Imagination' (1998), capitalising on the success
of her Booker prize-winning novel *The God of Small Things* (1997),
probably represent the most eye-catching ecocritical intervention by a
recognised postcolonial writer to date. The essays, first published sepa-
rately as cover stories for two mainstream English-language magazines,
Outlook and *Frontline*, and later re-packaged for the international mass
market as *The Cost of Living*, are clear attempts to reach out both to a
local readership familiar with their controversial issues (the Narmada
Valley Development Project in the first case, India's decision to go nuclear
in the second), and to an international audience possibly unaware of,
and probably uninformed on, either issue, but sufficiently attuned to
Roy's success to grant her work another look. The essays are deliberately designed, that is, as a politically motivated publicity venture which,
riding on the back of Roy's recently accorded celebrity status, seeks to
attract and, ideally, to convert large numbers of readers both in her
home country and elsewhere.

It would be easy here to categorise Roy as another media-hungry
Indo-Anglian cosmopolitan celebrity (Brennan 1997; Mongia 1997), or to
see her as having staked a claim in the latest popular humanitarian cause.
(The latest re-packaging of the essays, *The Algebra of Infinite Justice*

(2002), also includes suitably polemical essays on 9/11, in which Roy's populist anti-Americanism is brought to the fore.) Certainly, in 'The Greater Common Good', the essay on which we will initially concentrate here, Roy takes rhetorical liberties with her disempowered Adivasi subjects, converting them into mythologised victims in her own highly personal moral crusade against the tyrannies of the modern Indian state. And certainly, she is aware throughout the essay of the constitutive, but also distorting, role of the global media in constructing the latest, highly visible human/ecological catastrophe as a newsworthy 'event' (Roy 1999: 47, 50, 63; see also Rowell 1996: 282–86). But Roy, as in all her work, is not only interested in manipulating publicity for her own, and other people's, interests, but also in showing how publicity – or, in this case, the mediated language of the common good, the *national* interest – achieves its magical effects. Hence the ironic title of her essay, which reflects – as does Saro-Wiwa within the Nigerian context – on the ways in which a centralised state has not only commandeered national assets and resources, but also sought through media channels both to convey the fiction of a carefully monitored 'national progress' and to ally it to the greater (global) development cause. The fiction of 'national progress', as Partha Chatterjee would have it, demands that government be 'abstracted out of the messy business of politics', thereby releasing it for the utopian task of 'receiving inputs from all parts of society, processing them, and finally allocating the optimal values for the common satis- faction and preservation of society as a whole' (Chatterjee 1986: 160). Chatterjee's satirical view of the development process is crucially linked to technological know-how in the service of the state; and such expertise, in the hands of the few, requires the self-sacrifice of the many:

> Place all your prayers at the feet of the *sarkar*, the omnipotent and supremely enlightened state, and they will be duly passed on to the body of experts who are planning for the overall progress of the country. If your requests are consistent with the requirements of progress, they will be granted.
>
> (160)

Such classic developmentalist mythology provides the grounds for Roy's vivid ecological fable of the Narmada Valley Development Project: that ill-fated post-independence hydro-electric and irrigation scheme which, affecting hundreds of thousands of lives, is often considered to be 'India's Greatest Planned Environmental Disaster' (Roy 1999: 44); and which is sometimes seen, in the 'congealed mass of hope, anger, information, disinformation, political artifice, engineering ambition, disingenuous socialism, radical activism, bureaucratic subterfuge, [and] misinformed socialism' that surrounds it, as a metonymy for the self-consuming narrative of modern India itself (9).

A few facts may be helpful here. India is the third largest dam-builder in the world, having built over three thousand big dams in the sixty-odd years since independence (Roy 1999; see also McCully 1996). Of these dams, several of the largest and best known belong to the state-administered Narmada Valley Development Project, spanning three states (Gujarat, Maharashtra and Madhya Pradesh) in central India. This hugely ambitious project, first dreamed up half a century ago and still – despite mass protests – considered to be a viable proposition, conceives of building '3,200 dams that will reconstitute the Narmada [river] and her forty-one tributaries into a series of step reservoirs – an immense staircase of amenable water' (Roy 1999: 33). Two of these dams, the giant Sardar Sarovar in Gujarat and the Narmada Sagar in Madhya Pradesh, will hold 'more water [between them] than any other reservoir on the Indian subcontinent' (33). The project aims to provide electricity and safe drinking water for millions while irrigating millions of hectares of infertile farming land. From its inception, however, the project has been fraught with problems. Hundreds of thousands of local people, mostly Adivasis, have been ousted from their land, with irreparable damage being done to their daily lives, their economic self-sufficiency, and their culture. The evidence suggests that the project may consume more electricity than it produces, and that its state-of-the-art flood-warning and irrigation systems have had a damaging – in some cases, devastating – effect on the very dams they sought to protect, the very crop-yields they promised to increase. The astronomic cost of the project, heavily subsidised by the World Bank until its forced withdrawal in the early 1990s, has helped to push 'the country [further] into an economic bondage it may never overcome' (35). (More recently, the Maheshwar dam, India's first major private hydro-electric project, has been added to the scheme in a move suggestive of what Roy calls, in a slightly later essay, the 'privatization [not just] of natural resources and essential infrastructure [but] of policy making itself' (Roy 2002: 135).) As Roy suggests in the essay, the increasing privatisation of energy sources in India 'seeks to disengage politics from the market', thereby 'blunt[ing] the very last weapon that India's poor still have – their vote' (143). Roy calibrates this 'privatization of power' to the *dis*empowerment of the people, suggesting that the selling-off of energy stock to private companies in a country where 70 per cent of the population still lives in rural areas, amounts to a 'barbaric dispossession on a scale that has no parallel in history' (136).)

Notwithstanding, widespread dissent to all aspects of the project, mobilised around the powerful Narmada Bachao Andolan (Save the Narmada Movement), has been violently suppressed. All in all, as Andrew Rowell summarises it, the Narmada Valley Development Project,

> conceived in the dinosaur development era that deemed megaprojects the panacea for the world's energy problems, has been nothing short of a human and ecological catastrophe, [...] an example of the neglect of local communities' needs and views in the development equation and the state repression against dissent when communities want to have their voices heard.
>
> (1996: 282)

But the story, as Roy knows, is not limited to the facts, depressing though these are; for the project and, particularly, the big dams at its centre have also played a symbolic role in the development of India as a modern nation, a process in which – much as in Saro-Wiwa's Nigeria – the two equal-and-opposite faces of development, economic (corporatist-statist) and human (communal), are locked in battle as never before. As Patrick McCully puts it:

> Perhaps more than any other technology, massive dams symbolize the progress of humanity from a life ruled by nature and superstition to one where nature is ruled by science, and superstition vanquished by rationality. They also symbolize the might of the state that built them, making huge dams a favorite of nation-builders and autocrats. When a dam is given such a powerful symbolic role, its economic and technical rationale and potential negative impacts fade into insignificance in the decision-making process.
>
> (1996: 237)

Big dams, in other words, suggest a potentially deadly alliance between the modernist ideology of technological gigantism and the repressively authoritarian politics of state ownership and control (Roy 1999: 91–92). Transnational corporate interests also play a key part in the alliance. The international dam industry, as Roy points out, is

> worth $20 billion a year. If you follow the trails of Big Dams the world over, wherever you go – China, Japan, Malaysia, Thailand, Brazil, Guatemala – you'll rub against the same story, encounter the same actors: the Iron Triangle (dam-jargon for the nexus between politicians, bureaucrats and dam construction companies), the racketeers

who call themselves International Environmental consultants (who are usually directly employed by dam-builders or their subsidiaries), and more often than not, the friendly neighbourhood World Bank.

(35–36)

The national allegory of statist abuse Roy constructs around the Narmada Valley Development Project thus gradually widens out into an ecological 'war for the rivers and the mountains and the forests of the world' (52). At the same time, the narrative Roy spins takes on the dimensions both of anti-statist fable, quasi-Dickensian in its moral intensity ('[The state] is a giant poverty-producing machine, masterful in its methods of pitting the poor against the very poor': 28), and of cautionary tale on the ecological price to be paid when 'human intelligence [...] outstrip[s] its own instinct for survival', and 'twentieth-century emblems' such as big dams and nuclear bombs become 'malignant indications of a civilisation turning upon itself' (101).

If Roy's message is crystal clear, unashamedly partisan in its intentions, her text remains a curiously unresolved mixture: part hard-headed investigative report, part sentimental political fable; part historically situated postcolonial allegory, part universal Green manifesto and call to arms. The different narrative strands cut across and contradict one another. Facts are needed to illustrate the enormity of the story, but its teller also complains of suffocating statistics and the state's own version of 'fascist Maths' (72). The breathless language of fable is ironised on numerous occasions ('Nobody knows this, but Kevadia Colony is the key to the World. Go there, and secrets will be revealed to you' (73)), only to be reinstated, writ doubly large, on just as many again:

Who knows [...] what the twenty-first century has in store for us. The dismantling of the Big? Big bombs, big dams, big ideologies, big contradictions, big countries, big wars, big heroes, big mistakes. Perhaps it will be the Century of the Small. Perhaps right now, this very minute, there's a small god up in heaven readying herself for us.

(12)

Complex social, political and ecological systems – as if to counter the technocrat's with the storyteller's magic – are repeatedly reduced to the black-and-white dramatics of the children's morality tale (15, 24, 41). In the end, the standard format of the ecological heroes-and-villains story (Guha and Martinez-Alier 1997), however ironically manipulated, proves to be no match for contemporary postcolonial realities. Indeed, it raises the crucial question of for whom Roy believes herself to be speaking – Adivasi 'oustees'? The Narmada Bachao Andolan? The Indian people? Environmental activists and 'eco-warriors' from all over the world? – an open question that blurs the boundary between underclass victims of ecological disaster and their privileged supporters, and that makes Roy vulnerable to the criticism that she is silencing those on whose behalf she is determined to speak (Gadgil and Guha 1995; see also Omvedt 1999). Roy's tirade against the state seems to want to claim a victory for the people (Roy 1999: 48–49). But which people? As other commentators have pointed out, it is oversimplified to say that the political battle in the Narmada Valley is a basic conflict between 'the state' (in the Blue corner) and 'the people' (in the Red); there are also numerous conflicts between different sections of the people and different branches of the state, while even within the Narmada resistance movement there are factional splits between different groups, each of which sees itself as acting in the people's interests (Singh 1995: 1; see also Fisher 1995).

Roy's text thus draws attention to at least two modes of the 'worlding' of the Third World (Loomba 1994) to be found in certain postcolonially inflected forms of environmental protest writing.[5] The first of these launches a rightful (sometimes righteous) attack on a quintessentially neocolonialist Iron Triangle – politicians, bureaucrats and corporations, often with International Aid backing – which has exploited the progressivist ideologies of Third World economic development for its own immediate purposes; while the second risks amounting to a further 'subalternisation' (Spivak 1987) of some of the Third World's poorest people, whose stories are told – in English – so that we privileged First Worlders, and our Third World middle-class counterparts, might help them 'resist'. Still, 'The Greater Common Good', for all its pieties, remains a highly intriguing text, not least because, like the auto-cannibalising tiger that provides its first and most arresting image, it effectively deconstructs many of its own best arguments by drawing attention to itself as a playful piece of investigative writing: a highly *literary* text. This raises the larger question of how to harness the resources of aesthetic play to reflect on weighty ethical issues, as well as to serve a variety of real-world needs and direct political ends. This question, implicitly addressed throughout Roy's work, takes centre stage in what is sometimes seen as the companion piece to 'The Greater Common Good', 'The End of Imagination': a passionate jeremiad in which Roy tackles the durably topical, but also potentially hackneyed, subject of how to protest against India's 1998 decision to test the nuclear bomb.

As Roy admits at the beginning of the essay, 'There's nothing new or original left to be said about nuclear weapons. There can be nothing more humiliating for a writer of fiction to have to do than restate a case

that has, over the years, already been made by other people in other
parts of the world, and made passionately, eloquently and knowledge-
ably' (121–22). While this admission can easily be seen as an act of false
modesty, it also sets the tone for Roy's rehearsal of standard anti-nuclear
arguments, couched in what she calls her own idiosyncratic brand of
'Doomsday hyperbole' (125): the inevitability of total extinction; the
madness of those who deny it; and the fatuousness of arguments based
on deterrence and the need for military strength (124–25). As in 'The
Greater Common Good', Roy's arguments are assembled in a sometimes
grating conversational language, liberally sprinkled with capitalised
nouns and rhetorical questions, and directed at a largely like-minded
readership consisting first and foremost of her educated English-speaking
Indian peers. Roy's trademark combination of querulous populism and
confessional elitism is, as she herself recognises, intellectually and emotionally perilous, and always runs the risk of patronising the same illiterate
masses she promotes. It also entails a frequent shift in subject position,
seen most clearly here in the oscillation between Roy's self-announcement
as a committed Indian citizen and her alternative, freewheeling status as
a stateless 'citizen of the earth' (140). Similarly self-acknowledged contradictions are contained in her apportioning of blame for the existence of
the bomb. Is it the Americans' fault for having created it, or the Indians'/
Pakistanis' fault for threatening to use it? Or is it rather the West's fault
in general for the overweening cultural arrogance that lies behind their
invention of 'colonialism, slavery, ethnic cleansing, germ warfare [and]
chemical weapons', and for having 'more money, more food and bigger
bombs than anyone else'? (144).

For Roy, the nuclear bomb, a perverse symbol of national pride and
technological wizardry, represents both the metaphorical and literal end-
point of a developmentalist logic that has caused India to mimic the west
even as it flaunts its independence from it, and that has hoodwinked
India's masses into accepting the false promises of the Nation (capital N)
and its administrative henchman, the State (capital S). India, Roy asserts,
is 'an artificial State [...] created by a government, not a people', and
'created from the top down, not the bottom up' (148–49). 'The impoverished, illiterate agrarian majority have no stake in the State. And
indeed, why should they, when they don't even know what a State is? To
them, India is, at best, a noisy slogan that comes around during the
elections, or a montage of people on Government TV programmes wearing
regional costume and saying *Mera Bharat Mahaan*' (149). While Roy
insists elsewhere that she is 'not an anti-development junkie, nor a pro-
selytiser for the eternal upholding of custom and tradition' (8), it seems
safe to conclude that she sees Development (capital D) largely as an

instrument of state authority, and as a mechanism by which to force through large-scale, often foreign-funded government initiatives that are then falsely sold to people the government has never bothered to consult. Such policies, Roy suggests, cannot be other than self-destructive; peddling the postcolonial search for national selfhood as the panacea for continuing poverty, caste snobbery and illiteracy, they help to create a reified sense of collective suffering and victimisation that leads inexorably to the bomb (147).

At the same time, the bomb goes far beyond these insidious games of political brinkmanship and fundamentalist breast-beating, for nuclear war isn't the kind of war in which 'countries battle countries and [people] battle [people]', but is rather an *ecological* war in which 'our [eventual] foe will be the earth itself' (123–24). Here, as elsewhere in the essay, Roy's argument adopts that familiar form of 'environmental apocalypticism' (Buell 1995) which is the ecological revenge narrative: 'the very elements – the sky, the air, the land, the wind and water – will all turn against us. Their wrath will be terrible' (124). The narrative proceeds with Roy's customary gift for melodramatics and the journalistic clipped sentence:

> Our cities and forests, our fields and villages will burn for days. Rivers will turn to poison. The air will become fire. The wind will spread the flames. When everything there is to burn has burned and the fires die, smoke will rise and shut out the sun. The earth will be enveloped in darkness. There will be no day. Only interminable night. Temperatures will drop to far below freezing and nuclear winter will set in. Water will turn into toxic ice. Radioactive fallout will seep through the earth and contaminate groundwater. Most living things, animal and vegetable, fish and fowl, will die. Only rats and cockroaches will breed and multiply and compete with foraging, relict humans for what little food there is. [...] What shall we do then, those of us who are still alive? Burned and blind and bald and ill, carrying the cancerous carcasses of our children in our arms, where shall we go? What shall we eat? What shall we drink? What shall we breathe?
>
> (124)

The passage is characterised by a breathless emotionalism that is prevalent in Roy's writing: 'All I can say to every man, woman and sentient child here in India, and over there, just a little way away in Pakistan, is: take it personally. [...] The bomb isn't in your backyard. It's in your body' (131). (While Roy's emotionalism seems not to be specifically gendered in this essay, it certainly is in other essays, notably the mischievously entitled 'The ladies have feelings, so ... ', which focuses on the divisive impact of corporate globalisation on a country already at war with itself. 'The ladies have feelings, so ... ' is Roy's most forthcoming essay to date on what it means to be a writer in a country 'where something akin to a civil war is being waged on its citizens in the name of "development"' (Roy 2002: 169): a war which mistreats all citizens, but not men and women alike.) Roy is well aware that women in countries like India often bear the brunt of development's modernising strategies, strategies which often increase the strain on rural women, who were previously responsible for carrying out most of the agricultural work (Saunders 2002). Thus, while Roy's essays generally fall short of endorsing such post-development catchphrases as the 'feminisation of survival' and the 'double subjection' of poor Third World women, they are clearly alert to the link between development and patriarchy, and to the need to address the 'multiple oppressions of gender, [as well as of] class, race and nation that can form the basis for the new [ecological] visions and strategies the world needs' (Sen and Grown, quoted in Saunders 2002: 12).[6]

Roy's work, like Saro-Wiwa's, can be seen as a populist attempt to raise global consciousness of events and issues that go far beyond the immediate regional or national contexts within which they are set. While neither writer's work can be reduced to activism *tout court*, it certainly fits the bill of 'committed literature' – the literature of dissent – and both writers are consistently (in Saro-Wiwa's case, fatally) invested in campaigning for social equality and a clean earth. Both show, in the process, that ecological disruption is co-extensive with damage to the social fabric, and that environmental issues cannot be separated from questions of social justice and human rights (Huggan 2004). 'Development', one of the key terms under which their social and ecological protests gather, is primarily associated in their work with those top-down forms of economic management which, while retaining ties to the history of colonialism, are more obviously bound to the neocolonialist imperatives of global corporate commerce and the post-independence state. In both writers' work, the state's coercive allocation and management of natural resources can be seen as a postcolonial version of 'ecological imperialism' (Crosby 1986) in which it becomes clear that 'the forced march to industrialisation' has had disastrous cultural, as well as ecological, effects (Guha 2000: 196). Thus, for both writers there are two symbiotically related crises in their respective countries: an ecological crisis brought about by the use of resource-destructive technological processes and a cultural crisis emerging from an erosion of the social structures that make cultural diversity and plurality possible (Shiva 1991: 12, 235). These crises, in both cases, have hit *indigenous* societies hardest – societies subject both to the continuing expropriation and exploitation of their resources and to social/political exclusion by the centralised machinery of the state. Here, however, there is a crucial difference between the two writers' respective subject positions: for while both are self-acknowledged members of a cosmopolitan educated elite, only Saro-Wiwa can *also* claim membership of an indigenous community, with the blood-ties to land that membership implies (consider the title of one of his best-known interviews, 'We Will Defend Our Oil With Our Blood': Saro-Wiwa 1998). We will return later to the question of bloodlines and their significance in the struggle for what might be called ecological self-determination: the right to control the land and resources over which centuries, in some cases millennia, of continuous occupation have established a powerful entitlement. For the moment, though, we will press on with another example of the devastating effects of nuclear power on indigenous societies and cultures – in this case, the scattered peoples of the Pacific Islands – as these effects have been imaginatively captured in creative writing from the region, beginning with the Pacific's best-known literary figure and self-appointed spokesperson, the Samoan writer Albert Wendt.

In his 2005 report for the Brisbane-based Foundation for Development Cooperation, the Australian social scientist Anthony van Fossen distinguishes between two, not necessarily mutually exclusive, views of Pacific Islands development: a *globalist* view that hinges on the fluctuating fortunes of the world market, and an *Oceanic* view dedicated to the strengthening of regional consciousness and the collective self-determination of Pacific Islanders, many of whose lives continue to be shaped by a history of colonial racism and exploitation that has renewed itself in present, global times (van Fossen 2005: 4). Prominent among the latter group is Albert Wendt, a pioneer-figure in the development of Pacific literature (not so much writing by western travellers and writers, which has helped determine the west's often stereotypical perception of the Pacific, but rather writing about the region by Pacific writers themselves, which is self-consciously centred on their own particular experiences and visions of the world: Keown 2007; Sharrad 2003). For Wendt, as for his fellow Pacific writers Epeli Hau'ofa (Tonga) and Subramani (Fiji), cultural revitalisation is an essential accompaniment to economic growth across the region, whose future clearly depends not only on Islanders' responsible deployment of sustainable modern technologies, but also on their collective ability to recover and reinterpret their own traditional past (Hau'ofa 1993: 2–16; 2000: 453–71; see also Subramani 2001; Wendt 1983). 'Oceania' is thus as much the name for an ongoing cultural project as a geographical label, proceeding from the recognition that a new 'Oceanic imaginary' (Subramani 2001) needs to be created for the region, not least as a means of counteracting what several centuries of western colonialism have diminished or destroyed.

Contained within this history is *environmental* destruction, as captured in van Fossen's resonant phrase 'the ecology of doomsday', which refers both to an apocalyptic perception of the Pacific's future and to a continuing record of ecological abuses in the region, most though not all of them attributable to the military-industrial ambitions of the capitalist west (van Fossen 2005: 40). Probably the most flagrant of these abuses have been those practised in the name of 'nuclear colonialism' (Robie 1989: 146): the systematic programme by which the post-Second World War arms race turned large swathes of the Pacific into a military zone and, more specifically, a nuclear arena, with the mantra of 'national security' being invoked to justify sustained nuclear bomb and missile testing in Micronesia (especially the Marshall Islands) by the US and Britain, and in Polynesia (especially the Tuamotus) by France (Robie 1989; Fischer 1992). The devastating effects of nuclear colonialism can hardly be overestimated. Whole islands and societies were laid waste and, despite the discontinuation of nuclear testing in the region and the establishment of various resettlement and compensation mechanisms, much of the damage caused has been irreparable, with new forms of colonialism being practised under the guise of protective humanitarianism, and semi-permanent nuclear dependencies having been created in US-occupied Micronesia and French-governed Polynesia that continue to cater to the political and economic interests of the (former) colonial powers (Fischer 2002; see also Danielsson and Danielsson 1986; Dibblin 1988).

Not surprisingly, then, a symbiotic relationship has come to exist between decolonisation and the campaign for a nuclear-free Pacific: as Vanuatu's Deputy Prime Minister Sethy Regenvanu put it in the late 1970s, while pledging his support for the newly formed movement for a Nuclear-Free and Independent Pacific (NFIP), 'We are seeking a Pacific [...] free of every last remnant of colonialism. But freedom and independence will have no meaning if our very existence is threatened by the constant fear of total destruction' (quoted in Robie 1989: 147). Nor is it surprising that a sense of impending doom tends to hover over much of the creative writing that emerged during the key decades – the 1960s to the 1990s – of nuclear colonialism, despite many of the writers' stated commitments to regional self-empowerment and national independence, and despite their appeals to an 'Oceanic ecological ideology' which, implicitly rejecting the 'ecology of doomsday', links linear development to natural cycles, and sidelines imperial history by bringing the locally grounded oral narratives of indigenous Pacific peoples to the fore (Hau'ofa 2000: 465).

As good an example as any here is the work of Wendt, whose writing makes relatively few direct references to nuclear colonialism in the Pacific, but whose hallucinatory explorations of the 'dark side of paradise' (Sharrad 2003) are arguably haunted by a fear of annihilation linked to the ever-present nuclear threat. Probably the two clearest references to nuclear colonialism in Wendt's work are contained within the title of his futuristic novel *Black Rainbow* (1992), which draws on a series of protest paintings by the Māori artist Ralph Hotere that allude to French nuclear testing at Moruroa; and in the prophetic ramblings of the crazed old man who, ghosting through the pages of the earlier novel *Pouliuli* (1977), seems to embody the horrors of a modern post-Holocaust/post-nuclear world (Sharrad 2003: 110). Through portentous figures like the old man, Wendt links his dominant motif of the existential void to the threat of nuclear catastrophe, with the billowing mushroom clouds of Hiroshima and Nagasaki providing at least one version of Pouliuli, the 'Great Darkness out of which we came and to which we must all return' (Wendt 1977: 145).

As a number of different commentators have pointed out, there is a sharp contrast between the hortatory style of essays like 'Towards a New Oceania' (1976) and the bleak, corrosively satirical self-consciousness of Wendt's poetry and fiction, which is inhabited by a rogues' gallery of vicious con-men and self-destructive existential outsiders, and which is haunted by nightmare visions of disease, degeneration and death (Sharrad 2003; see also Keown 2007). Less fecund than faecal, the Pacific landscapes of Wendt's work are similarly scarred, either polluted sites that mirror psychic decomposition or sterile correlatives to uncompromising visions of existential truth (Sharrad 2003: 71). A typical scenario is the one depicted at the beginning of the 1974 story 'Flying Fox in a Freedom Tree', whose pathologically disillusioned narrator lies dying of tuberculosis in a local Samoan hospital:

> Through the window I see the plain on which this hospital stands, dropping down to the ravine, and on the other side the land rises up to the taro and banana patches and mango and tamaligi trees to palms at the top of the range. [...] On the ravine edge stands a shed surrounded by mounds of dry coconut husks. The shed has no walls and I can see [...] two old men stoking the fire in the big urn in that shed. Stink of burning meat, guts, bits and pieces of people from the surgery department. [...] On the platform outside the shed, which is what the nurses call the crematorium, I think, are kerosene drums full of rubbish and flies and stink. One of the old men [...] is foraging in one of the drums. He takes out scraps and puts them into a basket. Food for his pigs, I think. He eats some of the scraps himself.
>
> (Wendt 1999b: 95)

The scene is reminiscent of what Lawrence Buell calls 'toxic gothic', displaying the 'gothicized environmental squalor' that often accompanies traumatic accounts of 'contaminated communities' in a once incomparably beautiful but now irreversibly post-pastoral world (2001: 42–43, 36). 'Toxic discourse', as Buell explains in a chapter of his 2001 book *Writing for an Endangered World*, consists of an 'interlocking set of topoi whose force derives partly from the anxieties of late industrial culture, partly from deeper-rooted habits of thought and expression' (30). Toxic concern is not new, of course, but it is closely linked to recent events in 'the history of [the] postindustrial imagination that ensured that the environmental apocalypticism activated by Hiroshima and Nagasaki would outlast the Cold War' (32). Wendt's own particular version of toxic discourse is both anticipatory and confirmatory, combining repressed fears of nuclear annihilation with post-apocalyptic soundings of the despair and anger that follow on disastrous nuclear events. Similar 'traumas of pastoral disruption' (Buell 2001: 37) can be found in other contemporary works that emerge out of a nuclear Pacific context, many of them conforming to the literary sub-genres of 'toxic gothic' and 'moral melodrama' that arguably constitute the twin parameters of toxic discourse in its dominant 'ecocatastrophe' mode (Buell 2001: 39, 40, 42). In what follows, we want to look briefly at alternate examples of these sub-genres, beginning with the Australian feminist-activist Zohl de Ishtar's collection of Oceanic nuclear testimony, *Daughters of the Pacific* (1994), then continuing with the Hawai'ian-based author Robert Barclay's more self-consciously fictionalised, but no less emotionally powerful, account of a post-nuclear Pacific, *Meļaļ* (2002). We will then round off with some thoughts on two contemporary New Zealand whaling narratives – Ian Wedde's *Symmes Hole* and Witi Ihimaera's *The Whale Rider*, both published in the mid-1980s, and both concerned with the reframing of national culture in a nuclear space.

Aimed at a non-specialist readership and assembled by a globe-trotting Irish Australian feminist self-confessedly more interested in her activism than her writing (though aware, like Arundhati Roy, of the link between both), *Daughters of the Pacific* consists of more than 200 pages of testimonial stories gathered from all corners of the Pacific over a process of several years. Together, these stories confirm the author's ongoing commitment to what she calls 'the actual voices of Indigenous women [whose] lives have been ignored, erased, in a world that increasingly gives power to the written word' (Ishtar 1994: xviii). While some of the stories have narrative power, several amount to little more than mutually supportive declarative statements testifying to the continuing oppression of indigenous peoples, particularly indigenous women, in the Pacific region and elsewhere in the world. Trading on a gendered politics of affect (again, the link with Roy's work is apparent), *Daughters of the Pacific* has a cumulative impact that repeatedly slides into the melodramatic – a self-consciously hyperbolical style also employed by Ishtar as primary narrator, who enjoins women across the world, both indigenous and non-indigenous, to 'turn the acute pain [of] reading the stories [...] into positive anger [and] pure rage' (236).

Ishtar's approach is, broadly speaking, ecofeminist in inspiration, drawing on what she sees as indigenous women's shared commitment to the nurturing and protection of Mother Earth (9–11).[7] In a similar spirit to more academically minded ecofeminists like Vandana Shiva (a direct influence on Roy's work), Ishtar sees Third and Fourth World women as bearing the brunt of environmental crises that are inextricably linked to ongoing processes of colonial exploitation, and as leading the transnational feminist struggle for a more socially and ecologically just world. At the heart of this struggle lies what might be described as an ecological battle over contending interpretations of modernity, a battle also staged in *Daughters of the Pacific* in radical disjunctures both within and between the stories themselves. Thus, while some 'voices' in the text draw a clear line between 'modern' (western) and 'traditional' (indigenous) cultures, others insist on their productive inseparability; and a similar, almost structural inconsistency can also be found in arguments about development, seen by some as a force for liberation and by others as a tool of patriarchal/colonialist oppression which, in continuing to elevate men over women and to separate culture from economy, has had the ruinous effect of stripping entire indigenous communities of their wealth (227–30).

Probably the strongest of the stories revolve around the nuclearisation of the Pacific as seen through the eyes of those who have suffered directly from its consequences, and as experienced, 'to an extent beyond anything imaginable in Europe', by people whose lives and livelihoods have been placed at risk and whose ancestral homelands have been ravaged by colonial powers – the USA, France, Japan, Britain – which have historically 'pushed onto the Pacific the political, social and economic programs of the nuclear industry [that] were unacceptable at home' (7). The alarming effects of nuclear irradiation are graphically documented, for example, in a powerful section on the Marshall Islands:

I saw a child from Rongelap. Its feet are like clubs. And another child whose hands are like nothing at all. It is mentally retarded. Some of the children suffer growth retardation. Now we have this problem, what we call 'jellyfish babies'. These babies are born like jellyfish.

They have no eyes. They have no heads. They have no arms. They have no legs. They do not shape [*sic*] like human beings at all. But they are being born on the labour table. The most colourful, ugly things you have ever seen. Some of them have hairs on them. And they breathe. This ugly thing only lives for a few hours. When they die they are buried right away. They do not allow the mother to see this kind of baby because she will go crazy. It is too inhumane.

(Keju-Johnson, quoted in Ishtar 1994: 24)

Other witnesses in this section speak directly from personal memory, recounting their first, confused experiences of nuclear fallout, and their subsequent, unexplained removal to neighbouring islands often hopelessly unsuited for human habitation, creating the first wave of a 'nuclear nomadism' (24) that was to extend for several decades, and the devastating consequences of which can still be felt today. In Susan Najita's terms, we might call this 'traumatic realism' of a kind that has permeated Pacific writing in the post-nuclear era, with trauma being understood here in its classical sense as 'a symptom of, or delayed response to, an overwhelming event' (Najita 2006: 18). As Najita suggests, the Pacific region has produced a number of literary works, especially fiction, in which the European novel-form has been creatively transformed on contact with 'the orally-inflected narration of traumatic history' (20). One such novel is Robert Barclay's *Meḷaḷ* (2002), also set in the Marshall Islands, and a good example of an ecologically oriented post-nuclear narrative that self-consciously intermingles the expansive myths and legends of ancestral Pacific cultures with the more clipped style of the modern western investigative report.

'Meḷaḷ', revealed in the novel's frontispiece as the archaic definition for a 'playground for demons, not habitable by people', is an ironic name for the tiny, impossibly overcrowded island of Ebeye, bluntly described in *Daughters of the Pacific* as a 'slum of slums [...] a biological time-bomb waiting to go off' (Keju-Johnson, quoted in Ishtar 1994: 26). A semi-permanent home to some 10,000 people, many of them forcibly displaced from Rongelap and other neighbouring, nuclear-contaminated islands, Ebeye is the living embodiment of toxic casualty, a haphazard community of nuclear exiles living 'in the midst of the US war machine' (Ishtar 1994: 27). The island also sets the stage for Barclay's vivid dramatisation of 'toxic gothic' (Buell 2001). It is a haunted site, replete with 'soul stealers, decay makers, child eaters, sickness spreaders, brain suckers, the foulest of all conjurable demons clinging to people and things like sea slugs sucking the reef, feverishly intent in the service of their masters on wringing death from life, on replacing everything pure and natural and pleasurable with stinking rot and ruin, a living death, life inside-out' (Barclay 2002: 14). These malevolent spirits of nuclear fallout are the spectral emanations of a continuing toxic nightmare that the inhabitants of Ebeye seem condemned to rehearse (282–83). Yet the narrative of *Meḷaḷ*, against all odds, is a story of survival in which its lead actors, the impoverished Marshallese waste worker Rujen Keju and his two teenage sons Jebro and Nuke [*sic*], withstand the forces – both terrestrial and otherworldly – that appear to have conspired against them, ushering the novel to an emotionally satisfying conclusion in which a temporary balance between social death (the crushing legacy of several decades of nuclear colonialism) and cultural revival is precariously secured.

Barclay's novel illustrates the moral intensity of toxic discourse, its propensity for staging 'us-versus-them dichotomies' (Buell 2001: 41), but complicates this scenario by suggesting that the lives of the indigenous Marshall Islanders (Marshallese) and their American occupiers are inextricably enmeshed. The recent history of Pacific militarisation is similarly revealed to be just the latest stage in an epic battle between the region's mythological heroes and their implacable opponents, with the ecological future of the Islands as habitable spaces, but also imaginative entities, at stake. At least two different versions of ecological advocacy come into conflict here: an indigenous version, elemental in scope, that conforms to Hau'ofa's Oceanic vision of natural/environmental cycles, and a western version that presents animals as substitutes for human friends. Midway through the novel, this conflict assumes crisis proportions. Hurt by what he sees as disrespect for Marshallese custom, Rujen refuses to lend support to an American-led campaign to save the islands' dolphins, which are occasionally captured and eaten by local fishermen; this later escalates into his symbolic revenge killing of a saved dolphin now apparently destined to become an American's pet. The Americans see only animal abuse, Rujen only environmental racism. Barclay suggests, however, that both are right in their own way, and that their cultural beliefs are not necessarily incompatible. In a further illustrative sequence, Nuke spares a turtle that he and his brother have captured, taking pity on its condition and comparing it to the sacrificed lives of Marshallese boys who, in his brother's words, are caught 'in a hole between two worlds', with the suicide rope being their only way to get out (Barclay 2002: 130–31). Nuke acknowledges the dilemma, but offers a more positive solution: 'Turtles live in water but have to breathe air. […] It's like they can never decide which world they want to live in, so they try to live in both. I think it would be very hard to live as a turtle' (129).

Species protection, Barclay suggests, may yet benefit from such western anthropomorphic sentiment – sentiment abundantly reproduced in the novel's closing sequence, which improbably succeeds in incorporating nuclear irradiation's most virulent symbol – the jellyfish baby – into the harmonious vision of a spiritually interconnected world. In this mythic world, the tormented souls of jellyfish babies, previously rescued by the folk-hero Noniep and now being transported across the waters in his spirit canoe, are ingeniously accommodated by being coupled with the souls of whales, so that their afflictions might be eased and, in time, their fearful squalling might even turn into song (300). This theatrical conclusion risks dissolving toxic gothic into Disney-style anthropomorphic fantasy, but without suggesting that Noniep's attempted exorcism of Melaļ's demons, and his mission to save those afflicted by them, are necessarily definitive or complete. On the contrary, Melaļ/Ebeye will continue to struggle with the human and environmental legacies of its nuclear past, with its residually colonised present, and with its marginal location in an unevenly developed world.

The doe-eyed whales of *Melaļ*, typical of the 'charismatic megafauna' (Baker 2000) that light up twentieth-century environmental literature, present a stark contrast to the otherworldly, monstrous creatures that thrash a destructive course through any number of nineteenth-century travellers' and whalers' accounts. Probably the most celebrated, but also one of the most atypical, of these is Herman Melville's classic novel *Moby-Dick*, which – according to perspective – can be seen as the highpoint in a long history of whaling literature or as a radical departure from it, and in which 'transcendental' and 'naturalistic' versions of the great creature vie in the service of an even greater metaphysical cause (Zoellner 1973). Also following in this tradition is the New Zealand writer Ian Wedde's satirical novel *Symmes Hole* (1986), a heady brew of Melvillean South Seas fantasies that plays on the casual brutality and carnivalesque degeneracy of nineteenth-century colonial whaling accounts. More specifically, the novel weaves between the parallel journeys of an early settler in New Zealand, the beachcomber and whaler James 'Worser' Heberly, and his modern-day counterpart, an unnamed Wellington-based writer, whose compulsive research into the buried meanings of his country's history eventually opens doors onto an incriminating, if at times suspiciously fabricated, chain of symbolic associations between the corporate greed of contemporary America and the violence of New Zealand's colonial past.

At the centre of the puzzle is the eponymous 'Symmes Hole', the outlandish but nonetheless briefly influential theory that the earth had a secret core which was both hollow and potentially inhabitable, and which was accessible, for those intrepid enough to discover it, at either of its poles. The idea of a hollow earth was spread by, among others, the prominent early nineteenth-century American entrepreneur-philanthropist Jeremiah Reynolds, a rumourmonger of the first magnitude, who was similarly responsible for disseminating the sailors' legend of a fearsome Pacific leviathan called Mocha Dick (Greenspan 2001: 152). (Reynolds, the narrator also suggests, manufactured the aluminium for the nuclear submarines with which American polar exploration, and Pacific domination, are continued, a further unsubstantiated rumour that is mapped onto the novel's global marketing grid: Greenspan 2001: 160.) The novel latches eagerly onto these and other rumours, amplifying them into a full-blown imperial conspiracy aimed at securing and consolidating American cultural and economic domination of a morally hollow corporate world. This conspiracy is headed in the present – or so the narrator wants us to believe – by the ever-expanding McDonald's fast-food empire, seemingly dedicated to the Leviathan-like task of swallowing the entire world whole (Greenspan 2001; see also Williams 1990). In these and other ways, *Symmes Hole* reads as a scarcely controlled rant against the fatuousness, but also underlying violence, of the modern consumer lifestyle and the enormous wastage it produces: hence the novel's relentless scatological drive, its destructive obsession with those linked processes of incorporation and evacuation through which the capitalism/cannibalism nexus functions as a phobic means of assimilating its own enemies – phobic in the sense that total assimilation always carries the reverse fear of total contamination, the paranoid fantasy of alien invasion that is at capitalism's/cannibalism's core (Greenspan 2001; see also Barker *et al.* 1998).

At the level of both content and form, *Symmes Hole* plays between the complementary images of total incorporation (fusion) and total annihilation (fission) that are the stuff of the postmodern historical novel, but never to the extent of emptying out historical specificity, or suggesting that the omnivorous, Melvillean world its characters inhabit is either arbitrary in its workings or 'synonymous with the good' (Bohrer, quoted in Greenspan 2001: 162). Rather, like the great whale at its centre, Wedde's novel is intermittently subversive rather than transcendentally uplifting; halfway between material fact and unsubstantiated rumour, it is committed to the kind of counter-historical mischief-making that turns the unfinished – unfinishable – legend of Mocha Dick into a lingering 'spectre of revolt' (Wedde 1986: 289). As Mark Williams has rightly pointed out, there is more than a hint of nostalgia in the novel's playful, sometimes childish, acts of anti-establishment rebelliousness, and in its apparent belief in the transformative power of a subaltern, anti-colonial idiom that – as Heberly, the 'new' New Zealander, discovers – is neither civilised nor savage, neither imported nor indigenous, but somehow all of these at once (Williams 1990). Like most other commentators, however,

Williams underestimates the significance of the novel's *environmentalist* impact as a wide-ranging satire, both on the toxicity of contemporary global consumer society and on its co-existence with a residually nuclear world. This 'developed' world, quite literally, stinks, piled high with a variety of noxious industrial products, and with the effluent and waste – the humans as waste – that are unwanted evidence of development itself. Development in the novel is synonymous with waste: with what is rejected by the body, with rejected bodies. Also included among its victims is the whale, no longer subject to the licensed massacres of New Zealand's now defunct whaling industry, but still both living symbol and spectral reminder of the nation's violent colonial past. Perhaps appropriately, then, the last whale sighting in the novel is not of the legendary Mocha Dick, but of a deep-frozen sperm whale calf, illegally killed and now presumably awaiting human consumption, 'the Whaleburger of [Pacific] history' hypocritically saluted by the characters of the novel as they solemnly file past to pay their last respects (299). So much, then, for the narrator's earlier dreamy fantasy of

> what it might be like to be one of the great whales: sea-horizon all around, below the photic ocean fades into the sunless abyssal zones, above the constellations and star-charts [...] lunar and stellar tides, the subtle exertions of the planets [...] weather moving the mantle of the atmosphere [...] the enormous flows of warm surface and icy abyssal currents – your mature racial occupancy of the planet dates from a time when human ancestors were tree-shrews [...] your brain larger than a human's [...] you carry on simultaneous conversations in different modes of language over hundreds of miles of ocean [...] you don't have to think about having technology [...] you have songs without art, you have routes without highways, *you have life without time* [...].
>
> (111; emphasis Wedde's)

This Ishmael-like version of the whale in which, in Robert Zoellner's terms, 'power is redeemed by beauty', is not enough to displace its Ahab-driven counterpart, which is characterised by 'outrageous strength' (163–64). Rather, as in *Moby-Dick* itself, these two alternative whales underlie the novel's unresolved conflict between the vengeful desire to crush resistance (one of the primary bases for settler-colonial violence) and the more accommodating vision of a world in which settler and indigene might peacefully co-exist (Williams 1990). Heberly arguably achieves this accommodation, taking a Māori wife, but his twentieth-century counterpart is apparently more adrift than ever by the novel's end.

There is no place for him, or so it would seem, in a society he sees as the crude product of aggressive economic expansionism (the logic of development) and unchecked human greed (the logic of consumption). History's last joke in the novel is to suggest that cannibalism provides the link between them. In Brian Greenspan's words, the 'steady devolution of *homo oeconomicus* since the onset of late capitalism' has turned the clock on nineteenth-century fears of cannibalism as a regression into barbarism by showing that twentieth-century 'development' is just another form of barbarism; and that Ronald McDonald and his fellow Clown Princes have already done the job themselves (Greenspan 2001: 159).

A less cynical view of the link between development and consumption is provided in the work of Māori writer Witi Ihimaera, the 2002 film of whose 1987 novel *The Whale Rider* has been seen as exemplary of the shift from the culturalist perspective of the Māori Renaissance to a brazenly consumerist ethos in which the international branding of Māori culture has been adjusted, not least by Māori themselves, to the changing national cause (Prentice 2005; Webster 1998). As Chris Prentice among others has argued, the film is best seen 'in terms of the extent to which its cultural mode of production and representations travel inside the whale', swallowed by global capitalism; or alternatively, whether they remain 'outside the whale, refusing or contesting the forces of global capitalism' – a quintessentially postcolonial riddle that continues to tax the critics, and that gives every appearance of remaining unsolved (256). However, the earlier novel also engages with this question and the various ideological problems it raises: the commercially viable appeal to universal values; the fetishisation of the local; the sentimentalisation and objectification of the natural world (Prentice 2005). While these problems are all connected, we will restrict ourselves here to a few thoughts, in keeping with the spirit of this section, on the visible tensions between the novel's 'Oceanic' and 'globalist' dimensions as an environmental text (Buell 1995).

In several ways, *The Whale Rider* is an exemplary exercise in the ecologically oriented 'Oceanic imaginary' (Subramani 2001). Its human and animal characters, like its legends and myths, span the Pacific, from Hawai'i in the north to New Zealand in the south, taking in Antarctica at the extremities, and imaginatively traversing the 'huge seamless marine continent' that links the Te Tai Rawhiti people of Aotearoa's east coast to 'Hawaiki, [their] ancestral island homeland, the place of the Ancients and the Gods, the other side of the world' (Ihimaera 1987: 26). It is opposed to the arbitrary separation of human and animal worlds, and to the rationalist distinction between natural and supernatural phenomena (though this mutual exchange is trumped by the naturalistic whale simulation models in the movie, which suggest the imaginative possibilities of a further ontological category, the hyperreal: Prentice 2005: 265–66). It is nostalgically, but by no means impractically, committed to the dissemination of traditional environmental knowledge, and to the responsible, egalitarian management of its own subsistence needs (Ihimaera 1987: 40–41; see also Clarke 1990). It is keenly attuned to ecological abuses (e.g. whaling) but not necessarily immune from them, and aware that the price for the violation or neglect of environmental duties is loss (84, 57). And it is conscious, finally, of the need to revive atrophied kinships (e.g. between human beings and other living creatures) while forging new kinds of social and ecological relationships (e.g. in terms of race and gender: the 'new' whale rider, Kahu, upholds the traditions of her male ancestors, but she herself is female; her uncle Rawiri seeks alliances beyond his own culture, only to be rebuffed by others' ingrained attitude to his race).

As the mixed experiences of both Kahu and Rawiri testify, the transition between remembered and renewed worlds is far from easy, and Ihimaera's novel is arguably disabused of the nostalgia it otherwise seems so eager to create. A more pressing issue: nuclear testing in the Pacific (still happening at the time the novel was written) has created a world that is radically out of kilter, setting in motion destructive patterns of behaviour that may prove impossible to overcome. In one of the novel's italicised 'whale's-view' sequences, nuclear panic lures the whales into a near-fatal Antarctic detour, reconfirming their leader's worst fear that Hawaiki, the place of life and the Gods, has now become a place of death:

> *The herd was waiting for a sign from their ancient leader [...] but their leader was still mourning. Two weeks earlier the herd had been feeding in the Tuamotu Archipelago when suddenly a flash of bright light had scalded the sea and giant tidal soundwaves had exerted so much pressure that internal ear canals had bled. Seven young calves had died. The ancient whale remembered this occurrence happening before; screaming a lament of condemnation, he had led them away in front of the lethal tide that he knew would come. On that pell-mell, headlong and mindless escape, he had noticed more cracks in the ocean floor, hairline fractures indicating serious damage below the crust of the earth. Now, some weeks later, the leader was still unsure about the radiation level in the sea trench. He was fearful of the contamination seeping from Moruroa. He was afraid of the genetic effects of the undersea radiation on the remaining*

*herd and calves in this place which had once, ironically, been the
womb of the world.*

(48)

In a later, parallel scene, two fear-crazed whale herds are washed up on
a local beach, one of which (a real herd) is brutally slaughtered, and the
other of which (the mythic herd) is only spared by Kahu's intervention
in 'riding' its leader back out again into sea. Both incidents have environmentalist implications in a global era in which the protection of
endangered species has been co-opted by a number of transnational corporate bodies: the first stranding, which immediately attracts media
attention, also draws local operatives from Greenpeace, Project Jonah,
and Friends of the Earth (87). The second stranding, however, requires a
different kind of solution, in keeping with the Te Tai Rawhiti's belief
in whales as the mythic ancestors linking them to Hawaiki and, more
specifically, to Paikea, the legendary founding-figure who arrived from
Hawaiki on a whale's back. As the elder Koro Apirana says, 'our ancestor
Paikea was given power to talk to whales and to command them. In this
way, man, tipua [whales] and Gods lived in close communion with one
another', a communion he now fears has been irrevocably lost (95).
Kahu, the new Paikea, provides the missing link that allows the fable to
clinch its happy ending, but without suggesting that the cultural renaissance it implies is anything other than temporary, or that the ecological
crises it alludes to are definitively resolved. It is thus Ihimaera's novel
that first forges the uneasy alliance between 'Oceanic' revivalism and
'globalist' *realpolitik* that emerges more strongly in the movie, an alliance that counteracts the nuclear-driven 'ecology of doomsday' (van Fossen
2005) by suggesting that the twin goals of cultural and environmental
sustainability depend as much on forced responses to global pressures
as on local indigenous communities' continued ability to match their
traditional cultural and environmental practices to their modern social
needs. This squares, in any case, with at least some versions of 'Oceanic'
theory, like that of Subramani for example, who believes that while
'globalism's millennial dreams [have] become apparent with increasing
poverty, unemployment, crime [...] and environmental disruption' in the
Islands, local self-sufficiency needs to be balanced against the awareness
that the region exists within an overarching global system, and that 'no
amount of boycott, legal challenge, or moral outrage can completely
prevent [that system's] flow' (160). Ignoring globalism, then, is not an
option. Rather, the question is how best to respond to it; for not to
respond would be – as Vilsoni Hereniko puts it – to 'stand by and watch
as our tiny islands are swallowed, not only by the rising sea levels of our

own Pacific Ocean, but also by the tidal wave of globalization [itself]'
(Hereniko 2001: 168).[8]

The tourist and the native

By far the most significant form of global development in the Pacific Islands
over the last half century has been *tourism*, now generally if grudgingly
recognised to be an important means of economic diversification in the
region and a valuable if not always reliable source, especially in the poor
countries, of much-needed foreign exchange (Overton and Scheyvens 1999).
Fragile ecological zones such as the Pacific are dependent, however, on
the ability to create more sustainable forms of touristic development, the
hard-headed question being more of what particular kinds of tourism are
to be practised than of whether tourism, in whichever form, is acceptable or not. A typical 'Oceanic' view is that tourism can be beneficial if
it is moulded to local needs and interests; the key is thus to find alternative forms of tourism that benefit local people and have a relatively
low environmental impact rather than relying on those mainstream forms
that pander to international consumer fantasies, and that either wilfully
ignore the damaging ecological consequences of touristic development or
continue to treat the environment as if it were an endlessly replenishable
resource (Hau'ofa 1993; van Fossen 2005). Unsurprisingly, however, the
sustainability of tourism is no less controversial than the sustainability of
development, and justifiable fears remain that tourism is primarily a
'neo-colonial extension of economic forms of underdevelopment' rather
than an effective mechanism for the alleviation of north–south developmental discrepancies or a profitable basis for addressing southern social
and economic needs (Britton 1980: 149).[9]

Sustainable tourism notionally mirrors the combination of social,
economic and environmental factors at play in standard definitions of
sustainable development in general, encompassing global concerns for
poverty eradication and social justice as well as a locally situated acknowledgement of the deleterious effects of climate change, land degradation, and
biodiversity loss (Overton and Scheyvens 1999: 1). Thus, like sustainable
development, sustainable tourism is best understood as a compromise
option based on the not unreasonable but always potentially expedient
perception that environmental sustainability and economic development
are 'compatible, attainable and mutually inseparable' goals (Overton and
Scheyvens 1999: 3). One definition of sustainable tourism that follows
this logic runs as follows: it is 'tourism which is developed and maintained in an area [...] in such a manner and at such a scale that it
remains viable over an indefinite period and does not degrade or alter the

environment [...] in which it exists to such a degree that it prohibits the successful development and well-being of other activities and processes' (Butler, quoted in Brohman 1996: 58). But probably the clearest example of sustainable tourism is that cluster of alternative tourisms which, conveniently gathered under the loose heading of 'ecotourism', is organised around a conservation ethic aimed at 'increasing public awareness of the environment, maximising economic benefits for local communities, fostering cultural sensitivity, and minimising the negative impact of travel on the environment' (Ryel and Grasse 1991: 64; see also Fennell 1999). However, this idealistic view all too frequently butts against its opposite, namely that ecotourism is a 'new form of ecological imperialism in which western cultural values override local values and thereby oppose the [very] principles of sustainability which ecotourism claims to support' (Mowforth and Munt 1998: 104). Ecotourism, its opponents argue, is little more than a western middle-class luxury practice, rather like the international environment and conservation movements in whose globally responsible spirit it claims to operate, and from which it continues to enlist its primary ideological support (Dobson 1995). Also in keeping with these movements, it tends to promote an ethnocentric view of the environment that shows little of the cultural sensitivity it is so keen to foster, and that sometimes flies in the face of the local people it wishes to endorse. Finally, it is either given to legitimate the clash between environmental and cultural considerations – as in game parks that involve the forced eviction of local people – or, alternately, to promote the kind of convergence between them in which local people are themselves treated ('zooified') as curiosities, and are stereotypically represented as being at one with the natural environments they inhabit and protect (Mowforth and Munt 1998: 246).

While radical critiques such as these are an unfair dismissal of ecotourism's potential to counteract the damaging environmental consequences of other, less ecologically oriented forms of touristic development, they draw attention to a different sort of problem – namely the construction of the *local* both in developmentalist discourses and in the alternative, post-developmental paradigms that seek to redefine or replace them (e.g. by placing emphasis on sustainability or by insisting on local communities' self-given right to steer their own social, cultural and environmental course: Rahnema and Bawtree 1997; Saunders 2002). As our own vocabulary implies, both developmentalist and post-developmental discourses are inclined to fetishise local communities: in the first case as the beneficiaries of western development initiatives and, in the second, as primary agents or secondary partners in the establishment and subsequent monitoring of sustainable cultural/environmental projects and concerns.

Consider, for example, the following sentences taken from an essay that seeks to promote the virtues of alternative tourism within the context of 'appropriate' development:

- The success of a strategy of tourism development ought not to be measured just in terms of increased tourist numbers or revenues. Tourism should also be assessed according to how it has been integrated into the broader development goals of existing *local* communities, as well as the ways in which tourism-related investments and revenues have been used to benefit those communities. Tourism can indeed be positive for *local* communities if their needs and interests are given priority over the goals of the industry *per se*.
- Tourism should be seen as a *local* resource. Its management according to the needs and interests of *local* communities ought to be the principal criterion upon which its development is evaluated.
- Alternative tourism encourages community participation in *local/* regional planning concerning tourism and related development. By creating democratic institutions to allow *local* residents to participate in decision-making, it is expected that more appropriate forms of tourism development will be established that will be viewed positively by *local* residents. (Brohman 1996: 61–64; emphasis ours)

While it might legitimately be argued that there is no adequate replacement for the adjective 'local' in these instances, their cumulative effect is to reify locality as an object of developmental discourse, much in the same way that contemporary globalisation rhetoric effectively produces the localities on whose behalf it likes to speak (Appadurai 1996; Tomlinson 1999; Wilson and Dissanayake 1996).[10] As the geographers Martin Mowforth and Ian Munt have suggested, the mutual constitution of the global and the local in touristic and, more broadly, developmentalist discourses has had the paradoxical effect, not so much of demonstrating their complex entanglements and interactions, but rather of creating a series of separate spaces in which particular localities, acting on and in turn acted upon by global forces, are clearly delineated and marked out. Similar difficulties surround the symbolic construction of the 'native' in touristic discourses in which, despite mounting material evidence for the blurring of these categories, 'tourists' and 'natives' continue to be locked into antagonistic compartments sealed off by unambiguous references to outsider/insider perspectives and that tired pseudo-anthropological fiction, the 'native point of view'.

It is here that a literary-critical approach to tourism can be useful, both by illustrating the complexities and contradictions of contemporary touristic discourses as these are inflected by the shifting play of voices and perspectives, and by complicating essentialised distinctions between local cultural formations and holistic, 'ecological' understandings of the global system to which they are all imagined to belong. Ironically, as we shall see, one of the virtues of a more specifically *eco*critical approach to the postcolonial writing that engages with such discourses is to show how this writing offers, not just an ecologically informed critique of global-capitalist ideologies of development, but also a corrective to those reductive understandings of holistic patterns of interconnectedness and reciprocity that are popularly, but at times inaccurately, associated with ecology itself (Heise 2006).[11] In what follows, we propose brief ecocritical readings of two postcolonial texts which, while written from very different cultural perspectives, both disrupt the binarist vocabularies from which they initially appear to draw sustenance, and in which the twin 'ecological' myths of embeddedness (locality) and interconnectedness (globality) are historically resituated, even if they fall short of being comprehensively debunked. We shall then use the two texts – Patricia Grace's *Potiki* (1986) and Jamaica Kincaid's *A Small Place* (1988) – to draw some conclusions on the developmentalist ideologies examined in this section, and to suggest some ways in which these might be linked to postcolonial debates surrounding belonging and entitlement, which will go on to provide our main subject for the next.

Patricia Grace's 1986 novel *Potiki* has been read as a poetic meditation on the struggle between 'nativist' and 'developmentalist' understandings of land, the former being associated with the view of land as unchallengeable spiritual obligation and the latter with land as exchangeable material resource. Admittedly this view, at the level of plot, has something to commend it. Developers come in with a view to converting a stretch of coastal land into a lucrative theme park, but are rebuffed by the local Māori, who inform them that some of the land is theirs and cannot simply be annexed (Grace 1986: 97). All attempts to persuade the Māori fall on deaf ears and the developers resort to aggression; provoked beyond measure, the Māori eventually respond with aggression of their own. As John Beston hastily concludes, the 'moral of this parable is that one should fight back, with appropriate retaliation. Grace has joined the ranks of [...] Maori who believe that justice can only be obtained by direct action' (Beston, quoted in Fuchs 1994: 172). (Another apparent lesson is that the developmentalist language of opportunity, backed up by money and power, is also a language of dispossession; and that its nativist counterpart is a language of resistance, founded on the perceived entitlement to live where one traditionally belongs (Grace 1986: 132). The developmentalist view, in short, is that land belongs to people, and can be traded or transformed to suit their immediate purposes; while the nativist view is that people belong to land, which holds them in their trust and requires their care and custodianship in return (110).)

The problem with this confrontational view is, precisely, that it is plot-driven. But *Potiki* is not so much a discrete series of events as a 'percipient existence' (Fuchs 1994: 181), shaped both by the liminal presence of the *potiki* and by the sensibilities of other members of his adopted family, all of whom are characterised less by the individual actions they perform than by the collectively intuitive – part-inherited, part-invented – stories they relate. These stories are interlinked: inhabiting a Māori 'now-time' that effortlessly straddles past, present and future (Grace 1986: 39), they create the uncanny effect of a recital of genealogies in which nothing really happens because it has all happened before (Fuchs 1994: 174). Commentators have understandably been fascinated by the ways in which *Potiki* creates a 'spiral temporality' in keeping with traditional Māori attitudes to the death-birth continuum (DeLoughrey 1999); but equally important in the novel are the ways in which its stories, connecting across time, also bring together differing, sometimes conflicting, attitudes to place. *Potiki*, in this sense, is both a meditation on place and an ecology of stories in which the delicate balance between embedded ('rooted') and interconnected ('routed') narratives is continually renegotiated by a shifting community of tellers and listeners that is at once profoundly local and inextricably connected to the wider world (Grace 1986: 38, 44, 145; also DeLoughrey 2007b). This ecology is more than just a network; rather, as the term 'ecology' implies, it is a sphere of co-dependent interaction that connects people to the other ecological beings, both animate and not, that share their phenomenal life-world. And just as ecosystems tend to be characterised by neither homeostasis nor complementarity but rather by their susceptibility to disruption, so the ecology of stories in *Potiki* exists in a volatile condition, subject to sudden forms of profoundly unsettling mutation in which familiar stories inexplicably change. (As the novel shows, it is the *potiki* above all who is able to anticipate, but not necessarily facilitate, changes within the signifying system – social, cultural, spiritual – that the community had previously depended on to make sense of their daily lives.)

To see the interconnected stories that make up *Potiki* in these terms is to risk aestheticising ecology to the point of caricaturing it – an occupational hazard, it could be argued, of ecocriticism as a whole. As the Canadian ecocritic Susie O'Brien ruefully remarks, 'there is a temptation for many ecocritics, who tend not to be trained in science, simply to import such condensed ecological formulae as Barry Commoner's First Law of Ecology that "everything is connected to everything else" [...]

into a literary-critical context in order to talk about everything from textual representations of environments [...] to the ways in which formal literary structures reflect and/or interact with organic physical ones' (O'Brien 2007:182). O'Brien's point is well taken; however, our reading of *Potiki* hopefully points to a more complex performance of ecological mimesis in which the eco-populist paradigms of harmony and stability – never likely to have been endorsed by professional ecologists in the first place – are outstripped by systemic indeterminacy, cutting through illusions connected to romantic ideals of self-sufficiency and the fixity of place. These illusions are primarily associated in the novel with the character of Hemi, whose nostalgic land-based vision of the community is founded on what might be called a radical (anti-modern, organicist) form of environmental self-sufficiency: 'everything we need', he insists repeatedly, despite increasing evidence to the contrary, 'is here' (38, 69). The novel, however, fails notably to endorse this vision. Nostalgia is not the answer; rather, the community's most urgent struggle is for the freedom to negotiate the terms of its own engagement with a global modernity it cannot do without.

The ostensible ground on which this struggle is fought is development; more specifically, it is (mass) tourism. Development is largely filtered in the novel through economistic myths of progress: 'amenity', 'benefit', 'improvement', the self-satirising language of the 'Dollarman' who, while 'officially welcomed, was not in the heart welcome, or at least what he had to say was not' (88). The impact of development on tourism is understood to be both quantitative (the move from small-scale to mass tourism: 92–93) and qualitative (the move from low- to high-impact tourism, encapsulated in the increasing commodification of the natural world (97)). At the heart of the community's objections to the development plans is the right to control use of their own land, but also important is the need to protect the commons:

> The hills and sea did not belong to us but we wished to see them kept clean and free. We could only be objectors along with others who liked to swim and camp and fish, and who did not want the sea or land changed. We, like them, did not want the company to make zoos and circuses in the sea, or to put noise and pollution there, or to line the shore with palaces and castles, and souvenir shops, or to have restaurants rotating above the sea, lit up at night like star crafts landing their invaders on the shore. [...] Because soon there would be no fish, only pet ones that you went in lit underground tunnels to see at shark-feeding time, or any time you wanted. If you paid. [...] Well we wanted the fish to be in the sea like ordinary fish,

the stingrays to roam in the evenings as they always do. We wanted our eyes to know the place where they would meet the tide whether it was low or high.

(98)

At times like these, it is clear that the community (both Māori and *pakeha*) is practising a variation on the environmental ethic in which the value of the commons consists precisely in its accessibility to all those who use it, and in which the condition of this use is that the natural ecosystems already in place be left more or less untouched. This is, of course, a relative statement, the crucial distinction in the novel being that between modifying the environment in accordance with sustainable ecological practices and wilfully altering it in the sole interest of extracting profit from it, disfiguring it as a result (115–16). As with other manifestations of the environmental ethic, land use depends on, and is regulated by, the prior perception of environment, not as separate from those individuals and groups who inhabit it but as integral to them; in this sense, the term 'environment', with its inevitable connotations of externality, is a misnomer, even in self-consciously environmental texts (Buell 1995; Glotfelty and Fromm 1996).[12] *Potiki*, we want to suggest, is both an *ecological* text (in its broadest sense) and an *environmental* one (in its narrower definition as one that is both attentive and accountable to the natural environment(s) it represents: Buell 1995). However, it is perhaps most of all a *Māori* text, deeply inflected by indigenous ways of seeing and knowing, and to some extent uninterpretable by those without thorough knowledge of Māori language, customs and beliefs (Fuchs 1994). This might seem like a silencing mechanism, but there are signs in the text that it is not intended to be one. For example, the various Maui-Potiki creation myths that are woven through the text run in parallel with an idiosyncratic version of the Christian nativity. While this is what one might expect from a Christianised Māori community like the one that features in the novel, it also indicates that the stories of *Potiki* can be read on a number of different interpretative levels, and that no one level excludes the others, just as no one reader (or community of readers) is consciously excluded from the text.[13] Still, this does not suggest, as Miriam Fuchs implies in her detailed reading of *Potiki*, that the novel can be read according to the holistic principles that she sees as informing (western) ecology, where 'the diverse parts of ecosystems [are assessed for evidence] of patterns of interactivity and reciprocal change' (165). For one thing, the novel retains what might be called an indigenous core that remains inaccessible to the western reader; and for another, the practice of cultural holism, whatever its merits, does not correspond to ecological principles, being closer in spirit to the eco-populism already mentioned above. Fuchs's otherwise interesting reading might thus be seen as an example of the perils of a critical approach which seeks support from an ecology that it believes it understands but probably, at best, instrumentalises for the apparent purposes of universalising the methodologies (in this case, narratological) it wishes to enact.

If one of the problems of an ecocritical approach to *Potiki* is the risk that its ecological dimensions might be over-aestheticised, the opposite problem arguably obtains in *A Small Place*: that they are not aestheticised enough. Critical reception of Kincaid's text – a volatile mixture of semi-fictional autobiography and political travelogue – has been notable for its astonishing degree of literal-mindedness. Moira Ferguson, for example, calls the text a 'virtually unmediated anti-colonial polemic' (77), while other critics, seeing the narrator as little more than a mouthpiece for Kincaid, either condemn her biases accordingly (King 2002) or credit her with the kind of heightened insight that seems to be the product of liberal guilt's conversion into exaggerated praise (Scott 2002). Our own critical sympathies here lie with Alison Donnell who, while conceding that the text is at one level 'pure polemic', also draws attention to an 'underlying indeterminacy of meaning' connected to its duplicities of narrative voice (Donnell 1995: 107). For Donnell, *A Small Place* is both 'a direct political statement on neo-colonialism [in Antigua] and a consummate work of ventriloquism that deploys a whole series of [narrative] voices in order to debate the values and limitations of the cultural discourses and limitations associated with postcolonialism', not least the inbuilt tendency of at least some postcolonial critics to turn extreme cultural relativism into the kind of political paralysis that cannot see beyond celebration of the culturally particular, the representative 'native voice' (107–8). We would agree with the second half of this statement but also apply its protocols to the first. Whatever else *A Small Place* is, it is not 'unmediated polemic': rather, complex processes of mediation are apparent at all levels of the text. Our main task here is to suggest what implications this might have for the text's *ecological* message: a message, we would argue, that emerges less from the discursive interplay between its key terms – tourism, nativism, colonialism – than from the economies of scale and perspective that are contained within its disarmingly simple title: 'a small place'.

A Small Place's initial conceit is that it is addressed to a 'representative' (Euro-American) tourist in the name of a 'representative' (Antiguan) native; but neither of these positions, as one might expect, is allowed to hold for very long. First, as the narrator openly acknowledges, she is hardly a 'representative native' but rather an expatriate Antiguan who, having left her birthplace two decades ago, has only recently returned to it. Second, as she also concedes, 'every native of every place is potentially a tourist, and every tourist is a native of somewhere' (18). While this relativising assertion is immediately challenged by the view that 'most natives in the world cannot go anywhere', being too poor even to 'live properly in the place where they live' (18–19), this view merely reinforces the text's sustained assault on Europeans' and North Americans' privileged place within the global postcolonial economy: a place also shared by the majority of the text's readers, and which imparts obvious advantages to those 'natives' who happen to come from, and enjoy the conspicuous material benefits of, the so-called First World (Gauch 2002: 911–12). This move – a crucial one in the text – allows for connections to be made between tourism and colonialism, but also between both of these and what might be described as a postcolonial politics of reading in which the model reader is set up *both* as a literary tourist of Antigua *and* as a liberal critic of such touristic forms of reading, which have helped turn poverty such as Antigua's into an exotic variation on the picturesque (77–79). Literary tourism, the text suggests, is a product of the alienated relations of production and consumption within a global cultural economy, relations reproduced in the stereotypical cultural perceptions and divisive material practices of tourism itself (Donnell 1995).[14] 'Alienation', in fact, is a key term in the text in so far as both 'tourists' and 'natives' are presented as being psychically removed, with lastingly damaging consequences, from the physical circumstances in which they actually live. One symptom of this alienation is a perception of banality, of the empty routines of everyday living; another is an intuition of nostalgia, expressed most clearly in the text as colonial mimicry: either the attempt to structure the place where one lives according to another place's values or, what may amount in the end to the same thing, the will to imaginatively refashion the place one has definitively left (Kincaid 1988: 24–25, 30, 33).

Two tentative conclusions can be drawn from the text's emphasis on alienation, one individual and the other structural. The first, more personally oriented conclusion is that the text is self-consciously rehearsing a form of 'diasporic melancholy' (Brophy 2002) that is the joint product of a psychopathology of *colonialism* (the distorting effects of slavery, colonialism and their aftermath in Antigua, which arguably leads 'native' Antiguans to consent to their own abasement) and a psychopathology of *displacement* (the equally distorting effects produced by a shorter history of self-imposed exile, which arguably leads 'ex-native' Antiguans to articulate their own feelings of disconnectedness through a toxic combination of anger, anguish and contempt). The second, more general conclusion is that the text is offering an indirect commentary on the political implications of the radical perspectivism it also practises, and that this commentary revolves around the different meanings – socio-cultural, historical, ecological – that can be ascribed to a 'small place'. While these two conclusions are clearly linked, we shall focus on the second one here. The 'smallness' of Antigua can be seen in the text according to at least two, sharply differentiated perspectives. The first of these emphasises vulnerability and susceptibility to exploitation, reflecting the text's 'metonymic shift' from tourism to colonialism (Ferguson 1994: 84); the second highlights provincialism and small-mindedness, reflecting its (self-)accusatory exposure of Antiguans' collective failure to make connections between the place where they live and the wider world:

> For the people in a small place, every event is a domestic event; the people in a small place cannot see themselves in a larger picture, they cannot see that they might be part of a chain of something, anything. The people in a small place see the event in the distance heading towards them and they say, 'I see the thing and it is heading directly towards me.' The people in a small place then experience the event as if it were sitting on top of their heads, their shoulders, and it weighs them down, this enormous burden that is the event, so that they cannot breathe properly and they cannot think properly and they say, 'This thing that was only coming towards me is now on top of me,' and they live like that, until eventually they absorb the event and it becomes a part of them, a part of who and what they really are, and they are complete in that way until another event comes along and the process begins again.
>
> (52–53)

This second form of 'smallness' is later seen in terms of an inability to appreciate context, both in the historical sense of linking discrete events to broader patterns and in the environmental sense of not being overwhelmed by the immediacy of one's own surroundings:

> It is as if [...] the beauty of the sea, the land, the air, the trees, the market, the people, the sounds they make [...] were a prison, and as if everything and everybody inside it were locked in and everything and everybody that is not inside it were locked out. And what might it do to ordinary people to live in [...] such heightened, intense surroundings day after day? They have nothing to compare this incredible constant with, no big historical moment to compare the way they are now to the way they used to be. No Industrial Revolution, no

revolution of any kind, no Age of Anything, no world wars, no decades of turbulence balanced by decades of calm.

(79)

While these sentiments are disturbingly reminiscent of Naipaul's notorious dictum that 'nothing was ever created in the West Indies' (Naipaul 1962), they also mimic the colonial discourse that inspires them, projecting the small-mindedness of their own, sophisticated outsider's derision onto the self-limitations of those relatively uneducated insiders who are apparently unable to see beyond the immediate horizons of their actions, or to escape from the discursive as well as material conditions within which this immediacy, this sensory intensity, is couched. Here, as elsewhere, the text works towards undoing the colonial discourse it simultaneously inhabits, producing a rhetorical form of displacement that is the equivalent of its geographical situatedness in the diaspora, and that might help explain the continual shifting of positions by which its narrator is able to claim both insider and outsider status, or to pass – with what often seems like equal arrogance – as an articulate advocate of 'ordinary Antiguans' and as their greatest scourge. (This cultivated duplicity in the text might itself be seen as a form of mimicry, as when the narrator distinguishes, copying the 'revolutionary' Fanon rather than the 'reactionary' Naipaul, between the national consciousness of Antiguans and the self-interested nativism with which its neocolonial elite has co-opted the national cause: Kincaid 1988: 69; see also Lang-Peralta 2006.)

The double consciousness of *A Small Place* emerges from a clear awareness of the distance that separates the place *from* which it is written from the place *about* which it is written: an awareness which, in sliding between accusatory rage and agonised complicity, combines these apparently contradictory attitudes with predictably mixed results. The inherent slipperiness of the text has been seen as evidence of ambivalence or even hypocrisy but, like Donnell among several others, we would prefer to see it as the text's attempt to reflect on the diasporic consciousness from within which it is narrated, and on the significance of its own location within a global cultural/economic circuit in which its compromised (*neo*-colonial as much as *anti*-colonial) status as a postcolonial text is enmeshed (Donnell 1995; Lang-Peralta 2006; Simmons 1994). All of this makes Kincaid's book a very different kind of meditation on place to *Potiki*: one in which the awareness of (global) interconnectedness seems to prevent (local) embeddedness rather than to help produce it, and in which tourism operates as the sign of a fundamental 'place-disconnectedness' (Buell 2001) which, part-sustained by the developmentalist logic of global capitalism, is now shared, to their mutual frustration, by 'tourists' and 'natives' alike.

Both *Potiki* and *A Small Place* are enraged by the kind of developmentalism that merely panders to global-corporate interests, but neither
work suggests that globalisation, and the at times destructive kinds of
cultural/economic development it fosters, can simply be bypassed. The
problem addressed in both cases is of how to harness the demands of
global development to the ecological well-being of the local communities
that embrace it, given that these communities are frequently entangled
in a 'globally integrated system of resource use over which they cannot
exercise control' (Brohman 1996: 55). While neither Grace's nor Kincaid's
texts are able to show a way out of this dilemma, both go beyond the
simplistic equation of development with capitalism, or of tourism with
colonialism, by suggesting that the battle is not against development or
tourism as intrinsically harmful processes and activities, but rather
against the often flagrant human and environmental abuses that continue
to be practised in their cause. At the same time, like many of the literary works examined in this section, *Potiki* and *A Small Place* show
the inadequacy of discourses of human/environmental victimisation to
address the needs of local people whose historical reverses are out-
weighed by their future ambitions and initiatives, and whose continuing
commitment to the well-being of their communities requires a high degree
of self-determination that 'top-down' processes of social and environmental management are often likely to arrest. The anti-colonial rhetoric
of self-government may itself be abused, as Kincaid's mediated tirade
against corruption in post-independence Antigua clearly demonstrates,
but self-determination still remains the political platform upon which
most of the counter-developmental case studies in this section eventually rests. 'Counter-developmental', we would say, rather than 'anti-' or
'post-developmental', in so far as many of the examples treated here
point to the existence of alternative social and environmental knowledges that are neither endorsed nor necessarily understood by development experts in the west. It is one of the tasks of postcolonial
ecocriticism, as we suggested at the beginning of this section, to bring to
light these alternative knowledges and knowledge-systems, which often
underpin postcolonised communities' sense of their own cultural identities and entitlements, and which represent the ontological basis for
their politically contested claims to belong. Entitlement and belonging
are, at heart, ontological rather than juridical questions. The next section will consider whether western rights-based discourses are capable of
accounting for, let alone adjudicating on, questions concerning the very
being of postcolonised peoples, and will assess the contribution made by
postcolonial writers to these arguments – arguments which, as we shall
see, have profound aesthetic implications for postcolonial literature's

continuing pursuit of social and environmental advocacy across the historical faultlines of literary genre.

Epilogue: Eco-catastrophe, global warming and the crisis of the human

In the foregoing section we made the case for postcolonial writers as both 'underground' critics of mainstream development processes and unacknowledged legislators for alternative, often community-oriented, styles and modes of development that are uncoupled from neoliberal principles of market expansion and economic growth. Postcolonial literature, we argued, continues to play a valuable role not just in imagining more sustainable alternatives to the current world order, but also in prefiguring what happens when that order collapses, bringing planetary chaos in its wake. Catastrophes of different kinds – social, political, environmental, and all of these combined – have long been a staple of postcolonial writing, which creatively engages with the long history of catastrophes, not least those associated with colonialism, that operate in multiple temporal and spatial frames (Carrigan 2015). Importantly, though, catastrophe in postcolonial literature can also be seen as a *source* of energy and creativity, giving rise to new visions of human society and, in some cases, new understandings of the human itself. Perhaps the greatest catastrophe of our times falls under the general heading of global warming. However, both postcolonial theory and ecocriticism – if not necessarily postcolonial literature itself – have been decidedly, even reprehensibly slow in responding to global warming,[15] despite its current media- as well as climate-accelerated billing as 'the ecological trauma of our age' (Morton 2013: 9). There are several possible reasons for this. From a postcolonial perspective, as Dipesh Charkabarty notes, global warming presents a unique challenge to the ontological modes and models of human subjectivity and agency that have long been integral to postcolonial theory and criticism; for if human beings are now increasingly acknowledged to act as 'a geophysical force on the planet' – and if they are now increasingly seen to be part of that planet's natural history – then both ontological *and* non-ontological understandings of the human, as well as ways of thinking *beyond* the human, are urgently required (Chakrabarty 2012: 2, 10, 14; see also Chakrabarty 2009). Meanwhile, for ecocritics, who have long since questioned the planetary centrality of the human, a different problem obtains, of how to account for a megaphenomenon – in Timothy Morton's terms, a 'hyperobject' – which, while indubitably real, potentially exhausts the realist place-based credos that inform conventional modes of environmental representation: 'nature', 'habitat' and, not least, 'environment' itself (Clark 2010; Morton 2013).[16]

For both postcolonial theorists and ecocritics, then, global warming opens up a crisis that registers – as does the phenomenon itself – at many different levels, and that operates across a large number of seemingly incommensurable temporal and spatial scales. This crisis is ethical and political as much as it is definitional and representational. As Emily Brady suggests, the ethical dilemmas associated with global warming are closely linked to the dispersal of its causes and effects; for it is difficult to 'pin down responsibility and address issues of climate justice [when there] is a fragmentation of agency with emissions originating in individuals, institutions and industry across different parts of the globe at different times' (2014: 553). These dilemmas also have inevitably political dimensions: for if there is no single rational solution to the potentially devastating social and environmental problems posed by global warming, then a struggle for legitimacy ensues that involves a number of potentially conflicting political actors, all operating in the larger context of what remains a deeply divided and unevenly developed world (Chakrabarty 2012: 13; see also Narain and Agarwal 1991). Global warming, in this last sense, has particularly deleterious effects for those who are most vulnerable to suffer from it, while such contemporary developmental initiatives as carbon trading effectively double as new forms of colonialism through which 'land and resources in poor countries [are acquired in order to] sustain the profligate consumption of the rich' (Newell and Paterson 2010: 32).

As might be expected, postcolonial literature tends to focus on the conspicuous socio-economic inequalities that underlie politically motivated attempts to address global warming: attempts which, more often than not, use (sometimes fabricated) evidence of global warming as an opportunity to implement technocratic forms of 'planetary management' that reinforce boundaries between rich and poor, the 'developed' global North and the 'developing' global South (Escobar 1995; Ross 1991). However, postcolonial writers must contend at the same time with the inherent difficulties of representing a 'massively distributed' phenomenon (Morton 2013: 42) which, in Ursula Heise's words, 'poses a [serious] challenge for narrative and lyrical forms that have conventionally focused above all on individuals, families, or nations, since it requires the articulation of connections between events at vastly different scales' (Heise 2008: 205). As Heise among others suggests, novelists (among other creative writers) who seek to engage the contemporary realities of global warming are often given to fall back on stock motifs of catastrophe and apocalypse, playing out the familiar scenarios of genre fiction in futuristic settings where this world is folded into one or other version of the next (Heise 2008; see also Trexler and Johns-Putra 2011). The tropes of 'catastrophe' and 'apocalypse', however, need not be formulaic, nor are the temporalities that inform them necessarily future-oriented; rather, what Kate Rigby (2013a) calls 'the ineluctability of eco-catastrophe' can be addressed in a number of different, sometimes startlingly original, ways.

In what follows, we will look briefly at three postcolonial literary texts – Alexis Wright's multiple prize-winning 2006 novel *Carpentaria*, Kamau Brathwaite's fragmented narrative poem *X/Self* (1987), the third volume in a poetic trilogy also containing *Mother Poem* (1977) and *Sun Poem* (1982), and Curdella Forbes's 2012 futuristic fictional memoir *Ghosts* – all of which evolve formally experimental ways of engaging with global warming, even if only the last and most recent of these, Forbes's *Ghosts*, directly addresses its enduring effects and consequences for a socially and ecologically shattered earth. Indeed, these texts have been chosen in part because they dispel the illusion that it might be possible to write explicitly 'about' global warming; instead, each in its radically different way takes place within the general *context* of global warming, a context marked by a high degree of uncertainty and contingency, and by a strong ethical awareness of the issues at stake in the social staging of risk in a globally interconnected world (Beck 2009).[17]

Despite their differences, which demonstrate the urgency of addressing cultural specificity under the general conditions of global warming, the three texts all address the multiple colonialisms inscribed within contemporary discourses of global warming – colonialisms attached to the long history of mercantilist capitalism, but also to the longer histories still within which catastrophist visions of planetary destruction are entwined. As Ilan Kelman and J.C. Gaillard (2010) have rightly argued, global warming needs to be embedded within the larger social and political contexts of development, sustainability and disaster risk reduction; but it equally needs to be taken *out* of its contemporary contexts, re-inscribed within the millennial scales and glacial rhythms of geological change. This is presumably what the environmental historian Tom Griffiths means by 'deep time', which he links rather than opposes to social history:

> 'Deep time' and 'social history' seem to be the antithesis of one another, each operating on utterly different timescales and subject matter. One conjures up ancient evolutionary history, even a non-human world, while the other suggests the study of modern society. One deals in awesome geological eras, while the other takes its chronological scale from a human lifespan. It is one of the challenges of the emerging field of environmental history to connect

them, to work audaciously across time as well as across space and species.

(2000: n.p.)

Carpentaria, *X/Self* and *Ghosts* all explore the imaginative possibilities of deep time, even if they do so from a number of distinct social and cultural locations (in braiding the 'cultural' and the 'natural', they also offer a critical rejoinder to what Rigby [2013a] calls 'that modernist mind-set which seeks neatly to separate human from non-human causes and effects'). The three texts are also similar in deploying a magic-realist aesthetic – however problematically defined – to address a wide variety of social and ecological issues across vast realms of time and space. Finally, the texts all promulgate what might be described as an 'alter/catastrophist' vision of the world in which imperial/colonial legacies of natural destruction are symbolically countered, and global warming, while its apocalyptic threat is by no means negated, is incorporated into utopian presentiments of cultural homecoming on a radically transformed earth.

Carpentaria (2006), Alexis Wright's second published novel, is a multi-layered text, aptly described by Wright herself as a 'spinning multi-stranded helix of [indigenous] stories' (2007: 84), set in the Gulf country that Wright knows intimately – the place where she grew up. As several of the novel's commentators point out, *Carpentaria* makes few concessions to the non-Aboriginal reader, who is confronted with a complex world of shifting time and space in which 'the cosmological, cultural and spiritual relationship of indigenous people with their country' is highlighted in the novel's 'imagery, narrative point of view, characterisation and plot' (Brewster 2010: 90). Kate Rigby's response is characteristic of the nervousness of non-Aboriginal Australian critics who, in approaching the novel, feel they are 'eavesdropping on a tale that is being told to somebody else with far more familiarity with the world to which it pertains, and the language in which it is told' than they are, and who are painfully aware that any interpretative strategies they might bring to bear upon it constitute a narrow 'whitefella' reading that is ignorant to the many indigenous-specific nuances of the text (Rigby 2013b: 124; see also Brewster 2010, Devlin-Glass 2008, Ferrier 2008).

While this is true up to a point, Wright's novel is far from exclusivist in its intentions; rather, it fashions an appealing transcultural cross between the mordant northern yarn (*à la* Xavier Herbert) and the dreamy tropical fable (*à la* Gabriel García Márquez), even if both are assimilated to the distinct rhythms of Aboriginal storytelling and presented in an irreverent vernacular tone that 'belongs to the diction of the tribal nations of the Gulf' (Wright 2007: 88). These and other aspects of the text have led some critics to detect family resemblances between *Carpentaria* and the creolised fictions of Latin American magic realism, although the novel has also been held to demonstrate 'the unconsciously colonialist and European biases in the label *magic realism*', which tends to trivialise the sacred by lowering it to the status of the magical in ways similar to those found in some early anthropological texts (Devlin-Glass 2008: 395). The label certainly applies to Wright's text, though, at least in so far as magic realism is a 'literary practice [...] closely linked with a perception of living on the margins, encoding within itself [...] a concept of resistance to the imperial centre and its totalizing systems'; while the novel also draws on magic realism's paradigmatic reversal of the ideologically constructed relationship between colonial periphery and imperial core (Slemon 1988: 10; see also Zamora and Faris 1995).

This relationship takes several different forms in *Carpentaria*: that of north to south; that of Old to New Australia; that of a straggling coastal town (a colonial periphery itself) to its rubbish-strewn hinterlands (the periphery of the periphery, inhabited 'only' by Aboriginal people who are dismissed by the town's white-settler inhabitants, who delusively see themselves as belonging to the nation's core). But as soon becomes apparent in the text, it is these tip-dwelling 'edge people' (2007: 54) who, for all their conspicuous faults, have access to a richly experienced life-world in which the townsfolk are themselves peripheral figures – dangerously so, for they are both ignorant of the land that sustains them and insufficiently attentive to the fickle weather systems on which their lives ultimately depend. Indeed, it is the land itself that is the true centre, the main character, of Wright's novel. Perhaps a better word here would be *country*, a multi-faceted indigenous term which at once includes the material aspects of land and the spiritual figures, themselves fully material presences, that formed the land in an immemorial past and continue to co-create it in the present (Rigby 2013b; see also Rose 1996). Country takes in both the spatial coordinates of a given territory and the temporal mechanisms through which the various entities that inhabit it – whether living or dead, whether human or non-human – are ritually connected through ancestral kinship bonds (Rigby 2013b). If country encompasses both *ecology* and *cosmology*, these are then joined to a volatile 'weather-world' (Ingold 2011: 96-97) where the four cardinal elements (air, fire, earth and water) function simultaneously, often destructively, as geophysical force and cosmic energy.[18] This reflects the vicissitudes of climate change over deep time, which requires equally deep-seated ancestral knowledge to comprehend it (Wright 2007: 3). But even inside knowledge is not enough to forestall the next calamity, since both land and sea are filled with belligerent spirit-creatures whose running feuds involve random manipulations of wind and tide, thereby 'spurn[ing] human endeavour' (3) and ruining even the most carefully calculated of human plans (272).

In *Carpentaria*, extreme weather – notably the cataclysmic flood that washes the town away towards the end of the novel – is thus as much an act of the gods as a confluence of the elements; but crucially it is *both* of these things, and the text neither rejects modern meteorological understandings of local atmospheric phenomena nor disputes the accumulated scientific evidence for global climate change. On the contrary, its central Aboriginal characters are singularly adept at reading potentially destructive changes in their environment, a skill that harnesses scientific and mythological knowledge for both survival and regenerative ends (202). And they are aware, too, that there are larger changes afoot in which the earth is beginning to stir itself (372). For example, Will Phantom, the eco-activist whose spirited one-man-stand against the local mining corporation comes eventually to be supported by other members of the Aboriginal community who had previously ostracised him, recognises that 'the whole oceanic world seemed to be occupied in the Gulf. It was a grey painter's palette of tankers exchanging mining equipment for mined ore that came to the coast, after the flesh of the earth had been shunted there by pipelines, tying up the country with new Dreaming tracks cutting through the old' (388). This nightmarish vision of a global-capitalist empire, irradiated with industrial waste, has its meteorological equivalent in the sure signs of global warming: longer Dry seasons, the catastrophic effects of rising oceans as these intensify the already volatile atmospheric conditions of the Wet.

If in *Carpentaria* she only hints as much, Wright makes her position clear in a 2011 opinion piece in *Meanjin*. The piece shows scepticism towards, without necessarily rejecting, the technocratic accounts by which recent extreme weather events in Australia have been attributed to global warming; meanwhile it emphasises the enduring if neglected value of indigenous knowledge, which places such events within a deep time-frame that stretches back tens of thousands of years (2011: 78). Wright wonders aloud 'what the traditional Indigenous caretakers of the land [might] think about these extreme weather events of flood, fire and wind, where the whole geography of the country is considered sacred' (77–78). Her conclusion is that non-Aboriginal Australians have much to learn from such 'other ways of knowing, of understanding, of feeling the land and sea, environment and its climate' (78); and that it is in *stories*, through which 'Indigenous people struggle to retain their right to keep a strong cultural sense of what the environment is telling us', that this knowledge may best be disseminated today (79). *Carpentaria* offers one such story, and although it may not have much to say explicitly about the perils of global warming, it offers indirect evidence that climate is as much a cultural as a scientific phenomenon (cf. Hulme 2009), and that attitudinal transformation, including the willingness to learn from others, must be a key element in the ongoing struggle to combat global climate change.

The 'alter/catastrophist' vision of *Carpentaria* inscribes the contemporary environmental devastation of the Gulf within a long history of human and ecological catastrophes – catastrophes which are by definition destructive, but also carry within them a powerful regenerative force.[19] In the work of Barbadian poet and historian Kamau Brathwaite, catastrophe operates similarly as a catalyst for change and as an explosive outlet for creativity – literally explosive in Brathwaite's case in so far as his poetic oeuvre simulates the crash-and-burn of civilisations, pausing to gather the cindered fragments that result from this cataclysmic collapse. Also as in Wright's work – if more explicitly in Brathwaite's case – catastrophe is linked to the aesthetic and ideological credos of magical realism (his preferred iteration of the term), which he envisions as both a radical disruption of western progressivist history and as a creative exercise in cross-cultural cosmology: a bringing together, via the experimental poetic techniques of 'multiple representation, the plural instant, [and] collective improvisation', of apparently incommensurable historical moments and the hidden messages contained within them, their latent cultural codes (Brathwaite 2002 I: 302; see also Jenkins 2007).

Brathwaite has explained the rationale for this in a number of interviews, including one in 2005 with Joyelle McSweeney. 'Art comes out of catastophe', he says near the beginning of the interview: 'I'm [acutely] conscious of the enormity of slavery and the Middle Passage and I see that as an ongoing catastrophe. So whatever happens after that, like tsunamis in the Far East and India and Indonesia, and 9/11, and now New Orleans [the interview took place shortly after Hurricane Katrina], to me these are all aspects of that same original explosion, which I constantly try to understand'. As he goes on to suggest later in the interview, there is a further link between catastrophe and magical realism, which he clearly sees as carrying regenerative potential: 'That moment of utter disaster, the very moment when it seems almost hopeless, too difficult to proceed, you begin to glimpse a kind of radiance on the other end of the maelstrom'. It is important to understand that for Brathwaite, magical realism is much more than a literary style; rather, it is a kind of 'cultural gene' (2002 I: 66) linked to the 'two great continental cosmological catastrophes' of colonialism and slavery (2002 II: 475), to the broader existential notion of 'culture under crisis' (1987: 127), and to the fundamental inseparability of *cultural* and *natural* catastrophes, which he joins together by means of 'tidalectics', his loose-strung neologism for a revision of the Hegelian dialectic in ecological terms (Carrigan 2015; DeLoughrey 2009; Niblett 2014).[20] For Brathwaite, magical realism represents an unruly marriage of ecology and technology, a formally innovative means of 'holding a broken mirror up to broken nature' in such a way as to see the 'submerged fracture[s]' that exist beneath the surface of the so-called 'real world' (Brathwaite 2002 I: 2; see also Brathwaite 1997: 18 and Jenkins 2007: 168).

There is no space here to examine in detail how this approach, which is relational and non-systematic, works in practice across the large and at times bafflingly complex body of Brathwaite's writings; suffice to mention a few examples from *X/Self* (1987), which offers perhaps the clearest demonstration to date of how his oeuvre effects an 'alter/catastrophist' poetics through which a wide variety of simulated explosions produce an even wider variety of scattered fragments, and vast intuitive leaps are made across even vaster expanses of historical time and geographical space. As Brathwaite explains in his notes to the text, *X/Self* uses the techniques of 'magical montage' (1987: 115), musically inspired, to produce a radically creolised version of imperial history in which the military-industrial forces of 'Euro-imperialism' and 'Christine [*sic*] mercantilism' are destructively crossbred (118). 'Rome burns/and our slavery begins' (5) is the leitmotif that joins these two forces across time, allowing in turn for an uncanny play – what Brathwaite's fellow-Caribbean writer Wilson Harris might call an 'infinite rehearsal'[21] – of partial resemblances in which imperialism begets slavery, slavery begets the Holocaust, and a spiralling history of wars and genocides – a litany of catastrophes – encompasses them all and negatively energises the rest.

A typical hallucinatory effect is that produced in the poem-fragment 'Mont Blanc' (31–33), where Europe's highest peak and one of its most celebrated sources of poetic inspiration is dialectically attached to deadly counter-histories involving an obsessively expansionist (western) military-industrial complex and a rapacious capitalist ethic that finds its negative apotheosis in the Holocaust and the atomic bomb. Offering a further counterpoint to this ice-bound (white) world, in which 'factories [of death] blaze forth bergs and avalanches' (31), the speaker invokes a nightmarishly drought-stricken Sahara (32), in which

the dry snake of the harm
attan the harmattan reaches into our wells into our smiles into our cook

ing pot oil in/to the water re
flecting our walls in

to the bone
of the mutton in

to our dry
gully eyes

This hellish composite vision of stagnation/starvation echoes the epigraph to *X/Self*, in which the speaker (the eponymous x/self) asks his inter-locutors (x/self's Black Diaspora brethren) to contemplate what happens when, suddenly and without reason, 'you crops die' and 'you cant even see the sun in the sky' (n.p.). This apocalyptic rendering of a sick world in which 'ev'rything look like it comin out wrong' (n.p.) appears to mirror the calamitous ecological fallout of a long history of capitalist imperialism – one that continues to wreak havoc on humans and non-humans alike. And while it might be one intuitive leap too far to connect this history to the chain of circumstances, both manmade and not, that have produced contemporary global warming, this is surely another of Brathwaite's 'cosmological catastrophes': a vast disaster-generating complex, both human and non-human, that reaches back through the historical past into the seemingly unfathomable recesses of deep time.

The potential fatalism that might accompany such a vision is countered, however, by the 'episodic bursts of energy' (Davis 1999: 18) that attend all natural/cultural catastrophes. These bursts of energy, destructive though they are, are also potentially transformative. Thus, in the closing poem in *X/Self*, 'Xango', the eponymous Xango, described in the notes as the 'Pan African god of thunder, lightning, electricity and its energy' (130), becomes the presiding spirit – enfolding the many identities of x/self – for a *vodoun*-style healing ceremony into which 'book and bribe/bomb/blast and the wrecked village' are solemnly incorporated, (110), and the thunder of Xango himself, 'shattering outwards' in one final, redemptive explosion, eventually 'comes home' (111).

Sharing the redemptive magic-realist qualities of *Carpentaria* and *X/Self*, but engaging more directly than they do with the contemporary realities (and possible future consequences) of global warming, is Jamaican writer Curdella Forbes's latest published novel, *Ghosts* (2012). An alter-nately playful and melancholic merging of magic realism and speculative fiction in a fictionalised but still identifiable Caribbean island setting, *Ghosts* tells the multi-generational story of the Pointy-Morris clan, who are announced at the beginning of the text as carrying a 'wound' that may either be attributable to the family or, more generally, to the world itself (2012: 9). The private version of the wound manifests itself in the various deformations, both physical and psychological, that are passed down from one family generation to the next, although an alternative causality may lie in the family's seemingly congenital inability to deliver themselves from the ghosts, linked inevitably to slavery, of their ancestral past. The public version links the family metonymically to a terminally damaged earth featuring 'cataclysmic landscapes' (37, 53) of storm and flood: one in which the rainy season is out of season (55), and those too poor to escape to the cooler hills – or to other, less contaminated islands – are left to swelter in the sulphurous air of the lowlands, where they are also subject to severe UV radiation as a result of the mounting ozone threat (138).

As the saga moves forward in time, the threat realizes itself, confirming the family's dark premonitions of an out-of-control world of endemic violence in which 'the [ocean] deep is polluted beyond measure, the milk of breasts is [...] cancerous, and the hills fired with greenhouse gases are smoking away' – a world in which the only alternatives rest in the equally tenuous possibilities of seeking to be 'absolved' or of 'stubbornly staying [on], grasping after eternity, as if the violence of [...] longing can take it by force' (171–72). If this is standard eco-apocalyptic fare, the text complicates presentist understandings of global warming by insisting on the deeper catastrophist histories that inform it, creating – much as Brathwaite does – 'tidalectical' connections with both recent cultural cataclysms (e.g. 9/11) and more distant historical events (e.g. the Middle Passage). Global warming, in this sense, is envisioned as the latest stage in a continuing history of natural/cultural calamities which stretches back to the original catastrophe of slavery, while the polluted atmosphere is made to carry the wound, not just of the Pointy-Morrison family, but of industrial modernity and, back and beyond it, of humanity itself (124–25).

Ghosts' is a volatile realm of fire and ice, captured in Daniel Pritchard's expressionist paintings of 'clashing tornadoes' and 'the screaming blue hearts of hurricanes' (48), and balefully prefigured in his wife Tramadol's [*sic*] doomed romantic visions of 'faraway places [...] struck deep, like newly minted coin, with desert fire or the ice of fjords [and ocean-breaking] mountains of frost' (19). But, like *Carpentaria* and *X/Self*, it offers consolations in the form of an 'alter/catastrophist' vision in which natural destruction produces new, utopian modes of cross-cultural belonging and planetary consciousness. (In the case of *Ghosts*, this consciousness is explored through the caring relationship between Evangeline Pointy-Morris – herself a weird hybrid figure, part Mother Teresa part Nanny of the Maroons (123) – and a cyborg-like 'dwarf child' (135) who, having been incurably damaged by the planet's scorched atmosphere, must now learn to accommodate himself, as she herself does, to a technologically improved but ecologically impoverished earth.)

Also like *Carpentaria* and *X/Self*, *Ghosts* presents a temporally extended weather-world that shifts 'tidalectically' between an ancestral past and a post-apocalyptic future, and in which long histories of violence, both ecological and cosmological, intersect. These are not necessarily the histories *of* global warming, but they are certainly some of the histories that lie *behind* global warming, and all three texts offer postcolonial variations on the model of the 'environmental crisis narrative' (Buell 2003) – a narrative in which the multiple disjunctions of global warming are made visible, temporally and spatially, in and across a wide range of multidimensional sites. The differential effects these sites produce may be radically disruptive – of linear time, of bounded space, or even of the ontological status of the human – but they are not necessarily unimaginable, and the texts in their different ways all indicate why postcolonial literature is well positioned to examine the alternative ecological scenarios presented by a catastrophically warming world. One scenario, as suggested above, involves a rethinking of the human; another requires thinking beyond it. For Dipesh Chakrabarty, who is primarily concerned with the first, global warming poses a new challenge to postcolonial criticism in so far as it enjoins postcolonial critics to think, not just of the continuing history of inequality on the planet, but of the 'survival of the species' and the future of the planet itself (2012: 15). At another level, however, global warming requires postcolonial critics to do just the opposite: to return to basic questions of inequality, including those linked to histories of slavery and colonialism, but to re-think these in ecological terms.

Notes

1 In the introduction to his 1995 book *Encountering Development*, Escobar describes the book as a 'study of developmentalism as a discursive field' (6) in the manner of Saidian Orientalism, although he then claims to part company with Edward Said through his closer examination of the deployment of *discourse* through *practice*, with the discourse of 'development' resulting in 'concrete practices of thinking and acting through which the Third World is produced' (11). Escobar perhaps overstates the distinction between discourse and practice in Said's oeuvre, though he is certainly right to point to its 'culturalist' emphasis – an emphasis sometimes seen, especially by Marxist critics, as limiting the political effectiveness of postcolonial critical work.

2 On the historical relationship between development and neocolonialism, see Escobar 1995; also Young 2001, esp. Chapter 4. Young's general definition of neocolonialism is the one that will be adopted in this book – i.e. a form of colonialism by other means through which politically independent postcolonial states 'remain in a situation of dependence on [their] former masters' (45), in which metropolitan control continues to be exerted by economic

measures, and in which 'the ruling class constitutes an elite that operates in complicity with the needs of international capital for its own benefit' (45). A further argument that will be made in this book is that there are contemporary forms of environmental control and management that also operate under the sign of neocolonialism: forms of ecological neocolonialism, if you will, that bring Alfred Crosby's term 'ecological imperialism' fully up to date.

3 'Planetary management', according to the cultural theorist Andrew Ross, obeys a corporate logic 'continuous with the scientific perspective of quantitatively dominating the physical world' (Ross 1991: 208). It represents an extension of the ideology of human control, manipulated in global-corporate interests, in which 'questions of ecology [are not] answered by social theory or social action [but] resolved at the level of "resource management" by the logic of the multinational corporate state' (210).

4 For further thoughts on what Young rather grandly calls the 'new imperialist era of global capitalism', see the work of postcolonial Marxists, who often seem unsure whether to lambaste postcolonial criticism for its continuing 'ideological evasions' (Lazarus 2006: 22) in the face of an aggressive 'new imperialism' or to rehabilitate a properly materialist postcolonialism attuned to the social/environmental fallout of global capital and self-consciously placing itself within the historical context of anti-colonial struggle (see, for example, Lazarus and Bartolovich 2002; Lazarus 2006; also Parry 2004). For an overview of what is at stake in the 'new imperialism', see Harvey 2005; for an emergent 'eco-materialist' critique of its environmental implications, see also Mukherjee 2006.

5 The metaphor of 'worlding' is usually associated with the work of the Indian postcolonial critic Gayatri Chakravorty Spivak, who has exhaustively examined the different ways in which Third World people, especially women, and the figure of the 'Third World' itself are discursively produced. (In this sense Escobar's anti-developmentalist work, as discussed previously in this section, probably owes more to Spivak than Said.) A key figure in this discursive production is that of the 'subaltern', the historical dimensions of which are examined in the disparate work of the Indian-based Subaltern Studies Collective, a group with which Spivak has erratically affiliated herself. Like Spivak, the SSC suggests that 'subalternisation' – like 'worlding' – is a process related to the general psycho-social mechanism of (colonial) 'othering', with 'other' being understood here less as a *noun* than as a *verb*: i.e. the other is a product of 'othering'; he or she is an 'othered' subject. The process of 'worlding' acts similarly but in a collective manner, creating the 'world(s)' of which it speaks as objects of discursive management and control. This process is necessarily overdetermined: hence the tautologous implications of Loomba's Spivakian phrase, the 'overworlding' of the Third World (Loomba 1994). For more on the symbolic and material connections between 'othering', 'worlding' and 'subalternisation', see Spivak 1987, 1988, 1999.

6 On the link between ecological imperialism and gender subjection, see the inspirational work of postcolonial ecofeminists such as Val Plumwood and Vandana Shiva, both of whom posit a clear connection between what Plumwood calls 'the colonization of nature' and the 'range of conceptual strategies [...] employed within the human sphere to support supremacism of nation, gender and race' (Plumwood 2003). For a concise account of what is at stake within postcolonial ecofeminism, see also Young 2003: 100–108. Young's

emphasis, like Shiva's if not necessarily Plumwood's, is on those kinds of grass-roots social and environmental struggles in which women – particularly Third World women – resist *both* their emplacement within a patriarchal social order *and* their continuing subjection to the demands of the postcolonial state. For Young among others, postcolonial feminism draws attention to the con-temporary social injustices of the postcolonial state, not just the historical injustices of the imperial/colonial system; postcolonial *eco*feminism adds another layer to the struggle by insisting on the gendered interconnectedness of social and environmental struggle, and on the leading role played by women in addressing and providing often collectivised alternatives to abusive systems of imperial/colonial acquisition and state administrative control.

7 Probably the clearest bringing together of indigenous, feminist and envir-onmentalist perspectives is in the work of the Indian scientist-feminist-activist Vandana Shiva, who insists on the fundamental incompatibility of subsistence and market economies, and outlines the negative – sometimes devastating – impact of the latter on women in India and other parts of the so-called Third World. Shiva's ecofeminist work seems at times to be informed by deep eco-logical, at others by social-ecological perspectives, suggesting the wide range of not always compatible positions and perspectives that is contained within the umbrella term 'ecofeminism' itself. For a useful overview of these posi-tions and perspectives, see Merchant 1992, esp. Chapter 8; also Mies and Shiva 1993, Warren and Erkal 1997.

8 While the connections between environmentalism and globalisation are mul-tiple and complex, it is possible to argue, as Ursula Heise (2006) does, for instance, that 'environmental-justice ecocriticism is the only branch of the field that has addressed globalization issues in any depth' (513). Heise's own work goes some way towards redressing the balance, as does some of the work of Buell (2001, 2005) and, more recently, Marzec (2007). However, it probably remains the case, as Greg Garrard asserts, that the 'relationship between globalisation and ecocriticism [...] has barely been broached' (2004: 178), while Heise's worthwhile suggestion that ecocriticism is well placed to comment on the cultural dimensions of globalisation is speculative rather than proven, partly because, as she also suggests, there is a notable dis-crepancy between the environmentalist aspiration towards critical globalism and the ecocritical tendency to 'think globally' in one language – English – that has hegemonic status across the globe (2006: 513; see also Heise 2008).

9 There is a voluminous literature on the yoking of tourism and neocolonial-ism, but significantly less on tourism and *post*colonialism: see, however, Hall and Tucker 2004, Waters 2006, Winter 2007. For an excellent book-length dis-cussion of the imaginative potential of postcolonial literature to envision sustainable tourism futures, as well as to critique tourism's negative social/environmental influence on local (e.g. Third World) communities, see Carrigan 2008.

10 That globalisation works towards producing certain locales – that it is instrumental in what the anthropologist Arjun Appadurai (1996) calls the 'production of locality' – is a given, as is the fact that 'global' and 'local' discourses are mutually constitutive, inflecting one another in a variety of ways. However, as Appadurai avers, the production of locality under globalisation isn't just a matter of producing 'local subjects [and] the neighbourhoods that contextualize these subjectivities', but also suggests that 'time and space

[themselves are] localized through complex and deliberate practices of performance, representation, and action' (180). For some case studies of global/local dialectics, see the essays in Wilson and Dissanayake 1996; for a discussion of the environmental implications of these dialectics, see Heise 2008 (also note 8 above) and Buell 2001.

11 As Ursula Heise says in her useful overview article on ecocriticism, ecocritics have not always kept pace with changes within the very field – ecology – after which they see at least some of their work being modelled. Hence the tendency within certain strands – particularly romantic strands – of ecocriticism to posit ecosystems as working towards 'stability, harmony, and self-regeneration', even as ecological scientists part company with this outdated model, presenting instead a 'more complex image of [them] as dynamic, perpetually changing, and often far from stable and balanced' (510). While Heise rightly draws attention to the social and political instrumentality of earlier ideas of holistic, self-regenerating ecosystems, she also cites Dana Phillips' work, which – in her own words – 'lambasts environmental scholars for adhering to an obsolete notion of ecological science and for transferring ecological terms to literary study by means of mere metaphor' (510). Phillips' critique, while overdrawn, points to the hazards of an environmental populism – an eco-populism – that is often far less scientific than it claims to be, and that at its worst can hardly be said to be 'scientific' at all. For further reflections on the term 'eco-populism' and on the benefits and dangers of eco-populism for ecocriticism, see Garrard 2004, O'Brien 2007, and Szasz 1994.

12 As ecocritics are quick to acknowledge, there are several problems bound up with the term 'environment'. For one thing, as Cheryll Glotfelty suggests, it is 'anthropocentric and dualistic, implying that we humans are at the center, surrounded by everything that is not us, the environment' (Glotfelty 1996: xx). For another, 'environment' is now generally seen as a compound noun rather than a root verb plus a suffix, with the result that it is less likely to be considered as a multiple *agent* than as a composite *thing* (Mazel 1996b: 137–46). For a spirited attempt to wrest back the performative potential embedded within the term 'environment', see Mazel 1996a and b; for further discussion of the different – sometimes conflicting – meanings contained within the word 'environment', see also Buell 2005, especially Chapter 1.

13 The inclusiveness of *Potiki* works on several different levels. At one level, the text welcomes different communities of readers – both indigenous and not – with different outlooks and competencies, even if it simultaneously demonstrates the limits of non-indigenous knowledge systems and privileges indigenous (Māori) understandings of the self's relationship to others and the wider world. At another level, the text adopts a loosely communitarian perspective based on according equal value to all its members, whatever their physical and mental abilities, although the harnessing of physical disability to visionary capacity – made manifest in the special powers of the *potiki* – is neither romantically celebrated nor definitively confirmed (see also Barker 2012).

A few comments might be in order here on the links between postcolonialism and disability. The multiple intersections between postcolonial studies and disability studies have proved to be one of the most fruitful areas for ethically oriented postcolonial research, spawning a wide variety of books and articles too numerous to be summarised in this note (for recent work, see Barker 2012, Barker and Murray 2010; for earlier interventions, see Ghai 2002,

Quayson 2007, Sherry 2007). Three general observations will have to suffice here. First, most crossover work in postcolonial disability studies proceeds from the basis that postcolonial studies and disability studies have much to offer one another, not least as mutual correctives, with disability studies questioning postcolonial criticism's tendency to treat disability as 'prosthetic metaphor' (Barker and Murray 2010), and postcolonial studies contesting the assumed transportability of western understandings of disability, which pay insufficient attention to the variability of their cultural meanings and effects. Second, most of this work also warns against the 'conflation of disability with postcolonial experience' (Sherry 2007: 12) and the rhetorical manipulation of terms like 'disability' and 'colonialism' as generalised concept-metaphors for political oppression or social suffering in circumstances and conditions that are often very different from one another, and in which the very real hardships of disabled and/or colonised people are paradoxically obscured (Quayson 2007). And third, some of the more recent work – Barker's, for instance – argues for the reframing of disability as a 'mode of exceptionality', following on from Davis's influential observation that the disabled body is not so much a site of disempowerment and vulnerability as a catalyst for alternative readings of culture and power (Davis 1996; see also Barker 2012).

A single literary example – Indra Sinha's 2007 novel *Animal's People* – helps bring several of these general issues into critical focus, re-framing them in brutally raw and uncompromising terms. *Animal's People* is probably best seen as a Bhopal-inspired 'environmental picaresque' (Nixon 2011) combining social satire and moral outrage, and toxically laced with eco-apocalyptic visions of a world seemingly doomed to extinction or at least damaged beyond all reasonable repair (Sinha 2007: 333). Bestriding this world – on all fours – is the eponymous protagonist, an orphan boy whose twisted body seems to operate as an analogue for corporate atrocity (his disability is linked to a Bhopal-type toxic event) and the equally twisted tales that are now being told by the authorities to cover it up.

At another level, though, the text actively resists this metaphorisation of disability or its translation into the liberal discourse of 'difference' and 'special ability': Animal simply is who he is, and his tale is the unvarnished account of a life lived in society's margins, seen and sensed from the ground up (350). Similarly, while disability can certainly be seen in the text as the basis for a radical interrogation of the human, Animal repeatedly pronounces that he has no *wish* to be human – or at least not in conventional bourgeois-liberal terms (23). Nor does he want to be labelled as a 'humanitarian victim' (27) and, in this last sense, the text is both a tale about the abuse of human rights and the equally shocking exploitation of the humanitarian discourses through which such rights are publicly articulated and politically deployed (131).

While *Animal's People* has been rather lazily read as a transparent allegory for Bhopal (e.g. Mukherjee 2011), the text – like its protagonist – will not allow for direct allegorical equivalence, and disability functions in this context as a *non*-metaphorical marker for a condition that is what it is, not what others would like it to be, e.g. an index of marginality, a sign of special ability, or an alternative site for the reading of community engagement and social power. Thus, in keeping with this cautionary tale to end all cautionary tales, we would argue against ecological readings of the text that seek to recuperate the figure of Animal in order to gesture towards more inclusive models of multispecies community and personhood (Mukherjee 2011); for at the end as at the beginning, Animal remains fundamentally *dis*figured, resisting figuration in either individual or collective terms.

14 There are links as well – as Donnell suggests – between literary tourism and postcolonialism. Some critics (see, for example, Huggan 2001 and Brouillette 2007) see postcolonial writing as being niche-marketed to those kinds of internationally minded readers who are likely to take pleasure in exotic location(s) and cultural difference(s) while recognising the historical price that others have paid in offering these commodities – hence the double-edged sword of postcolonial guilt. For an up-to-date and carefully modulated discussion of the postcolonial guilt industry and its complex associations with literary tourism, see Brouillette 2007.

15 The term *global warming* will be used here rather than its more generic counterpart *climate change*. Global warming, simply put, refers to a rising temperature trend associated with pressure generated on the earth's atmosphere by a build-up of greenhouse gases, whereas climate change – the most obvious contemporary manifestation of which is global warming – involves a variety of visible and invisible effects that are responses to external and internal 'forcing mechanisms' (Maslin 2008: 15), some of which are the product of natural cycles (e.g. variations in the earth's orbit around the sun) while others are manmade. For our purposes here, it will be assumed that anthropogenic climate change – the various processes by which human beings have become 'weather makers' (Flannery), acquiring the collective capacity to transform global climate – is beyond reasonable doubt, although the historical timeframe for this acquisition, as well as the timing and degree of its anticipated effects, remains uncertain (Crist 2007; Litfin 2000; Maslin 2008; see also Huggan 2015).

16 Objections might be raised here, both to the scientific looseness of Morton's theoretical understanding of global warming as belonging to the class of 'hyperobjects', which he defines as 'things that are massively distributed in time and space relative to humans' (2013: 1), and to the philosophical extremism of Clark's view that global warming effectively spells an end to ecocriticism as we know it, further marking the 'exhaustion or closure of [those conventional forms of] environmental politics [that are] embedded in the modernist, liberal tradition' (Clark 2010: 146–47). For both Morton and Clark, the sheer size and scale of global warming dwarfs all attempts to find a *scientific* language in which it can be adequately described or a *literary* language in which it can be convincingly represented. This kind of thinking, which ironically embraces the apocalyptic rhetoric it claims to reject, is not particularly helpful; nor does it give enough credence to the different languages available to both science and literature/literary criticism that might go some way towards accounting for, if not necessarily explaining, the highly variable effects of global warming and other current manifestations of climate change. An argument could be made, for example, that literature has a capacity to work across different spatial/temporal levels and scales that makes it well suited to representing global warming, while ecocriticism is neither as place-specific nor as wedded to realism as Clark asserts. Clark is equally mistaken that ecocriticism has failed sufficiently to engage with global warming; there are numerous examples to the contrary, not least Jonathan Bate's influential 1996 essay 'Living with the Weather', which was later incorporated into his classic

2000 ecocritical study, *The Song of the Earth*. For a further rejoinder to Clark, see Huggan 2015.

17 Drawing on the work of Frederick Buell, the American ecocritic Ursula Heise makes a useful distinction between *apocalyptic* and *risk* perspectives on global warming in the wider context of a socially precarious and ecologically endangered world. Apocalyptic perspectives, Heise says, tend to suggest that 'utter destruction lies ahead [but that it might be] averted and replaced by an alternative future society', while risk perspectives stress that 'crises are already underway all around, and while their consequences can be mitigated, a future without their impact has become impossible to envision' (Heise 2008: 141-42; see also Buell 2003). As Heise goes on to note, apocalyptic and risk perspectives are by no means mutually exclusive, but the latter are more likely than the former to 'emphasize indeterminacy, uncertainty, and the possibility of a variety of [crisis] outcomes' (142). While it is probably true, at least to date, that apocalyptic perspectives tend to dominate in creative (e.g. literary) responses to global warming, risk perspectives – including the kinds that are associated with the seminal work of the late German sociologist Ulrich Beck – are not difficult to find. For a closer analysis of some of these perspectives in postcolonial 'risk narratives', see Huggan 2015.

18 'Weather-world' is the British anthropologist Tim Ingold's multi-faceted term for the ways in which wind, rain, sunshine and other weather elements are not *external* to human existence but *co-extensive* with it, combining in a 'co-constitution of being' in which material substances and the supposedly immaterial medium in which they operate interact (Ingold 2011: 121; see also 96). While Ingold's is primarily a western phenomenological approach to how human beings interact with their environment and with the elements, it also resonates with sacred-spiritual understandings such as those instantiated in the indigenous 'Dreaming Ecology' (Rose 1996) of Alexis Wright. Thanks to Kate Rigby for drawing our attention to Deborah Bird Rose's work and for sharing her own work with us.

19 The largely hopeful ending of *Carpentaria* is a case in point, although there are several different ways in which the final scenes might be interpreted: as the prelude to a family reunion; or as the basis for a new order; or as the confirmation of a terminally damaged earth. Wright's most recent novel at the time of writing, *The Swan Book* (2013), picks up on some of these themes, offering a set of characteristically complex Aboriginal perspectives on a futuristic world irreversibly altered by climate change.

20 We are indebted to Anthony Carrigan and Michael Niblett, some of whose views we are parsing here, for pointing out to us the central relevance of Brathwaite's work to both contemporary and historical understandings of natural/cultural catastrophe. Our respective approaches differ slightly. Niblett's and, to a lesser extent, Carrigan's focus is on the critique of capitalist imperialism embedded in Brathwaite's oeuvre; our own is on Brathwaite's seemingly intuitive understanding of the temporal cycles within which natural/cultural catastrophes operate – an understanding that requires an appreciation, not just of historical transformation, but of the secret workings of deep time.

21 'Infinite rehearsal' (also the title of one of Harris's idiosyncratic novels) refers to the continual revision process by which the past – especially though not exclusively the New World past – is creatively re-imagined and intuitive connections are found between previously disparate 'cultures, places, times

and characters' (Lewis 1995: 83). There is much in common between Brathwaite and Harris, who share an overriding sense of history as catastrophe, but also the view that catastrophe provides a creative catalyst by which imprisoning ideologies – such as those upholding slavery and colonialism – can be shattered and imaginatively transformed.

2   Entitlement

Some versions of the postcolonial pastoral

The New Zealand poet Allen Curnow's ironic ballad 'House and Land' (1941) is frequently taken to be an exemplary study of postcolonial white settler anxiety: of the crisis of belonging that accompanies split cultural allegiance, the historical awareness of expropriated territory, and the suppressed knowledge that the legal fiction of entitlement does not necessarily bring with it the emotional attachment that turns 'house and land' into home. After all, to assert one's right to live in a place is not the same thing as to dwell in it or inhabit it; for assertion is possession, not belonging, and dwelling implies an at-homeness with place that the genealogical claim to entitlement may reveal, but just as easily obscure (Bate 2000; Read 2000). In Curnow's poem, it is the 'English' landowner, Miss Wilson, who takes illusory refuge in this particular version of the genealogical imperative: 'People in the *colonies*, she said / Can't quite understand [...] / Why, from Waiau to the mountains / It was all father's land' (39). Miss Wilson is entitled to her land, but whether she belongs to it is another matter. Her notion of entitlement, deeply colonial in spite of her felt contempt for 'colonials', takes the form of an openly expressed patrician privilege, historically if not morally vouchsafed by romanticised appeals to English cultural heritage and the preservation of the colonial past. As the poem implies, entitlement operates as a legislative mechanism for the recognition of affective ties to land and place that are confirmed by historical continuity of association (Griffiths 1997). But affect and experience, vital though these are to a sense of belonging, are rarely enough to guarantee entitlement. Entitlement is much more, or sometimes much less, than the imaginative and/or emotional possession of a place based on a perception of belonging. But then again, it isn't just about property and the laws that govern ownership either. Rather, entitlement is both of these things and usually encompasses the tensions between them. *Pastoral*, we want to argue in this section, is the literary mode in which these tensions are most evidently expressed.

There are at least three excellent reasons why the pastoral mode should be unamenable to postcolonialism. First, as is generally agreed, the pastoral mode has served as a vehicle for sublimated (sometimes more directly articulated) bourgeois ideology (Empson 1935; Patterson 1987; Williams 1973). William Empson, whose 1935 study still remains one of the most incisive on the pastoral, points to the deployment of 'ironical humility' in its affectionate representations of supposedly 'simple' to much more obviously 'complex' people, representations primarily designed to reassure patrician or bourgeois audiences that these 'simple' lives contain truths and insights which, being universally applicable, are relevant to themselves (159). Pastoral, suggests Empson among several others, is heavily dependent on the very class system it claims temporarily to suspend; thus, while it generally appeals to fictions of contentment and social harmony through its pleasingly domesticated images of working farm and fruitful garden, it conveniently forgets the division of labour that makes such productivity possible, allowing instead for the charming development of a 'beautiful relation between rich and poor' (17).

Second, this strategy of avoidance carries over into pastoral's characteristic coyness in the face of social injustice. Thus, while pastoral can certainly be, and frequently is, an instrument of social critique, it is hardly likely to be a catalyst for the active transformation of established social structures (Alpers 1996). Joseph Meeker, for instance, sees pathos and resignation as features of a mode unable to see beyond the inherent contradictions in its own values, illustrating the dilemma with an extended anecdote:

> The sensitive aristocrat who turns toward Arcadia and away from Rome often discovers that Rome is really within him. Though he can leave behind the fearsome environment of civilization and its cities, yet the psyche of civilization remains to guide his responses to nature. He cannot reject civilization without rejecting his own humanness, so he seeks a compromise in the halfway house of a pastoral Arcadia, somewhere midway between the horrors of wilderness and the horrors of the city. His choice of the garden-farm is this exact midpoint, a place of mediation between nature and civilization but also the point where the two worlds make contact and where both continually tug at him. His fear of wilderness is as intense as his fear of cities, and the garden merely intensifies the contrast without providing a solution. In his total alienation from both worlds, his only response is self-pity and despair at ever resolving the contradictions

which he has now discovered to be internal as well as environmental. He cannot achieve tragedy, for he has not risked enough. The end of the pastoral cycle is pathos.

(Meeker 1972: 91–92)

Third, as Meeker implies, pastoral is predominantly European in sensibility and form. The stylistic conventions of pastoral are not easily mapped onto non-European landscapes that often appear to be in direct opposition with them, and their value-systems likewise; meanwhile, traditional pastoral forms – the eclogue, for example – can easily be co-opted for a benign version of Euro-imperialism, usually expressed through the idea of unchallengeable social and cultural hierarchies, or through the watchful figure of a non-authoritarian (often invisible) overseer/landlord, whose duty it is to see that the work is done and everything remains in its proper place (Ettin 1984: 152–53). Pastoral, in this sense, is about the legitimation of highly codified relations between socially differentiated people: relations mediated, but also mystified, by supposedly universal cultural attitudes to land. Through these and other means, pastoral ideologies tend to emphasise the stability, or work toward the stabilisation, of the dominant order, in part through the symbolic management – which sometimes means the silencing – of less privileged social groups (Patterson 1987: 8–10).

None of this bodes well for the practice of either postcolonial literature or postcolonial criticism; and yet, as we aim to show in this section, practitioners of both are heavily invested in the pastoral mode. One reason for this might be that pastoral, for all its apparent political quietism, has always retained a utopian dimension to it that is attractive to writers and critics looking for alternative, more socially and environmentally conscious visions of the world (Buell 1995; Garrard 2004). Pastoral is usually associated with nostalgic retreat into the past, but its idealism may also have an oppositional character, or – most notably in America – an imaginative potential for the assertion of a new, and better, world (Buell 1995: 52; see also Marx 1964). Pastoral, in the USA and elsewhere, has also had obvious relevance for the more recent development of an ecological ('green') consciousness, although historically speaking pastoral perceptions of the world have always been more inclined to be narrowly anthropocentric than broadly ecocentric, and just as likely to be interested in the cultivation of the (urban) intellect as the cultivation of (rural) land (Alpers 1996). The problem, however, with a generalised view of pastoral is precisely that: of generalising across a mode that is traditionally characterised by a high degree of ideological flexibility, as well as a large number of possible permutations of literary form. What

Lawrence Buell calls the 'ideological grammar' of pastoral is always contingent, always shifting, and there is no reason to dismiss it as an inherently conservative or complacent bourgeois form (Buell 1995: 50).

A second reason, however, has rather to do with the built-in inadequacies of pastoral. As Raymond Williams (1983) suggests, the 'natural order' in pastoral tends to disguise a crisis of ownership, a crisis that arguably traverses the contemporary postcolonial world. Pastoral, as is perhaps most evident in the former settler colonies, affords a useful opportunity to open up the tension between ownership and belonging in a variety of colonial and postcolonial contexts: contexts marked, for the most part, by a direct or indirect engagement with often devastating experiences of dispossession and loss. The myth of pastoral fulfilment, in any case, had always lived under the shadow of irony: pastoral, if it is anything, is an intrinsically ironic form. The ironies of pastoral are intensified, however, in contexts of contested entitlement and embattled ownership, where the plaintive search for 'lost pastoral havens' might well be seen as belonging to the originary structure of colonial violence itself (Griffiths 1997: 118). Pastoral, in this last sense, is a spectral form, always aware of the suppressed violence that helped make its peaceful visions possible, and always engaged with the very histories from which it appears to want to escape.

In what follows, we want to look at three examples that explore pastoral's constitutive ironies as these are played out in and across contemporary postcolonial literary texts. Surprisingly perhaps, each text can be seen in terms of a partial rehabilitation of the pastoral, either in terms that are self-consciously ecocentric or that work towards a re-appraisal of more pragmatic, though not necessarily non-idealised, pastoral modes.

Pastoral in black and white

At first sight, Australia seems to be a case of pastoralism without the pastoral; for, as Paul Kane wryly remarks, 'nothing is more likely to drain the genre of its charm than actually having to deal with [140 million] sheep on a daily basis' (Kane 2004: 269). Nor is the Australian landscape particularly welcoming to the attenuated cadences and aesthetic mannerisms of pastoral; the desert and the bush have their charms, certainly, but these are unlikely to be refracted through the pastoral, which is apparently suited neither to the land itself nor to the people who inhabit it, both of these being seen, not least by Australian writers, as singularly lacking in the qualities 'vital to pastoral as it is traditionally understood' (Indyk 1993: 838). Not that these writers – especially poets – have necessarily given up on the attempt to offer their own 'representative anecdotes' of the pastoral, or to invest Australian landscapes with the types of bucolic sentiment and idealised imagery that are in alignment with European pastoral norms (Alpers 1996). However, pastoral literature in Australia has tended, for good reason, to accentuate the irony already prevalent in, even intrinsic to, the pastoral mode. The most obvious reason has to do with the history of settler colonialism in Australia, which has involved the violent 'displacement of an indigenous population by the settlers of a colonizing power' (Indyk 1993: 838). In a context such as this, pastoral nostalgia takes on an almost pathological quality, either conjuring up visions of pre-colonial harmony in a series of virtually unrecognisable pseudo-Arcadian settings or recuperating idealised images of European classical antiquity in order to superimpose a largely invented version of the Old World onto an equally fabricated version of the New.

This kind of pastoral, unleavened by irony, might well be accused of being little more than the blunt instrument of a colonial imaginary that seeks to secure hallowed ground for an emergent white settler society, and to forge racial myths of emplacement and belonging – 'land rites', the Australian environmental historian Tom Griffiths half-mockingly calls them – which are designed to make the case for 'peaceful annexation' by laying counter-claim to an emotional and spiritual possession of the land (Griffiths 1997: 151–52, 109). However, Australian pastoral has never quite managed to shake off the shadow of colonial violation, and more often than not it has actively engaged with it. It is shot through with the ironies of dispossession, never more so than when it invokes the 'figure of the dispossessed [Aborigines] whose presence unsettles the affirmations of the [traditional] pastoral song' (Indyk 1993: 838). As Ivor Indyk suggests,

> Though there have been times when [Aborigines have] played no part in Australian pastoral, this effacement has been limited and partial. For the most part it is the persistence of the Aboriginal figure which is remarkable – appearing sometimes as a shadowy, spectral presence, sometimes dramatically heightened by fear or guilt, more recently as a figure arguing on its own behalf for a revision of the pastoral order – and always as the embodiment of an aboriginal claim, a claim to priority.
>
> (1993: 838)

As Indyk goes on to show, white Australian attempts to accommodate the unsettling figure of the Aborigine have tended to result, either in an ironic recognition of the impossibilities of pastoral harmony or in a more drastic 'derangement of the foundations of the pastoral order', usually based on an acknowledgement that 'the Aboriginal and the shepherd', to both of whom might be accorded a differential custodianship of the land, are 'mutually exclusive types' (841).

Part of the dilemma obviously revolves around competing claims to belonging and entitlement, but part also consists in the perceived unassimilability of Aborigines, even suitably poeticised Aborigines, to pastoral codes of productivity and fulfilment based on the dominant white-settler ideology of cultivated land. Thus, in the colonial poetry of Harpur and Kendall, among several others, 'the "wild" pastoral of the Australian bush and its indigenous inhabitants [was felt to be] by nature undefined, unformed [and therefore to be a malevolent] force working against the traditional pastoral economy, unsettling and negating its priorities' (Indyk 1993: 841). For later postcolonial primitivists such as Katharine Susannah Prichard, Xavier Herbert and, above all, the mid-twentieth-century Jindyworobak poets, the tables were turned, and now it was 'the whites who [were] portrayed as the intruders into a timeless Aboriginal idyll, with the [Aborigines] representing those qualities of spontaneity, freedom, reciprocity, and ease denied by the relentless capitalist urge of white settlement' (Indyk 1993: 845). Indyk sees here the first signs of a decisive shift from *pastoral* to *georgic* as a symbolic counterpart to the white-settler commitment to working the land for profit, a shift arguably sustained in Australian literature right up to the present day (Kane 2004).[1] Meanwhile, from mid-century onwards, Aboriginal writers themselves began to experiment with modified pastoral forms, particularly though not exclusively pastoral elegy, ironically deployed both as a means of lamenting an atrophied present and of seeking imaginative sustenance from the myths and rituals of a fondly remembered past. After this admittedly over-generalised prelude, let us now turn to some of the more specific ways in which two modern Australian writers – one white, one black – manipulate the conventions of pastoral elegy in such a manner as to reflect both on the contemporary politics of conservation and on the interconnectedness of white-settler and Aboriginal versions of the Australian past.

A word first on the choice of 'conservation': a term that has come in for a fair amount of criticism recently, but one to which the two poets we have in mind here – Judith Wright and Oodgeroo Noonuccal (Kath Walker) – were fully committed for much of the course of their working lives. In several of her own essays, Wright spells out what she means by conservation, a concept inextricably connected with the complex world-view expressed in her poetry as a whole (Wright 1975, 1991). Conservation, according to Wright, entails a 'new kind of responsibility towards our environment', one based on a committed 'consideration for the needs of things [and creatures] other than ourselves' (1975: 215). Conservation, while technically concerned with the responsible management of resources, also consists for Wright in the wider possibility of 'a renewed humility and a revival of imaginative participation in a life-process which includes us, and to which we contribute our own conscious knowledge of it, as part of it, not as separate from it' (1975: 194). This conservationist view (probably more likely today to go by other terms such as 'ecological') is of a piece with Wright's conviction in the capacity of poetry to counteract the instrumentalism of hyper-rationalist and materialistic values, and to celebrate 'the totality of nature' by engaging with human feelings and sympathies in a broadly intersubjective, mutually beneficial way (1975: 202, 254; see also Bennett 1991).

Wright, like Oodgeroo whom she was to befriend, and who shared a similar concern for the protection of the environment and the sustainable management of natural resources, espoused what we might call a form of pragmatic idealism in which the often glaring ideological contradictions embedded within global conservationist movements were weighed against the need to enlist the public's interest in what they believed, however naïvely, to be the common conservationist cause (Wright 1975). Unlike many of today's professional conservationists, both Wright and, in a rather different context, Oodgeroo had little difficulty in wedding ecological sentiment to a broadly conceived humanist vision in which 'human and humane co-operation and creativity' were urgently needed to avoid the pitfalls of 'technologizing' the earth (Wright 1975: 256). This largely holistic view (inflected, in Wright's case, by what she called her 'vaguely Buddhist' sympathies) ran the risk of overlooking structural inequalities in late twentieth-century global-capitalist society, but it enjoyed the distinct advantage of making a clear link between environmental and social issues, nowhere more apparent than in the shared concern for indigenous justice that underpins both writers' work. In keeping with the liberal integrationism of the times, Wright and Oodgeroo campaigned tirelessly for racial harmony and a peaceful world, both of which possibilities they saw as being threatened by self-destructive tendencies within a militaristic world order, and by the more specific reluctance of Australia to keep pace with global debates on decolonisation and civil rights.

However, even if we accept the consensus view that Wright and, particularly, Oodgeroo were poet-activists well aware of their performative role as public representative/celebrity figures, due care needs to be taken with the specificities of the two authors' written work. Our argument here would be that the closest link between their work – a link that also allows us to look at the relations between their respective views of the creative imagination and their conservationist sympathies – is their complex use of pastoral and, more specifically, pastoral *elegy*. As Paul Alpers argues in his comprehensive study of pastoral, pastoral elegy is particularly useful for defining pastoral conventions because 'death is the ultimate form of the separations and losses that pervade pastoral poetry' as a whole (Alpers 1996: 91). Pastoral elegy also has particular resonances in the context of postcolonial settler societies which are marked by the death and/or dispossession of their original inhabitants; as Indyk remarks ruefully of Australian colonial pastoral, one of its most common motifs is the Aboriginal grave (Indyk 1993: 842).

Pastoral elegy, in Wright, is mostly used to look back at a white pioneer history of her 'blood's country' (Wright 1996: 11), the climatically harsh but starkly beautiful New England Tableland region where she grew up. Early poems such as 'Bullocky' and 'South of My Days' are usually seen as celebrating the heroic nature of pastoral conquest, what the critic Shirley Walker calls the 'progress achieved by suffering and self-sacrifice' (Walker 1991: 19), in a landscape whose lineaments are fondly recalled even though much of its beauty has now been compromised or lost. At the same time, this landscape is haunted by the expulsion of its former Aboriginal custodians, who establish a powerful spectral presence in Wright's poems, ensuring that the heroic spirit that sometimes inspires them is violently undercut.[2] 'Did we not know', the speaker asks in 'Nigger's Leap: New England', one of several memorials to white-settler atrocity in Wright's poetry, that 'their blood channelled our rivers / and the black dust our crops ate was their dust?' (Wright 1996: 8). Such historical events are indelibly scored into what might otherwise become a white mythic consciousness of embattled colonial origins, embodied in such toiling anti-pastoral figures as the crazed bullocky, whose prophetic vision of himself as a latter-day Australian Moses is accompanied by 'fiends and angels' of his own making, and who finally adds another ghostly presence to a haunted landscape where grass now grows over what were once the pioneers' wagon-tracks, and pastoral 'vineyards cover all the slopes / where the dead teams were used to pass' (9).

Poems like 'Bullocky' use the double-edged qualities of elegy – which is never far short of mocking what it mourns – to enact what might best be described as an ironic counter-pastoral in which the redemptive power of rural labour works towards counteracting an awareness of displacement and separation, propagating the idea that belonging is as much created as retrieved. A different version of this counter-pastoral can be found in later poems such as the autobiographical 'For a Pastoral Family', in which the speaker plays part-ironically, part-affectionately on the conflicting registers that are contained in the multivalent term of 'pastoral' itself. The poem, like much of Wright's later work, takes on a distinctly, even bitterly ironic stance toward the legal fiction of white-settler (pastoralist) entitlement:

> A certain consensus of echo, a sanctioning sound
> supported our childhood lives. We stepped
> on sure and conceded ground.
> A whole society
> extended a comforting cover of legality.
> The really deplorable deeds
> had happened out of our sight, allowing us innocence.
> We were not born, or there was silence kept.
>
> (226)

At the same time, these alibis are incorporated into a larger process of elegiac recall that partly reinstates the pastoral nostalgia it otherwise cannot help but mock. This process is irreversible: 'horses have changed to land-rovers', and 'what swells over us now is a logical spread / from the small horizons we made / the heave of the great corporations / whose bellies are never full' (226–27). But there are pastoral residues, even if these are far from innocent or uncontested:

> Well, there are luxuries still,
> including pastoral silence, miles of slope and hill,
> the cautious politeness of bankers. These are owed
> to the forerunners, men and women
> who took over as if by right a century and a half
> in an ancient difficult bush. And after all,
> the previous owners put up little fight,
> did not believe in ownership, and so were scarcely human.
>
> (226)

The stanza – like several others in the poem – has a sting in the tail, but the wound is never mortal. The original theft of the land is not condoned, but nor is the land entirely alien to those who have acquired it; rather, it is continually refashioned in the image of those generations of white pastoralists who have effectively bequeathed it to themselves. Refashioned, but also cared for in its own way, as a bequest, however fraudulent its origin, implies a continuing commitment. The poem thus works towards a version of reconciliation even if that version largely restricts itself to the settling of family differences; it is much too aware of unamended crimes, and of continuing injustices, to allegorise the kind of broader intercultural reconciliation that might bring whites and Aborigines together in a mutual alliance in which each proves capable of meeting the other's needs.[3] Such reconciliation, Wright insists (1991: 78), is contingent on the transfer of ownership, even if the idea of ownership – the founding fiction of colonial possession – is itself largely a product of the modern industrial-capitalist West. Wright's fierce commitment to Aboriginal land rights occasionally clashed with her conservationist message, and she was dedicated to the view that conservationist issues could not be pursued over Aboriginal people's heads. What this meant – and it can be seen as much in her poetry as her activist work – was that the holistic view enshrined in her conservationist philosophy always risked foundering on her awareness of the structural inequalities between different categories of people that capitalism had helped to create and colonialism to intensify, and that then played into selective visions of an Australian nationalism in which the country itself became another tradeable commodity, to be treated as a 'source of profit' rather than as a 'parent to be loved' (1991: 47). This awareness is displayed in Wright's Aboriginal pastorals, which are often marked both by an apprehension of incommensurable cultural difference and by what Griffiths calls a personal intuition of 'double dispossession', based on the localised recognition that 'her forebears and the Aborigines had at least one shared thing – a love for [the] land – yet the descendants of neither now lived there' (Griffiths 1997: 268).

Probably the best known of these pastorals, 'Bora Ring', effectively ironises its own nostalgia by staging a self-incriminating version of the standard romantic-primitivist 'vanishing native' trope. The poem thus begins in familiar terms that rework the pseudo-Aboriginal themes of Jindyworobak poetry:

> The song is gone; the dance
> is secret with the dancers in the earth,
> the ritual useless, and the tribal story
> lost in an alien tale.

The last stanza, however – as is often the case in Wright's verse – turns the tables on the poem's elegiac vision of a lost (indigenous) pastoral idyll, making it clear that the broken connection with the earth that it invokes is the product of white colonial guilt:

> Only the rider's heart
> halts at a sightless shadow, an unsaid word

that fastens in the blood the ancient curse,
the fear as old as Cain.

(3)

Walker confidently interprets 'Bora Ring' as acknowledging 'with compassion the destruction of the Aboriginal race which preceded the establishment of the great pastoral enterprises celebrated in "Bullocky" and "South of My Days"' (27). But 'Bora Ring', at least in our own reading, is more an articulation of white fear than an acknowledgement of black loss, and that fear lies at the heart of a colonial consciousness split between its emotional attachment to a land for which it has suffered – the basis of white pastoralist mythology – and its awareness of an even greater suffering in which, in Wright's own words, 'the love of the land we have invaded and the guilt of the invasion' are impossible to prise apart (1991: 30). Poems like 'Bora Ring', 'Nigger's Leap', and, in an urban context, 'The Dark Ones', make little attempt to enter into an Aboriginal consciousness, and yet they betray knowledge of the originary crimes which, stemming from the destructive colonial blood-knot, tie both white and Aboriginal Australians to the apocalyptic vision of a terminally desecrated land.

The idea of desecration – integral to Wright's view of conservation as atonement and 'sacred responsibility' (1991: 139) – infuses pastoral elegies like 'Bora Ring' as well as later, more obviously ecological poems ('Lament for Passenger Pigeons', 'Australia 1970', 'Cedar Creek', 'Interfaces') that chart the violence done to nature, a violence partly mirrored in nature's dualistic capacity both to destroy and to regenerate itself. Poems such as these explore, not so much the idea of spiritual belonging as the potentially devastating consequences of a materialist worldview that ignores, or actively disturbs, the fine equilibrium in which the world is precariously held. Intensified violence to this system may result in its definitive destruction ('The Two Fires', 'Patterns'); while in other poems, notably 'Two Dreamtimes', directly addressed by Wright to her 'shadow-sister' Oodgeroo, pastoral's regenerative vision is invoked in the face of possibly irretrievable loss:

Over the rum your voice sang
the tales of an old people,
their dreaming buried, the place forgotten ...
We too have lost our dreaming.
We the robbers, robbed in turn,
selling this land on hire-purchase,
what's stolen once is stolen again

even before we know it.
If we are sisters, it's in this –
our grief for a lost country,
the place we dreamed in long ago,
poisoned now and crumbling.

(168)

Yet pastoral reminiscences of an 'easy Eden-dreamtime' are now made to confront a 'changed world' in which the 'once-loved land' is now 'doomed by traders and stock-exchanges / bought by faceless strangers', and in which the stories and songs that might celebrate it are 'bought and sold too [...] / black or white at a different price' (168). The elegiac perception of an irremediably degraded world is imagined as bringing the two poets together, but not as equal partners: 'I am born of the con-querors', the speaker (Wright) confesses, 'you of the persecuted'; 'we can exchange our separate griefs / but yours and mine are different' (168). The poem thus identifies a common cause – the protection of an increasingly ravaged country – while acknowledging a continuing record of white injustices for which individual gestures of friendship are not enough, and will never be enough, to make amends (Wright 1991: 30). Pastoral nostalgia thus remains haunted by the very privileges – abused privileges – that help to make it possible, revealing a divisive history of entitlement that cannot be erased even when it is symbolically withdrawn:

My shadow-sister, I sing to you
from my place with my righteous kin,
To where you stand with the Koori dead,
Trust none – 'not even poets'.
The knife's between us. I turn it round,
the handle to your side,
the weapon made from your country's bones.
I have no right to take it.

(169)

'Two Dreamtimes', like Wright's other Aboriginal pastorals, is primarily driven by a politics of affect in which the restorative power of human sympathy is not enough to bridge the distance between culturally incommensurate worlds. At the same time, Wright mobilises the critical conventions of pastoral – the satirical component often embedded within its dreamy recollections of rural idyll – to challenge her own white-settler privilege and to posit an ecological alternative to what she sees, in more general terms, as a destructively technocratic world.

This ecologisation of the pastoral can also be seen in Oodgeroo's work, which, like Wright's, draws heavily on the ironic resources of elegy – nowhere more so than in her best-known, but arguably worst interpreted, poem. 'We Are Going' (1964) is usually read as a tragic confirmation of cultural loss in the European romantic-pastoral tradition:

> We are nature and the past, all the old ways
> Gone now and scattered.
> The scrubs are gone, the hunting and the laughter.
> The eagle is gone, the emu and the kangaroo are gone from this place.
> The bora ring is gone.
> The corroboree is gone.
> And we are going.
>
> (1970: 74)

But while its falling cadences are plaintive, this final incantation, read within the overall context of the poem, proves to be anything other than an admission of defeat. For one thing, it caps an affirmative recital of shared cultural properties that establishes clear lines of continuity between past and present: 'We are the corroboree and the bora ground. / We are the old sacred ceremonies, the laws of the elders. / We are the wonder tales of Dream Time, the tribal legends told' (74). For another, it cannily simulates, only to subvert, white assumptions of Aboriginal confusion and defeatism, as in the dramatic shift from third- to first-person in the poem, in which expectations of estrangement are accusingly pro- jected even as they are ironically performed: 'They sit and are confused, they cannot say their thoughts: / We are as strangers here now, but the white tribe are the strangers' (74). And for a third, the poem re-establishes a connection with the land that the 'white tribe' has lost; that it does not even see in its frenzied search to turn developable areas into profit, and to jettison everything else:

> They came here to the place of their old bora ground
> Where now the many white men hurry about like ants.
> Notice of estate agent reads: 'Rubbish May be Tipped Here.'
> Now it half covers the traces of the old bora ring.
>
> (74)

'We Are Going', in these and several other ways, is a performative poem, and what it offers – like many of Oodgeroo's poems – is a form of *counter-mimicry*: an ironic version, which is also an inversion, of the

white ventriloquism of Aboriginal loss. As Oodgeroo herself explains in
a 1977 interview,

> [The poem] is a double-header. Saying we are going was a warning
> to the white people: we can go out of existence, or with proper help we
> could also go on and live in this world in peace and harmony. It was up
> to the whites. Now the whites have proved to us that they're going the
> wrong way about it. But the Aboriginals will not go out of existence;
> the whites will. We are going to live; the whites are going to die.
> (Davidson 1977: 433; also quoted in Shoemaker 1994: 168)

As Adam Shoemaker, who quotes this interview extensively in his 1994
article, suggests, Oodgeroo is first and foremost a performer who, in
shifting her mostly white audience between positions of apparent
accommodation and outright condemnation, finds clever ways of alternating 'diplomacy and directness, humour and accusation' in the
exchange (168). In 'We Are Going', the skill in the performance consists
in pitting the conventions of white European pastoral elegy against those
of Aboriginal Australian storytelling/oratory: the result, in Anne Brewster's words, is a poem which only appears 'to be mourning the passing
of Aboriginal culture', but actually 'affirms the continuity of Aborigin-
ality through the poet's reading of the land' (Brewster 1994: 98–99).

   This assertion of continuity in the face of change – change often mis-
takenly assumed to spell the end of traditional indigenous life-ways – is
at the centre of Oodgeroo's poetry, much of which plays ironically with
white expectations of the inevitable absorption of a 'primitive' culture
into modern, technologised life. In some poems, this process is ironically
enacted with an apocalyptic twist, as in 'No More Boomerang', which
mimics a white-pastoral version of indigenous simplicity ('One time
naked / Who never knew shame'), only to mock it by suggesting that the
modern technological advances that have supposedly outstripped it are
rapidly working towards producing the simplest solution of all:

> Lay down the woomera,
> Lay down the waddy,
> Now we got atom-bomb,
> End *every*body.

> (1970: 33)

Other poems like 'Then and Now' propose an elegiac vision of the past
that is classically pastoral in its opposition to the time pressures of
modern industrialism ('Children of nature we were then / No clocks

hurrying crowds to toil': 87), but then turn nostalgia on its head by suggesting that a characteristic of the modern-industrial ethos is its propensity
to mourn what it has itself destroyed ('Here where they have memorial
park / One time lubras dug for yams': 87). These twists and turns in
Oodgeroo's verse imply a residual defiance that masquerades as performative acquiescence, a defiance by no means restricted to her more obviously
adversarial 'protest poems' ('Whynot Street', 'Acacia Ridge', 'Aboriginal
Charter of Rights'). There is genuine pathos in Oodgeroo's work:

> The tall surrounding trees that stir in the wind
> Making their own music,
> Soft cries of the night coming to us, there
> Where we are one with all old Nature's lives
> Known and unknown,
> In scenes where we belong but have now forsaken.
>
> ('The Past', 1970: 94)

But this pathos is rarely, as Meeker suggests, the exasperated end-point
of pastoral's contemplative process; rather, it re-energises the present by
maintaining a strong associative connection with the past:

> Deep chair and electric radiator
> Are but since yesterday,
> But a thousand thousand camp fires in the forest
> Are in my blood.
> Let none tell me the past is wholly gone.
> Now is so small a part of time, so small a part
> Of all the race years that have moulded me.
>
> (94)

The speaker's self-pride is coterminous here with what Tom Griffiths
calls a heuristic understanding of 'deep ecological time' – that visceral,
even primordial confirmation of belonging which registers a 'symbiotic
connection between human and environment [that apparently] recognises
no formal point of beginning', and certainly no formal end (Read 2000:
180–81). Wright's resonant phrase 'blood's country' comes to mind again
here but, as Read suggests, 'while Aboriginals remain dispossessed [and]
while governments seek continually to retreat from the Mabo judge-
ment and complicate or obstruct Native Title claims, no non-indigenous
Australian can belong legitimately to deep Australian time' (181; also
Griffiths 1997, 1999). Wright herself acknowledges this, both in her essays
and in her poetry. The affective force of colonial genealogy, she suggests,

is never enough to establish what Read calls 'belonging-in-parallel': the mutual acceptance that white and Aboriginal Australians are entitled to the country where they and their forebears have lived, and where both parties can claim the right – can claim to have *earned* the right – to belong (Read 2000: 210). Conservation, she further suggests, is crucial to the formative process of non-indigenous belonging: '[Australia] is a haunted country. We owe it repentance and such amends as we can make, and one last chance of making those amends is to keep as much of it as we can, in the closest state we can to its original beauty' (Wright 1991: 30).

Oodgeroo's Australia, too, is haunted, and the spirit of violence is in the land. But conservation, for her, is less about the task to exercise 'sacred responsibility' towards nature (Wright 1991: 139) than about the ongoing battle to control cultural resources; and this battle, once joined, may itself show violence: a 'violent love of land' (Oodgeroo Noonuccal 1970: 95):

> But time is running out
> And time is close at hand,
> For the Dreamtime folk are massing
> To defend their timeless land.
> Come gentle black man
> Show your strength;
> Time to take a stand.
> Make the violent miner feel
> Your violent
> Love of land.

> (95)

South African counter-pastoral

In South Africa, as in Australia, pastoral myths have been entangled with their opposites; anti-pastoral – and often an extreme version of it – has been a dominant literary mode. In the most comprehensive and influential study of white South African pastoral to date, J.M. Coetzee asks why it is that the idea of the Cape Colony as a garden – 'the home of the earthly paradise' – never took hold in South Africa (Coetzee 1988: 2). The answer, he suggests, is that Africa was not a new world, resplendent with the promise of a recovered Eden, but rather a 'Lapland of the south, peopled by natives whose way of life occasioned curiosity or disgust but never admiration' (2). The Cape Colony, in other words, was an *anti*-pastoral space, a site of barbarism and degradation, a space repeatedly explored in white South African literature, in which pastoral values and romantic myths have always co-existed uneasily, 'under a sardonic scrutiny' that questions them both (Christie, Hutchings and MacLennan 1980: 55).

Pastoral, nonetheless, has remained useful for white South African writers to reclaim this space as their own, with the farm, in particular, deployed to hold up 'the time of the forefathers as an exemplary age when the garden of myth became actualised in history' (Coetzee 1988: 4). The apogee of this development is the Afrikaner farm novel (*plaasroman*), a sub-genre that peaked during the early to mid-part of the twentieth century, and in which the garden-farm became both the 'bastion of trusted feudal values [and the] cradle of a transindividual familial/tribal form of consciousness' (4). Over and against this are the degenerated colonial farms of white South African anti-pastoral, for which Olive Schreiner's satirical late nineteenth-century novel *The Story of an African Farm* (1883) serves as a model, and in which the problem of the relationship between white ownership and black labour is brought to the fore. As in Australia, the incorporation of blacks into white pastoral fantasies has proved to be deeply troubling, for, as Coetzee puts it in the South African context, 'how can the farm become the pastoral retreat of the black man when it *was* his pastoral home only a generation or two ago?' (1988: 5). The problem can only be resolved, Coetzee suggests, by the occlusion of black labour: 'Blindness to the colour black is built into South African pastoral', which works instead to uphold the values of a Dutch peasant rural order by positing the 'organic mode of consciousness [of] a people who, from toiling generation after generation on the family farm, have divested themselves of individuality and become embodiments of an enduring bloodline stretching back into a mythicized past' (6).

For Coetzee, the myth of return to the family farm still functions as an 'isolationist romance' in white South African culture, and is wholly compatible with the more recent liberal-individualist tradition, compromised as it is by its association with 'the get-rich-quick exploitation of the country's resources and with the anomie of the [industrial] boom-towns' (6). This pastoral fantasy, however, is persistently contradicted by the rebarbative nature of the land, which resists human cultivation: 'To Schreiner and a line of writers after her, Africa is a land of rock and sun, not of soil and water. What relation is it possible for man to have with rock and sun?' (7). The landscape tradition of South African poetry and the history of the farm novel both arguably belong to this vain search for reciprocity: between the colonial descendants of the first white European settlers and what remains a largely intractable, impenetrable land. In the first tradition, the landscape is frequently rendered empty or silent; in the second, it is peopled, but only at the expense of removing the labour of 'those [black] hands that [might] make the landscape speak' (9). Both traditions are linked, according to Coetzee, to a 'literature of failure' in which no apparent language can be found to accommodate the white settler to black Africa, and in which, in both its pastoral and anti-pastoral varieties, there is no place for dispossessed blacks in the (anti-)idyll of African pastoralism as a whole (8, 71–72). White South African pastoral is thus, like the serpent in the garden, always already contaminated; or, to switch metaphors, it is like the black corpse in Nadine Gordimer's novel *The Conservationist* (1974), which keeps floating up out of the earth to provide a reminder of an alternative history of (black) occupation and entitlement that obsessively re-emerges until it ends up capsizing the entire genre (Coetzee 1988: 11).

Coetzee, among others, sees *The Conservationist* as following in the white South African tradition of the anti-pastoral novel, but disagrees with A.E. Voss's assessment that it 'lays the ghost' of the traditional South African pastoral, asking, tongue half in cheek, whether it is ever really 'in the nature of the ghost of the pastoral to be laid' (1988: 81; see also Newman 1988, Voss 1977). All the same, *The Conservationist* does raise the problems of the pastoral to the point where they might well seem to be terminal: the problem of patriarchy and inheritance, linked to the non-perpetuation of the 'natural order'; the problem of alienated relations to land and labour under the conditions of a late, global capitalism that might seem antithetical to the pastoral, but on which its continued existence actually depends; the problem of demography, in which pastoral enclosure is consistently threatened by the encroachment of unwanted, unknown 'others'; and, not least, the problem of semantics: the questioning and, ultimately, dismantling of the pastoral system of natural correspondences through which nature and the natural order can be reliably categorised and read.

At the centre of these problems – their infected source – is the false 'conservationist' Mehring, a corrupt industrialist through whose fractured consciousness the events of the story are narrated, events revolving around the day-to-day management of his increasingly imperilled farm. The farm is at first sight a classic modern pastoral retreat, a privileged space created out of the surplus of industrial capitalism, and managed by a mixed cast of mostly transient black labourers whose names (Solomon, Phineas, Izak) combine biblical and classical models, and who are effortlessly enlisted for the task of performing obedient pastoral routines (Barnard 2004). In a series of mock-pastoral epiphanies, the farm confers romantic illusions of communion on those, like Mehring, who are wealthy enough to afford them:

> The unexpected warmth of the spring evening, a premonition of summer [...] Reaches up to his shirtsleeves and down from the neck

of his half-buttoned shirt to the navel. He has been sitting so still he has the fanciful feeling that so long as he does not move the farm is as it is when he is not there. He's at one with it as an ancestor at one with his own earth. He is there and not there.

(Gordimer 1977 [1974]: 161)

As soon becomes apparent, however, the farm is a space outside the control of its privileged absentee owner, and it increasingly becomes the site of his deepest fears and anxieties: fears of intrusion, depletion and, eventually, destruction that the narrative, visiting upon him the worst nightmares of his diseased consciousness, ironically plays out. Mehring is deserted by the people (his wife, his son, his mistress) he had previously treated as possessions; even nature (drought, floods) seems to conspire against him; and then, in a final reverse, the pastoral idyll collapses into an anti-pastoral scene of abjection in which the would-be conservationist is exposed as an environmental spoiler who, ousted from his own protected paradise, is pitched unceremoniously onto one of his own industrial dumps (258).

As numerous critics have pointed out, the circular logic of the narrative enacts a kind of counter-pastoral revenge fantasy through which the dominant white narrative of social (especially, sexual) and ecological exploitation is subverted on contact with black (Amazulu) fertility and creation myths (Clingman 1986; Newman 1988). This reading supports the view that the land reverts, symbolically if not yet materially, to its original black inhabitants in a reverse process of white pastoral entitlement, and that in so doing it undoes the colonialist/capitalist logic of accumulation and development on which pastoral fantasies of vicarious productivity (farm) and bourgeois domesticity (garden) are based. *The Conservationist* thus completes the recovery process initiated in Gordimer's earlier short story, 'Six Feet of the Country', in which an unidentified black corpse, officially discarded but finally given a makeshift local burial, symbolically reclaims the space from which it was previously evicted – at the white authorities' expense.

The symbolic geography of the novel, however, is much more complex than that of the story, pitting at least three partly mythologised spaces against each other in a multifaceted ecology of survival: 'the city', the farm ('the country'), and the rapidly expanding township ('the location') which, at least for the fearful white characters in the novel, provides an unwanted bridge between the two poles of urban and rural space. The competition for limited resources that this ecology implies requires different modalities of conservation. One mode is allied to the global-capitalist ideology of 'possessive individualism', represented here in pathological form by the arch-accumulator, Mehring (Newman 1988). In this ideology, the ethic of pastoral care is displaced onto a hypocritical desire to protect (endangered) animals. 'Cattle apart,' Mehring complains of his black farmhands, 'you can't get them to care for any animal' (Gordimer 1977: 69), echoing his earlier concern that guinea-fowl eggs are being stolen from his property, thereby disrupting the pastoral idyll – the 'closed system' (75) – of self-perpetuating social and ecological relations that the farm represents for him. Another mode, purely survival-driven, is characterised by the practice of scavenging:

> Thousands of pieces of paper take to the air and are plastered against the location fence when the August winds come. The assortment of covering worn by the children and old people who scavenge the rubbish dump is moulded against their bodies or bloated away from them [...] The scavengers are patient – leisurely or feeble, it's difficult, in passing, to judge – and their bare feet and legs and the hands with which they pick over the dirt are coated grey with ash. Two of the older children from the farm go to school in the location. They could return as they come, across the veld and through the gap cut in the fence by gangs who bring stolen goods in that way, but they lengthen the long walk home by going to have a look at what people are seeking, on the dump. They do not know what it is they would hope to find; they learn that what experienced ones seek is whatever they happen to find.
>
> (84)

Just as some environmental theorists like to distinguish between so-called 'full-belly' and 'empty-stomach' environmentalisms (Guha and Martinez-Alier 1997), so the struggle for survival in a socially/economically segregated South Africa throws up both luxury and subsistence types of conservation, the first always liable to fall back into some mythology or other of self-preservation, and the second always looking for creative ways of recycling the waste products of the first. (Ironically, as Mehring finds out, the two forms are not mutually exclusive, and he himself becomes expendable, unable to accommodate himself to the changing conditions of a rapidly industrialising South Africa that his passion for economic development has helped create.)

As Irene Gorak rightly insists, it is necessary to see this struggle in its appropriate social and historical context – not just that of apartheid South Africa, but more specifically the volatile period of the early to mid-1970s, when 'executive greed, government mismanagement, and black protest combined to push the country further and further behind its competitors; but while it lasted, this luxurious life-style reinforced a pastoral division of labor and a pastoral sense of the separation from the squalor of black life' (Gorak 1991: 246). But while Gorak praises the novel as a powerful attack on one particular form of pastoral escapism – what she calls the 'Nationalist pastoral myth' (244) – she takes Gordimer to task for her failure to provide a radical alternative, accusing her instead of 'unleash[ing] one pastoral in order to drive out another without producing a vantage point from which to criticize either' (244). This accusation bears looking into. Is Gordimer guilty, as Gorak implies, of setting up a sentimental 'black' pastoral counterpart to the unacceptable 'white' one and, in the process, of mythologising them both?

For Gorak, the false conservationism of Gordimer's white protagonist is ranged against the 'true acceptance of natural realities of her black farmworkers' (249), setting up a counter-myth of black authenticity and rural self-sufficiency that belongs to the same pastoral symbolic economy the novel is otherwise so quick to mock. Yet there is not much evidence in the novel to support this. For one thing, the black characters in the novel are as sharply differentiated as the whites; and for another, many are obvious outsiders to the neighbourhood (the nameless dead man found down in the reeds is dismissed by Mehring as 'one of them', a generic 'city slicker' (Gordimer 1977: 15), but a much harder question – unanswered in the novel – is who makes up the 'us'). The novel thus works against the essentialisation of race that is a counterpart to the Nationalist myth of separate and hierarchical development – a myth enshrined in the 'closed system' of inherited familial space. It bears reminding, too, that Mehring is doubly displaced from this self-privileging (Boer) mythos: first, as an outsider himself – as he says, his name vaguely suggests that he is of German (colonial South West African?) extraction – and second, as a city-living industrialist, whose ties to the land are self-consciously mystified even as they are self-ironically embraced. This 'closed system' is also interrogated at the level of form, through what Brian Macaskill calls Gordimer's 'interruptive aesthetics': her repeated use of ambiguity and ellipsis to open up spaces in the narrative that its dominant voice – here, that of Mehring – tries unavailingly to plug (Macaskill 1990; see also Huggan 1994). Finally, it is clear throughout the novel that physical boundaries are both arbitrary, however staunchly defended, and dangerously porous: fences are cut, borders crossed, and even the orifices of the body (illegally) penetrated, revealing the violence that underlies the pastoral ideal of protected private space.

This last point suggests that Gorak's other main criticism of the novel – that it establishes a pseudo-radicalism of form that legitimates its author's own border-crossing sexual/racial libertinism – is off the mark as well. For Gorak, *The Conservationist* espouses a form of 'libertine pastoral' in which sexual and racial freedoms – associated, as so often in Gordimer's work, with a progressive younger generation (e.g. Mehring's apparently homosexual son Terry) – are substituted for more concerted political action, and 'the political realm [ends up being naturalised] just as effectively as [in] apartheid by [being turned] into the biological mystery of sex' (Gorak 1991: 243). This would be a valid criticism if it were true, but once again there is little evidence to warrant it. Just to compare the novel's two most obvious libertine characters, Terry's political 'innocence' is ironised just as surely as Antonia's (Mehring's mistress's) sexual 'experience', sexual free play and racial permissiveness being grist to the mill of Mehring's all-consuming cynicism (a cynicism by no means reserved for 'good' whites; witness his withering condescension towards his 'loyal' black overseer, Jacobus, as well).

Gorak is surely right that *The Conservationist* is not a revolutionary work, but that is hardly the novel's claim, nor is it within the range of its ambitions. Rather, like some of Coetzee's novels – as we will shortly see – it opts for a deconstructive approach to the white-settler ideologies within which it remains bound, such as the ideology of the pastoral, the unquiet ghost of which may not eventually be pacified, but the self-serving, potentially self-destructive elements of which are efficiently emptied out.

Mehring half-jokes at one point in *The Conservationist* that since his farm will likely be expropriated to make way for the expansion of the location, he wants to make sure he gets a decent price. But land reclamation for a newly empowered black population in South Africa is no laughing matter, nor is the question of the price to be paid, both materially and symbolically, for a long history of exploitative white attitudes to place (Barnard 2004; Darian-Smith *et al.* 1996). Land dispossession was a key element of colonial and apartheid regimes and, in a cornerstone of early apartheid policy, black ownership of land was forbidden as part of the 1936 Native Land Act (Wenzel 2000: 93). In the postapartheid era, few issues are more contentious than land and the bundle of conflicting rights that is attached to it. A land reform programme has been launched, but its major implication, the surrender of land by white to black South Africans, remains unclear to date.[4] Meanwhile, the fear of forfeiting land has led to a sequence of evictions of black tenants and labourers on white farms, and, responding in kind, frustrated blacks have hit out against their (former) white landlords: as Jennifer Wenzel reports in a 2000 essay, 'since the historic 1994 elections, more than 500 white farmers have been murdered in South Africa, 35 of them killed in the final two months of 1997 alone' (90). As Wenzel (among others) argues, land reform implies the need, not just for an equitable redistribution of property, but also for a fundamental shift in inherited cultural attitudes to place. Pastoral can be seen here as part of the emotional survival kit of a beleaguered white landowning class threatened, on one side, by the latest developments in the market economy and, on the other, by the real possibility that the reconfiguration of land ownership in the post-apartheid era may result in the definitive loss of valuable family property, secure over several generations (Wenzel 2000; see also Barnard 2004).

J.M. Coetzee's work, both fictional and non-fictional, has been heavily engaged with these issues from the outset. More than any other living South African writer, Coetzee has attempted to unravel the historical and ideological complexities of white South African pastoral, and to gauge the cumulative emotional affinities – no less powerful for being tied up with a long history of conspicuous injustices – to which several generations of living on the land attest. Pastoral tends to thrive, Coetzee suggests, at moments of crisis when previous, self-accorded entitlements to land and livelihood are increasingly threatened; its primary ideological function is thus to shore up or, perhaps better, strategically re-invent a mythologised view of the peasant order that provides a 'transcendental justification for the [white] ownership of land' (Coetzee 1988: 106). However, pastoral myths of return tend to live in the shadow of loss, and what this suggests in the contemporary South African context is that the 'pastoral promise of the return *to* the land' is always likely to exist in tension with the 'political imperative of the return *of* the land' (Wenzel 2000: 95; emphasis ours). In what follows, we want to look briefly at two fictional responses to this dilemma, Coetzee's Booker prize-winning novels *Life & Times of Michael K* (1983) and *Disgrace* (1999), each of which needs to be seen within its own particular context as the bringing-to-crisis of pastoral ideals that initially seem unable to survive, and are possibly unworthy of surviving, their latest historical test. Both novels, in different ways, offer a radically deconstructive approach to what Gorak calls the 'Nationalist pastoral', a mode that has proved to be an ideological mainstay for the propagation and perpetuation of self-justifying white-supremacist myths. But more controversially, both also offer ways of thinking beyond this particular, ideologically contaminated version of the pastoral. Can the pastoral be rescued, and is it worth rescuing? We want to suggest that novels like *Life & Times of Michael K* and *Disgrace* indicate – counter-intuitively perhaps – that both questions can be answered with a tentative 'yes'.

Life & Times of Michael K, as might be expected from the arch-ironist Coetzee, bears ironic relation to its own title. It is an anti-*Bildungsroman* in which the protagonist appears to learn little, and an anti-chronicle in which we learn equally little about the times (of war) in which the protagonist lives. In a novel of multiplied ironies, we might reasonably expect the text to ironise the other genres/modes on which it draws, including the pastoral, and at first sight it does not disappoint. In fact, the whole novel seems to offer a series of mock-exercises in what Empson calls the pastoral rendering of the complex in the simple. The slow-witted K graduates from being a part-time gardener in Cape Town to a self-styled 'cultivator' on a farm he temporarily occupies in the Karoo while he is on the run from the authorities. In both cases, the pastoral myth of being at one with the earth, and of persuading it to yield its fruits, is severely limited. K struggles to survive, and little happens by the end of the text to suggest that he either will or wants to. Meanwhile, his attempted self-explanations, no more successful than those imposed on him by others, take the form of dreamily oracular pronouncements on the purpose of his life:

> K knew that he would not crawl out [from his hiding place] and stand up and cross from darkness into firelight to announce himself. He even knew the reason why: because enough men had gone off to war saying the time for gardening was when the war was over; whereas there must be men to stay behind and keep gardening alive, or at least the idea of gardening; because once that cord was broken, the earth would grow hard and forget her children. That was why.
>
> (Coetzee 1998 [1983]: 109)

K is aware enough to recognise that there is a gap in his logic, 'a dark-ness before which his understanding baulked' (110), and agile enough to keep escaping from the euphemistically called 'resettlement' camps into which he and others judged to be of 'no fixed abode' are put (78). Still, he seems unable to fulfil his aim – if that is his aim – to escape from the clutches of history, and equally unable to live out his myth – if that is his myth – of returning to the earth. Instead, he seems to spend most of his time in mute reaction to other people's ideas and fantasies of him; like his namesake, Kafka's K, he is neither his own man nor, strictly speaking, his own character, rather a drifting consciousness to which various, more or less interchangeable functions and significances are attached.

In short, K appears enslaved by the pastoral myths he thinks will guarantee his freedom: the myth of return to origins; the myth of sacra-mental stewardship; the myth of an atavistic ('transcendentally justified') attachment to the land. Pastoral freedom – from this negative view-point – turns out to be another form of servitude, while the traditional pastoral figure of the shepherd/gardener turns into a puppet in someone else's fantasy of 'refuge', 'peace', 'land', 'home'. K's performance, notwithstanding, deviates from standard versions of the South African pastoral script. As Rita Barnard suggests, *Life & Times of Michael K* presents a dystopic counter-image to the Afrikaner's 'dream topography', the central feature of which is 'the family farm, ruled by the patriarch and guarded as a legacy for his sons' (Barnard 2002: 388; see also 2004). This counter-image – the carceral landscape of the camps – is distinctly anti-pastoral, but K does just enough in the text to suggest that he is capable of offering a counter-pastoral of his own. This counter-pastoral variant is *maternal*, retaining the idea of attachment to the land but rejecting the twin ideologies of white proprietorship and patriarchal authority on which more conventional modes of South African pastoral are based. Maternal care, rather than patriarchal self-perpetuation, is the basis for K's engagement with the country; indeed, he actively resists the notion of furthering his line, insisting instead that, in coming from a 'line of children', he has 'nothing to pass on' (Coetzee 1998: 105). This variant is also *minimal*, replacing the idea of pastoral plenitude with that of anti-pastoral privation, and apparently gesturing towards an ascetic ideal of total relinquishment or renunciation that entails K living 'nowhere' (1998: 120), working for no one, and 'only taking back as food what he has put into [the earth] himself' (Wright 1992: 437).

Derek Wright connects this minimalist philosophy to what he calls 'a special *chthonic* mythology, with its own ahistorical order, into which "the wheels of history" have been rerouted' (437; emphasis his). This mythology, revolving around repeated images of 'an original, amorphous Earth-Mother', turns the earth into 'a constant touchstone and referent for [K's] existence, so that he feels "like an ant that does not know where its hole is" [Coetzee 2000: 114] when removed from it to the camp' (437–38; see also Head 1998). Such a perspective, though partly ironised in its turn, turns away from the patriarchal mythology of the pastoral towards a feminised version of ecopoetics, which, in Jonathan Bate's Heideggerean terms, registers the impossible attempt to heal the divide between nature and consciousness by reconciling instrumental and immanent apprehensions of the earth (Bate 2000: 263; see also Heidegger 1971, Rigby 2004). This healing process requires a 'letting-be of Being' that allows for a rediscovery of familiarity with nature in which the idea of 'dwelling', immanently 'revealed' rather than instrumentally 'narrated', becomes the utopian expression of a non-instrumental relation between (individual) people and the earth (263–64). Ecopoetics, suggests Bate, is about imagining the dwelling-place, bringing it into being and, through this generative process, reflecting on what it might mean to 'dwell with', as well as to 'build upon', the earth (266, 282).

While there is certainly evidence enough for an 'ecopoetical' reading of *Life & Times of Michael K* (see, for example, Coetzee 1998: 98–99), such a reading invites the troubling consideration that the earth myths around which the novel is structured are primarily ecological, not political, and that 'the mythological drift of the novel – although it is problematic for a white writer [J.M. Coetzee] to use a black figure [Michael K] to say it – is that the land is not to be returned to the blacks but to the earth itself' (Wright 1992: 440). However, as is typical for Coetzee, the text appears to challenge its own mythologising impulses without necessarily subverting them completely, and without offering a clearly situated socio-political analysis in their place. While some of Coetzee's detractors have seen this strategy as little more than cultivated elusiveness (Knox-Shaw 1996; Rich 1984), it is better seen as an attempt on his part to reflect on the impossible necessity, as a 'white writer', of articulating alternative, 'non-white' ideas and ideologies that might unsettle dominant, explicitly or implicitly, colonialist relations between people, property and place (Coetzee 1988). This option is explored in *Life & Times of Michael K* through the supposedly supportive figure of the medical officer, whose vain attempt to explain his patient's (K's) actions requires an elaborate form of sustained ventriloquism that finally amounts to a colonising of the consciousness of the patient himself. One term by which this ventriloquism might go is 'pastoral'; for pastoral, after all, has traditionally involved 'speaking through' the aestheticised figure of the shepherd in order to counterpose an idea/ideal of rural virtue against the perceived insufficiencies of city life. Pastoral, in this sense, might even be held to be a form of epistemic colonialism, a version of the by-now-familiar postcolonial paradigm whereby the self strategically silences the other on whose behalf it wishes, largely for its own benefit, to speak (Spivak 1988; Parry 1996).[5] The analogy is far-fetched, perhaps, but as Wright among others points out, there is a connection that runs throughout Coetzee's work between the spatial practices of colonialism (confinement, containment, etc.) and the domesticating strategies of the pastoral – a mode that imprisons others within its own visions of peaceful cooperation, and that siphons off others' labour to promote its own ideals of self-sufficiency and enlightened self-critique (Wright 1992; Barnard 2004).

Coetzee's more recent novel *Disgrace* (1999) continues his strategy of dismantling pastoral as a colonialist discourse of obedience while partially reinstating it as an ambivalent vehicle of moral education attached to the utopian possibility of a reciprocal, mutually uplifting relationship with the earth. However, unlike in the earlier novel, this self-educative process requires the acceptance of a radical shift in power, with some of the old colonial myths of patriarchal authority and territorial entitlement now having been usurped by a new, post-apartheid generation of semi-independent black farmers keen to establish a managerial role over shared property, and keener still to acquire, control and distribute property of their own (Coetzee 2000 [1999]: 76; see also Barnard 2004, Wenzel 2000). This black counter-pastoral is firmly divorced from what Coetzee calls the white 'scenic tradition' in South Africa (Coetzee 1988: 97), a tradition most obviously associated in the novel with the ousted Cape Town university professor David Lurie, whose return to the country (in this case the Eastern Cape, where his daughter Lucy has a smallholding) is heavily overdetermined by pastoral/romantic visions of organic community and rural simplicity filtered through the various, but invariably European, literary/artistic fantasies by which his overheated urban imagination is fed (Coetzee 2000: 61, 170). It also has little truck with the dreamy nostalgia and romantic technophobia that often fuel contemporary versions of the pastoral: Petrus, Lucy's black co-proprietor, who finishes by taking over the title deeds to the property, is self-consciously 'forward-looking' (76) in his calculated approach to both the future acquisition and the provisional management of what he knows will eventually become his farm (Barnard 2002: 389).

Fanciful white pastoral/romantic visions of the land, however, are not jettisoned entirely; rather, they are combined with pragmatic discourses of black self-determination in an uneasy transhistorical amalgam in which ideologically manufactured oppositions and boundaries of all kinds – between black and white, city and country and, above all, strangers and kinsfolk – are consistently presented in the text as being on the verge of collapse (Barnard 2002: 389). Caught in the centre of this discursive web is the controversial figure of Lucy's unborn mixed-race child, the product of a violent rape that, the text leads us to believe, may go unpunished in the interests of securing an alternative future in which the penalty has been paid for past injustices and the right to redress for more recent counter-abuses is strategically given up (Coetzee 2000: 205). This renunciative idea of 'paying the price' is deeply troubling, linked as it is to Lucy's view of black violence as an historically specific form of 'debt collection' (158), and apparently reinforcing images of black brutality that circulate throughout the text (see, for example, 95). Over and against this is an ethic of care displaced onto the figure of the suffering animal: David Lurie's last act in the text is to give up a crippled dog placed under his protection, a gesture that can alternately be seen in terms of regenerative sacrifice or as the final confirmation of his own instinct for self-preservation, ironically contrasted with the (animal) other's unconditional love.[6]

As Rita Barnard among others has argued, Coetzee's text holds equal-and-opposite readings like these under seemingly permanent tension, never permitting the luxury of interpretative clarity and constantly alluding to the difficulties of translating from one medium to another in a novel in which different languages and registers – European and African, human and animal, secular and sacred – are demonstrably opaque to one another, and yet just as conspicuously mixed (Barnard 2004: 207; see also Sanders 2002). Barnard's view is that this discursive entanglement indicates the need for a new lexicon to describe transformed relationships in the context of the 'new' South Africa – a lexicon that the novel's principal narrating consciousness, David Lurie, proves congenitally unable to present (2004: 212). Pastoral's ideologically reassuring patterns of call and response are no longer valid in such a volatile context, although the momentary aesthetic gratifications of pastoral idyll, however delusional their apprehension of timelessness, are never quite cancelled out:

> Lucy straightens up, stretches, bends down again. Field-labour; peasant tasks; immemorial. His daughter is becoming a peasant. [...] The wind drops. There is a moment of utter stillness which he would wish prolonged for ever: the gentle sun, the stillness of mid-afternoon, bees busy in a field of flowers; and at the centre of the picture a young woman, *das ewig Weibliche*, lightly pregnant, in a straw sunhat. A scene ready-made for a Sargent or a Bonnard. City boys like him; but even city boys can recognize beauty when they see it, can have their breath taken away.
>
> (Coetzee 2000: 217–18)

As Barnard points out, the motif of *das ewig Weibliche* ('the eternal feminine'), taken from the end of Goethe's *Faust*, is typically double-coded, suggesting the almost comic mismatch between Lurie's Old World intellectual heritage and the social demands of the 'new' South Africa, but also gesturing towards the speculative possibility of his own redemption. As she puts it:

> [T]he erotic is displaced [in the womaniser Faust] by penitential devotion, and the desiring gaze is transformed into the gaze of religious epiphany. [...] It is therefore possible to discover in Coetzee's beautiful scenic moment not only a desire to suspend time and cling to the [pastoral/romantic] codes of the past, but the possibility of sudden transfiguration – a passage into a different state of being.
>
> (2004: 219)

Whether this redemption is actually achieved is something that Coetzee's novel leaves open; certainly, the final scene in which the dog is offered up suggests the possibility of a vicarious release from the burdens of the past, the subject of one of Lurie's academic monographs, and a motif reconfirming Coetzee's more-than-academic interest in the transmigration of human/animal souls (Coetzee 1990, 1999). This imagined release – which is quite possibly only the last of Lurie's delusions – might be seen in terms of a general disengagement from linear history (*à la* Michael K) or a more specific break from the 'sluggish no-time' of apartheid, in which 'an already anachronistic order of patriarchal clans and tribal despotisms would be frozen in place' (Coetzee 1988: 209; also quoted in Barnard 2004: 210). Coetzee's oeuvre suggests a link between this 'sluggish no-time' and the ossified rituals and routines of the pastoral, which often appears to turn its back on historical progress or to pursue the more active illusion that such progress has never taken place. However, the idea in pastoral of a sacred interconnectedness between human and animal lives – an idea of ancient origin – presents a viable alternative to the crude instrumental rationalism with which animals are treated, and with which people are treated as animals, under the compartmentalised conditions of apartheid and other colonial regimes. Characteristically for Coetzee, pastoral thus offers an insight into a durably exploitative mindset and a horizon of imaginative possibility for more equitable future times.

Hating nature properly

In former settler colonies like Australia and South Africa, pastoral has been a lens through which to view the native landscape that defies the imported vocabulary mapped onto it, and for which – as we have seen – the language of either realised accommodation or imagined refuge cannot readily be found. In other postcolonial societies like those of the Caribbean, these problems are intensified. Much has been written on the inadequacy of a European Romantic lexicon to account for the regional specificities of the Caribbean, and to absorb the full complexity of Caribbean ecologies that have been profoundly shaped both by historical experiences of European colonialism and genocide and pre-colonial geographies that, to put it mildly, are not remotely European in kind (DeLoughrey, Gosson and Handley 2005; Benitez-Rojo 1992; Dash 1998). The Renaissance literature of 'Discovery' registers a number of often unintentionally hilarious attempts to bridge these obvious discrepancies; a prime example would be Walter Ralegh, whose pastoral invocations of Guiana are a calculated political inducement rather than a genuine effort to document peoples and landscapes which, the evidence suggests, he may never even have found (Campbell 1988).

Modern Caribbean writing, in this context, involves a history of ecological reclamation – less a history that seeks to compensate for irrecoverable loss and dispossession than a history re-won. As the term 'ecology' suggests, this is a history of place as much as it is a history of people, and Caribbean writers have played a major role in re-establishing it, both for their kinsfolk and themselves. They have done so, in large part, by rejecting the terms that had previously been imposed on them, or by adapting them in such a way as to discard their assumptions of superiority: a process we might call, after Raymond Williams, the 'unlearning of the inherent dominative mode' (Williams 1983). One form this has taken is the rejection of the Caribbean 'island paradise', that tiresome trope that has historically overdetermined European aesthetic appreciation of the Caribbean, and that has exerted a similar stranglehold over its romantic-primitivist correlate, the South Seas. Another has been the rejection of the pastoral ideal of rural tranquillity: the peaceful country hamlet; the touristic snapshot, still wet from the beach, of smiling workers tending diligently to their fields. These fantasies of domination – for that is what they are – are ruthlessly dismantled in works such as Jamaica Kincaid's *A Small Place* (1988), which confront their readers by challenging their complacency, and by revealing the immiserated conditions under which reluctant Caribbean 'hosts' are forced to retail their poverty, converting it into the currency of authenticity, for the aesthetic delectation of their pampered European 'guests'.

In another context, Tim Brennan has called this process the 'aestheticization of underdevelopment', and no doubt, in its own way, it might be seen as contributing to the pastoral mode (Brennan 1997). But it would be a mistake, in any case, to see Caribbean writers as having turned their backs on the pastoral. Michael Dash has pointed out the 'prominence of discussions of nature, landscape and pastoral in Caribbean literature and criticism' (quoted in Casteel 2004: 15), and Sarah Phillips Casteel, partly drawing on Dash's work, has shown how a number of Caribbean writers have either undercut the conventions of (European) New World pastoral or, adapting them to their own interests, have forged 'a new Caribbean pastoral that re-imagines identity as conditioned by a dynamic interaction between place and displacement' (2004: 16; see also Bongie 1998, Casteel 2007). Casteel's examples are mainly drawn from the current work of Gisèle Pineau and Shani Mootoo, both of whom self-consciously fashion a diasporised version of the pastoral, but plenty of other Caribbean writers, both those who have left and those who have stayed, come readily to mind. Several classic Anglo-Caribbean novels, from Merle Hodge's *Crick*

Crack Monkey to Andrea Levy's *A Small Island*, feature scenes redolent of pastoral simplicity, while the championing of rural labour is even more evident – with Marxist inflections – in the work of Francophone writers like Jacques Roumain (*Les Gouverneurs de la rosée*) and Simone Schwarz-Bart (*Pluie et vent sur Télumée miracle*). In poetry and drama, similarly, pastoral themes are often treated, if often with a requisite note of irony, in the work of writers as different as Derek Walcott and Olive Senior, while other examples of the pastoral can easily be found in most anthologies of Caribbean verse. However, perhaps the writer to have engaged most systematically with the pastoral is Caribbean literature's original Grumpy Old Man, V.S. Naipaul. The rest of this sub-section considers the nature of this engagement, culminating in Naipaul's most ostensibly pastoral work, the novel *The Enigma of Arrival* (1988), and enquiring into the ideological conditions that underpin an oeuvre that presents alternately as pastoral, anti-pastoral and 'post-pastoral' (Gifford 1999); or sometimes, as in *The Enigma of Arrival*, as all of these at the same time.

Naipaul's work is no haven for the literary nature-lover. His despoiled landscapes tell of centuries of human cruelty, greed and plunder; for the most part, they are neither invested with the mock-simplicity of the pastoral, in which nature features ambivalently as contemplative site or ideal refuge, nor with the grandeur of the sublime, in which nature's annihilating/regenerating capacities are always in excess of any emotion that attaches to them, and for which the most readily available compensatory feeling is awe (Bate 1991, 2000; see also Eagleton 2005).[7] Crudely put, nature is not very beautiful in Naipaul, nor is it even pleasingly functional; in fact, it is much more likely to be ugly, either providing a painful record of the histories of violence – often colonial violence – that have been inscribed upon it (*Guerrillas*, *The Loss of El Dorado*, *A Bend in the River*), or a recalcitrant reminder of the limits of human endeavour itself (*A House for Mr Biswas*, *Miguel Street*, *An Area of Darkness*). Nature is to be ignored or, if it can't be, it is resolutely to be fought against; place, meanwhile, is the temporary respite between alternative experiences of displacement. For Naipaul, and in Naipaul, all places carry the mark of some enduring insufficiency; all places, for the resident as much as for the traveller, are the wrong place (Porter 1991; Nixon 1992). And, despite the geographical range of Naipaul's work, all places are the same place. They are shadowed, that is, by the originary trauma of the Middle Passage, whose burden of cultural memory is mapped onto a series of ravaged geographies, objective correlatives for the writer's repeatedly self-advertised 'colonial nerves'. Naipaul appears to be a writer, then, for whom – loosely adapting Adorno – nature is to be hated properly (Adorno 1978: 52; see also Lazarus 1999: 3). His work invites neither the luxuries of contemplation, encapsulated in such hoary figures as the solitary romantic traveller, nor a detached appreciation of the ritual pleasures of country living, embodied in such equally overdetermined genres as the provincial novel or the pastoral romance.

An emblematic figure here is 'B. Wordsworth', the neighbourhood poet in Naipaul's eponymous story in *Miguel Street*, whose life ambition is to compose, one line per month, the greatest poem in the world. The 'B' stands for 'Black': 'Black Wordsworth. White Wordsworth was my brother. We share one heart. I can watch a small flower like the morning glory and cry' (Naipaul 1974: 40). All the narrator (and, one suspects, most readers) want to do here is cry with laughter, but with his characteristic rhetorical skill Naipaul turns biting satire into a kind of reinstated wistfulness, so that the story eventually achieves a degree of romantic apology despite its anti-romantic sympathies, and the failed poet's life is made to reveal an unlikely poetry of its own. It is this combination of satire and wistfulness, and the default romanticism it reinstalls, that is of interest here, mainly because it challenges the regulation view of Naipaul as a comic – if also intermittently self-destructive – assailant of hypoc-risy, a dissector of the pretensions with which people reach for the symbolic capital of culture, as well as for the imagined consolations of the natural world. This view implies that Naipaul's attitude to the pas-toral, with its flagrant idealisation of both culture and nature, will turn out to be contemptuous. But such a view clearly underestimates the flexibility of the pastoral, as well as the profound ambivalence towards it that runs throughout the body of Naipaul's published work.

Our main example here is *The Enigma of Arrival* (1988), Naipaul's accomplished semi-fictional memoir, seen by several critics as a self-conscious retrospective, less on his own life than on his previous work. Ostensibly, the text is an elegiac tale of class relations in a rural community in western England, in which Naipaul, who both is and is not the tale's narrator, seizes the opportunity to replay some of his favourite writers' fantasies of England as civilisational hub and imaginative retreat. Fittingly, then, the text begins by deploying, only to deflate, some classic English pastoral imagery. 'Water meadows' and 'rolling downs', stripped back, reveal a 'narrow river' and 'flat fields' – not much for the eye to feast upon (Naipaul 1988: 5). And yet this unspectacular landscape, once divorced from the washed colours and gentle cadences of pastoral (visually repre-sented here by Constable), is permitted to take on a gentle beauty of its own. It is a landscape of decay, ruin even, dotted with the remnants of a once more glorious history; but also a landscape in which old and new structures achieve an aesthetically satisfying compromise, and where the faded grandeur of ancient (feudal/imperial) seigneurial systems has given way to a kind of ramshackle democratism in which successive generations of farm labourers have slowly but surely established their own social entitlements and property rights (13). It is a landscape, finally, that apparently supersedes the outdated conventions of the pastoral: '[S]heep-shearing was from the past. Like the old farm buildings. Like the caravan that wasn't going to move again. Like the barn where grain was no longer stored' (13). And yet, despite or possibly because of this evidence of anachronism, it is still tinged with the romance of 'old English country ways', reminding the narrator of his 'literary life in another country', and corresponding to 'an image of perfection, located at another time in another place' (18, 116, 131).

This mock-pastoral becomes, for the narrator, a simulacral reality filtered through borrowed visions from other writers' fantasies; even though these visions are corrected by experience, they restore a secondary pastoralism which, disappearing by design, re-emerges by default. This isn't the pastoralism of colonial envy, despite pleasing country views in which 'black-and-white cows against the sky [recall] the design on the condensed-milk label I knew as a child in Trinidad, where cows as handsome as those were not to be seen, [and] where there was very little fresh milk and most people used imported condensed milk or powdered milk' (36–37, 85). Rather, it is a pastoralism that links centuries of unrecognised achievement, joining the histories of twentieth-century English farm-workers to those of their earlier American counterparts who, 'intrud[ing] into the evenness of history on the other side [of the Atlantic] went back [and] changed the world in that part forever' (44).

Pastoral has other historical resonances as well and, as the narrator comes to recognise, it acts as a medium for painful cultural memory rather than comforting cultural myth. The text moves, in this respect, towards a 'synthesis [of the different but interrelated] worlds and cultures that made me' (157) – an uneasy synthesis that ends in anti-climax with the narrator, health seriously damaged by the weather, occupying a rented cottage on the margins of a faded English manorial estate. (As he tells us matter-of-factly, 'I, who did nothing in the grounds, lived there' (61).) The estate itself, not what it once was, produces little of note and some of the people there, like the gardener Pitton, are similarly archaic remnants of an older order, precipitated against their will into the realities of a modern working life. The sequence of Pitton's life is made to appear inevitable: he is discarded, like the rubbish he never quite seems able to dispose of. (An unresolved question: confusing 'refuge' with 'refuse' as he does, is it possible that Pitton subconsciously realises that the (false) sanctuary he is guarding for others will eventually cast out the guard himself?) The image of the ruined garden – a common trope in Caribbean literature (Casteel 2004; Collett 1998) – can be seen here as a degenerated version of the pastoral, symbolising the impermanence of privilege and containing within its own, superseded idea of perfection the seeds of its eventual decay. The garden, like other pastoral motifs, also carries unwanted memories for the narrator: of the yawning gap between rich and poor in modern Trinidad, or the link between growing and serving in an agricultural colony 'in which the point and explanation of everything, the houses, the style of government, the mixed population', is the brute fact of the plantation itself (Naipaul 1988: 224, 238; see also Collett 1998, Kincaid 1999).

Trinidad, a 'wooded land laid bare, its secrets opened up' (Naipaul 1988: 352), is resistant to the blandishments of the pastoral – it is too poor, too desiccated, too reminiscent of the historical origins from which its current inhabitants sprang. And yet the text still manages against the grain to create another version of the pastoral: one based on the dignity of transnational labour – a counter-pastoral variant on georgic – and on the enduring if by no means ineluctable qualities invested in people's personal, as well as professional, relationships with the land. ('Land is not land alone, something that simply is itself', suggests the narrator at one point; rather 'land partakes of what we breathe into it, is touched by our moods and memories' (335).) This version, which manages simultaneously to be romantic and undeluded, can be linked to what Terry Gifford calls the 'post-pastoral'. Post-pastoral, for Gifford, is a complex form that rejects the easy clichés of Arcadia in favour of a 'more knowing [or] adversarial sense of "environment" rather than "nature", "countryside" or "landscape"' (Gifford 1999: 174). It is a pastoral informed by ecological principles of uneven interconnectedness, as well as an educated understanding of the symbiotic link between environmental and social justice, at both the local level and beyond. While post-pastoral depends on a public rather than private apprehension of its own significance, it also involves the recognition of an individual relationship with nature in which there is a mirroring of, or at least a dynamic interplay between, inner and outer worlds (156). Naipaul never abandons this private version, nor should we expect him to. But his book arguably works towards placing the self-serving vision of pastoral as a fantasy of country living – a projection of the individual imagination – with a broader perspective that accepts the inherent value, if changing standards, of communal existence, and that gauges the interconnectedness of land and labour in pursuit of a socially responsible life.

These, on the face of it, are most un-Naipaulian sentiments; still, we would insist that this is the moral the book is gamely trying to impress on us, even if the uplifting rhetoric of its final sequence seems out of kilter with much of what precedes it, and the revealed motive for writing the book, while appropriately belated, still seems strangely out of place. Then again, the book's journey from reclusiveness to reconciliation – in accordance with its dominant de Chirico motif – is not linear but cyclical, and it would be stranger still if the narrator, having paid his last tributes to his family, were not to retreat to his study to 'write fast about Jack and his garden', reverting as much by personal inclination as professional necessity into a recluse again (354). This, too, is close to what Gifford calls the 'dialectical experience' of post-pastoral, which he reads in terms of 'the circle of postmodern mobility' (174). 'The paradox with which the post-pastoral engages', says Gifford, is 'the fact that retreat informs our sense of community' (174); and if, as we have been suggesting, *The Enigma of Arrival* can be taken as a test-case, it seems only logical that the writer's definitive confirmation of the worldliness of his own narrative should coincide with the originary moment of his own retreat.

Other paradoxes are always likely to accompany Caribbean literary invocations of the pastoral. After all, the violence that brought the modern Caribbean into being cannot be expected to be compatible with nostalgic Anglo-European notions of pastoral return (Bongie 1998; Dash 1998). Caribbean ecocriticism must contend with the fact that the Caribbean, as Elizabeth DeLoughrey puts it, is 'one of the most radically altered land-scapes in the world', if also, significantly, 'the space from which our current understandings of environmental conservation emerged' (DeLoughrey 2007a: 64; see also Grove 1995).[8] The Caribbean is a fractured space in which the 'natural' relationship between people and their environment was wrenched apart, not only by the brutalities of the plantation system, but also by the moment of 'Discovery' and the sickening violence it brought in its wake (DeLoughrey 2007a; Glissant 1989). Caribbean ecocriticism is charged with the task of negotiating the profound physical and psycho-logical effects of this double fracture; but it is also charged, at the same time, with looking at the new relationships between nature and culture that have emerged out of it – relationships which, often loosely categorised under the rubric of 'creolisation', involve a complex 'hybridization of diverse cultural and environmental forms' (DeLoughrey 2007a: 64).

These relationships are post-pastoral in the sense that pastoral's idea-lised ('natural') connection to the land is as impossible to uphold in the twin contexts of imperial genocide and colonial plantation slavery as its mystified apprehensions of gender and, especially, race (DeLoughrey 2007a; Glissant 1989). In any case, the Caribbean's traumatic origins make the whole idea of return all but untenable (not that this has pre-vented some Caribbean writers from exploring it, or from attempting an equally impossible recovery of the lost Edenic past). What purpose is to be served by the memory of pre-contact ecologies in a context in which the native landscape was altered beyond repair – transformed for ever – and in which native people were not only indiscriminately slaughtered, but also expunged from the European historical record, as if there had been no Caribbean history at all? Why celebrate nature when it has been systematically taken away from you, or when its beauty has been routinely invoked to mystify, while effectively reproducing, the ideological conditions under which you were originally dispossessed? In contexts such as these, the diasporic nostalgia for origins seems bound, as Derek Walcott has suggested, by the unfulfillable wish for revenge or the self-defeating lapse into remorse (Walcott 1998).

Such rhetoric, however, seriously underestimates Caribbean writers' capacity for an imaginative transformation of history – one which may yet involve some kind of emotional re-attachment to landscape, even if it generally avoids the primordial conflation of native and environment that has traditionally functioned as an additive to imperial/colonial desire (Glissant 1989). In this sense, the twin impulses of postcolonial criticism – what Ashcroft, Griffiths and Tiffin (1989) call its deconstructive and recuperative dimensions – may be usefully harnessed to those of eco-criticism to provide an alternative reading, not just of the *cultural* history of the Caribbean, but of *natural* history itself. As DeLoughrey says:

> Postcolonial ecocriticism helps destabilize the universalist conceit of the Anglo-European human subject by examining the ways in which this anthropocentricity is constituted by a limited conception of the natural universe. One of the field's most important contributions is to foreground the human bias of historical narrative [...] [and one of its] most profound challenges[s] [...] is to provide an alternative rendering of 'natural history' [itself].
>
> (2007a: 63–64)

What might such a natural history look like? It might appeal, as DeLoughrey suggests, to an indigenous (if always already hybridised) environmental ethic that links pre-contact landscapes to an ancestral folk memory, as in the experimental novels of Pauline Melville and Wilson Harris, which provide ways of thinking about history – both 'cultural' and 'natural' – in defiantly non-linear, determinedly syncretistic terms (DeLoughrey 2007a; Lewis 1995). Or it might reinstall, as we have suggested via our reading of Naipaul, a transatlantic pastoralism that overrides obvious geographical and historical (e.g. 'Old' versus 'New World') differences. Such a pastoralism might connect a changing native workforce to similarly changing material circumstances, circumstances under which workers may recover some degree of agency for their actions, as well as some amount of individual and collective proprietorship over their land. To rehabilitate pastoral in a Caribbean context might seem bizarre, but perhaps this is better than hating nature properly; maybe it is the pastoral itself that needs to be hated properly in the dialectical (Adornian) sense that it must be imaginatively inhabited before being intellectually eviscerated – always with the option of being critically restored. There is no such thing of course as a single, readily identifiable version of the Caribbean pastoral; but if there were, it would probably be based, like Gifford's 'post-pastoral', on the idea of land as collective resource, not individual luxury; on the idea of a transnational, not western-globalist, environmental ethic; and on the idea of an 'imagining of survival' (Gifford 1999: 174) already implicit in most forms of pastoral literature – a survival Caribbean peoples, both locally and in the diaspora, are historically well equipped to account for, and from which others among us may well have a lot to learn.

Conclusion

In *London Calling*, his book-length study on V.S. Naipaul, the critic Rob Nixon suggests that 'in composing *The Enigma of Arrival*, Naipaul invents postcolonial pastoral' (Nixon 1992: 161). 'There is decidedly no other British writer of Caribbean or South Asian ancestry,' says Nixon, 'who would have chosen a tucked away Wiltshire perspective from which to reflect on the themes of postcolonial immigration and decay' (161). While this may well be true, the suggestion that Naipaul has invented postcolonial pastoral is inaccurate. As we have seen, pastoral is a mode that appeals to a number of different postcolonial writers, who have turned it to their own uses in a number of different regions of the world. While pastoral is traditionally a mode that tends to emphasise the fixity of place and the security of belonging, its stated certainties are by no means unchallengeable; indeed, it is persistently troubled by anxieties of its own. These anxieties have been well exploited by a number of post-colonial writers, and not only those who are keen to contest complacent pastoral ideologies, but also those who are looking to reconcile experiences of dislocation, dispossession even, with the need to establish an idea of home. The idea of home has always been important for postcolonial writers, particularly those with first-hand experience of displacement, and while it is true that postcolonial criticism has sometimes tended to exaggerate displacement, it might be more accurate to say that differentiated experiences of dislocation have provided the basis for radically revised conceptions of 'belonging' and 'home' (Casteel 2004: 13; see also George 1999). Hence the attempt to refashion the pastoral as a conduit for *both* dwelling *and* displacement in a variety of colonial/postcolonial contexts in which land is often intimately connected with identity and, as Jonathan Bate has suggested, 'home is a house in which one does not live but dwell' (Bate 2000: 274).

In such contexts, entitlement – whether legally claimed or emotionally experienced – is always likely to be challenged, and in much postcolonial writing, these challenges are explored through alternative modalities of belonging, as well as ecological understandings of the relationship between human beings, the environment that surrounds them, and the other creatures with whom they share their world. Entitlement here is not synonymous with the acquisition of, nor with the continued control over, property – indeed, the notion of property, and the ideology of possession it embodies, may be antithetical to 'rooted', as well as 'rootless', understandings of the relationship between people and place (Bate 2000). But however it is conceived of, landed property, which remains the unspoken basis for most articulations of the pastoral, is not so much 'a relation between people and things [as] a relation between people, concerning things' (Buckle 1995: 66; also quoted in Wenzel 2000: 96). It is this relation, and the contested rights it involves, that is of interest to postcolonial writers in their efforts both to understand the spatial dynamics of colonialism and to question the material and symbolic (material as symbolic) entitlements that colonialist attitudes to landed property – attitudes to do with *people* – are always likely to confer.

Postcolonial approaches to the pastoral explicitly or implicitly recognise both its generic and its ideological flexibility. As Terry Gifford suggests, pastoral

> can be a mode of critique of present society, or it can be a dramatic form or forms of unresolved dialogue about the tensions in that society, or it can be a retreat from politics into an apparently aesthetic landscape that is devoid of conflict and tension.
>
> (1999: 11)

For Gifford, it is the very versatility of pastoral that helps to make it interesting, its very adaptability as an ideological tool that guarantees the multiple perspectives that are applied to it, as well as its own malleable form. The evidence suggests that pastoral will continue to be of interest to postcolonial writers, whether they are attacking its reactionary tendencies or are reworking it into more socially and/or environmentally progressive forms. Pastoral's radical potential is often dismissed and its idealisations derided. For committed ecocritics like Greg Garrard, the problem also resides in the different meanings attached to such multivalent terms as 'radical' and 'pastoral':

> We are less sure than Marxists what would *count* as 'radicalism': Advocacy or idealization; pathetic fallacy or naturalism; social ecology or the dream of relinquishment. Thus the radical problem of pastoral: It may cloud our social vision, or open out a human ecological one; it may help in the marginalization of nature into 'pretty ghettoes' [Buell 1995: 4] or engender a genuine counter-hegemonic ideology. If pastoral can be radical, if it has been so, it is not as a finished model, exhortation or ideology, but as a questioning, as itself a question. [...] 'Radical pastoral?' appears as the political, poetical question of be/longing, of the root of human beings on this earth.
>
> (Garrard, in Coupe 2000: 186)

The radicalism of postcolonialism is equally contested, and the possibilities of a postcolonial pastoral will continue to mean very different things to different people (while for others, one suspects, it may end up meaning very little at all). Perhaps the only point of agreement might be the need to assert the political instrumentality of pastoral while retaining its capacity to ask fundamental questions about the nature of human rootedness, the possibility of reconciling place and placelessness, and the need to find or at least imagine a dwelling-place in which human beings can both respond to and creatively refashion their relationship with the earth (Bate 2000: 282). For postcolonial writers and thinkers, at any rate, there can be no pastoral without politics; by definition, the pastoral they countenance is an interrogative as well as an affective mode. It is difficult to imagine pastoral without either the irony or the idealism; one of the self-given tasks of postcolonial literature, and the criticism that responds to it, is to ensure that there is some play of both.

Coda: Staging entitlement

In his 2003 study *If This Is Your Land, Where Are Your Stories?*, Canadian critic Ted Chamberlin makes a powerful case for the reversion to what he calls 'underlying [Aboriginal] title' (Chamberlin 2003: 229), not just as a means of redressing historical injustices, but also of accepting alternative belief-structures that are not necessarily our own. Settler societies like Canada's, he suggests, have grown used to believing in another kind of story, one based on the fiction of exclusive ownership, in which the acquisition of title to land has brought with it the conviction that it is then ours, and we can do with it what we will (228; see also Harris 2002). Indigenous literature and, perhaps above all, indigenous *theatre* can be seen as an enactment of the conflict between these two sets of stories or, as Chamberlin calls them, these two 'ceremonies of belief' (2). It is simultaneously a theatre of loss – land, language, cultural heritage – and one of resistance and reclamation, in which the stage becomes a contested space in which conflicting spatial fantasies and histories are accumulated, and the land is revealed both as speaking subject and as object of discursive management and material control (Gilbert and Tompkins 1996: 156). Thus, while the indigenous performance traditions of First Nations Canadian, Aboriginal Australian, and New Zealand Māori peoples are by no means readily compatible or interchangeable, each involves a 'reconceptualisation of space and place that challenges the history of white settlement' (Gilbert 1998: 53): one which, as in other forms of postcolonial theatre, has profound consequences for the semiotic network of visual representation as a whole (Gilbert 1998: 235; also Balme 1999, Tompkins 2006).

The postcoloniality of indigenous theatre is the product of a linked set of colonial histories in which indigenous peoples were summarily eliminated or expropriated, and in which those who survived were systematically displaced. Justification for dispossession and/or displacement was usually provided on one or more of three possible grounds: the self-accorded rights of 'conquest' or 'discovery'; the perceived inability of Native peoples to use land 'properly'; and the still more skewed perception that the land was 'empty' and could therefore be occupied at will (Harris 2002: xxi). The prosecution of land rights in postcolonised societies is part of the ongoing attempt to counteract a colonial history of dispossession that has had a disastrous impact on indigenous peoples, not just in terms of loss of land but deprivation of cultural connection and political sovereignty as well (Dodds 1998: 188). It is also part of an ongoing struggle over the very meaning of 'indigeneity', in which competing claims to indigenous status are mediated through what Chadwick Allen calls 'the blood/land/memory nexus', establishing the contest over land as one of definitional, not just territorial, control (Allen 2002: 9, 16). In these and other ways, land rights can be considered co-extensive with the history of indigenous theatre. As Helen Gilbert and Joanne Tompkins put it, 'Almost without exception, Aboriginal, Māori, and First Nations Canadian playwrights stage, in some way, the historical displacement of their people as a consequence of imperialism': a part-elegiac, part-defiant performative process that reconfirms the spatial dynamic of settler colonialism itself (Gilbert and Tompkins 1996: 154; see also Carter 1987).

The politicisation of space in indigenous theatre can take many different forms, from the provision of a minimal background that focuses attention on the embattled movements and gestures of the actors to the co-presentation of segregated areas in which the official demarcation of boundaries is deliberately overstepped (Gilbert and Tompkins 1996; Gilbert 1998). For Joanne Tompkins among others, these spatial techniques are 'alternative means of managing the production of space in a spatially unstable nation', and are brought out in various enactments of an 'uncanny landscape' in which the historical anxieties surrounding colonial settlement, and its postcolonial legacies, are performed (Tompkins 2006: 5, 35; see also Gelder and Jacobs 1998). One instance Tompkins cites is the work of the Nyoongah (Western Australian) poet and playwright Jack Davis, whose plays rode the crest of a wave of Australian political theatre in the 1980s, and which now rank among the best-known examples of an indigenous theatre of anti-colonial resistance today. *Kullark* (1984), for instance, is a wide-ranging historical play that powerfully dramatises the Nyoongah people's subjugation to incoming European settlers in the first half of the nineteenth century, and the violence and dispossession that were the almost inevitable result. The play's double time frame also allows Davis to explore the consequences of this fractured history for contemporary generations of Aborigines, who are increasingly insistent on asserting their human and territorial rights. At the same time, plays like *Kullark* show the limitations of rights-based discourses that remain in thrall to a white European legislative system; as one of the main characters, Alec Yorlah, puts it later in the play, after institutional restrictions on his movements have been lifted: 'I seen a lot of blokes die in the war from freedom. Citizenship don't sound much like freedom to me' (Davis 1984: 63). Alec's recidivist son Jamie is left to fight the system, but ironically ends up joining it, making the play's final Black Consciousness anthem seem more than a little out of place (65–66). 'Kullark', the play's title (which means 'home'), rings equally hollow in a context of repeated dislocation in which a 'settlement' is effectively a prison, and 'protection' is synonymous with the denial of freedom and territorial rights. However, the play – in keeping with the remit of resistance theatre – moves beyond the self-conscious moralising of white-oriented protest vehicles which, as Zakes Mda argues in another context, are given to make 'statements of disapproval or disagreement, but [generally] don't go beyond that' (Mda 1998: 257).[9] Mda's arguments are in the Black South African context, a wholly different demographic to Aboriginal Australia. Still, what Mda sees as the distinctive characteristic of resistance theatre – its direct call to the oppressed rather than its mediated appeal to the oppressor – arguably holds good for the majority of Davis's early work. Further points of contact are that resistance is in *symbolic* as well as material terms, and that this symbolism is often *spatial*; as Tompkins demonstrates, *Kullark*'s battle for belonging (not quite the same thing as its battle for entitlement), which is initially organised around conflicting versions of the early history of the Swan Colony, is graphically illustrated in the gradual displacement, if never the fully achieved erasure, of the self-identifying Aboriginal rainbow serpent by the self-authorising British flag (Tompkins 2006: 34–35).

Another of Tompkins' key examples is the non-indigenous Australian Katherine Thomson's 2004 play *Wonderlands* which, though not ostensibly based on any particular Native title claim or outcome, follows in the footsteps of the historic 1996 Wik ruling, which found that underlying Aboriginal title was not extinguished by the Crown's granting of a long-term pastoral lease (Reynolds 2004: ix; see also Dodds 1998). As Tompkins suggests, the stage in *Wonderlands* is a tenuously shared space in which rival claims to rightful occupation are enacted, and the idea of legitimate co-tenancy is explored (Tompkins 2006: 26–27). Set on a rural Queensland homestead, the play operates according to a split time frame in which the past eventually catches up with the present, re-establishing a shared history of continuous interconnection between whites and Aborigines that had been systematically repressed (Thomson 2004: 64). However, while the play ends by making a plea for co-tenancy on the grounds of mixed bloodlines, the most important questions it asks remain necessarily unanswered. Under what cultural and political conditions can entitlement to land be established or extinguished, and under which code of law ought such decisions to be made? Western property law? Traditional Aboriginal law? What constitutes evidence of continuous occupation? Is inheritance biologically or culturally coded? What is the relationship between juridical and ontological claims in a context where rival parties both insist they are of the land, not just on it, and where traditional rights and cultural practices are as insistently re-interpreted as they are inconsistently maintained? (Thomson 2004: 48). These questions remain open in the play, despite its suggestion of a continuum of white–Aboriginal co-existence that re-annuls the legalistic absurdities of *terra nullius* by recasting whites as tenants on Aboriginal ground (Dodds 1998).[10] Mutually constitutive but unevenly represented, the tangled stories of *Wonderlands* go beyond an expedient 'Aboriginalism' that serves white emotional and economic interests, in large part by contesting the so-called 'bastard complex' through which the notion of shared illegitimacy is used to mask continuing inequalities, and through which enduring white anxieties over underlying title are temporarily circumvented by professed respect for indigenous land rights (Hodge and Mishra 1991: 25–26).[11]

A very different kind of play that engages with not entirely dissimilar issues is the Cree (First Nations Canadian) playwright Tomson Highway's characteristically rambunctious 2005 historical melodrama *Ernestine Shuswap Gets Her Trout*. As in his best-known play, *The Rez Sisters* (1988), Highway taps into the counter-historical energies of everyday female experience: a collective agency, seemingly generated as much by spite as solidarity, that is contained within the ranks of his permanently quarrelling all-female cast. Also as in *The Rez Sisters*, *Ernestine Shuswap* involves a ritualistic implementation of the principles of a transcultural 'syncretic theatre' in which indigenous cultural practices and mythologies are transposed onto the modern western stage (Balme 1999: 58). Set in the early twentieth century, the action of the play is organised around the upcoming visit of Canadian Prime Minister Sir Wilfrid Laurier to northern British Columbia: a visit that will provide the opportunity for the local (Thompson River) Native communities to complain – with justification but little hope of legal action – about the loss of their ancestral territories, the abrogation of their traditional hunting, fishing and grazing rights, and the *de facto* 'cancellation' of their languages without their consultation or consent (Highway 2005: 68; see also Harris 2002: 225–28). The play's opening monologues establish underlying title through a series of ritualistic incantations and repeated gestures:

> [Can you see that] river [...] in the distance away over yonder? That winding, greenish-bluish river that's so busy just a-weaving its way through the mountains over yonder, down, down, and down, down, down, and down, right through our hunting grounds, right through our pastures, right through our fields and fields and fields *and* fields of wild saskatoons, right through our houses, through our windows, through our doors, through our children, through our lives, through our dreams, our hearts, our flesh, our veins, our blood.
>
> (16)

Entitlement is soon extended to other ecological actors in the region, taking in all those who occupy the land, whether human or animal, whether animate or not (19–20). Yet this view of Native title – this ancestral 'ceremony of belief' (Chamberlin 2003: 2) – has recently been surpassed by the counter-fiction of Crown title, turning the Thompson River people into trespassers in their own country, as the official deposition (the so-called 'Laurier Memorial') which provides an accompanying aftermath to the play makes plaintively clear (91–92). The play reacts, however, against its own fatalistic impulses, and its last comic image is that of its lead figure, Ernestine Shuswap, defiantly fishing in the now-forbidden river 'till the cows come home' (90). As so often in Highway's plays, comedy and tragedy are balanced on a knife-edge, both presided over by the ubiquitous – if physically absent – figure of the Trickster, the half-laughing half-crying deity of Native North America who is at once motor force and emotive spirit behind most of his theatrical work.[12]

In *Ernestine Shuswap*, history is replayed simultaneously as farce and tragedy, with more than a nod to the 'territorial uncanny' that lies behind more obviously naturalistic plays like *Wonderlands*, and that 'epitomizes the political and emotional effects of battles regarding native title on both sides' (Tompkins 2006: 26). Unlike Thomson, however, Highway seems to be suggesting in this play at least that reparation and/ or reconciliation are not possible; and what exists in their place is a continuing history of resistance in the face of damage that has already, irrevocably, been done. At the same time – as in other Highway plays – resistance tends to be distilled into isolated moments of almost manic cheerfulness in the face of adversity, a resilience that offers few political alternatives, and that has led some of Highway's critics to complain that his predominantly white audiences, while dutifully scandalised, are still left relatively comfortable with the message they hear (Filewod 1992: 23; also quoted in Balme 1999: 59).

A far less comfortable experience, in this respect, comes in the community-centred plays of the Anglo-Canadian director-activist David Diamond, in which the audience is invited to exchange roles with the actors, and the pain of oppression is experienced collectively on stage. Diamond's work is particularly interesting for this book in so far as it deploys a self-consciously ecological approach to theatre. Drawing freely on the systems theory of physicist Fritjof Capra, Diamond's theatrical practice not only looks at how a 'theatre company [might] function in the ecology of many interconnected communities' (Diamond 2007: 51), but also at how theatre itself might model communities as 'living, conscious organisms', providing the 'symbolic, primal language' through which these communities' different stories can be told (23). 'Forum Theatre', as Diamond calls it after the Brazilian director Augusto Boal, provides a stage for the communal working-through of urgent social problems, with the further aim of re-integrating and re-invigorating the community itself. Implicit in this conception of the 'organic community' is the view that 'living communities have fallen into a stupor, hypnotized by a steady diet of manufactured culture' (20). The task of theatre in this context is to restore the community to itself by creating the conditions under which people voluntarily come together to engage in a theatrical dialogue about relevant social issues, proceeding from an exchange of individual stories to an interactive public event (59).

This dialogue is intended to be empowering for the community, but not necessarily to resolve its problems. A typical procedure is for workshop participants to create a short play, performed all the way through, then re-run with audience members stepping in to replace certain actors, much in the spirit of Boal's 'Theatre of the Oppressed'. However, unlike in Boal, there is no clear dividing line between the oppressed and their oppressors. Rather, it is assumed that 'the binary poles of oppressor and oppressed are part of the same large organism living in some kind of dysfunction'; the play is intended to reveal the destructive behavourial patterns that have created this dysfunction, with a view to changing these behaviours for the greater good of the community itself (Diamond 2007: 38–39). Diamond's theatrical practice is loosely based on what might be described as eco-socialist principles: in imitating the model of ecological inter-connectedness towards which it aspires and which it explicitly advocates, it also makes clear that social and environmental issues are inextricably enmeshed (Harvey 1997; Pepper 1993). This is eco-populism, no doubt, rather than scientifically accurate ecologism, operating on the possibly naïve assumption that environmental values are always compatible with indigenous rights (Perrett 1998).[13] Diamond's theatrical philosophy is self-confessedly inconsistent, in any case, if consistently practice-based; it also takes in very different kinds of theatre, as in probably his best-known production *No'Xya' (Our Footprints)* (1987), which, while certainly a piece of community-oriented theatre, runs more along the politically predetermined lines of agitprop (Diamond 2007: 50).

Set in a similar area of northern British Columbia to *Ernestine Shuswap*, *No'Xya'* first emerged from Diamond's dialogues with Gitxsan and Wet'suwet'en Heriditary Chiefs; these then turned into a four-year project culminating in the play, which is self-consciously designed as an agitprop vehicle in support of Gitxsan and Wet'suwet'en self-government, and articulating their perspectives on their relationship to land (51, 210). While the play enjoyed successful runs in New Zealand (as part of an exchange between the Gitxsan and Wet'suwet'en and the Māori) as well as in Canada, its main claim to fame was the instrumental role it played in pushing for Native title in the region, a sustained campaign that eventually resulted in the historic 1998 claim that granted the Gitxsan and Wet'suwet'en jurisdiction over their own ancestral lands (210). However, *No'Xya'* is an accomplished play in its own right: one which, employing techniques derived from both the theatre of resistance and syncretic ritual theatre, paints a broad historical canvas using a pared-down set and an alternating white/Native cast. The play, spanning the period between the early and late twentieth centuries, focuses on early clashes between (proprietorial) settler and (holistic) indigenous socio-environmental perspectives, and on the later escalation of conflict arising from profit-driven developmental policies on expropriated Crown land. While it might initially appear to create an unbridgeable gulf between competing white-settler and indigenous agendas, the play increasingly complicates such readily racialised distinctions, and in the end the mixed cast comes together (to some extent as in Thomson's *Wonderlands*) to agitate for the right to regional self-government and an unpolluted earth.

While *No' Xya'* is designed to carry a clear message, its collectivist spirit looks forward to later Forum Theatre vehicles in which the theatrical community is more conspicuously integrated, and which challenge the artificial dividing line between oppressors and oppressed (Diamond 2007: 24). As Diamond argues in his more recent book *Theatre for Living*, such challenges represent the point at which Forum Theatre (or his own particular version of it) begins to separate itself from Theatre of the Oppressed, where the distinction between oppressor and oppressed is fundamental, and in which audience members can only replace the latter category of actors, with the immediate goal of breaking the cycle of oppression and the wider aim of investigating its root cause (Diamond 2007; Boal 1988). This is also the point at which Diamond begins to develop an ecological model of theatre that focuses on systems break-down rather than oppositional conflict, and that is aimed at showing the complexity of struggle rather than the moral superiority of its victims – an occupational hazard of Theatre of the Oppressed.

A good example of this is the unexpected moment in Diamond's refugee play *¿Sanctuary?* (1989), when, in a re-run of the original action, a woman from the audience asks to replace the leader of a death squad that has been terrorising Guatemalan political 'subversives', and whose victims are the main subjects of the play. As Diamond explains in *Theatre for Living*, this moment presented him with a dilemma. The woman's intervention was clearly intended to humanise an oppressor, although it did not condone his actions. As Diamond says, reflecting back on this transformational moment:

> For me, it threw into question, for the first time, whether or not it was appropriate to be creating characters who were so clearly oppressor or oppressed. *¿Sanctuary?* was a very successful and popular project. But were its characters too one-dimensional? In retrospect, the answer to this question is yes. The characters were mostly either the 'good oppressed' or the 'bad oppressor'. By making such clearly defined and unrealistic distinctions, we were making the situation too simple

and therefore, ironically, harder than it needed to be to dig into the root causes of the problems we were presenting on stage. As a result, we were creating theatre that, as powerful as it was, did not accessibly represent the complexities of life; something I believe all good theatre should do.

(2007: 67)

Diamond's subsequent experiments with Forum Theatre have tried to reflect this complexity by creating the conditions under which both actors and audience are made to feel part of a single, organic community, the dysfunctional character of which it is incumbent on all of them to address. This dysfunction is the cause of rifts within the overarching social system: rifts revealed in the mistreatment of those the system marginalises and exploits. Hence Diamond's continuing interest in issues that tend to exacerbate social fragmentation and division: the controversies surrounding Native land claims, for instance, or the prejudicial treatment of asylum seekers and refugees. *¿Sanctuary?* belongs, in this last sense, to a mounting wave of Canadian refugee theatre, much of it performed by refugees themselves, and usually designed to highlight the social problems faced by a growing category of people that mainstream society tends to ignore or, in more extreme cases, to vilify and reject.

By definition, refugee theatre produces a very different kind of spatial dynamic from indigenous theatre. As Joanne Tompkins explains in the Australian context, where compelling evidence exists that asylum seekers are subject to human-rights violations in their home *and* their (intended) host countries, refugee theatre confronts the extreme difficulty of claiming space when lived experience is fundamentally ungrounded and where, in contradistinction to indigenous theatre, there is no land to be occupied at all (Tompkins 2006: 115; see also Gilbert and Lo 2007, Manne 2004).[14] Refugee theatre thus tends to focus on the experience of confinement, using the carceral imagery of the stage to examine 'the non-space in which asylum seekers are contained' (Tompkins 2006: 116). Drawing on a range of contemporary Australian examples – including *Citizen X* (2002), a powerful agitprop play that addresses the aftermath of the notorious *Tampa* crisis – Tompkins shows how refugee theatre uses memories of other places to counteract the overwhelming experience of placelessness, and how it asserts entitlement by the mere fact of physical presence on stage (116–17). In some cases, similar techniques are used to those of Forum and other types of community-oriented theatre, with audience members being coaxed, or coerced, into sharing the space of detention with the actors, and with the theatre performance being supplemented by the activities of anti-detention lobbying groups (122, 125). Like indigenous drama, refugee plays make a clear connection between the denial of freedom – especially freedom of movement – and the denial of humanity; in both forms of theatre, place and identity are constitutively enmeshed. Thus, while the claims of indigenous and refugee theatre clearly exist on a different historical plane, they are motivated by the same conviction that the right to live in a particular place is an *ontological* necessity; and that the most basic entitlement of all is the right to live one's life.

The colonial history of settlement was often little more than an alibi, either for the exclusion of people considered to be extraneous – sometimes actively detrimental – to the needs of the emergent nation, or for the displacement of people perceived to be unsuited – sometimes actively opposed – to the task of extracting maximum profits from the land (Harris 2002; Trigger and Griffiths 2004). Recent evidence suggests that these openly divisive perceptions and practices continue, to differing degrees in differing countries, in the postcolonial (ex-settler) societies of the present day. Settler entitlement, in this context, can be seen to amount to a continuing record of justified dispossession couched in the language of historical necessity – or its modern neoliberal equivalent, economic rationalism – and sustained by the self-perpetuating victim rhetoric of a 'paranoid nationalism' in which majority culture is seen, and depends on being seen, to be under permanent threat (Hage 2003).

The effects of 'paranoid nationalism' are currently more evident in Australia than in either Canada or New Zealand, although all three countries are still obviously struggling to overcome the conceptual legacies of their colonial past. Meanwhile, the increasing impact of globalisation has brought with it a heightened awareness of social and environmental problems that apparently require new conceptions of entitlement and belonging; new modes of cooperation and affiliation that confront, without necessarily resolving, the formidable difficulties that accompany the awareness of living among unshared values in a shared space. The theatre, perhaps more than any other medium, can bring these dilemmas to life, illustrating the 'spatial instabilities' (Tompkins 2006: 5) that underpin them. At the same time, theatre has an unrivalled capacity to demonstrate 'the recuperative power of spatial histories' (Gilbert and Tompkins 1996: 155), histories that are continually reworked even as they are repeatedly performed. Postcolonial 'remapping[s] of stage space' (Gilbert and Tompkins 1996: 154) may not necessarily contribute to a more inclusive sense of belonging, but their alternative stagings of entitlement are a significant part of the necessarily conflicted process by which postcolonised societies may be imaginatively transformed.

Notes

1 For an interesting, fairly recent work by an Aboriginal writer that takes account of this shift, see Alexis Wright's prize-winning novel *Carpentaria* (2006), which is discussed in detail in the Epilogue to the 'Development' chapter. The novel practises what might be described as a form of anti-corporate indigenous ecologism (for a slightly different form of this, see Patricia Grace's *Potiki*, discussed in section 1). Drawing on a number of readily identifiable anti- and counter-pastoral motifs, *Carpentaria* puts these into the service of its anti-colonial attack on indiscriminate resource extraction (commercial mining operations) in the Australian North – a corporate perversion of georgic ideals of working the land for profit – and its equally mythologised insistence on the need for indigenous self-regeneration and resistance. For a useful essay that brings out these and other issues in the novel, see Ferrier 2008.

2 Spectrality is a common feature of white Australian (and other 'settler colonial') representations of Aboriginal people, who are frequently co-opted for the task of cultural haunting (Huggan 2007b). Probably the key text here in an Australian context is Gelder and Jacobs 1998, but see also Hodge and Mishra 1991 and Nolan 1998. In a North American context, see Sugars 2004 (for Canada) and Cheah 2004 (for the USA).

3 Pastoral is arguably ill-equipped for reconciliation projects given its historical reliance on uneven power relations – the same relations it systematically mystifies (see section 1). However, it might also be argued in the Australian context that reconciliation is *itself* a mystifying process that overlooks systemic discrimination against Aboriginal people that continues to the present day. On some of the contradictions embedded within (white) reconciliation discourses in contemporary Australia, at least some of which shelter under the misleadingly neutral label 'multiculturalism', see Povinelli 2002.

4 For relatively recent information on the 'land question' in South Africa, see Hall and Ntsebeza 2007, who concede that while '[t]en years of democracy in South Africa have seen some impressive achievements in addressing the debilitating legacy of apartheid, [the pace of land reform] has been painfully slow' (2–3). Land reform remains a speculative goal as much as a recorded actuality in post-apartheid South Africa, although the ANC government has pledged its commitment to the state-led redistribution of land. Meanwhile, however, problems persist both with the aggressive (white) tenure of farmland and the exploitative treatment of (black) farm-workers, with widespread cases continuing to be cited of evictions and other abuses of rights (see Wegerif, Russell and Grundling 2005).

5 The classic essay here is Gayatri Chakravorty Spivak's much-quoted essay 'Can the Subaltern Speak?' which argues *inter alia* that silencing is an operation central – indeed, crucial – to the process of colonial subject formation, more specifically the formation of the colonial subaltern (on the figure of the subaltern, see also section 1, Note 5). Silencing is not necessarily the literal withholding of speech – although it certainly can be – but that particular form of ideological overdetermination through which a subject position, e.g. that of the 'Third World woman', is symbolically pre-assigned for the purposes of material control. This mechanism works for *any* subject, human or non-human: see, for example, Part II of this book for a discussion of the silencing of the *animal* subject.

6 For more on the post-Biblical motif of animal sacrifice, see Scholtmeijer 1993 and, especially, Wolfe 1998, who argues (following Derrida) that the sacrificing of the animal 'other' is the very basis for self-understandings of the human; for postcolonial applications of this motif, see also Tiffin 2001 and the Introduction to this book.

7 The sublime has discernible links with imperial ideology; see, for example, the work of Laura Doyle, who argues that '[t]heories of the sublime negotiate the turn in Western aesthetics from classicism to nativism to racialism', legitimating the imperial doctrine of racial uplift by converting the sublime 'savage figure' into 'the imperial, metaphysical, civilized European, fit to conquer and uplift the savages of other lands' (16). On the instrumentality of the sublime for imperialism, see also Suleri 1992.

8 As Grove argues, 'it has simply been assumed that European and colonial attempts to respond to tropical environmental change derived exclusively from metropolitan and northern models and attitudes [whereas the] converse is true. The available evidence shows that the seeds of modern conservationism developed as an integral part of the European encounter with the tropics and with local classifications and interpretations of the natural world and its symbolism' (3). However, as critics of his work like Ruth Blair (2007) have pointed out, Grove is less convincing in offering *indigenous* alternatives to metropolitan models, however modified or transplanted, and there is thus some substance to the claim – sometimes also made of Alfred Crosby, with whose work Grove's stands in critical dialogue – of residual Eurocentrism in their work.

9 Mda's distinction, made in the context of the emergence of the Black Consciousness movement in 1970s' South Africa, is that Protest Theatre (which he capitalises) was primarily a 'theatre of complaint [...] self-pity [and] mourning [that] did not offer any solution beyond a depiction of the sad situation in which the oppressed found themselves', whereas Resistance Theatre took up the cudgels on behalf of oppressed people, addressing them directly and encouraging them to mobilise against their oppression (Mda 1998: 257). The distinction is as much ideological as aesthetic, seeing Resistance Theatre as a form of agitprop for the black masses, although Mda also acknowledges its success in building solidarities with white audiences abroad. Davis' theatre is not agitprop, although it probably owes more to Resistance than Protest Theatre; the important point to make here is that Aboriginal plays, like their Black South African counterparts, take a number of different forms, not all of which can be corralled by (white?) academic labels, but at least some of which – Davis' included – complicate over-easy distinctions between mainstream and marginal, oppressor and oppressed.

10 *Terra nullius* might best be described as the legal fiction by which early white settlers in Australia – and a good number of their descendants – justified their claims to occupation by citing their belief that British settlement had effectively extinguished indigenous entitlement to land. Since the historic Mabo ruling of 1992, the pseudo-doctrinal status of *terra nullius* has been overturned, opening the door to other land claims and providing an unparalleled if, as yet, inconsistently exercised opportunity to right the wrongs previously done to Aboriginal people in Australia (for more on Mabo and its aftermath, see Attwood 1996).

11 As Hodge and Mishra see it, the 'bastard complex' supports a structure of national illegitimacy which confirms that colonial racism is 'unfinished business'

148   *Entitlement*

(Hage 2000) and that Aboriginal people, by being assimilated in this way, are being robbed of their custodial rights. For more on the 'bastard complex', see Hodge and Mishra 1991, esp. 23–24; see also Huggan 2007a: 161–80.

12 For more on the Trickster, see Radin 1956, Ryan 1999 and, above all, Hyde 1998.

13 The conflation of indigenous and environmental issues is often associated with the figure of the 'Ecological Indian', described by the American historian Shepard Krech in terms of a transhistorical set of cultural stereotypes that promotes 'the dominant image of the Indian in nature who understands the systemic consequences of his actions, feels deep sympathy with all living forms, and takes steps to conserve so that earth's harmonies are never imbalanced and resources never in doubt' (Krech 2000: 21). For further discussions of the 'Ecological Indian', see Garrard 2004, esp. 120–27, and Goldie 1989.

14 Gilbert and Lo's Australian-based work is particularly useful in showing how refugee and asylum-seeker theatre, by representing 'refugee stories in the flesh', has been singularly effective in producing what they call an 'edifying shame' about the nation's continuing failure to 'include some of the world's most vulnerable people in its humanitarian embrace' (Gilbert and Lo 2007: 206). However, they also point out the range of different representations, not all of which produce the desired effect of solidarity, and at least some of which flirt with exoticism (205–6). See Gilbert and Lo Chapter 7 for an excellent overview of recent refugee/asylum-seeker theatre and performance in Australia.

Part II
Zoocriticism and the postcolonial

Introduction

Throughout western intellectual history, civilisation has consistently been constructed by or against the wild, savage and animalistic, and has consequently been haunted or 'dogged' by it. The wild man of the seventeenth and eighteenth centuries lurked at the dangerously liminal fringe of a consolidating European Enlightenment civilisation; and if, during the eighteenth and in the early nineteenth centuries, slavery, and its accelerating racism, both necessitated and enabled Europeans to exile the animalistic to Africa and the New World, this was to return at the end of the nineteenth as the terror of a primordial Heart of Darkness: civilisation, it was feared, might be no more than a veneer over a still savage European 'inner man'. Theories of European degeneration in both metropolis and colony, and the capacity of European visitors and settlers to 'go native' in the tropics, seemed to bring such reversions home; but it was also in the second half of the nineteenth century that the impending disappearance of the wild – in the form of wilderness – became imaginable through the American experience, leading to the 1864 establishment of Yosemite Valley as the world's first national park.

While the Enlightenment trajectory of humanist essentialism demanded the repression of the animal and animalistic in all its latent and recrudescent forms, it is not until our own century, in the urgent contexts of eco-catastrophe and the extinction of many non-human species, that a radical re-drawing of this foundational relationship has occurred. Contemporary humanity, having materially destroyed vast areas of wilderness – and many other animals – is now routinely configured as spiritually hollow, as lacking the essence of the human through the repression, withdrawal, destruction or absence, rather than latent threat, of the 'inner wild'. This repression is expressed, in both literal and spiritually refractive terms, as a result of the all too successful extermination of that earlier Heart of Darkness; and so it is that what had initially been banished by the Enlightenment in order to constitute human civility – the animal and animalistic – is now paradoxically being returned as its essence, its inner core.[1]

In such current reconfigurations of both outer and inner relations, postcolonialism is well positioned to offer insight. Postcolonialism's major theoretical concerns: otherness, racism and miscegenation, language, translation, the trope of cannibalism, voice and the problems of speaking of and for others – to name just a few – offer immediate entry points for a re-theorising of the place of animals in relation to human societies. But dominant European discourses have expressed that dominance by constructing others – both people and animals – as animal, both philosophically and representationally. The history of western racism and its imbrication with discourses of speciesism, the use of animals as a basis for human social division, and, above all perhaps, the metaphorisation and deployment of 'animal' as a derogatory term in genocidal and marginalising discourses – all of these make it difficult even to discuss animals without generating a profound unease, even a rancorous antagonism, in many postcolonial contexts today.

Following on from this, we want initially to consider four examples of the ways in which serious consideration of the status of animal seems to be fundamentally compromised by the human, often western, deployment of animals and the animalistic to destroy or marginalise other human societies. First, human individuals and cultures at various times have been and are treated 'like animals' by dominant groups, and both human genocide and human slavery have been, and in some cases continue to be, predicated on the categorisation of other peoples *as* animals. In condemning human genocide and slavery, we are thus almost inescapably colluding – albeit obliquely or implicitly – in the idea that it is acceptable to treat animals cruelly, but not to treat people *as if they were animals.* And in so doing we are also colluding in the fiction that the species boundary[2] is a fixed one. This fiction of irreducibility is reproduced through the language we use in spite of our knowledge that some peoples considered 'human' by some have been dubbed 'animal' by others; and in spite of our awareness that the species boundary is not fixed at all, but always temporally and politically contingent, continually constructed and policed by the processes of representation itself.

Animal categorisations and the use of derogatory animal metaphors have been and are characteristic of human languages, often in association with racism and sexism: 'you stupid cow'; politicians with their 'snouts in the trough'; 'male chauvinist pig'. The history of human oppression of other humans is replete with instances of animal metaphors and animal categorisations frequently deployed to justify exploitation and objectification, slaughter and enslavement. It is thus not surprising that human individuals and societies reject animal similitudes and analogies and insist instead on a separate subjectivity. To offer a particularly pertinent example: any direct or metaphorical connection between the treatment of Africans as slaves and the treatment of animals today is a politically dangerous one to argue, whatever the obvious analogies. In her 1988 book *The Dreaded Comparison: Human and Animal Slavery* Marjorie Spiegel confronts this difficult issue. That Spiegel was well aware of the minefield she was entering is evident in the title (*The Dreaded Comparison*), as well as in the inclusion of a preface by Alice Walker, without whose endorsement Spiegel's comparison, by the usual terms of the racism/ speciesism nexus, would probably have been dismissed as outrageous. But as Walker writes:

> Marjorie Spiegel tellingly illustrates the similarities between the enslavement of black people (and by implication, other enslaved peoples) and the enslavement of animals, past and present. It is a comparison that, even for those of us who recognise its validity, is a difficult one to face. Especially if we are descendants of slaves. Or of slave owners. Or of both. Especially so if we are responsible in some way for the present treatment of animals – participating in the profits from animal research (medicine, lipstick, lotions) or animal raising (food, body parts). In short, if we are complicit in their enslavement and destruction, which is to say, if we are, at this juncture in history, master.
>
> (Spiegel 1988: 9)

Spiegel's comparison is hardly new, but her book when it first appeared in the 1980s entered a world much more conscious of the material consequences of representation and of the multiple uses made of the species boundary in racial genocide and racial vilification – uses that had created an even greater scepticism towards the comparison than before.

A second problem arises when, as in so many contemporary instances, humans are pitted against animals in a competition over decreasing resources. Peoples forced off their land to provide game parks for foreign tourists (or sometimes more insidiously included in 'native' displays as part of the local flora and fauna) understandably resent not just the implicit 'animal' comparisons, but also the physical presence of animals themselves. They are also likely to be particularly unsympathetic to western conservationist attempts at protecting endangered species from destruction, particularly so where conservation initiatives are in conflict with traditional indigenous hunting practices. But western exploitation, both past and present, has resulted in the murder, displacement and impoverishment of people, animals *and* their environments; and it has also generated apparently 'either/or' situations in contexts of land and resource scarcity or degradation. Emel and Wolch cite as one contemporary example the establishment of a reserve in Sulawesi, 'which entailed the eviction of some seven hundred families from the area, many of whom were indigenous Mongondow who had (already) been forced into the highlands because of pressure from the resettlement and migration of other Indonesians' (10).

The third category of difficulty inherent in any attempt to interrogate the species boundary in postcolonial contexts concerns the ways in which the treatment of animals that have special status in one human society is used to vilify, incriminate or marginalise other human groups – for example, immigrants in western societies – that regard those animals differently. Elder, Wolch and Emel (1998) cite the state-wide furore and anti-immigrant sentiment evoked in California by the beating to death of a puppy by a Vietnamese man whose wife was very ill, and who believed he could restore her health in this manner. Cruel though this custom is, such 'animal-linked racialisation' (Elder, Wolch and Emel's phrase: 73–74) works to sustain power relations between dominant groups and to subordinate immigrants, since, as the authors put it, 'violence done to animals and pain inflicted on them are almost inevitably interpreted in culturally and place-specific ways' (74). Such racialisations are both inappropriate and hypo-critical in a society with abattoirs, scientific experiment, and commercial exploitation, and it is consequently 'both difficult and inappropriate to characterise one type of harm or death as more painful or more humane than another' (73–74). But as the authors also note, 'this does not imply that animal suffering, agony and death are mere social constructs; *they are only too real*' (74; emphasis theirs). Elder, Wolch and Emel's critique of such 'animal-linked racialisations' is thus directed at 'a profound rethinking of *all* "savage practices" toward animals', as well as towards all those who are 'othered' under the sign of the animal (74).

All of the previous examples explicitly or implicitly invoke questions of priority. Crudely put, a fourth objection contained in such instances is this: why worry about animals when children are starving, or when other people are still being killed, raped and abused? The answer to this goes back to the point with which our argument began: that while there is still the 'ethical acceptability' (Wolfe 1998: 39) of the killing of non-human others – that is, anyone represented or designated as non-human – such abuses will continue, irrespective of what is conceived as the species boundary at any given time. Nor are these 'either/or' matters. As African women writers in the 1970s reminded their male colleagues, some of whom wanted to prioritise anti-colonial nationalism over anti-patriarchal feminism, there is no political purchase in such issues being addressed by a 'first-things-first' approach. They must proceed together.[3]

Let us now turn to the question of representation, since it is the *representation* of animals, rather than the animals themselves, which has historically resonated as racism and which – along with consumer capitalism – continues to determine and sustain the species boundary to the present day. This boundary is shifting and contingent, but most of us are still given to act as if it were obdurate, continually re-drawing the line between humans and simian primates or, in an opposite move, including domestic animals with ourselves as farm animals (Fiddes 1992; Fudge 2008). And because, as Steve Baker (2001) argues, 'our' animals are represented as domestic or wild, good or bad, savage or tame, brave or cowardly, there are further orders of classification within the primary category 'animal' that subtend or even violate the first. It is tempting to conclude that the collective term 'animal' is absurd, incorporating as it does anything not recognised as human, from orang-utans and elephants to grasshoppers and bacterial forms.

Our representation of animals, especially in the present, is characterised by blatant and unresolved contradiction (Baker 2001). Baker clinches his point by considering what he calls the 'glaringly contradictory' figurations of animals and the animalistic in adjacent articles in the popular press (167). He discusses the ironic placement of two such items: 'Sex Beast Caged' and 'Shake on It, Old Friend'. The first item concerns 'the return to jail of a man who had been "freed to prey on little girls"', while the second is about '"Tripper the Wonder Dog" who had recently saved the life of his "master"' (167). In accordance with the 'conventions of the popular press, the dog's praiseworthy actions are automatically humanised (and its image correspondingly anthropomorphised) while the sex offender can only be comprehended as beastly' (167).

Such representational anomalies are indicative of our attempts to reconcile, and thereby come to terms with, the contradictory attitudes to animals that most human societies harbour. For example, in the contemporary western world a fundamental disjunction often occurs between our eating habits and our objections to cruelty to animals.[4] Butcher shop windows decorated with printed borders of lambs dancing across a green meadow, a display of chops behind, or cheerful chickens beckoning customers into fast food outlets are images that help to naturalise the incarcerations of industrialised agribusiness and the pandemic slaughter of animals, even though we scrupulously avoid applying such incriminating terms. While torture, killing and eating are the actual processes involved, we routinely dissociate slaughter involving animals from that involving humans, and our eating of animal flesh from human flesh, confirming such dissociations in the everyday language we employ.

Representation has also proved crucial in the destruction of animal species, and is central to the contemporary preservation of others. As the fate of the now extinct 'Tasmanian Tiger' demonstrates, this small and relatively harmless carnivorous marsupial's designation, particularly in the popular press, as a 'wolf' or 'tiger' only helped to hasten its extinction (Paddle 2000; Freeman 2005). The logo of a 1999 Tasmanian exhibition[5] makes the point by depicting, against the background of the rising moon, a huge upstanding and howling wolf-like shadow for a creature represented in the foreground as small and frail with a pathetically hangdog head. This image prefigures the 'tiger's' fate at the hands of humans; its representation as a dangerous carnivore effectively sealed its fate.

While cruelty, death or extinction are not the necessary results of the human representation of animals – many such representations are sympathetic or benign – it is difficult for animals to escape anthropocentrism because they exist in modern cultures much more in representation than in 'the real' (Baker 2000). Conservation legislation, and/or the treatment of particular species, often depend on public response to representation rather than to the animals themselves or their environments since, for most urban-based voters, there has been little or no experience of the 'real thing'. Moreover, our training in 'reading' animals, from childhood on, tends to ensure that we interpret texts of all kinds about animals anthropocentrically, trapping them in distinct representational categories, e.g. animal-specific literary genres. Above all, most animals – though some more obviously than others – exist for modern-day populations as primarily symbolic: they are given an exclusively human significance, a 'whole repertoire of metaphoric associations' (Mitchell 1998: 67), the primary and often only referential context and field of purchase of which is 'man'.

Notes

1 Sections of this introduction have already appeared (in slightly different form) as 'Unjust Relations: Post-Colonialism and the Species Boundary' in Greg Ratcliffe and Gerry Turcotte (eds) (2001) *Compr(om)ising Post/Colonialism(s): Challenging Narratives and Practices*, Sydney: Dangaroo, 30–41.
2 The term 'species boundary' refers to the *discursive construction* of a strict dividing line between 'human' and 'animal' in terms of the possession (or lack thereof) of traits such as speech, consciousness, self-consciousness, tool use and so on. It is not being used in the strictly scientific sense (still arguably discursive) of Darwinian species differentiation based on the ability of individuals within a particular group to produce fertile offspring.
3 For an account of and comments on this debate see Kirsten Holst-Petersen, 'First Things First: Problems of a Feminist Approach to African Literature', 1984.
4 Eating and eating habits are central to critical understandings of the postcolonial politics of exploitative incorporation (see section 2 to follow). Indeed, food in

general has long been a staple of postcolonial criticism, which has focused with what some might see to be an unhealthy appetite on the cultural politics of eating, the contemporary and historical use of culinary metaphors, and the critical analysis of the multiple connections between cuisine and individual/ collective identity in which food frequently operates as a signifier for ethnicity in multicultural contexts characterised by the symbolic power of consumption in a framework of national containment and control (Gunew 2000; Mannur 2009). Mintz's classic 1986 study on sugar is a relatively early example of the formative role of food in the development of mercantilist colonialism, while there is more recent work on postcolonial 'food sovereignty' (Mount and O'Brien 2013) and, above all, food security, which has rightly been seen as one of the most urgent problems of our times (Deepak 2013). Current considerations of food security belong to what Barkawi and Laffey (2006) call the 'postcolonial moment in security studies'; they are also part of a wider debate on the pros and cons of sustainable development in which 'food aid' is increasingly recognised, at worst, as representing a new and virulent form of biocolonialism and, at best, as playing an ambivalent humanitarian role (Clay and Stokke 2000; see also Shiva 1999, 2007).

Postcolonial approaches to food tend, by and large, to be sceptical towards the view that food operates as a source of 'affective nourishment' (Mannur 2009: 224), acknowledging its power as a cultural signifier without necessarily assuming that it has the capacity to effect material change. And even when changes *are* seemingly effected through the agency of food, these are often individually or collectively destructive – eating is frequently *pathological* in postcolonial literature and criticism, which is given to figure colonialism as a loose amalgamation of literal/metaphorical eating disorders in nervous times. A paradigmatic example is Tsitsi Dangarembga's 1988 novel *Nervous Conditions*, which features a character, the rebellious Rhodesian teenager Nyasha, whose life-threatening anorexic condition becomes symptomatic for a colonial society in transition struggling to 'reconcile [the] competing and conflicted narratives' ranged against it, which are as much effects of internal patriarchal dynamics as they are of external colonial power (Bahri 1994: n.p.). Food, throughout the novel, is both a symbol of wealth and power and an instrument of social control. To *feast*, in such a hierarchical context, is to pay homage to the (male) provider; while to *fast* is ostensibly to protest against that social dispensation, but also paradoxically to absorb imported ideas about what the beautiful (female) body should look like, for Nyasha's conscious decision not to take in food seems to be driven at the unconscious level by the desire to imitate western cultural and aesthetic models, just as her similar-aged relative Tambu struggles to assert autonomy against the impress of continuing colonial power (Bahri 1994: n.p.; see also Wolf 1991).

A similar dialectic is set up in Anita Desai's 1999 novel *Fasting, Feasting*, which juxtaposes the stories of a stay-at-home Indian protagonist, Uma, and her pampered younger brother Arun, who is dispatched to the US to stay with the Patton family, thereby furthering his education in a consumerist 'land of plenty' the diversity of whose opportunities is schematically contrasted with the lack of her own (Poon 2006: 34–35). As 'land of plenty' implies, the novel is a veritable cornucopia of metaphors of consumption in which food and eating become the primary symbolic means by which its Indian and American characters measure themselves and their personal relations against a gendered semi-colonial background of uneven social power. As in *Nervous Conditions*, 'feasting' and 'fasting' are similarly unacceptable alternatives; as fringe forms of eating disorder, they reveal the hollowness of the socially stratified rituals that support them, functioning as mechanisms of unfulfilled (and unfulfillable) desire. As Angelia Poon observes, the Pattons' bulimic daughter Melanie brings these two hypertrophied rhythms together, representing both in the overdetermined figure of the damaged female body caught up in a vicious cycle of 'gorging and purging' that can only be broken by an equally violent external force (2006: 45). This problem of overdetermination remains unresolved; thus, like Nyasha in *Nervous Conditions*, Melanie is turned into an unwanted carrier of society's ills, with food and the rituals surrounding it becoming the primary conduit for uneven processes of social negotiation and exchange that merely reinforce what she seemingly wants to rebel against – the mutually informing circuits of parental authority and institutional power.

5 'The Tasmanian Tiger: The Mystery of the Thylacine.' The image for the exhibition was Patrick Hall's. For more on the connections between representation – both written and pictorial – and extinction, see Paddle 2000 and Freeman 2005. (A later debate between Freeman and Paddle can be found in *Australian Zoologist*, 34.4: 459–70 and 271–75.)

1 Ivory and elephants

Ivory

In the post-1492 European acquisition of colonial territories for strategic bases, raw materials and markets, Belgium was not a direct competitor with the Dutch or the French, the Spanish or the English. Nevertheless, in the late nineteenth-century Scramble for Africa, King Leopold II acquired vast areas of the Congo, a territory rich in minerals and ivory.[1] In contrast to England, Spain and France, Belgium had made little investment in colonial settlement. Instead, Leopold's interest in the Congo was purely one of asset stripping. The legacies of what was widely critiqued at the time as piracy are evident today as the still rich resources of the region are fought over by international speculators, corrupt post-independence governments, and Congolese and neighbouring militias. Even Leopold's use of forced African labour is replicated in the current 'mining wars' over the extraction of gold and tantalite,[2] the latter an essential component in the manufacture of computers and mobile phones.

While other imperial powers, to a greater or lesser degree, rationalised their asset stripping as the duty of saving souls or as a civilising mission, Leopold's rapacious and brutal raiding of the Congo was openly condemned by non-Belgian writers and politicians. Two of his most famous critics were Mark Twain in his savage satire *King Leopold's Soliloquy* (1905), and Joseph Conrad in *Heart of Darkness* (1901). Unlike *Soliloquy*, however, *Heart of Darkness* initiated a colonial trajectory of its own which ultimately had less to do with Belgium's colonies than with Britain's, and with the motherland itself.

Heart of Darkness is unequivocally a critique of Belgian colonialism and, by extension, European[3] colonialism, something often forgotten since the Nigerian writer Chinua Achebe's stinging attack on Conrad's racism in his 1977 essay 'An Image of Africa', and his more oblique literary response to Conrad in his 1958 novel *Things Fall Apart*. Throughout

Heart of Darkness, the Belgian 'pilgrims' (as Conrad's narrator Marlow calls the Belgian employees of the Company[4]) are represented as mendacious, quarrelsome and cowardly. The results of the Company's forced African labour policies are poignantly described by Marlow in the 'grove of death' scene, while Company administrators are bluntly satirised: 'Can't say I saw any road or any upkeep, unless the body of a middle-aged negro, with a bullet-hole in the forehead, upon which I absolutely stumbled three miles farther on may be considered as a permanent improvement' (20). For Marlow, only the legendary Kurtz seems to offer some redemption from this otherwise disgraceful Company enterprise and its obsessive dedication to the acquiring of ivory. While Kurtz is also a very successful ivory collector for the Company, his methods are described as unorthodox, he does not mix with other collectors, and he is primarily known for his impressive voice and striking pronouncements (though on what exactly, the enthralled pilgrims seem unclear). Kurtz, it turns out, had acquired some evangelical fervour for the mission of civilisation; but as Marlow discovers when he arrives, Kurtz's time upriver has effected a terrifying alteration. Kurtz's 'primitive' instincts, apparently catalysed by contact with African 'savagery', have led him to become a participant in 'unspeakable rites'; no longer the emissary of European enlightenment, he has succumbed to the condition of *animality*, characterised in the text by unbridled savagery and the temptations of the flesh.

But there is another side to Conrad's critique of the imperial enterprise. A painting made by Kurtz and left in a way station on the Congo points to the naïveté of Europe's civilising mission in Africa. In the picture, reminiscent of Kurtz's Intended, is a western woman, blindfold, holding out a candle into an area of darkness. Read allegorically, this figure stands for Europe's good intentions in Africa – civilisation, salvation – but the portrait suggests that these (imagined) motives are as misguided as the (real) relations behind them are exploitative and murderous in intent.

In the orthodox modernist reading of Conrad's novel – an interpretation exported via education curricula throughout the English-speaking colonial world in the first half of the twentieth century – *Heart of Darkness* is about the primitive instincts always lurking in the human heart, and the danger of atavistic reversion. Alone (i.e. without fellow whites), Kurtz has reverted to the condition of a brute, while civilisation is revealed to be a mere veneer over the underlying Heart of Darkness. For all their best efforts, the text suggests, human beings may not really have overcome their original condition as animals at all.

Counter-intuitive as it may initially seem, Achebe's aforementioned attack on Conrad homes in on a particular image of Africa – an image that had been presented to much of the English-speaking world via *Heart of Darkness*, as a work of 'great literature' supposedly dealing with universal themes. As Achebe had previously argued elsewhere, such apparent universals were in fact profoundly Eurocentric and, in the essay, he directly challenges the 'greatness' of a text he considers to be racist. His argument is based on three main points. The first of these is that Conrad, via his narrator Marlow, depicts Africa as a blank, a *terra nullius*,[5] not because it was not inhabited, but because such inhabitation was of no consequence to Europeans. (As the Marxist historian Basil Davidson would later pithily express it in a television series (1984), 'nothing exists until a white man has seen it'.) Second, the Africans described in the novel are virtually without language; though they may gabble[6] among themselves, there is little occasion or avenue for their speaking, and the only memorable phrases they utter are the much cited 'Mr Kurtz he dead' and, perhaps more significantly, 'catch 'im. Give 'im to us [...] Eat 'im!' – a comment elicited by Marlow from his native crew about *other* Africans, fleetingly glimpsed behind a seemingly impenetrable jungle screen (41). Even their apparently domesticated fellows are, in Marlow's view, by definition cannibals, and he duly wonders at the restraint they demonstrate. Left to secure their own food or starve during their journey in the service of the Company, they manifest no desire to attack and eat the pilgrims; however, this proves to be less of a comfort to Marlow than it might have been, since it provokes speculation not on the absolute difference that cannibalism indicates, but on the even more disturbing possibility of similarity – a humanity 'like yours [...] ugly' (36–37).

Achebe's third charge is that Africans are rendered absent in Conrad's novel by that most popular and widely promulgated modernist interpretation of *Heart of Darkness*, according to which their role can only be as surrogates for a European malaise. As Achebe bluntly puts it, Africa and Africans became 'mere metaphors for the break-up of one petty European mind' (Achebe 1988: 257). Read as the animality lurking in the civilised European heart, Africa's darkness is made symbolic of Europe's fears of evolutionary reversion; tethered to this symbolism, Africans cease to exist as independent entities, becoming – as many animals do in fiction – representative of some earlier moment in evolutionary history or some primordial human trait. (The magnificent African woman who mourns Kurtz's departure also evokes a wildly animal antithesis of the civilised Intended, suitably 'out of it' in Brussels.)

Achebe rejects the bitter pill of Conrad's novel having been presented to Nigerian readers (and English readers world-wide) as uniquely authoritative in its insights. He also understands that such authority, endorsing as it does the counter-models of European civility and African brutishness, is merely reinforced in the traditional modernist interpretation. Thus, for Achebe, Conrad's critique of Belgian colonialism, and colonialism in general, is vitiated by the essentialist basis of his thought – Europeans may lapse into some version or other of African savagery, but that savagery resides *essentially* in the Africans themselves.

The power of representation to influence the policies and practices of Empire, as well as to energise the imperial impulse, is further examined in Achebe's 1958 novel *Things Fall Apart*, now generally acknowledged as being a canonical work in its own right. In his concluding reference to the District Commissioner's proposed memoir, *The Pacification of the Primitive Tribes of the Lower Niger*, Achebe suggests the insidiousness of the politics of the government official's representation. The District Commissioner wants to interpret Ibo society, character and customs for his (western) reading audiences, presenting Ibo cultural complexity – to which readers have already been introduced in the novel – from a position of ignorance and bias accepted, nonetheless, as authoritative and complete. This interpretation is strategic; for in portraying the Ibo as interesting anthropological subjects – as exotic savages – the District Commissioner's account, however painfully inaccurate, will play its small part in legitimising the further conquest and colonisation of Africa to take place in decades to come.

Representation need not operate in this way; but where, as in coloniser/colonised or human/animal contexts, there is a marked imbalance of power, it will almost always do so. Achebe's critique of *Heart of Darkness* effectively establishes Africans' status as absent referents, a manufactured absence that merely serves to reify the presence of the European civility they are imagined to oppose. But there is another significant absence in *Heart of Darkness*. While ivory is central to narrative and even character in Conrad's novel (we are told that the 'brutalised' Kurtz has sickened to the colour of ivory), those from whom the ivory has been extracted – by slaughter – are conspicuous by their absence from the text. Nor, for that matter, do they appear in Achebe's critique of Conrad or in his 1958 novel. Since Europeans – for all the destruction they cause – remain on the periphery of *Things Fall Apart*, a critique of ivory extraction is not part of Achebe's purpose; and in any case, by the time Achebe was writing, Iboland was no longer a viable elephant ground. Elephants hardly appear in most other re-writings and responses to *Heart of Darkness*, whether hostile or dedicatory, either, although there are one or two notable exceptions, as will be seen in our later discussion of Canadian writer Barbara Gowdy's 1998 novel *The White Bone*.

Elephants *did* appear in many European accounts of African hunting, a lucrative sport, which, as John MacKenzie (1988) notes, was of great

ideological as well as commercial significance in the European and, particularly, the British imperial enterprise. Herbert Ward's *A Voice from
the Congo*, published in the same decade as *Heart of Darkness*, is an
unremarkable and much more typical account of European adventures in
Africa than is Conrad's. Here we find no critique of colonialism and little
danger of atavistic reversion, however exceptional or fleeting. Instead,
the reader is treated to a standard Great White Hunter adventure with
elephants and natives as bit players to the author's heroic lead. Embellished by the author with sketches of a dead elephant, an African sorcerer
and a native fighting knife, the 'Voice from the Congo' is none other
than Ward's own, which, in the spirit of the day, emphasises not the
commercial rewards of elephant hunting but its fashion as adventure:
'Elephant hunting alone and on foot, in spite of numerous obstacles in
the shape of dense vegetation and boggy ground, with the physical strain
of tramping, climbing and wading is an exciting sport' (Ward 1910: 19).
Predictably, the country Ward enters in the Upper Congo 'had never
before been visited by a white man' and so 'we were far from confident
of a friendly reception from the cannibals' (19). (It is only when Conrad's speculations on cannibalism and restraint are placed alongside
Ward's unthinking assumptions about Africans that we can appreciate
Conrad's ability to interrogate at least some of the accepted ideas of
his time.)

Ward's Bangala natives are variously described as 'ill-favoured savages',
'an ugly mob', and 'cannibals', but this does not stop his being dependent on them for his knowledge of, and eventual transportation to, an
elephant ground. There he is left to do his own stalking, experiencing a
'feeling of loneliness' (24) in being 'fully five hundred miles from the
nearest white man in the dead of night and in the land of capricious
savages' (24). A storm breaks and, crouching in a cane patch, Ward can
hear 'the frightened squeals of baby elephants as they plunged and
stumbled in the swamp' (25). Revived by daylight, Ward's spirits lift and
he manages to wound two elephants that crash 'through the dense foliage
like giant locomotives' (26). As the Cartesian simile – animal as machine –
indicates, Ward is interested in the animals only for the experience of his
own power; the elephants he kills are neither for profit nor his sustenance (though they serve as the latter for the Bangala, this being their
payment for transporting Ward upstream).

> Trembling with excitement I fired point-blank at the forehead and
> quickly stooping below the smoke I caught sight of a jet of blood
> spurting from the wound. The ponderous animal fell slowly to the
> ground – dead. Reloading in haste I took two snap-shots at an elephant

rushing past me, without other effect however than to stop his progress.
He stood for a moment gazing at me and twitching his tail.

(26–27)

Ward's dead and wounded elephants are most likely to be 'her', not 'his',
since this is clearly a matriarchal group, but such details are meaningless
to Ward, whose 'cannibals' eventually return to collect him and their due.
Ward then spends an uncomfortable few hours in a canoe 'laden almost
to the gunwale with reeking meat' (27). The Bangala, having arrived
back in what to Ward appears to be their hundreds, are unsurprisingly
never individualised; indeed they seem to him to be so many ants swarm-
ing on his prey, and within 'an incredibly short time the huge carcase
was stripped of meat' (27). The tusks are also taken, not to be immediately traded (by the Bangala) or carried off as trophy (by the Great White
Hunter) but, as becomes clear in a later story, to be buried in a swampy
region near the Bangala village in case they are needed to redeem villagers captured by Arab slave traders or neighbouring hostile groups. (In a
more materialist sense, the trades in ivory and slaves had long been
intrinsically interwoven. Even though patterns were by no means uni-
form across the African continent, the two trades had been traditionally
linked through both Arab and Swahili entrepreneurialism well before the
Scramble for Africa took place. While the trade in slaves was catastrophic for Central Africans and West Africans especially, the trade in
ivory had already drastically reduced elephant populations at least forty
years before *Heart of Darkness* was published.)

It is worth including Ward's work for its representative nature. For him,
it is the excitement of the kill and the display of technological dominance
rather than the possibilities of commercial gain that are important. As
MacKenzie (1988) recounts at greater length, hunting ventures such as
Ward's were not only pandemic in the context of Empire but also played
central symbolic roles in imperial display and colonialist control. Ward's
elephants are first ghostly in the dawn light, then reduced to mere automata. Once the kill has been accomplished, the meat is left to the 'lesser
beasts', the Bangala, who then proceed to swarm on it like flies. Elephants
and Africans, both described as 'noisy', are simultaneously depicted as
being without any comprehensible language, and, as Robinson Crusoe
does with Friday, Ward conducts business with the Bangala through gesture
alone since technologically and linguistically they are 'inferiors' serving
his needs.

Ward claims typically to have been the first white man in the region,
but succeeding administrators were also able to indulge themselves,
especially in Africa and India, justifying their activities as responsible

stewardship of the villagers they ruled (MacKenzie 1988). Meanwhile, as elephants and other animals were increasingly driven from their traditional forest and plain areas and forced to raid gardens, they were conveniently termed 'rogue' animals, to be eradicated by the local administrator. Within the wider contexts of colony and empire, the shooting of the rogue beast had a further significance. Since the celebrated trial of Governor Warren Hastings in India, the fear of colonial officials adopting native customs (reinforced by Conrad's time through strategic mis-applications of Darwin's evolutionary theory) had been a continual source of anxiety for those, like Kurtz, who were situated at the place of temptation, and for imperial officers who were stationed back home. In shooting the rogue elephant, colonial administrators – if not the Great White Hunters – were laying to rest their own potential bestiality at the same time as they were reinforcing, through graphic displays of technological superiority, their managerial control.

Elephants

At the time Ward published the account of his exciting butchery, elephants were still to be found in relatively large numbers in some regions of the Congo, although they had been virtually exterminated from southern Africa and most coastal regions in the west. Writing thirty years before Conrad published *Heart of Darkness*, Joseph Thompson had already warned of their imminent extinction in East Africa: 'The fact that the trade in ivory and slaves now almost entirely depends on the distant countries to which these routes lead, suggests a woeful tale of destruction. [...] Over that vast region hardly a tusk of ivory is to be got' (MacKenzie 1988: 150). We will return to that same casual comparison of 'slave' and 'ivory' as inanimate trade goods in subsequent discussion, but it is worth noting here in passing that Thompson's warning in relation to ivory was not totally ignored by the colonial governments in place. As ivory became scarce, and hence more profitable, Europe bought into the trade in various ways, e.g. through licensing and arm's-length capital ventures, while making feeble, easily adjustable attempts at conservation of their elephant populations. The Belgians, however, did no such thing; and the Congo continued to offer more or less open season for ivory hunters well into the 1920s (MacKenzie 1988: 154).

Just as 'Africans' and 'cannibals' or 'slaves' became not interchangeable terms but similarly metonymic in these accounts, so 'elephants' disappear to become *their* metonyms – ivory and meat. To argue then that elephants, slaughtered in their millions to provide fodder for human (Arab, African and European) greed, are the crucial absent referents[7] in *Heart of Darkness*, and its many postcolonial re-writings and re-readings, is neither a frivolous proposition nor one which can be dismissed as a merely sentimental extension of ethical and philosophical consideration to yet another category of the oppressed. Since, as Derrida and others have shown, speciesism underpins racism, the latter cannot be addressed without reference to the former, as even the traditional linkage of ivory and slaves implicitly suggests.

As we have insisted throughout this book, the racism/speciesism nexus is particularly important in terms of representation, with specific relation to the human/animal symbolic economy. It is thus ironic that literary critics should have been so slow to take up this connection, and more ironic still in the areas of postcolonial and eco/environmental studies. Admittedly, its virtual absence in the latter can be in part explained by genre constraints and the vexed question of the human in eco-literature and criticism. But in the case of the former, it seems worth reiterating a point made in the introduction to Part II. While the 'dreaded comparison' requires careful handling, it is clear that the term 'savage' has often been deployed, not just to signify an *animal*, but also to impute the *human*, albeit in a primitive form. The characteristics of the savages that trouble Marlow and Ward are basically those of the animal, though Marlow, a more thoughtful (fictional) character than (real-life) Ward, broods on similarities. For Ward, however, his 'superiority' is built in direct proportion to the natives' 'inferiority'. The central point here is that in colonialist contexts the terms 'animal' and 'savage' are not always synonymous in relation to the species boundary; rather it is the property of the *animalistic* that is shared by, even characteristic of, savages and animals alike.

As Achebe has famously stated, *Things Fall Apart* was not written specifically to rehabilitate the African image in the eyes of the wider reading public so much as to 'teach *my* readers that their past – with all its imperfections – was not one long night of savagery from which the first Europeans, acting on God's behalf, delivered them' (1975: 72; emphasis added). He thus concentrates in his novel on presenting a portrait of the complexities of Ibo culture, relegating Europeans to the margins and showing *them* as the people capable of a savagely retributive genocide, e.g. in the punitive massacres at Abame and elsewhere. Effective though these inversions are, Achebe, like Conrad, is arguably locked within a binary paradigm that never seriously challenges the crucial basis of the savage/civilised dichotomy. To have done so, he would have needed to interrogate the value ascriptions of the terms – 'human', 'animal', 'savage' – themselves.

Like *Things Fall Apart*, Canadian writer Barbara Gowdy's 1998 novel *The White Bone* is not a direct critique of *Heart of Darkness* though, like a large number of twentieth-century works, it is significantly responsive to it. *The White Bone* tackles the fundamental question of the human/animal dichotomy, addressing precisely some of those issues that had impelled Achebe's critique of Conrad as racist – but this time in terms of elephants and humans rather than Africans and Europeans. Whereas in *Heart of Darkness* and *A Voice from the Congo*, elephants are little more than absent referents of their dead remains, it is Gowdy's self-given task to bring elephants into genuine presence. However, she immediately faces a number of difficulties peculiar to the form she chooses (fiction), while at the same time working towards an imaginative liberation from the constraints of other conventional animal genres (science writing, nature documentary, etc.). Foremost among these challenges is the western approach to the reading of fictional animal tales featuring animal characters. Stories about animals have generally been written for children or, in cases such as George Orwell's *Animal Farm*, the animals have been read as stand-ins for human beings. Since the reception of *Animal Farm* has been particularly instructive, it seems worth pausing for a moment to reflect on it here.

Animal Farm has traditionally been read as a political satire, particularly of Stalinist Russia, or, more generally, human political democratic failings. This goes against Orwell's own claim that one of his major aims in writing the novel had been to protest against human treatment of animals, especially farm animals.[8] This statement of purpose, however, has had notably little impact on the novel's critics, who have generally persisted in reading *through* the animals to extract a purely human message from the book. In the classical fables of Aesop, now generally accepted as having been brought to Greece from West Africa, animal traits – e.g. the persistence of a thirsty bird in reaching water, as in 'The Crow and the Pitcher' – teach *us* lessons of determination. Robert Bruce, hiding in a cave, learned from observing a spider building a web that 'if at first you don't succeed, try, try again'. Animal fables, as the Jamaican writer Erna Brodber demonstrates in her novel *Myal*, were often used as a means of slave and colonialist control: for example, the rebellious animals in the tale of Mr Joe's farm come home with their tails between their legs after a foray into the outside world, where they discovered that freedom was not so valuable after all.

Thus, in *The White Bone* Gowdy must take account of our naturalised tendency to read through her elephant principals as if they were mere metaphors for humans, and she addresses this problem in a number of telling ways. First, *The White Bone*, subtitled 'A Novel of Elephants', is told from the elephant point of view, and follows individual elephants as they move across a drought-stricken landscape in search of group members and the white bone, the relic of a newborn that is rumoured to guide its finders to the 'safe place' away from the depredations of the ivory hunters by whom they are being relentlessly pursued. Humans ('hindleggers' in the novel) are – to the elephants – inexplicably savage, seemingly delighting in desecration and lacking any language that can be understood. Elephants, we are told, were once able to read the minds of hindleggers, but after the Fall and the Darkness – a two-stage process during which the original hindleggers were 'unrepentant and wrathful' (42) but became still worse as they took to 'massacre and mutilation' (43) – all communication between the two species ceased. Gowdy reverses the human/animal dichotomy in relation to savagery and civilisation in line with the transposition of point of view, but this is only one of a number of strategies adopted. After the terrible massacre, protagonist Mud finds herself hurling clods of earth at an outcrop of rock, 'something humanly barbarous fermenting within her' (93). The elephants are also given language, complicated consciousness, prescience, cultural complexity, memory and rituals of mourning, the experience of trauma and the possession of a form of religion, with several of the above attributes attested to by scientific observations, while a number of the others are imaginative anthropomorphisms with some basis in observed elephant behaviours. As Gowdy herself puts it, 'rather than being a social satire, *The White Bone* is an attempt, however presumptuous, to make a huge imaginative leap', one of 'fully imagining', as she tells an interviewer, 'what it would be like to be that big and gentle, to be that imperiled and to have that prodigious memory' (Gowdy, in an interview on www.bookreporter. com/authors/au-gowdy-barbara.asp).

Europeans (as in *Things Fall Apart*) and humans in general are relegated to the sidelines, however destructive their effects on the elephants. All the while, in *The White Bone*, as in *Things Fall Apart*, a complex culture is in the process of being destroyed by a largely off-stage but apparently unstoppable incursion, the human protagonists of which are acquisitive, destructively self-seeking, and potentially genocidal in intent. Significantly however, hindleggers are never distinguished by their colour. Rather, the reader can trace the history of elephant killing through various kinds of human contact (as the stories have come down to the present-day elephants), and by their particular murderous technologies, with those employed in the recent past and present having a far greater ferocity and impact than those of several generations before. And since the elephants' contemporary killers are likely to be both black *and* white, race is of no importance – it is the species itself that, after the advent of the Darkness, has become evil. By writing humans, and their inexplicable murder and destruction, into the text, Gowdy discourages us from reading the elephants *as* humans or as metonymic of human traits; and, as in *Things Fall Apart*, the destroyers are usually off-stage, only occasionally erupting into 'civil' elephant society with devastating results.

Second, in *The White Bone* the deliberate violation of the representational categories we use to keep animals in their place disallows easy compartmentalisation, forcing us to see the elephants in a more holistic manner, as well as interrogating those forms of authority embedded in the different generic approaches themselves. For example, we would not expect either medical or behavioural scientists to write in the same way as poets, dramatists or novelists, and the intellectual and affective impacts of particular genres or forms of representation are expected to vary enormously. In medical science, to take one prominent example, animals, which are not usually the intended beneficiaries, are often regarded as mere objects, instruments of a greater human purpose. It would thus not generally be thought appropriate to represent laboratory rats as suffering individuals who can evoke our sympathies in the way that a work of fiction dealing with rats might. Animals in most human societies are virtually powerless; we can do as we please with them – exploit, enslave, murder or vivisect to improve *our* lot in life. And, like Achebe's District Commissioner in *Things Fall Apart*, we can also represent animals as self-servingly as we please, in ways that rationalise or justify their continued subjection. Within representation *and* in medical and behavioural experiments we depend on stressing varying degrees of similarity and difference between the human and the animal; and if we are unable to perceive some similarity between ourselves and the activities of crow or spider, the very basis of a fable's lesson is undermined.

There is an implicit irony here, but one that is more immediately evident in the practices of medicine and behavioural science: because animals are not humans we may subject them to pain, loss of freedom, destruction of their environments, or the cruelties of contemporary agribusiness. Yet it is only because we ourselves are animals that we can gain material, physical or psychological knowledge and rewards from their ill-treatment. The significance of each so-called animal group's (constructed) difference from us is not so much cultural, anatomical or physiological as it is one of power. Science is the dominant discourse of our time. In science philosopher Bruno Latour's vivid formulation, we live as those in Plato's cave, sending out our representatives, the scientists, to bring back knowledge of the outside world and interpret that world for us. In very general terms, these interpretations depend on a structured interplay of similarity and difference between the various animal groups and ourselves. Thus, apparently radical differences facilitate the dismissal of animals as beings of no moral concern while their similarities, on which the very practices of these disciplines (and their heroic discoveries) depend, can just as easily disappear.

The genres of natural history also stress differences between ourselves and other animal groups, although they are sometimes deliberately anthropomorphic. Inevitably, too, wild animal behaviours – mothering, playing, fighting, eating – will to some extent be read or seen anthropomorphically; but natural history genres tend also to focus on difference, however great their affective appeal. In the popular-scientific works of Jane Goodall or Biruté Galdikas we feel we read the minds of chimpanzees or orang-utans, and we do so through behavioural analogues. These may indeed be accurate interpretations, but since we have no way of confirming them, observer-scientists such as Goodall were regarded until recently as outcasts within the scientific community for methodologies and conclusions considered insufficiently objective.

Yet in 'reading' animals through all such genres we depend on generic indicators to dictate our appropriate responses. Talking animals *belong* in satire, fable, cartoons or children's stories, while anatomical descriptions of bodily functions generally do not. Anthropomorphism – generating sympathy or empathy through similarity – would be inappropriate in accounts of eye-brain experiments on primates or octopus; and while vocal animal communication may be acknowledged as being complex in natural history programmes, even here these sounds are rarely referred to as 'language'. Science has always espoused an interested objectivity, with its methodologies claiming to produce unemotional and unbiased fact. But science offers us only one approach to reality that, like all others, has its own protocols and boundaries. Our attitudes to animals are as contradictory and conflicted as those offered by the different genres of science and fiction; but we negotiate these differing responses through the particular nature and tone of the representations of animals they present. Mixing these animal genres and/or categories, as Gowdy does so skilfully in *The White Bone*, forces us to re-think the ways in which the animal, and by extension the animalistic, is presented to us, and how their very different approaches enable us to live with and act out of quite contradictory views. From Ward we *expect* a purely instrumental attitude to elephants, just as, quite contradictorily, we are not surprised to read of a near-contemporaneous outpouring of emotion in London over the projected sale of England's favourite captive elephant, Jumbo, to the USA. (Interestingly, Jumbo represented both the reach of Britain's Empire and its submission to the imperial centre: he was the colonial exotic and, at the same time, the representative of Britain and her 'greatness'.)[9] Drawing on anatomical science, natural history, personal observation and imagination, *The White Bone*'s holistic approach challenges representational compartmentalisation of this kind.

A third strategy adopted by Gowdy to discourage readers from reading her elephants as human stand-ins is a more complex and interesting one. Gowdy's elephants have their own religion in the worship of the 'She' since the society itself is matriarchal. However, they have no clergy and no particular place or time of worship. The hymns they sing, which are passed down from one generation to the next, are reproduced in the novel as doggerel in a nineteenth-century mode that appears to pay ironic homage to Rudyard Kipling. Although, without clergy or church, elephant 'religion' is recognisably based on what we regard as a human proclivity – the need to construct some higher order or greater force beyond our ken – there are enough echoes of Christianity, combined with just as many determined differences, to reap the benefits of anthropomorphic association while presenting sufficient distance for the elephants not to be read as humans in the text. Nor can their quest for the white bone be read as a kind of elephants' *Pilgrim's Progress*. Salvation for the elephants means escaping the murderous hindleggers to a place where, so the elephants believe, human behaviour is more benign. (The elephants speculate that the hindleggers who merely stand and look may be doing so in an attempt to regain their elephant status, lost in the original Fall.) Though this view is perhaps too elephant-centric, the faculty of interpretation exercised by the elephants is highlighted throughout. Although they certainly possess such a human-comparable speculative faculty, the elephants are also depicted as retaining the capacity to question symbolic and/or allegorical readings. Thus, Torrent, the so-called 'Link Bull', comes to doubt the interpretation of patterns of omens because 'the links may be infinite', while Mud wonders whether symbolic interpretation might not encourage distraction from more survival-significant sense-based clues.

If these techniques discourage allegorical or anthropo*centric* interpretations, anthropo*morphism* is nevertheless important. Before considering the question of animal language and the ways in which imaginative writers have dealt with the familiar western Cartesian separation of mind and body, it is worth reflecting further on the idea of anthropomorphism itself. Like sentimentality, anthropomorphism is frequently employed as a controversial charge against those who argue for animal consciousness, agency or intelligence. Its practice in, for instance, cartoons or satire invites a different form of animal dismissal in the reading of animal figures as human; yet in *The White Bone*, Gowdy harnesses the positive potential of anthropomorphism – always there in children's literature but usually outlawed in adult writing – paradoxically to liberate the elephants from metonymic, metaphorical or fabular enclosure in the text.

While children's stories unashamedly espouse anthropomorphic animal portraiture, science as the reigning epistemology of the last two centuries has denigrated and dismissed anthropomorphic interpretations of animal behaviour for at times contradictory reasons. In order to maintain what Bernard Rollin has termed the 'moral agnosticism' of an allegedly value-free science (because moral judgements are *contra* scientific principles and practice, i.e. unverifiable), science has been forced to deny similarities between humans and many animal groups (2000: 109). On the other hand, it has also sometimes been claimed that in likening animals to ourselves, we deny them a separate integrity. But as the 1987 American Veterinary Medical Association Report belatedly acknowledges, 'all animal research which is used to model human beings is based on the tacit assumption of anthropomorphism; and if we can in principle extrapolate from animals to humans, why not the reverse as well?' (Rollin 2000: 109).

Very much a two-edged sword, anthropomorphism in representation is wielded in a number of contradictory guises. For Gowdy in *The White Bone*, or for J.M. Coetzee's fictional novelist Elizabeth Costello, the complex interplays of similarity and difference that inform our attitudes to animals can best be harnessed by the literary imagination. Practised as writers are, in extrapolating otherness from self – be it in terms of gender, race, ethnicity or disability – the leap required to read observed animal behaviour and imagine animal being is perhaps not as profound as we conveniently like to believe. Indeed, our emphasis in differentiating ourselves from animals has rarely stressed the anatomical or physiological; rather, we prefer to designate animals as 'lesser' through mentality, singling out those traits we regard as peculiar to ourselves – a practice which is not just anthropocentric but often ethnocentric as well. Such confidently drawn if self-fulfilling distinctions are also related, at least in the west and in western-influenced societies, to Cartesian dualisms – separations of mind and body – and it is these dualisms, and the self-distancing ideologies that drive them, that writers like Gowdy and Coetzee challenge in their literary texts.

In *The White Bone*, we are encouraged throughout to empathise with the elephants through their very recognisable individual traits, both good and bad – their social solidarity, their mental complexities and emotions – with such empathy effectively counteracting any ingrained tendency we might have to 'other' elephants in the text. Perhaps two of the most important technologies of 'othering' involve European ideas of language and colonialist projections of the Cartesian separation of mind and body. The three paradigmatic fictions of colonial encounter remain Shakespeare's *The Tempest*, Daniel Defoe's *Robinson Crusoe* and Joseph Conrad's *Heart of Darkness*. Speech, or the lack thereof, is crucial to all three: Caliban (in *The Tempest*) 'doth gabble like a thing most strange', and Caliban appears to concur in Prospero's assessment, telling his master not 'You taught me *your* language', but 'you taught me *language*' (emphases added), while Robinson Crusoe and Friday communicate initially by signs whose interpretation Crusoe alone controls. That Friday has a language of his own is acknowledged, but only in the brief and belated encounter with his father; and there is never any question that Caliban should 'naturally' become Prospero's servant, even though Caliban and his mother Sycorax were the island's original inhabitants. Friday – named for the day of his arrival in European time – is more than content to be his master's slave forever, or at least as Crusoe reads it, and Crusoe soon teaches Friday the language of the master.

Where the language of 'savages' was sometimes acknowledged as such by Europeans venturing into other environments, the assumption was that the language of indigenous people was purely instrumental and simple: composed, like animal sounds, of words and phrases exclusively concerned with food, sex and the threat of danger. Australian writer Randolph Stow addresses this linguistic stereotype in *Visitants*, a 1981 novel set in Papua New Guinea. The Trobriand Islanders speak Biga Kiriwini, as does Patrol Officer Cawdor, who has explained to the raw recruit Tim Dalwood the complex significance of the word 'yamata' in the Trobriand Islanders' language. While the staple of the peoples' diet *is* yam (though this is the English, not the Kiriwini word for the vegetable) the choice of 'yamata' to counteract the stereotype is strategic. Dalwood contemplates the various meanings of the word as he walks behind his two companions:

> I couldn't have said, then, why I watched them so possessively, those two. But I think now that he had already told me. Because once he said to me that the most tender word in their language was *yamata*, which is to keep watch over, guard, and has in it the word for hand. So to watch over someone was to handle or stretch out a hand, he said, and also, he thought, to hold in one's hands, to have one's hands full. That, anyway, is what he made of it; and I think when I looked after them and thought about them in that way I was holding them too, so as not to be empty-handed.

> (55)

Yamata, then, is a very complex concept and its echoing of the word 'yam' works in *Visitants* to disprove that dismissive European view that the language of native peoples (and indeed of animals) was or is only able to encompass the survival basics, yams and sex. However, the word *yamata* in Biga Kiriwini conveys a highly sophisticated understanding of *agape*, *eros* and fulfilment more generally, a nuanced combination we understand but which it takes Dalwood a couple of sentences to explain satisfactorily in the text.

Let us return now to *The White Bone*. In a novel exclusively concerned with elephants like *The White Bone*, the representation of language is necessarily problematic. Jane Goodall or Biruté Galdikas, for instance, through their extreme familiarity with chimpanzees or orang-utans, can translate their sounds, looks and gestures into a language we understand; but the animals themselves cannot be represented as communicating through the English language. In children's books concerned with animals or in adult satires, speaking animals are expected. But in a novel like *The White Bone*, representation of elephant language is both necessary in humanising the animals, yet dangerous in inviting infantilisation or ridicule. Still, without a voice, without some direct speech, the readers' inhabitation of the elephants' world would be strictly limited. *The White Bone* contains much direct speech, but interweaves dialogue with a third-person narration which can incorporate comments on that communication, reminding us that this is a form of translation from a very different vocal source:

> 'I must tell you something,' Torrent rumbled.
> 'Several things. Vital [...] Vital things [...] There are links you know nothing of.'
> 'Which links are these?' Tall Time said, affronted. Unconsciously he had dropped the formal timbre.
> Torrent jerked his head towards the She – Ss.
> Trunk up, he took a long inhalation. 'Any number of them,' he rumbled. [...]
> Torrent turned back around.
>
> (63)

While the elephants always use an English modified by their own particular point of view ('hindleggers'; 'roar-fly' for helicopter; 'big grass' for bamboo, and so on), in this passage, where there are no such specific noun changes, Torrent does not 'say'; he 'rumbles'. Though much less formalised in English than in some other languages, different kinds of address – formal and informal – are familiar to us. But here the words are not inflected to represent formal dialogue; it is the timbre that conveys the tonal distinction. Even in the phrase 'Torrent turned back around' (instead of the more usual 'Torrent turned around' or 'back'), we have conveyed to us the sense of a very large body manoeuvring to speak.

Gowdy also makes speech only one of many forms of communication, others among which are of greater significance. Much of the novel is couched in the form of reportage of what is going on in the minds of Mud, Date Bed and Tall Time. Some forms of elephant communication, such as infrasonic rumbling, the group and individual rituals of mourning the dead, or touching each other with their trunks, have the imprimatur of scientific authority. Gowdy also attributes to her characters telepathic skills that we, as humans, lack. Mind talking and visionary capacities are not shared by the entire group, but if the group's mind-talker is killed or lost, the gift passes to another member in a manner similar to that recorded in other animal groups when an individual with a singular role (or sex) is lost and another takes their place.

While the conversational exchanges of the elephants are rendered credible in this way, their speech allows human readers to identify more easily with them and to see them as individuals rather than a species, one of the most significant ways in which westerners in particular distinguish between humans (individuals worthy of moral concern) and animals (a collectivity or, at best, species to be preserved or eradicated at human will). The anthropomorphism Gowdy employs in *The White Bone* is erected on the basis of natural history and/or scientific observations of elephants, and the acknowledgement of this basis – one made clear in the apparatus of the book as a whole – destabilises a reliance on genre. Moreover, she exploits the possibilities offered by fiction to address the question of other languages, particularly in relation to animals. After all, animals are never without language even if we prove unable to translate their speech.

In colonialist discourse a further important separation – not just between 'language' and 'gabbling' but mind and body – is also evident. Friday is Crusoe's slave and, even though he is able to ask some awkward questions of his master, he still 'naturally' plays the labouring body to Crusoe's reflective empire building, just as Caliban had done to Prospero's in Shakespeare's earlier work. As commentators have noted of both works, the closer a people to the natural world, the further from civilisation and closer to brutishness – at least to Europeans – they appeared. Such associations have also determined women's inferiority to men, since women have been thought closer to nature, particularly through such bodily activities as childbirth and child rearing, and consequently less concerned than their male counterparts with the activities of the mind. Indeed, it is now commonplace to suggest that women and colonised subjects have been identified with the body and the animalistic, while the 'natural' supremacy of men – and, by extension, male colonisers – is evidenced by their apparent transcendence of the body (Plumwood 2001).

In *The White Bone* the elephants, represented as having complex spiritual and telepathic connections with their surroundings, possess a consciousness that arises out of their extraordinary capacity for memory, one that well exceeds the human. The elephants think this accounts for their size: 'that under that thunderhead of flesh and those huge rolling bones they *are* memory' (1; emphasis in the text). When their 'memories begin to drain their bodies go into decline, as from a slow leakage of blood' (1). Even humans who know virtually nothing of elephants know that they 'never forget'. This is true, as Gowdy notes in her prologue, because the slow process of memory draining is almost never allowed to occur since 'nine out of ten [elephants] are slaughtered in their prime long before their memories have started to drain. I speak of the majority, then, when I say it is true what you've heard; they never forget' (1). For elephants, however, memory, regarded by us as a function of mind, is not a capacity that can be separated from the body, while metaphysical speculation and dreaming are also products of the same embedded sensory experience:

> Every odour they have ever sucked into their trunks, every flicker of sunlight they have ever doused with their tremendous shadows is preserved inside as a perfect and instantly retrievable moment. They rarely ask, Do you remember? The remembering is taken for granted. It is the noticing they question: Did you smell that? Did you see it? [...] the precise tenor of the wind that lowed in the acacias that day, how the sun slammed down through the foliage. [...]
>
> Suppose, to one side, waves of salt dust had swirled up from the pan. In memory they can turn their gaze on the waves and ponder this phenomenon of a lake bed dreaming its lost lake.
>
> (1–2)

While human memory also invokes senses other than sight, and leads to speculation upon the past, we associate this process with mind rather than with body. Gowdy's novel deliberately breaches the mind/body dichotomy that forms the basis of much of western understanding (as well as its speciesist, racist, colonialist and gender biases and prejudices). Even though we are sometimes forced to acknowledge the indissoluble embeddedness of mind in body, that reluctant acknowledgement is indicative of the persistence of this basic western separation. In *The White Bone*, by contrast, the huge bulk of the elephant body, its physiological functions, the desires and sufferings of fleshly being, are represented as intrinsic to the complexities of mind.[10] Although it was René Descartes who most famously encapsulated the western division of mind and body in his *cogito ergo sum*, such a separation was already a part of the west's philosophy and religion in the works of Aristotle and in early Christian thought. To become fully human was to transcend one's animality, one's earthbound substance. *The White Bone* challenges this construct, which has been historically instrumental in claims to racial, gender and species superiority, and has underwritten the separation of (human) being from (extra-human) environments as well.

Australian novelist Elizabeth Costello in J.M. Coetzee's *The Lives of Animals* (1999) uses the occasion of her lecture at an American college to deny this separation and to draw attention to the ways in which animals and the animalistic have been regarded and treated by (western) humans. Referring to Descartes' claim that animals are mere automata, machines – the kind of thinking that generates Ward's elephant-locomotive analogy – Costello suggests the following:

> 'Cogito ergo sum' he [Descartes] also famously said. It is a formula I have always been uncomfortable with. It implies that a living being that does not do what we call thinking is somehow second-class. To thinking, cognition, I oppose fullness, embodiedness, the sensation of being – not of consciousness of yourself as a kind of ghostly reasoning machine, thinking thoughts, but on the contrary a sensation – a heavily affective sensation – of being a body with limbs that have extension in space, of being alive to the world. This fullness contrasts starkly with Descartes's key state, which has an empty feel to it: the feel of a pea rattling round in a shell.
>
> (33)

In her two lectures on the lives of animals, Costello also addresses the function of writing, paying particular attention to the kind of self-serving philosophical fiction practised by Descartes. Such philosophical fictions are different in each age, Costello suggests, but they nearly always emerge in practice as being to human benefit at animal expense.

In counteracting Cartesian dualism through the representation of animals *as animals,* Gowdy and Coetzee also work towards undermining the bases of racial and gender inferiority, confirming this inseparability of mind and body in both the material and metaphysical realms. Inextricably connected as it has been to concepts of animality, this triple lack – language, consciousness and mind – is best interrogated by the kind of imaginative writing that questions, through the ways in which it represents animals, the dominant science paradigms whose contrasting generic approaches deliberately foreclose knowledge other than their own. Science has been instrumental, these two writers suggest, in giving us our current ideas of animality – ideas that classical philosophical theories and Christian doctrine have reinforced.

Notes

1 From 1884 Leopold II extended his personal territory in the Congo region through forced treaties with local chiefs, some of which included the provision of what was virtually slave labour by the 'signatories'. Leopold's *personal* control of this 'Congo Free State' was formally relinquished to the Belgian Government on 15 November 1908. The area then became known as 'The Belgian Congo' until its independence in 1960 when it became the present Democratic Republic of the Congo.

2 'Coltan' is the local African term for the substance known as columbite-tantalite, a metallic ore extracted from niobium and tantalum. The mineral concentrates which contain tantalum are generally termed 'tantalite'. Tantalum from coltan is used in consumer electronic products such as cell phones, DVD players and computers. Export of coltan from the eastern Democratic Republic of the Congo to European and American markets has been cited by experts as helping to finance the present-day conflict in the Congo.

3 The term 'European' has a broad usage, ambiguous especially from the British point of view since it may be used to include *or* exclude the United Kingdom. It is also frequently used, not to designate particular geographical or national borders or peoples, but as synonyms for 'western' and 'white', the latter rather unstable terms themselves. It is well known that Conrad thought far more highly of British colonial policies and practices than he did of those of other European colonial powers, and those of Belgium in particular. When Marlow remarks that all of Europe had contributed to the 'making' of Kurtz, he may (or may not) be including Britain since Kurtz's initial 'civilising' idealism is regarded, at least by Marlow, as a saving grace, redolent of the idealism Conrad attributed to at least some aspects of the British colonial enterprise.

4 Conrad's portrait of the Company is based, at least in part, on Leopold II's *Association Internationale Africaine* and its successor association and company: 'fronts' for the amassing of Leopold's private wealth so brutally extracted from the environment and peoples of the Congo region.

5 More correctly in this context, perhaps, *terres vacantes* – i.e. vacant land, defined by Leopold as anything on which no European was living. It thus has a slightly different specific meaning here from the broader *terra nullius*, although the attitude to and effects on the lands and peoples in question remain the same.

6 'Gabble' is used here to deliberately invoke one of the earliest of English works dealing with colonial encounters, Shakespeare's *The Tempest*, where Prospero finds Caliban to 'gabble like a thing most strange'.

7 See in particular, Carol J. Adams' *The Sexual Politics of Meat: A Feminist Vegetarian Critical Theory* (1990).

8 As Jeffrey Moussaieff Masson (2003) comments: 'Literary critics and ordinary readers alike have seen this tale of farm animals as merely a device, an engine for the story. Orwell however saw it in another light, explaining in a preface

written for the Ukrainian translation, that the story came to him when he saw a little boy, perhaps ten years old, abusing a carthorse. He was struck with the force of a revelation "that men exploit animals in much the same way as the rich exploit the proletariat". He went on to explain that he turned Marx's fundamental insight on its head: "I proceed to analyse Marx's theory from the animals' point of view. To them it was clear that the concept of class struggle between humans was pure illusion, since whenever it was necessary to exploit animals, all humans united against them: *the true struggle is between animals and humans*."' (9, emphasis Masson's).

 9 For a fuller account of Jumbo and his imperial significance see for instance Koenigsberger 2007.
10 There has always been a popular perception of elephant memory, intelligence and emotion, and elephant 'mourning' over the remains of dead elephants is well documented. There is, however, increasing evidence of individual and social trauma in elephant communities consequent upon human-induced social anomie and the overall threat of ultimate extinction. For an account of trauma in contemporary elephant communities see Siebert 2006 and 2008. See also *The White Bone*, Acknowledgements (329–30) for Gowdy's scientific and other sources, and Wylie 2008.

2   Christianity, cannibalism and carnivory

Origin myths

In *Not Wanted on the Voyage* (1985), Canadian novelist Timothy Findley returns to a key source of anthropocentrism in the Christian story of Noah's Ark. By re-writing this parable in the form of a modern novel, Findley draws attention to the ways in which such foundational texts have served to naturalise human–animal separation. More specifically, *Not Wanted on the Voyage* exposes the strategies through which a story of the *destruction* of the unfettered imagination, the mass extinction of non-human species, and the devastating loss of a more inclusive, non-anthropocentric conception of community, ethics and value, has been contradictorily interpreted as a story of *salvation*.

In Genesis, at God's bidding, Noah builds an Ark to save his family and pairs of animals from the impending flood, the latter having been issued as a punishment for human disobedience of God's laws. Within the Old Testament tradition, this is regarded as an example of God's mercy, with the focus on God's alerting of Noah and his family rather than on his destruction of the rest of creation; it is a story of salvation. However, in Findley's novel, this so-called 'mercy' is exposed as the initiating of processes of human patriarchal domination: of the operations of sexism, speciesism, racism, torture and – finally – murder. When, at the end of the novel, signs of land are glimpsed, Mrs Noyes (Noah/Noyes' wife in Findley's novel) and the surviving animals pray for more rain, for they know that once they land the self-serving tyrannies of Noah and his hierarchy established on the Ark will become law.[1] This hierarchy will eventually be accepted as 'natural', indeed as what constitutes the very 'nature' of human beings, through the systematic suppression of animals, the patriarchal dominance of women, and the indoctrinated notion of inferior races, here represented by Ham, the only one of Noah's sons to take animals' and women's side. Animals, once an intrinsic part of the community before the flood, will be enslaved or at best relegated to mere 'environment' in a self-perpetuating human drama of inter-generational violence and self-love.

In the world before the flood, in the wonderfully diverse community Findley conjures, species and racial divides did not exist. All species had their different ways, their different forms of interaction, but there were no fixed hierarchies. Moreover, strict dividing lines were complicated by the presence of various 'in-between' creatures: half-ape half-human children, semi-divine angels, and the like. Humans could communicate with other animals (especially Mrs Noyes with her cat Mottyl) but this was not a completely peaceable kingdom. Some individuals and species did not like each other but at least they agreed, sometimes warily, to co-exist. There was, in Tzvetan Todorov's formulation, difference in nature but equivalence in value. All this is to change, however. Living entities we no longer regard as real, such as fairies, demons and unicorns, all banished to the realms of the mythological after the flood, are cruelly disposed of by Noah/Noyes; but it is the human–animal hybrids, the so-called 'Lotte children', who must be done away with if a definitive species boundary is to be effectively established and maintained. Since the very definition of humanity is the 'not-animal', such human–animal hybrids cannot be allowed to exist. Findley's re-writing of the story of the Flood thus exposes the moment of instantiation of the species boundary, a moment that also reifies humanity through the literal and figurative sacrifice of animals for the human cause and dispenses with the 'now' (the 'now-time' of mythology) in favour of human history and scientific fact. For it is representation that is Noyes' main weapon, just as the story of Noah's Ark has operated in western cultures as a means of bolstering patriarchy and of consolidating and protecting a strict human–animal divide.

Noyes' methods of asserting his dominance over the members of his family and his non-human passengers also replicate imperial processes. The patriarch uses physical punishment, torture, ritual and, in particular, the control of textual interpretation to subdue his subjects. Early on in the novel, God sends a message to Noyes on which he immediately acts, without revealing the text of the message to those who will be so drastically affected by it. This gives him sole interpretative authority to carry out God's word. Moreover, interpretative power and the historical record work together to control meaning, not just at this moment but for the future, through their inscription as fact, which then becomes the sole province of the writer-interpreter himself. This self-privileging process is exposed in the early sections of the novel when an apparently inexplicable phenomenon occurs:

Here it was the end of summer and though it hadn't rained, it had already snowed. Or so it had seemed. Small white flakes of *some-thing* had fallen from the sky and everyone had crowded onto the porch to watch. Doctor Noyes at once had proclaimed a miracle and was even in the process of telling Hannah to mark it down as such, when Ham went onto the lawn and stuck his tongue out, catching several of the flakes and tasting them.

'Not snow,' he had said. 'It's ash.'

Ham, after all, had the whole of science at his fingertips and Mrs Noyes was inclined to believe that it had been ash – but Doctor Noyes had insisted it was snow – 'a miracle!' And in the end he'd had his way. Hannah had been instructed to write: TODAY – A BLIZZARD.

(21)

The only interpretation to be recorded is Noyes' and hence, as his wife has already pointed out, 'the only principles that matter here are *yours*'(13). The ways in which texts – the inscribed word – can be used to harness reality to a dominant ideology are exposed and demystified, much as they were in *Things Fall Apart* with the District Commissioner's pseudo-educational treatise, *The Pacification of the Primitive Tribes of the Lower Niger*. The 'power to narrate', as Edward Said notes, 'or to block other narratives from forming and emerging, is very important to culture and imperialism, and constitutes one of the main connections between them' (Said 1993: 2). But it is also significant that in most contemporary interpretations of *Not Wanted on the Voyage* the novel is read allegori-cally, not just as a gloss on Biblical legend, but as a thinly veiled attack on processes of *human* domination – imperialism, sexism, colonialism – that are still powerful today.[2] In this sense, animal or part-animal characters in the novel have generally been interpreted as standing in for humans or as being aligned with women and blacks against a persisting racist and homophobic patriarchy; and the novel is rarely thought of as being about speciesism and the establishment of human dominance over animals themselves.

In *Not Wanted on the Voyage*, God destroys the world he had formerly created in a fit of pique after his orders have not been obeyed and his carriage has been pelted with 'excrement, eggs and rotten vegetables' (64). Understanding that he has become 'the object of the world's derision' (70), God, after witnessing an entertainment offered by Noah/Noyes which involves a bottle and a penny, suddenly finds he has his solution: 'Yahweh was saying to Noah; "that trick of yours [...] the bottle [...] the penny [...] by the sheer application of the water [...] It disappears"' (111). Meanwhile, as in *The White Bone*, communication between humans and other species (Mrs Noyes had previously taught the sheep to sing) has been lost after the holocaust that precedes the flood; and in the rigid orders later enforced on the Ark, the animals, Ham and Lucy (Lucifer in drag), Mrs Noyes and, indeed, all of the women except the sycophantic Hannah are confined to lower decks, for authoritarian (patriarchal/human) values have arrived to replace more egalitarian ones, and once the Ark makes land, these values will predominate as *the* western way of being for all time to come.

A primal flood is also the key motif in First Nations writer Thomas King's *Green Grass, Running Water* (1993), and water provides the basis of both the original First Nations creation myth and the account of a dispute over the building of a dam on Native land in the twentieth century which are interwoven through the text. In King's novel, present-day First Nations people meet with Coyote the trickster and a wonderfully heterogeneous group of re-animated fictional figures drawn from the classics and appearing in the novel as four Indians escaped from a lunatic asylum (Lousley 2004: 21). All four – Robinson Crusoe, Ishmael, Hawkeye and the Lone Ranger – are named after characters from texts where they are masters of another race, having relationships that are similar to the Crusoe/Friday one mentioned in the previous sub-section.

Like Findley, King also re-writes the Biblical Genesis by shifting its base from the Middle East to North America where Coyote, a figure analogous to the Middle Eastern Yahweh of Findley's novel, is a generator of both creativity and chaos. Here, rather than encountering Yahweh, Noah meets Coyote, and together with Changing Woman (the North American earth mother figure) they prove more formidable adversaries than did Ham, the animals and Mrs Noyes on the Ark. 'Man-Christianity' (in Bhabha's provocative phrase) is similarly challenged in King's novel, contrasting as it does with indigenous beliefs incorporating humans as part of animal being and 'wilderness' rather than in opposition to them, as they are in many white North American texts. As the first-person narrator explains to Coyote, he is definitely not wanted on the voyage:

'Wait, wait,' says Coyote. 'When's my turn?'

'Coyotes don't get a turn,' I says.

'In a democracy, everyone gets a turn,' says Coyote.

'Nonsense,' I says. 'In a democracy only people who can afford it get a turn.'

'How about half a turn?' says Coyote.

'Sit down,' I says. 'We got to tell this story again.'

'How about a quarter turn?' says Coyote.

(327)

Pitting his own version of Native American theology against the Biblical story, King replaces Adam and Eve with First Woman and Ah-dam, and God with Coyote – at least until Coyote's bad dream gets loose and the Old Testament God re-appears by mistake. Arguing that it, and not Coyote, is 'in charge of the world' (2), the personified Dream wishes to supplant its adversary. Told that this is impossible, but that it can be a dog instead, the Dream is manifestly unsatisfied and gets 'everything backwards':

> 'That looks like trouble to me,' I says.
> 'Hmmm,' says Coyote. 'You could be right.'
> 'That doesn't look like a dog at all,' I tell Coyote [...]
> I am god says that Dog Dream.
> 'Isn't that cute,' says Coyote. 'That Dog Dream is a contrary. That Dog Dream has everything backward.'
> But why am I a little god? Shouts that god [...] I want to be a big god!
> 'What a noise,' says Coyote. 'This dog has no manners.'
> Big one!
> 'Okay, okay,' says Coyote. 'Just stop shouting.'
> There, says that G O D. That's better.
> Where did all that water come from? Shouts that G O D.
>
> (2–3)

What E.M. Forster in *A Passage to India* dubs 'poor talkative little Christianity' (1924: 150) is unleashed here on Native North America, muscling its way in and claiming everything. While Noah spends his time in the Ark in lecherous pursuit of First Woman, the new G O D is fencing in 'unused' land and damming up the waters. 'It starts with a void. It starts with a garden' (41), one which quickly becomes 'my' garden, enclosed and blocking other people, animals and wilderness – and other stories – out. As soon as G O D is loose he turns proprietorial: '"That's my garden. That's my stuff," says G O D' (41). In the comically interwoven past-present that King portrays, First Woman offers to share, having tasted not just apples but 'melons, fry bread and pizza' from G O D's orchard. But G O D won't share, so First Woman, Ah-dam and the animals just leave, heading west in the face of this determinedly selfish Euro-Christian incursion.

Such claims of possession and use-value signal the destruction of not only Native American ways, but also the land and its animals. 'Empty land', as Cheryl Lousley notes, 'not only refers to a racist erasure of indigenous cultures and political communities, but also represents a particular configuring of nature in the service of national development' (19). The ironic title of King's novel refers, similarly, to the breaking of the Indian treaties of the settler-invader governments, which had promised to honour them for 'as long as the grass is green and the waters run'. But the running waters are dammed up by the invaders, whose stories block out those that had formerly been regarded as foundational – and, as King suggests, stories, like dams, have a profoundly material impact on land, people, animals; on the fabric of others' lives.

> This is a Christian world, you know. We only kill things that are useful or things we don't like.
> 'He doesn't mean Coyotes?' says Coyote.
> 'I suspect that he does,' I says.
>
> (196)

Nevertheless, trees and animals have no intention of surrendering easily. Trees are capable of talking and answering G O D back, while the animals resist Ah-dam's attempt to name them. Noah, in *Not Wanted on the Voyage*, might have got away with recording the ash from the burning of Yahweh's altars as 'snow, a miracle', but here the animals quickly protest at their own misrepresentations:

> You are a microwave oven, Ah-dam tells the Elk.
> Nope, says that Elk. Try again.
> You are a garage sale, Ah-dam tells the Bear.
> We got to get you some glasses, says the Bear.
> You are a telephone book, Ah-dam tells the Cedar Tree.
> You're getting closer, says the Cedar Tree.
>
> (41)

Ah-dam 'gets closer' with the cedar tree, whose eventual use may well be as paper; for the conversion of environment and animals into capital profit is a hallmark of the new regime.

In *The Location of Culture*, Bhabha argues that 'the political and theoretical genealogy of modernity lies not only in the origins of the *idea* of civility, but [also in the] history of the colonial moment. It is to be found in the resistance of the colonised populations to the Word of God and Man-Christianity and the English language' (1994: 32). As Bhabha suggests, the transmutations and translations of indigenous traditions in their opposition to colonial authority demonstrate how the 'desire of the signifier, the indeterminacy of intertextuality' are deeply embedded in the postcolonial struggle against dominant relations of power and knowledge (33). Similar resistance is shown in *Green Grass, Running Water* in the sweeping away of settler dams by Native traditions, religion and philosophy, and in the retrieval of Indian sovereignty through the symbolic unleashing of Coyote's flood. The flood, both a creative and a destructive event, and the burst dam provide the novel's central metaphors, reflecting the washing away of western barriers, and the release of Native imagination and culture in its more holistic perception of living being. The reasons for those barriers in the first place – the Judaeo-Christian separation of body from spirit, and the arbitrary demarcation of animal from human – are similarly revealed through King's riotous purification ritual to be alienating tropes.

Cannibalism and carnivory

If colonialism can be said to have its own origin myths, none is more powerful than the suppression of the threatening 'other' – the disavowed animal rival, the cannibal gnawing at the human heart. In Conrad's *Heart of Darkness*, Marlow assumes the Africans aboard his steamer to be cannibals; while Ward, in his anecdotes from the Congo, is convinced the Bangala are, even though he shows little sign despite this of fearing for his life. In King's *Green Grass, Running Water* the colonialist origin myth of the cannibal 'other' is brilliantly lampooned. In Latisha's Dead Dog Café, this myth is subversively redeployed as twentieth-century tourist attraction. Decorated in the modern style, the café is advertised with a 'neon sign of a dog in a stewpot' (109) – carnivory as metonym for cannibalism – while the area boasts 'old Indian ruins and the remains of dinosaurs', trumping both with a 'real Indian reserve to the West' (149). Over a century earlier, Herman Melville's *Typee* had played similarly with expectations of cannibalism, the inevitable serpent in the American author's Pacific Eden. In one scene in the novel, Tommo enters a native hut and sees some long bones in a string basket hanging from the rafters, reading this as tell tale 'evidence' of human remains. Characteristically, he flees without stopping to investigate, leaving the reader to reflect on those other classic European encounters with cannibalism: the remains but not the deed, the mediated (hearsay) but never the direct (eye-witness) report. Finally, going back further in what is generally considered to be one of the first novels written in English, Daniel Defoe's *Robinson Crusoe*, the archetypal fear of being eaten is also apparent if, in this particular instance, it is also followed by qualification or distanced realisation of some kind. Shipwrecked in foreign seas, Crusoe is cast ashore on what is eventually established to be a human-free island. He survives by clearing land, by growing crops with seeds salvaged from the wrecked ship, and by hunting and eventually domesticating local livestock. The key elements of colonialism are all present in this early narrative: the assumption of ownership of foreign land (typically constructed as *terra nullius*); the expenditure of labour to make the new land fruitful; the use/abuse of the environment and animals for the benefit of the settler; and, not least, the fear of consumption by the 'other' – the dreaded footprint in the sand. This fear is apparently realised when Crusoe apprehends that natives occasionally visit the island and, later, when he rescues Friday from them after assuming that they are about to kill and eat him, in reward for which – or so Crusoe chooses to imagine it – Friday binds himself to his master for life.

As is well known, *Robinson Crusoe* was written at a time of European territorial and capitalist expansion, and it has become almost commonplace to read it as paradigmatic of colonial encounter (*terra nullius*; the cannibal 'other'; land use; race relations; attitudes to animals; personal labour as the route to salvation; the conversion of others to western/ Christian values; the efficacy of capitalist accumulation over mere exchange). Taken for granted, such powerful and popular narratives not only establish obdurate stereotypes, but also – repeating Said – 'block other narratives from forming and emerging' in their place (1993: 2). Teaching Friday 'language' as well as the Bible, Crusoe aims to wean him from a cannibalism he typically interprets as being his servant's exclusive diet. By instructing him to eat goat instead, Crusoe seeks to save him from the sin of cannibalism through conversion to carnivory. (By contrast, Patrick White's similarly shipwrecked Englishwoman Eliza Fraser, a couple of centuries later in his novel *A Fringe of Leaves*, relishes gnawing the bone of a murdered Aboriginal woman – an experience that satisfies both physical and spiritual hunger but one which, as she afterwards cautions herself, '[i]n the light of Christian morality she must never think of [...] again') (1997: 244).

As numerous commentators have suggested, the routine assumption that the people westerners encountered in the 'new worlds' they conquered and occupied were cannibals demonstrated the fear of cannibalism rather than its actual practice – not that cannibalism did not exist as a reality, but its paramount significance was as a self-authorising myth (Arens 1979; Hulme 1998). In support of the argument that cannibalism was – and to some extent still is – a European obsession, the anthropologist William Arens notes that it was one of the few 'native' practices that was abandoned with ease on actual contact with Europeans: 'Other customs which the agents of western morality also fail to appreciate, but which have actually been encountered, somehow manage to remain a vital part of the culture despite determined attempts by others to stamp them out' (Arens, quoted in Hulme 1998: 7). Arens's larger point is that the real significance of cannibalism, particularly since the fifteenth century, is *discursive*. As Peter Hulme notes in keeping with Arens, cannibalism

> exists as a term within colonial discourse to describe the ferocious devouring of human flesh supposedly practised by some savages. That existence, within discourse, is no less historical whether or not the term cannibalism describes an attested or extant social custom. [...] [The] overriding question remains, why were Europeans so desirous of finding confirmation of their suspicions of cannibalism?
>
> (4)

As one of the most potent 'term[s] within a discourse of othering' (Slemon 1992: 165), the eating of the flesh of one's own (human) species is the ultimate crime; utterly beyond the pale, it constitutes irrefutable evidence of an unregenerate animal savagery. There are four further interesting things to note about this discourse, however. First, its practice is not and never has been widespread among either humans or animals. Second, almost from the beginning of New World colonial encounters, writers like Montaigne had wondered who was really eating whom: as he was moved to observe in his seminal essay 'Of Cannibals' (1958),

> I think there is more barbarism in eating men alive, than to feed upon them being dead; to mangle by tortures and torment a body full of lively sense, to roast him in pieces, to make dogges and swine to gnaw and tear him in mammocks than to roast and eat him after he is dead.
>
> (112)

Third, while there was little evidence of native anthropophagous practices, there *was* some evidence of European cannibalism, albeit in extreme situations of shipwreck and starvation, while – as several commentators have pointed out – symbolic cannibalism became, and to a large extent remains, the core ritual of Christian practice (Kilgour 1990; Hulme 1998). And fourth, because many non-European cultures identified their self-hood in relation to animals – e.g. as totems or ancestral continuities rather than as their absolute antithesis – the force of cannibalism *as discourse* had considerably less significance for them than it did for their European counterparts. (Indeed, many of these cultures assumed that *Europeans* were cannibals because of their obsession with the topic.) Eating the flesh of one's own kind has generally been proscribed throughout human history, since no community could subsist by living exclusively off its own, as critics have pointed out in relation to Crusoe's assumption that Friday's only food was human flesh. Thus, while the rare practice of eating the flesh of one's enemies, or of one's own dead, might have had great ritual importance for some non-western cultures, it could not possibly carry the same kind of significance it had for the west. Such native practices were primarily symbolic and had nothing to do with (western) human self-definition in relation to animals, the latter of these generally being regarded as edible, the former as taboo.

Employing the familiar motifs of shipwreck and cannibalism, the Canadian writer Yann Martel in *Life of Pi* (2001) complicates the distinction between cannibalism and carnivory in a number of different ways. *Life of Pi* contains many intertextual references, including Edgar Allan Poe's *Narrative of Arthur Gordon Pym* and its many predecessors and – of course – *Robinson Crusoe*. Like Crusoe, Pi is shipwrecked, but unlike him, he is not cast ashore but rather adrift in a lifeboat in the Pacific, where he is accompanied not by other humans but by a tiger, albeit one with a human name.

The novel begins with the Pondicherry childhood of Piscine Molitor Patel (the eponymous Pi), son of a zoo director. Outraged by Indira Gandhi's Emergency measures, Pi's parents decide to migrate to Canada. The animals are duly sold to foreign zoos, and the family embarks in the Japanese freighter *Tsimtsum* with the animals, all of them bound for North America. One of these is the full-grown Bengal tiger, oddly named Richard Parker. It is important, however, that readers remain unaware for quite some time that Richard Parker is an animal. In an inversion of readerly expectation, it is Piscine Patel (Pi) who is denoted by a symbol – something standing in for something else – while the tiger has first and family names, apparently due to a bureaucratic error in India shortly after he was caught.

After the freighter sinks, Pi, a wounded zebra, a hyena, an orang-utan saved by climbing onto a raft of bananas, and Richard Parker find themselves quite literally in the same boat. Richard Parker, after recovering from an initial bout of seasickness, dispatches the orang-utan and the hyena, after the latter has killed the zebra. The only remaining survivors, Pi and Parker, then drift across the Pacific in the lifeboat for over two hundred days. Initially a 'gentle vegetarian' (as he describes himself), Pi is forced during this time to fish actively for food and, finally, to catch and eat a turtle. Like Findley's Noah/Noyes, he also learns to control the accompanying animals, in this case Richard Parker. But he does so – indeed is forced to do so – by acknowledging and re-inhabiting his own animality, not by divesting himself of it, however much he might wish this. Though his awareness of being human initially discourages him, he increasingly eats like Richard Parker and marks the limits of his territory in the same manner. Starting the voyage in terror of Parker, Pi realises by the end that it has been the tiger's presence that has saved him by keeping him alert and providing him with essential company, continued motivation, and a model for survival.

At the end of *Life of Pi*, two Japanese insurance agents, Mr Chiba and Mr Okamoto, come to Toronto to interview Pi about the shipwreck of the *Tsimtsum* and his subsequent experiences in the lifeboat. The story they have heard – which is also that recounted to the reader in careful detail by the Canadian narrator of Pi's tale – is rejected. 'Mr Patel', they announce, 'we don't believe your story' (324). Amazed, Pi asks why not? Their immediate response is that 'bananas don't float', but the major sticking point is their inability to believe that Pi could have lived for such a length of time on the open ocean with a Bengal tiger. 'So', says Pi, 'you didn't like my story?' No, the agents reply, they *did* like it; they just didn't *believe* it. What they need, they say, are facts. However, arguing that any use of words, indeed any human apprehension of the world, is already an invention, Pi counters slyly: 'I know what you want. [...] You need a story that won't surprise you. That will confirm what you already know. [...] You want a story without animals' (336). As in *Not Wanted on the Voyage*, the animals are surplus to requirements; all animal stories are to be read, according to convention, as mere allegories of human traits.

Though the Crusoe-esque detail of Pi's story appears to militate against such easy allegorical equations, Pi eventually complies with what his interlocutors expect by offering, as a brief alternative, an allegorical rendering of the quasi-realist narrative of his voyage with Richard Parker that makes up the bulk of the novel we have been reading so far. In the revised account, animals do not feature at all except as occasional food. The shipwreck survivors are now Pi, his mother, the cook and a sailor. There is no hard-won co-operation over scarce resources and, instead, the lifeboat's members behave in precisely the way expected of the genre. The story becomes one of murder and cannibalism and, ironically, the humans in this alternative story are said to behave 'like animals'. The cook kills and eats Pi's mother, then is killed (if not eaten) by Pi himself. The cook, Pi remarks wryly, 'had gone too far even by his own bestial standards' (334). Here, in negotiating the actual and metaphorical complexities of the species boundary, Pi performs a common transfer across it: bad behaviour on the part of humans – in this case, that precise behaviour (murder, cannibalism) which allegedly marks the outer limits of the human – is metaphorically re-applied to humans, but only after its 'real' basis has been exiled to the animal (the 'beast'). Human cannibalism turns people into 'animals' or 'beasts', but without jeopardising human distinctiveness since the deed has already been categorised as 'animal': humans can thus behave *like* animals or beasts while at the same time the species boundary, with its operational distinction between animals and non-animals, is kept firmly in place. Needless to say, Chiba and Okamoto are well pleased with Pi's new story, which contains all the elements expected of it, and now that Pi has taken the animals out of his narration, they can comfortably accept that the earlier version he had told them was no more than an allegory designed to help him escape from his own conscience or a delusion occasioned by the extreme conditions of shipwreck and starvation.

Life of Pi links our attitudes to animals with the ways in which our classic narratives have dealt with animal subjects, i.e. by relegating them to the background of human activity or reading them as more-or-less transparent allegories of ourselves. Either way, the animal *as animal* becomes invisible. As we have seen, Martel's novel plays complex inter-textual games with Genesis, *Robinson Crusoe*, and numerous other classic tales of shipwreck and cannibalism. Prominent among these is Poe's *Narrative of Arthur Gordon Pym*, in which the mutinous survivor of the slaughter on the *Grampus* is called Richard Parker. It is Poe's Parker who first voices the need to draw straws (unluckily for him, he draws the shortest and is promptly eaten by Pym and his two companions). By playing mischievously in this way on Poe's grisly tale and other classic narratives of shipwreck, *Life of Pi* erodes the apparent certainties of the species boundary, with Martel's tiger being given the name of that human (fictional) character who introduces the possibility of eating others only to be eaten himself.

Many eighteenth-century travellers believed that the Pacific was another Garden of Eden. Pacific Islanders, or so it seemed to these Europeans, did not have to cultivate or even seek out food; they just lay back and let the abundance of the tropics fall into their laps. But the original sin of the Garden of Eden, as we all know, was the eating of the forbidden fruit, and serpents continue to lurk even in the most apparently innocent of tropical island paradises, symbolising the biological necessity of consumption itself. Late in the voyage, Pi and Richard Parker come upon a floating island composed entirely of giant algae. The algae throw up huge branches around a central lagoon, giving it the appearance of an island covered in trees. The only inhabitants are – improbably – meerkats, who forage during the day but take to the trees at night. The reason soon becomes apparent to Richard Parker (who gorges himself on the meerkats) and Pi (who gorges himself on the algae). For in this anti-Eden, the harmless-looking algal mat of which the island is composed becomes nocturnally carnivorous, with only the trees offering an apparent refuge.

But these strange trees bear equally strange fruit. At the centre of what initially appears to be a giant green hairball, which turns out to be made of densely packed layers of leaves, Pi discovers a human tooth, and, understandably panicking, he and Richard Parker flee the island, believing the tooth to be that of a former shipwrecked sailor who had been consumed by the algae in his turn.

Both of Pi's versions of the story centre, as in *Robinson Crusoe*, on eating, being eaten and the fear of being eaten. Although Pi, in version one, obviously fears that he is the one who will be consumed – be it by Richard Parker or the algae – the presence of the human tooth at the centre of the 'forbidden' fruit yields a rather different interpretation from the one Pi seems to imagine for himself. For the serpent in Martel's tropical (anti-) Eden is revealed as nothing other than the voracity of human consumption itself, with the tooth adverting not to the science-fiction fantasy of carnivorous algae on a mysterious floating island, but rather to the everyday horrors of human eating on an industrial scale. Interestingly, the algae have enclosed, not incorporated, the human tooth, whereas cannibalism and carnivory result in full incorporation of the other within the – now indistinguishable – self. The tooth-enclosing fruit can thus be seen to literalise the paradox of cannibalism in the imperial context, where western explorers and adventurers – Crusoe's real-life equivalents – attempted to save themselves from the fate of being 'swallowed' in the tropics. Unsurprisingly, Crusoe's account includes numerous references to the fear of being swallowed: by the elements, by wild beasts, by cannibals. In actuality, however, it is Crusoe himself who increasingly dominates, taking over the land, animals and people and incorporating them into his new capitalist economy. Consumption, in particular *capitalist* consumption, is the real serpent in the garden here, and it remains the crucial problem for any attempt to redress the continuing inequities of human and animal subjects, First and Third (colonial) worlds.

Life of Pi, in Pi's longer version, also substitutes the threat of cannibalism for that of carnivory, and here again Richard Parker's name turns out to be significant. Edgar Allan Poe himself drew on a number of non-fiction sources for the name of his cannibal victim. Elsie Cloete for example notes, 'in 1846 the *Francis Speight* sank in Table Bay and a crewman, Richard Parker, lost his life. In the 1870s [...] the *Mignonette* sank and the crew drifted in a dinghy for 19 days. After drawing lots, the captain and crew killed the youngest crewman, Richard Parker, and ate him' (2007: 319). This precursory nomenclature 'raise[s] the question that *Life of Pi*'s Richard Parker is actually the [...] victim in terms of [these] extratextual historical coincidences' (319).

In Pi's secondary version of the tale – the stereotypically embroidered yarn of post-shipwreck cannibalism – Richard Parker (the tiger) disappears completely, falling victim to the conventional anthropocentric reading Pi's interlocutors expect. Here, the beast resides *within* the human, and is brought to the surface by exceptional circumstances: murder and cannibalism comprise the 'bestial' Heart of Darkness lurking within the apparently 'civilised' human heart. In some sense, then, Martel's novel reverses the Heart of Darkness trope by insisting, in Pi's main story, that the beast is externalised: tiger and human forge a truce for the sake of survival, a pact by which each tacitly agrees not to kill and eat the other. In so doing, the novel disturbs the familiar pattern by which the nature of the human is constituted *against* that of the animal; in *Life of Pi*, on the contrary, human and animal must forge an uneasy alliance of mutual dependence. Pi's behaviour becomes ever more animal-like as the voyage progresses, while Parker constrains what might be assumed to be his natural tendency to kill and eat his human rival.[3] Above all, perhaps, the textual prehistory of Parker's name suggests, as Cloete also intimates, that the victim of the standard cannibal story turns out to have been the 'other' – the *animal* 'other' – all along.

Carnivory

Like cannibalism, carnivory has its inherent paradox. The separation of 'man' from nature, and the firm belief in human-species exceptionalism and individual autonomy have always been problematic because, as Maggie Kilgour argues, '[eating], like all acts of incorporation, assumes an absolute distinction between inside and outside, eater and eaten, which however breaks down as the line "you are what you eat" obscures identity and makes it impossible to say for certain who's who. Paradoxically the roles are completely unreciprocal yet ultimately indistinguishable' (1990: 7). In introducing *Cannibalism and the Colonial World*, Peter Hulme refers to 'the rich metaphorical hinterland in which the term [cannibalism] flourishes: appetite, consumption, body politic, kinship, incorporation, communion' (1998: 4–5). Strangely absent from this list is that to which cannibalism seems closest, carnivory. But as Hulme's summary of the discursive formations into which cannibalism penetrates suggests, the two are rarely to be found in close proximity even if both generally involve the same process, the eating or consumption of another's flesh.

Despite these obvious similarities, it is often claimed that native (rather than, say, survival) cannibalism is primarily symbolic, whereas carnivory – especially human carnivory – is not. But it remains the case that humans do not need to eat the flesh of others in order to maintain their own well-being; indeed, millions depend completely on other food sources to survive. Moreover, from an environmental perspective, meat is a very expensive form of protein consumption, a wasteful way of acquiring energy from an increasingly limited resource. Animal meat eating by humans can be seen then – much like cannibalism – as a symbolic practice rather than a necessity (Fiddes). Most human meat eating is ultimately an expression of power over others, in particular women, animals and the poor. As Carol Adams (1990) has demonstrated, meat eating is interwoven with various forms – violent forms – of sexism and anthropocentrism, while there is evidence to suggest that as individuals within communities, or communities themselves, become wealthier a dietary shift from vegetarianism to carnivory occurs. However, there are still some notable exceptions. (Western) humans do not generally eat the flesh of three classes of animals: pets, primates and carnivores. This, Nick Fiddes speculates, is because they are so close to us, albeit in different ways, with primates being anatomically and physiologically similar to humans while pets are often treated as part of the family fold. Eating either of these seems to border on something like a cannibal transgression. Carnivores, meanwhile, are, like us, top of their particular food chains, so that eating *them* comes in turn to be considered 'not quite right'.

One literary example where the paradoxes informing both cannibalism and carnivory come into play is yet another re-writing of *Robinson Crusoe*, Trinidadian Sam Selvon's 1975 novel *Moses Ascending*. In the novel the eponymous Moses, originally from the Caribbean, has managed to buy his own house, if a very ramshackle one, in London. To help him run his establishment – he rents rooms to a motley collection of Commonwealth immigrants, both legal and illegal – he engages Bob, an illiterate white man from the Black Country. Moses resolves to teach Bob – his Man Friday – to read and write while, also like Crusoe, he is working on his memoirs. When Faizull, one of his boarders, brings a sheep into his backyard in order to slaughter it for a religious festival, reactions are divided. Moses, a keen anthropological observer of 'his' subjects, hopes to get a chapter of his memoirs from the episode (with a few choice cuts thrown in if he succeeds in turning a blind eye to the proceedings (57)). English Bob, on the other hand, is horrified when the fate of the sheep is revealed to him. The episode can be read in part as a satire on imperial anthropological practices, especially the twin documented obsessions with cannibalism – in this case displaced onto carnivory – and hunting in the wilds. It also reveals the hypocrisy of the west in condemning animal slaughter in an age of agribusiness and the industrial destruction of farm animals.

In a comic lead-up to the kill, Farouk (the slaughterer), Faizull and Moses – notebook in hand – advance towards the tethered quarry:

> We went out into the yard with all the necessary paraphernalia, tripping over all kinds of rusty junk and battling through the undergrowth. Now and then Farouk, in the lead with his butcher's knife, would slash at a branch or a bramble or a liana that impeded our progress. I put my foot in a set of stinging nettles that sting me even through my trousers. At last, panting and exhausted, we reach the small clearing. The sheep was laying down, but the eyes was open watching we.
>
> (61–62)

Moses looks about for a piece of board to back his notebook so he can record the process for posterity, wondering at the same time how his predecessors might have managed the task. Meanwhile, 'Messrs Farouk and Faizull was getting ready for the dark deed [...] Farouk was kneeling down, facing the pearly light of dawn in the East, and with the weapon in his hands as if he was proffering it to the sun to make the *coop de grace*' (62, *sic*). After Faizull has tied the feet of the sheep,

> Farouk start up a oriental chant in one of them strange tongues. [...]
> What is he saying? I ask Faizull.
> 'Shh,' he say. 'It is a prayer. Try not to make noise. If the sheep becomes excited and nervous, the muscles will get tense and stiff, and the meat will be tough.'
> 'It's the sheep that should be praying,' I say.
>
> (62)

As the deed is done, 'a solitary shriek of horror rent the atmosphere' (63). Its source is none other than Bob, Moses's English Man Friday. 'I will get the RSPCA to arrest you!' Bob declaims, '[and] you too, Moses'. As Moses witheringly tells us, 'everything was going nice and smooth until the white man run amok' (63).

Moses's share of the sheep is its 'fresh liver', but Bob refuses any part of it, looking instead 'as if he want to throw up' (65). 'It's good for you' I say. 'It will make your cock stand up' (65). This puts a new perspective on the matter, and Bob, as Moses notes, now starts to look interested. 'You could,' Moses acidly comments, 'fool a white man with any shit if he believe it will prolong the sexual act' (65). Bob eventually compromises on the promise of enhanced virility and cooks and eats his share, '[tackling] the meal with gusto' but still keeping up his original tirade. '"It's the principle of the thing, Moses", he say, with his mouth full of liver. "It's not that I'm not partial to a bit of fresh meat"' (65). This comic scene of the Great Black Hunter-cum-anthropologist in his own (English) backyard hints at the fuss the west makes over cannibalism while taking carnivory more or less in its stride.[4] (Such equanimity is less likely, however, if one has to perform – or witness – the actual killing, as J.M. Coetzee's Michael K discovers when he tries to kill a goat himself.) Selvon's episode also invokes racist myths of black (here white) virility and the inevitable association between meat eating and male power (Adams; Fiddes). It is the promised enhancement of the latter that persuades Bob to overcome his hypocritical scruples, given that he eats animals – killed 'off-stage' of course – on a regular basis anyhow.

By contrast, Michael K attempts, throughout the novel to which he gives his name, not to become an all-consuming predator. Forced by hunger to kill a goat with his own hands, he finds it almost insufferably difficult and repugnant, vowing never to attempt it again and to grow his own (illegal) pumpkins instead. K's is an extended attempt, however unsuccessful in terms of sustainability, to abjure predation and consumption, while it also tacitly registers resistance to the practice of carnivory as an expression of the power of self over other, and – paradoxically, as in cannibalism – of the absorption of the power of the other into the self. Carnivory, as we have seen, is also an expression of the power to dictate the categories of 'edible' and 'inedible' and a potent symbol in the discourse of 'othering' – one which many human communities are reluctant to relinquish even at the expense of preserving the planet itself.

Moses's Man Friday objects to seeing his 'meat' killed; but there is also a sense in which the sheep, while hardly a pet, has been singled out as an individual, and once animals become individual subjects rather than stereotypes or species it becomes much more difficult to dismiss their claims upon the world. Pets *are* individualised, of course, as an integral part of human families, particularly though not exclusively in the west.[5] Our prohibition against the killing, eating and general ill-treatment of pets can, as already noted in the Introduction, be used to vilify other human cultures that do not regard certain species as sacrosanct in this way. Thus, in King's *Green Grass, Running Water*, the Dead Dog Café caters to present-day tourists who are able to enjoy the apparent violation of one taboo (pet-eating) with just the frisson of another (cannibalism) among modern-day Native Americans, who can be imagined to be former cannibals themselves.

The restaurant, as previously noted, is located in an area promoted in the tourist literature as having 'Old Indian ruins and the remains of dinosaurs' and 'a real Indian reserve to the West' (149). Gone, like the dinosaurs, into a now nostalgically sought-after past, Indians have become interesting relics to amuse tourists. The café trades, quite literally, on these and other stereotypes, backing these up with the kinds of images drawn from hunting magazines where 'a couple of white guys are standing over an elephant or holding up a lion's head' (109). The difference here is that the photographer, Will Horse Capture, has substituted Indians for whites and dogs for elephants or lions. The owner's favourite, we are told, was a 'photograph of four Indians on the buffalo runners chasing down a herd of Great Danes' (109). Simultaneously a parody of imperial hunting culture, the western obsession with cannibalism, and the exemption of family pets from the west's otherwise ferociously carnivorous diet, the Dead Dog Café comically threatens the species boundary on a number of different fronts. At the same time, it satirises modern (western) tourism's nostalgic search for that authentic world of 'natural man' for whose loss western incursion has been responsible.

Perhaps it is not surprising that two of the most important writers and philosophers of our age, J.M. Coetzee and Jacques Derrida, both deeply interested in the human–animal boundary and its racial implications, should also be concerned with carnivory. Robert McKay has drawn attention to what he calls 'intriguing coincidences' (2003: 1) between Coetzee's 1997 Tanner Lectures at Princeton University, later published as *The Lives of Animals* (1999), and Derrida's 1997 address at a colloquium on his work in France. As McKay notes, among the several consonances of these lectures are:

> [a] critique of the anthropocentrism of Reason; criticism of canonical philosophers such as Aristotle, Descartes and Kant for their theorizations of the animal; the comparison of factory farming and the industrialisation of animal death to the Nazis' treatment of Jews; and the meaning of authorial self-disclosure.
>
> (2003: 1)

Citing Matthew Calarco's reading of Derrida's essay 'Eating Well', McKay argues that in this work, 'Derrida aims to complicate the strict distinction between the constitutive symbolic sacrifice inherent in the logic of discourse and the actual sacrifice of animals [themselves]' (1). Within the complex terms of this argument, it is not even possible to consider vegetarianism as a more ethical practice just because it avoids animal sacrifice; rather, the best we can do – or so McKay argues after

Derrida – is 'to determine "the best, most respectful, most grateful, and also [...] most giving way of relating the other to the self"' (1). For Derrida, then, the crucial moral question is not whether we 'should eat or not eat, this and not that, the living and the non-living, man or animal', but rather how we should go about 'eating well'. What does this last question imply, Derrida asks; what constitutes 'eating'? 'And in what respect does the [very] formulation of these questions give us still more food for thought? In what respect is the question, if you will, still carnivorous?' (1). For Coetzee, too, though himself a vegetarian, the question of whether we should eat meat or not is not a serious one because

> [i]t is on the same level of logic as posing the question 'should we have words?' We have words, the question is being posed in words; without words there would be no question. So if there is going to be a question at all, it will have to be a different question, one I have not even begun to frame.
>
> (1995: 46)

For the imaginative writer and philosopher, then, the main difficulty in re-imagining an ethically inclusive community is linguistic cognition itself, since linguistic cognition, as an apparently inescapable condition of humanity, is inherently 'carnivorous', necessarily 'sacrificing' the animal that, nonetheless, is also ourselves. It is in *The Lives of Animals* (1999) and, particularly, *Elizabeth Costello* (2003) that Coetzee begins to frame his question. Costello, in her two lectures on the lives of animals (and in other 'lessons' in the later novel), seems to be exploring the issue of how to 'eat well' or, as Derrida might put it, how to live in ethical relation to the 'other' in the face of a linguistically cognitive carnivorousness. But as Derek Attridge among others has noted, *The Lives of Animals* and *Elizabeth Costello* are novels, not philosophical discourses; and the words in these novels are *about* Costello, not just narrated *by* her. Her life is also the 'life of an animal' and, like her two lectures ('The Philosophers and the Animals' and 'The Poets and the Animals'), it is about eating or, more particularly, about the dilemma of 'eating well'. How then *should* one eat well? Is there any possibility of escaping the 'carnivorousness' of a linguistic condition that consumes the 'other', more specifically the racial and/or animal 'other'; is there any possibility of an alternative to this condition at all?

One way in which Coetzee addresses this seemingly irresolvable problem is to explore the unstable relationship between signs and things in themselves, e.g. between the idea of linguistic carnivorousness and literal flesh eating, or between the metaphor of consumption and the actual eating of animal flesh. A similar relationship is explored in Findley's *Not Wanted on the Voyage* when Noyes interprets the screeching of a peacock as divine affirmation of his decision to sacrifice a ram to God. His commonsensical wife rightly points out that the peacock has not the slightest interest in Noyes' intentions: he is 'only calling to his mate, for God's sake!' (13). Undeterred, Noyes calls on their son Ham to make the sacrificial offering. By deliberately slashing his arm together with the sheep's throat, Ham – the only male character on the side of the angels/ animals in the novel – attempts to atone for the literal sacrifice of an animal by performing a metaphorical reconciliation, the sharing of the animal's pain through his own flesh. Significantly, this gesture is physical, not verbal; its equivalent in Coetzee's fiction would be that culminating moment in *Foe* where Friday's lifeless body becomes 'the place where bodies are their own signs' (1986: 157).

The eight 'lessons' that comprise *Elizabeth Costello* all address, in their different ways, the notion of community and, through this, the fundamental relations between self and other. Similarly, Costello's lectures at Appleton College (*The Lives of Animals*), which appeal for the exercise of the sympathetic imagination in relation to animal 'others', centre on the potential that shared embodiedness might have to bypass linguistic-cognitive carnivorousness. Costello's daughter-in-law Norma's antagonism towards her is based on her attitude towards animals and what she (Norma) reads as Costello's militant vegetarianism. Norma will not allow her own children to eat with their grandmother because of her belief that eating meat is 'only normal' and because she is exasperated by Elizabeth's insistence to the contrary, which prompts the children to ask irritating questions about the rightness of consuming animal flesh.

Costello's own beliefs are held to account in the final 'lesson' of the later novel. Here, as a novelist, a lifelong purveyor of words, she presents herself to her Kafkaesque jury of inquisitors as someone through whom the voices of others may speak; and as a neutral conduit for those whose suffering may otherwise go unheard. But this proposition has itself already been interrogated in an earlier 'lesson'; and what emerges from this one is that she begins to hear a different voice, that of her own body:

> For the moment, all she hears is the slow thud of blood in her ears, just as all she feels is the soft touch of the sun on her skin. That at least she does not have to invent: this dumb, faithful body that has accompanied her every step of the way, this gentle, lumbering monster [...] this shadow turned to flesh that stands on two feet like a bear and laves itself continually from the inside with blood.
>
> (210)

She is not only *in* this body; she *is* this body. Thus, just as Derrida reformulates the Cartesian 'I think therefore I am' as 'the animal therefore I am', Coetzee has Costello practise reformulating her credo for her judges as 'I believe that I am. I believe what stands before you today is I' (210–11). But this too, she thinks, 'may be too much like philosophy' (211). Casting around for a way to proceed, a chilling episode from the *Odyssey* occurs to her. This, too, is a scene of animal sacrifice that provokes the sympathetic imagination; and she consequently imagines, as a fellow animal, suffering the fate of the king of Ithaca's ram:

> The pool of dark blood, the expiring ram, the man, at a crouch, ready to thrust and stab if need be, the pale souls hard to distinguish from cadavers: why does the scene haunt her? What, coming from the invisible, does it say? She believes, most unquestionably, in the ram, the ram dragged by its master down to this terrible place. The ram is not just an idea, the ram is alive though right now it is dying. If she believes in the ram, then does she believe in its blood too, this sacred liquid, sticky, dark, almost black, pumped out in gouts on to soil where nothing will grow? The favourite ram of the king of Ithaca, so runs the story, yet treated in the end as a mere bag of blood, to be cut open and poured from. She could do the same, here and now: turn herself into a bag, cut her veins and let herself pour on to the pavement, into the gutter. For that, finally, is all it means to be alive: to be able to die. Is this vision the sum of her faith: the vision of the ram and what happens to the ram? Will it be a good enough story for them, her hungry judges?
>
> (211)

Yet even this seems to her too abstract, too literary. At the point where she realises she has lost her appetite, she offers her 'hungry' judges a different answer. In telling them about the life cycle of the aestivating frogs of Dulgannon, she does all she can to avoid turning their real lives into a human allegory of rebirth. Instead, her account is, as she says, a 'story I present transparently, without disguise [...] [for] the life cycle of the frog may sound allegorical, but to the frogs themselves it is no allegory, it is the thing itself' (217). 'The thing itself': this is perhaps the closest a human character can come to apprehending animal being, and to disengaging it from the human/linguistic/cognitive shackles in which that being is generally held. However, alerted by Costello's claim to a story without disguise, the reader understands that while her creator (Coetzee) may share her desire for such disengagement, he can never fully effect it; not that this cancels Costello's belief in the autonomous existence of the frogs: 'They exist whether or not I tell you about them, whether or not I believe in them. [...] It is because of the indifference of those little frogs to my belief [...] that I believe in them' (217). As usual, Coetzee fails to provide any solution to the problems his fiction raises. The evidence Costello presents here is circumstantial; and yet by depicting her as grounding her own identity in the very indifference of the frogs to her existence, Coetzee gestures towards a world that does not even acknowledge our presence; where we (humans) must learn to stand alone without the co-operation or co-optation of animal 'others'; and where, like those of Gowdy's elephants, our 'essences' are no longer defined in opposition to others', and we no longer define ourselves by the animal we are not.

Findley's *Not Wanted on the Voyage*, Martel's *Life of Pi*, and Coetzee's *Elizabeth Costello* and *Lives of Animals* are all attempts to radically re-imagine the relations between humans and animals. Though their approaches to the task are very different, all regard linguistic cognition, carnivorousness and animal sacrifice as key areas to be addressed in the ongoing attempt to fashion less anthropocentric and imperialist ideas of community. For no closer relation can exist between animals and humans than the literal one of consumption: blood of my blood, bone of my bone, flesh of my flesh. And this is the paradox implicit in both cannibalism and carnivory; the paradox contained in such clichés as 'you are what you eat' and 'all flesh is grass'.

Notes

1 Earlier versions of this account of *Not Wanted on the Voyage* appear in *The Empire Writes Back* (1989) and 'Unjust Relations: Post-Colonialism and the Species Boundary' in *Compr(om)ising Post-Colonialism(s): Challenging Narratives and Practices,* ed. Greg Ratcliffe and Gerry Turcotte, Sydney: Dangaroo, 2001.
2 For a full account of various critical approaches to Findley's novel see Brydon 1998.
3 For a very different interpretation of *Life of Pi* – one which regards the novel as much less 'animal friendly' – see Armstrong 2008.
4 For a more detailed discussion of Selvon's politically and linguistically comic retelling of Robinson Crusoe's 'colonial' adventures, see Tiffin 1995.
5 For further discussion of human/pet relations see Fiddes 1991 and Fudge 2008.

3   Agency, sex and emotion

The lives (and deaths) of tigers

In the second version of Pi's tale (*Life of Pi*), the tiger Richard Parker disappears altogether, not into the Mexican jungle, but as a character in the narrative *tout court*. Humans supplant animals; animal is obliterated by human drama. This allegorical reading is quite plausible, since there are reasons – both psychological and legal – why Pi might have wished to transpose a story of human 'brutality' into an animal tale. Yet the forms in which Pi presents the two versions of his story are very different. The original account, notwithstanding the bizarre 'carnivorous island' episode, is told in realist mode; but version two is stereotypical, cartoonish even, with all the grisly elements of murder and cannibalism one might normally expect. Nevertheless, most readers of Yann Martel's novel – like the insurance agents – would probably *prefer* the first and *believe* the second. Survival at sea with a Bengal tiger beggars belief; the equally incredible human story must therefore be the 'real' one.

Competing human–animal priorities also come into play in another contemporary tiger story, which forms an integral part of Amitav Ghosh's multi-layered novel *The Hungry Tide* (2004). In this work, however, the tiger is not sacrificed to anthropocentric narrative expectation but rather to its pre-designated ideological positioning between the rights of local peoples and western conservationist objectives – the subject of an increasingly important postcolonial debate. As we have already seen several times in this book, such conflicts of interest have attracted the attention of both postcolonial and environmentalist critics, who are alert to the dilemmas involved in conserving endangered ecosystems and animals when the livelihoods of local (subaltern) peoples are simultaneously put at risk. The problem often seems intransigent, with either humans or the 'extra-human' environment demanding prioritisation (Cribb and Narangoa 2004: 1093–1102). Nor has the situation of these peoples necessarily improved with Independence. Instead, numerous instances can be cited worldwide of subaltern groups being targeted by their own governments in league with global capitalist ventures, through internal political corruption or on behalf of international conservationist NGOs. Whether or not such collusion against one's own nationals occurs with the co-operation of international corporations, it is often precisely those animals and humans allegedly being protected who are the first to suffer from its destructive effects.

A case in point is the historical background to Ghosh's novel. In 1979, the West Bengal government was keen to secure the support of the WWF (World Wildlife Fund) in order to carry out its task of evicting thousands of refugees from the island of Marichjhapi in the delta region of the Sundarbans, also the last refuge of the Bengal tiger, hunted to near-extinction in other parts of India, especially during colonial times. By this period, a large section of the region had been reserved for a tiger conservation project, with WWF both rewarding and pressuring the incumbent Left Front government to protect the area from human incursion. Unlike the tiger, the Marichjhapi refugees were not indigenous to the area but had been forced into it, first by displacement during Partition and later, in the early 1970s, by the break-up of East and West Pakistan and the founding of Bangladesh. These refugees, while not initially a cohesive group, were brought together through their neglect and eventual persecution by the West Bengal government. Economic blockades were instituted but, when these failed, the government resorted to more draconian measures, employing off-duty policemen and even criminal gangs to 'remove' the refugees. Carried out unofficially, this drastic 'removal' campaign resulted in murder and rape on a massive scale (Mukherjee 2006).

While European instrumentalist attitudes towards the environment and the corporate exploitation of land continue, counter-moves – themselves often inspired by western attitudinal changes – have had catastrophic results for people violently co-opted into western systems and world views. The environmental historian Richard Grove has provocatively contended that it was in colonised areas of the world that European naturalists, scientists and administrators first apprehended the need for conservation measures and, in recognising the finite amount of flora and fauna at their disposal, began to implement strategies of preservation. Whether one agrees or not with Grove's hypothesis, it is certainly the case that as long-established scientific hierarchies and 'predator-prey' models of relationships in nature came increasingly to be challenged during the twentieth century, pressure to preserve non-human animal and plant species grew with it. Ironically, however, this shift of emphasis from anthropocentric to environment-based (ecocentric) philosophies and practices not only failed to benefit those very peoples whose pre-colonial apprehension of being-in-the-world had been systematically deni-grated by Europeans, but also consistently provided justification for their colonisation, the 'primitive' being distinguished from the 'civilised' pre-cisely by its proximity to the natural world. Indeed, as Robert Cribb has shown in relation to Dutch environmental legislation in Indonesia, 'the creation of national parks and the protection of endangered species have both excluded indigenous peoples from regions they have occupied and managed for centuries and [have] hampered them from using natural resources as an economic base from which to seek modernity' – a mod-ernity into which European incursion had already propelled them (Cribb 2007: 49).

While the dilemmas such conflicts raise have been important to both postcolonial and environmental studies, they are particularly so at the intersections of the two related areas. Neither the 'Marichjhapi massacre' refugees nor their descendants (the villagers in Ghosh's novel) were or are indigenous to the region, but they had suffered a history of violent displacement that initially brought them to the area – one which, con-stantly shifting between a state of land and a state of water, provides an objective correlative for their own unstable past. *The Hungry Tide* offers a superb evocation of the region: of the sights, smells and sounds of the great delta beyond Kolkata, and of the ways in which the lives of the people who live there are attuned to its ever-shifting rhythms and moods. And it is into this area that Ghosh (2004) propels his two protagonists, Piya (an American citizen of Bengali descent) and Kanai (a city-based translator and self-styled cosmopolitan), whose apparently incompatible approaches to environmental and social issues, tested by the material realities of the region, are eventually resolved.

Local knowledge plays a key role here: Piya, the educated metropolitan scientist, falls in love with Fokir, an illiterate local fisherman, partly because of his intimate knowledge of the region and his intuitive under-standing of the habits of the endangered river dolphins that live there, creatures she has come to study in her turn. Fokir proceeds to save Piya's life not once but twice, first when she is at the mercy of a corrupt park warden and his partner, a local captain, and second at the cost of his own life, when he shields her from a great storm that threatens to engulf them both. While Ghosh is sympathetic towards Piya, he is also impli-citly critical of her, as he is of Kanai, for their shared tendency to dismiss local social/ecological knowledge. This attitude is not shared by the latter's social-activist relative Nilima, who admits that she knows nothing about dolphins or environment conservation, but whose views are shaped by the daily lives of the people who live in the region, as she does, and who are attuned to both the pleasures and perils it affords. Piya eventually realises that she doesn't want to 'do the kind of work that places the burden of conservation on those who can least afford it' (2004: 327). By corollary, the novel appears to advocate the sensible policy of no conservation without local consultation and participation (and to attack the alternative of interventionist arrogance, an arrogance matched by the brutal indifference of some of the Indian government park wardens, exemplified in the episode when, in pursuit of villagers who have burned alive a captive tiger, they accidentally run over a river dolphin – Piya's symbol of hope for the survival of the species – in their boat).

But the real clash of interests is displaced – perhaps deliberately – in Ghosh's novel. In recent decades, the strongest international pressure on the Indian government has been for tiger, not river dolphin, conservation, in large part because the Bengal tiger represents a prime example of a global signature species at mortal risk. In the novel, however, because both refugees and locals are dependent for their survival on the fickle delta environment, they frequently encroach on protected tiger territory – and some are killed by tigers when they do. Thus, when the villagers capture a tiger, they feel entitled to take revenge on the now defenceless animal – a traumatic scene the reader witnesses through Piya's horrified eyes. Hurried away by Kanai and Fokir before she can intervene, Piya is simultaneously shielded from the realisation that her wish to protect the tiger has been based on a revulsion against cruelty that fails to take into consideration the number of local people whose lives have been taken by tigers in the past. People, Ghosh seems to assume, necessarily take precedence over animals. Piya's decision at the end of the novel to become a 'rooted cosmopolitan' rather than a 'footloose expert' (Shalini Randeria's terms, 2007) is only possible because the local people have no particular issue with the dolphins; the much more intractable problem of tiger sanctuary is thus displaced by the relatively easy 'dolphin solution', and neither a practical nor a philosophical answer to the situation of the tiger is offered in its place.

Thus, even when a provisional solution to the social/ecological preservation of the Sundarbans is found at the end of Ghosh's novel, it fails to dispel the residual unease surrounding the earlier episode of the tortured tiger. Ghosh's implication is that this is a further lesson Piya has to learn: not to regard Fokir as a 'noble savage' living in harmony with his environment in order to persuade herself of their shared environmentalist ideals. Fokir's mother had been a victim of the Marichjhapi massacre and his enthusiastic participation in the torture of the tiger suggests that while the villagers are certainly taking revenge on a 'man-eating' animal, they are also symbolically avenging their persecution at the hands of the Bengali state. As is so often the case with 'man-eaters' (among other examples of 'pest species'), human responsibility is elided and scapegoats are found in the shape of the animals on whose territories they encroach. Meanwhile, although Ghosh depicts the local environment as being mightier than either humans or tigers – at one point Piya and Fokir attempt to shelter from the ferocious storm in a tree, as does a nearby tiger – the endangered Bengal tigers are not generally seen as being an essential part of an ecosystem – including humans – or as sharing characteristics with humans as fellow-inhabitants of a decidedly hostile but also unusually fragile place.

Arguing that Ghosh has sought, in both his creative and critical work, to present us with 'the disenchanting [of] the divisive and destructive borders and boundaries propagated by colonial and post-colonial modernity', Pablo Mukherjee adds that such 'disenchantment' cannot take place outside of an 'eco paradigm' since this necessarily opens up

> ways for us to assess the central issues faced by 'second-wave' poco/
> eco theories – how to analyse contemporary post-colonial political
> crises as being continuous with ecological crises; how to excavate a
> history of bio-regional modernities; how to centre refugee migrants
> and not 'hybrid cosmopolitanism' as the paradigmatic post-colonial
> framework.
>
> (2006: 146)

While Ghosh certainly provides us with such a paradigm in *The Hungry Tide*, the figure of the tiger arguably remains outside both the various (local) human communities in the novel and the environmental ethic its author apparently seeks to propose.[1] Mukherjee (2006) argues further that Piya, 'kitted out with the latest GPS monitor [...] and binoculars, literally embodies the pan-optical knowledge machine of colonialism' (148). The scene involving the torture and killing of the tiger is therefore of crucial importance in her coming to recognise a difference between her own attitude to the environment and that of Fokir, precisely because there is a 'gap between her environmental ethos and any properly ecological ethics' (148). However, while the episode certainly reminds Piya of the fundamental differences between her environmentalist views and Fokir's, any 'properly ecological ethics' (148) should surely include the right of the tiger to occupy its traditional environment, as well as an acknowledgement of the significant role it plays in the Sundarban ecosystem to which it belongs.

In his novels, Ghosh frequently draws attention to the absurdities and tragedies of borders; yet in *The Hungry Tide* the most crucial shadow line – that between animals and humans – remains undisputed throughout. Instead, the tortured tiger becomes a scapegoat for the past-and-present sufferings of the refugees and is implicitly presented as being expendable in individual, if not collective, terms. Moreover, the novel gives us to understand that previous violence against the refugees has been perpetrated by Bengali politicians *in the name of the tiger*, which makes it difficult to come to any other conclusion than that the tiger is being turned into a sacrificial symbol of violence itself.

The question of non-human agency

As Divya Anand notes, Ghosh explores the 'tensions between and within human communities, their respective relations with the natural world, and the extra-discursive reality of nature that changes and is simultaneously acknowledged by humanity' (2008: 22). Anand's essay highlights the different ways in which water acts as an agent – the most powerful agent – in the Sundarbans and, correspondingly, in Ghosh's novel. Citing the influential American environmentalist critic Lawrence Buell, Anand argues that ecocritics explore literary texts as 'refractions of physical environments and human interactions with those environments, notwithstanding the artifactual properties of textual representation and their mediation by ideological and other socio-historical factors' (21). Water, tides and winds – furiously combined in the fateful storm at the end of Ghosh's novel – certainly bespeak an agency the destructive potency of which has often been neglected at its peril by the post-industrial west. In the history of the Sundarbans, however, such natural agency could never be ignored. As much a character as the human protagonists, water is a constant actant in the novel, for, as Piya discovers,

> [the] proliferation of aquatic life [in the Sundarban region] was thought to be the result of the water itself. The waters of river and sea did not intermingle evenly in this part of the delta, rather they interpenetrated each other, creating hundreds of different ecological niches, with streams of freshwater running along the floors of some channels, creating variations of salinity and turbidity.
>
> (125)

Wind and water, however, also prove to be a lethal combination in the violent storm during which Fokir is killed. As the wind rises, a mangrove leaf, blown two kilometres across the water, gives warning (371). Facing its full force, Piya is reminded of the raw power of environment, even in the face of such political juggernauts as the USA (372). The water – itself an agent – is outdone by the power of the wind but remains destructively collusive with it, while, as the gale worsens, it 'no longer sounded like the wind but like some other element [...] [emitting] a deep, ear-splitting rumble, as if the earth itself had begun to move' (377, 378–79). Tied together to a tree branch, Piya and Fokir experience a displacement of elemental realities that Piya at least could never have imagined, while the synaesthetic imagery used to describe the tempest reflects a dissolution of the very binaries on which her known world had previously been constructed: earth and water, solid and fluid, east and west (382–83).

Agency has been a problematic issue for both postcolonial and environmental studies since, in the anthropocentric version of this problem, 'others' may speak but their speech is often pre-positioned so as not to be heard by those in power (Spivak 1988: 271–313). Animals, similarly, are rarely seen as independent actors, a sometimes strategic human failing that reminds us that 'what is at stake [in recognising animal agency] is our own ability to think beyond ourselves' (Fudge 2002: 22). To speak of 'non-human agency', however, immediately invites the allegation of anthropomorphism, potentially imputing to non-humans a capacity for choice, decision-making and conscious planning often considered by human beings to be unique to themselves (P. Armstrong 2008: 3). Yet such a definition of agency is itself open to charges of anthropocentrism, as Ghosh's remarkable evocation of the 'hungry tide' indicates. If we define agency less by the essentialist capacities apparently required to effect change than by the effecting of change itself, we have not only a less anthropocentric but also a less circular definition of agency. As Philip Armstrong suggests, following Wilbert and Philo, 'many people (outside the West, but in it too) have [now] started to deconstruct seemingly obvious claims about the privileged status of the human, in contradistinction to the animal, as *the* source of agency in the world'; what is needed therefore is 'a reconsideration of the term and concept [of agency] itself' (Philo and Wilbert, quoted in P. Armstrong 2008: 3–4).

Since at least the Middle Ages, animals have not been accorded moral agency, nor – until recent revolutionary legislation in Spain[2] and elsewhere – any rights whatsoever. This situation is imaginatively redressed in Robyn Williams' novel *2007* (2001), in which animals both domestic and wild stage a revolt, to some degree against animal slavery and sundry other human torments, but the chief purpose of which turns out to be a planetary protest against the impending catastrophe of global warming and its associated crimes. In this globalised *Animal Farm*, there are no particular leaders, nor are the animals motivated by any political ideology or purpose other than that of drawing attention to destruction (for themselves) and planetary apocalypse (for us all). As the revolt breaks out, whales attack a Japanese ship in the Antarctic while huge flocks of birds shut down Heathrow airport; then Melbourne airport is also closed when cows defecate all over the airstrip. The showdown is in New York's Central Park where children – the natural inheritors of our predisposition to planetary vandalism – negotiate, with those adults who are willing to participate, for a different future. As in other fables of this kind, 'bad' scientists rub shoulders with 'good'. Hector Breen – a corporate descendant of Findley's Dr Noyes – proposes to kill off all 'non-useful' animals in the interests of cost saving, but is countered by Julian Griffin, who, like Ham in Findley, favours negotiation with animals as long as conditions allow. Breen goes further, proposing 'faunicide' and a Brave New World where 'pastoral land [will be] freed up' for human usage and there will be 'no crowded species jumping from over-confined shrinking habitats to do mischief [to man]' (156). That this formula might also prove to be the 'final solution' for humanity obviously does not occur to Breen, whose proposed animal-free world is a fascist state in which sympathetic or even tolerant attitudes to animals, like the animals themselves, will have no place (157). Instead, a virus that renders all vertebrates – with the exception of humans – sterile will be engineered using the latest biotechnology, with the eventual elimination of animals being the destiny towards which industrial modernity has been working, and that it has now finally – triumphantly – reached (219). Once Breen's plan is revealed, there is unsurprisingly strong reaction against it, and after a further round of negotiation the rebellious animals and children return to their homes temporarily unscathed, but keeping a watching brief. Though often playfully absurd, *2007* has a serious message. Species other than our own, the novel suggests, register potentially devastating environmental changes (just as some animals tend to do before other natural catastrophes), while the fear of environmental apocalypse is a real one, as is humans' readiness to scapegoat animals – think SARS, think the 'mad cow' outbreaks – for their own immediate interests and long-term goals.

Scientists, animal agency and the vexed question of inter-species communication also come together in the Australian writer Peter Goldsworthy's remarkable novel *Wish* (1995), about the growing intimacy of a man, John James (JJ) and a female gorilla, originally called 'Eliza' but later renamed 'Wish'. Employed by Wish's current owners, Stella and Clive Kinnear, to teach her sign language, JJ – the son of deaf parents – discovers to his horror that she had previously been altered *in utero* as part of a commercial laboratory project designed to produce half-human, half-ape hybrids: potential slaves for industrial assembly lines. Learning from JJ, Wish turns out to be a gifted pupil, one able to invent new signs to express *her* consciousness, and revealing in the process an inner animal world that humans, until recently, have denied. And, like Wish, the reader also learns some 'Auslan' signs, both through JJ's descriptive accounts of them and his inclusion of illustrations of hand signs that accompany the text.

The principal task of the novel is to convey one form of communication (signs) by means of another (words) and, in so doing, to show that the power of the sign lies in its embodiment; writing about signs, rather than actually performing them, is thus like 'pin[ning] a pair of fluttering hands – the wings of a butterfly, a bird – to a flat page' (4). The differences between sign language and words in turn suggest the different means of communication between those groups we categorise as human and those – such as gorillas – we do not.[3] The crucial question Goldsworthy's novel raises, however, is whether Wish is animal or human, and what ethical standards consequently apply to her treatment: as adopted daughter to the Kinnears, then as lover to JJ. As the emotional bond between teacher and pupil deepens, the gorilla makes sexual advances to the man, who responds; Clive Kinnear then seizes the opportunity to turn this into a *cause célèbre* for animal rights by arguing that it is not a case of bestiality but rather the seduction of a minor (Wish is eight years old), a charge that will accord Wish the same rights that a human would have. The outcome is tragic: JJ is jailed and Wish is transferred to a zoo, where she exercises the ultimate act of (human) agency, suicide. This brief summary does scant justice to a complex text which, like the fictophilosophical works of Coetzee or Derrida, is primarily concerned with the question of ethics in a post-Christian society: the ethics of relating to the underprivileged and disadvantaged, whether animal or human; the ethics of scientific experimentation; the ethics of the species boundary; the ethics of human meat-eating; and the ethics of activist reform, where the individual is sacrificed for the many: here, the causes of animal liberation and animal rights.[4]

Animal sex, human emotion?

Like Coetzee and Derrida, Goldsworthy has few answers if any to the moral dilemmas he explores; still, he insists as they do that these dilemmas are neither perverse nor preposterous – they deserve to be taken very seriously indeed. Thus, while JJ's captors (the police) regard him with little more than amused contempt, 'a lonely fat man in love with a gorilla' (259), the novel reminds us that the regulation of human sexuality has a long history, in which miscegenation and/or its results – like Noah/Noyes' 'Lotte children' or the intelligence-enhanced Wish – threatens boundaries important to racial colonialist controls. The French code which differentiated one hundred and twenty-eight possible shades of colour, so that people one part black and one hundred and twenty-seven parts white were still people 'of colour', may now seem an historical curiosity. But racist laws between blacks and whites were only abolished in South Africa in the second half of the twentieth century and the spectre of prohibition lingers: such racist taboos still exist in many countries and cultures today.

Legislation against bestiality – sexual intercourse between a human and an animal – has long been established in most societies. As Keith Thomas's scholarship has demonstrated, violations of this code in the Middle Ages were punishable by death, to the animal as well as the human, since the animal was also held to be morally responsible for the act. However, as people and animals became increasingly separated – by enclosure movements, by the industrial revolution, by the categorisation of animals as species – their apparent lack of capacity for either consciousness or intelligence was accepted as granting them immunity from responsibility while ironically enslaving them (e.g. through the Cartesian figure of the animal as automaton) all the more.

But just as it is hard to argue for what Spiegel calls the 'dreaded comparison' because the very notion of animality has condemned human 'others' to ill treatment, so bestiality is a profoundly difficult subject to confront. For a start, one of the ways we have long distinguished ourselves as humans is to claim emotional lives while denying these to animals. Animals mate (i.e. have sex), and those that mate for life are regarded as aberrations. And while there has been increasing acknowledgement of animals' ability to suffer pain – though we generally prefer not to think about this – there is still widespread denial that animals can lead emotionally complex lives. This situation is further complicated by two factors. First, hesitant as we are to accord complex emotions to animals, we are equally reluctant to admit our own involvement with them. We may acknowledge our love for particular pets (though we may be equally tempted to dismiss this as sentimentality) but we *necessarily* disguise our feelings towards animals from ourselves. If we did not, the structure of most human societies, dependent as they are on animal products, would collapse. Chinks in this armour have appeared: popular outcries against industrial farming and support for farm animals that manage to escape slaughter; the emotional outpouring that is a successful whale rescue; the uncomplicated way children treat animals, not necessarily with kindness, but as partners in their environment, moral equivalents of themselves.

Meanwhile, increasingly incontrovertible evidence of both wild and domestic animal emotions – elephant mourning, for instance – has begun to provoke scientific reconsideration of animals' emotional capacities.

(Pet owners have long testified to animal emotion; even those engaged in animal slaughter have traditionally understood animal emotion, but science, after all, is the dominant paradigm of our times.) The problem is not necessarily one of anthropo*morphism*, though animals can only be perceived and represented through our eyes; it is rather one of anthropo*centrism*, the limited view that animals are not capable of having the emotional relationships we have ourselves. While the presence of complex animal emotions must remain to a degree speculative and always runs the risk of being dismissed as unscientific, the increasing recognition of our own emotions in relation to animals seems to be part of a wider epistemological shift. Since the Enlightenment reification of reason, disciplinary protocols, e.g. in the social and medical sciences, have been faced with a paradox, one succinctly expressed by Elizabeth Costello in *The Lives of Animals*: 'Of course reason will validate reason as the first principle of the universe – what else should it do? Dethrone itself?' (25) she asks, appealing not to animal rights but to the 'sympathetic imagination' as a way of exercising feeling in relation to others and of linking others to ourselves.

Costello is predictably accused of being sentimental, which raises the important issue of where this term originates and what it has come more recently to imply. To be called a 'man of feeling or sentiment' in the eighteenth century was a compliment, but as the term was gradually feminised, it increasingly suffered from derogation by association with women. *The Oxford English Dictionary* defines 'sentiment' broadly as the expression of more feeling than a particular object or occasion demands, but this is oddly circular, for who or what decides on the appropriate amount of feeling, or for which particular objects we may appropriately feel? More recently, literary critics and theorists have been keen to take up these questions. Theories of affect have joined increased scholarly interest in memory, mourning and trauma, and the latter areas have become the twenty-first century's epistemological Trojan Horses in relation to the time-honoured 'reason-versus-emotion' debate. The evidence suggests, not so much that feeling might be making some kind of comeback, but rather that feeling *together* with reason might now be reconfiguring the original terms of the debate.

To return to the vexed topic of bestiality – an offence which, if not widespread, is much more common than reported – the legalistic problem of discriminating intention from preparation, the rarity of establishing *in flagrante delicto*, should not detract from the broader picture of animals being used, and sometimes purchased, for the purpose of satisfying (usually male) sexual desire.[5] As previously suggested, this picture is blurred by the continuing gap between human and animal sexuality; for, aside from instances of non-consensual sex, humans are held to 'make love' while animals have 'instinctual sex'. This division goes back at least as far as the Great Chain of Being, which hierarchised species differences, and was later connected to popular understanding of Darwinian evolutionary theory, which like Christian doctrine considered cross-species sex to be a perversion, thereby disallowing the possibility that either human or animal might feel emotion even if the one or the other could feel pain.

Why is it that postcolonial writers have entered this distinctly tricky territory? While no definitive answers can be supplied, some preliminary insights can be gathered from works such as Zakes Mda's *The Whale Caller* (2005) and Marian Engel's *Bear* (1976). *Bear* created a double scandal, not only when it was first published, but also later when it was selected for the Canadian Governor General's Award. In the novel, Lou, a Toronto librarian who has been involved in an unsatisfying affair with the director of the institute where she is working, is sent to a remote island in the Canadian North Country to catalogue the estate of Colonel Jocelyn Cary, who has left his property and its contents to the library as a bequest. The standard interpretation of the novel is that it is about the transformation of Lou from a state of urban *ennui* to a more vital, embodied contact with the world – and, especially, the wilderness – via the unlikely agency of the estate's resident bear. The bear, previously looked after by an old Native woman, now becomes Lou's charge, and, as in *Wish*, an emotional bond develops, followed by a number of sexual experiments (but when Lou offers the bear penetration, he categorically refuses, swiping her back with an apparently admonitory paw). The bear's motivations are unknown but, in spite of her sexual rejection, Lou returns to Toronto re-invigorated, having had awakened her previously deadened emotional world. She has also seized the opportunity to go through clippings about bears in Colonel Cary's library, a series of clues – legends, anecdotes and other ephemera – that offer multiple, if ultimately futile, ways of pinning the mystery of 'bearness' down:

> In Wales, the bear was used as a beast of chase. The name Penarth means bear's head [...] To the Lapps, the bear is King of the Beasts. Hunters who kill him must live three days alone, else they are considered unclean.
>
> (Engel 1976: 68–69)

Or:

> In the Linnaean system [...] Ursus comes between Mustela and Didelphis. The order includes Arctos, the true bears; Meles the badgers;

Lotor the raccoon; and Luscus the wolverine [...] Claws for digging, non-retractable. Senses acute. Cylindrical bones more similar to man's than those of other quadrupeds, espec. the femur. Therefore able to rear up and dance. Tongue has longitudinal groove. Kidneys lobed as in bunches of grapes; no seminal vesicles. Bone in penis. In the female, the vagina is longitudinally ridged.

(43)

And:

The Norwegians say 'The Bear has the strength of ten men and the sense of twelve'.

(55)

In the British Isles, Lou learns from yet another clipping: 'Caledonian bears were imported by the Romans and used as instruments of torture. In Wales it was a beast of chase' (Engel 1976: 120). However, for all Lou's enthusiasm, the novel suggests that she has made little progress in understanding bears; and though the eponymous Bear is in some sense a human captive, it has not proven possible to capture his essence in all the different representational genres, including the novel itself. Lou comes to recognise in the end that she could 'paint any face on [Bear] she wanted, while his actual range of expression was a mystery' (78–79). Thus, although Cary's clippings suggest a persisting interest in the nature of bears, they offer very little insight into either animal difference or animal similarity. Lou's intimate, sense-based knowledge of Bear possibly brings us closer to his nature, suspending unachievable knowledge of the animal 'other' for just long enough to suggest that genuine human–animal interchange and communication can take place. But Bear still retains his protean character – which is arguably not 'his' at all, but rather the result of repeated human attempts to incorporate him scientifically, or even metaphorically, into anthropocentric paradigms: 'Ursus', 'Arctos', the 'King of the Beasts'.

Bear is last seen leaving in a boat with his former guardian, Lucy, the Native woman, and appears to be hunched like an old woman himself. This enigmatic ending reconfirms the mystery that precedes it. Like Goldsworthy's *Wish*, Engel's *Bear* is the story of a relationship between a human being and a large animal; but while the possibility of reading Wish herself as something other than an intelligence-enhanced gorilla is precluded by Goldsworthy's fictional treatment, Bear has, for most critics and commentators, effectively disappeared from his own narrative, leaving only the limited interpretative possibilities of an avatar of the

Canadian wilderness or, still more anthropocentrically, a mere catalyst for the sexual awakening of the human protagonist in the text.

The problem of what Steve Baker (2000) calls the 'instrumental characterisation' of animals in human narratives is also taken up in the South African writer Zakes Mda's 2005 novel, *The Whale Caller*. Human jealousy occasioned by the intimate bonding of man and animal is a factor in *Wish*, and is more obliquely hinted at in *Bear*; but in *The Whale Caller* it becomes a major issue, with the 'eternal triangle' extended in this case to include man, woman and female whale. The eponymous Whale Caller is never given a first or family name, and the sobriquet appears indicative of his Ahab-like monomania; however, the obsession this time is one of love, not hate. Further parallels between Mda's novel and Melville's prove irresistible; for, as surely as *Heart of Darkness*, *Moby-Dick* haunts twentieth- and twenty-first century fiction,[6] particularly those works concerned with relationships between animals and men. Current western attitudes towards whales tend to range between the sympathetic and the awe-struck, and it is no coincidence that while Williams' *2007* is mainly concerned with terrestrial and avian species, emblematic episodes of whale hunting supply the novel's main narrative frame. Like the other animals in Williams' fable, whales resist both their literal and textual capture by humans, thwarting human intention when it becomes necessary. However, animal agency – relatively unproblematised in Williams – becomes a central problematic in Melville, for whom the great white whale is the object of a hatred so extreme, so all-consumingly pervasive, that it becomes a perverse, obsessive love.

Love and hate also interfuse in Mda's later novel, which otherwise demonstrates the drastic change in human attitudes to whales over the century and a half since Melville published *Moby-Dick*. In the small South African town of Hermanus where *The Whale Caller* is set, whales are still – as in Melville's day – thoroughly commodified, but now it is the tourists who pursue them, viewing them less as a source of profit than of wonderment and awe. A local whale caller is also used to lure the whales, but the eponymous Whale Caller is not a servant of the commercial tourist industry; his luring is of a different, unequivocally sexual kind. Using a traditional kelp horn, the reclusive Whale Caller awaits the arrival of his true love, a southern right whale, Sharisha, who comes temporarily to rest in Hermanus Bay on her annual migratory journey. The Whale Caller dresses formally in a tuxedo on these occasions, often blowing himself into a state of sexual ecstasy with his horn, and communing with Sharisha through what he interprets as call-and-response patterns of breaching and blowing by the aroused whale. Although the Whale Caller is apparently the apex of his own particular love triangle, he frets insistently with jealousy when other (whale) suitors surround his loved one. On such occasions, 'he holds the horn close to his heart. He dare not press it too hard against his cheek, lest it break' (Mda 2005: 5).

It is Saluni, the town drunk, who eventually upsets the Whale Caller's relationship with Sharisha when she becomes obsessed with him. From a natural (vegetarian) simplicity, the Whale Caller is civilised (into piscivory, carnivory and tablecloths) by Saluni, and he becomes increasingly involved with her, without forgetting his old love, disparagingly referred to by Saluni as 'that ugly fish' (62). 'I am not going to be part of any triangle', Saluni insists, 'the fish must go' (80). Because of his affection for Sharisha, the Whale Caller cannot make love to Saluni at first, but he eventually succumbs to her. Tragedy awaits, however, when Saluni deliberately blinds herself by looking directly at the eclipse so that the Whale Caller will be obliged thereafter to give her, and not Sharisha, his full attention. Saluni is eventually killed by an enigmatic female duo known as the 'Bored Twins' and, equally tragically, Sharisha strands herself in responding too strongly to the Whale Caller's horn. When rescue proves impossible, the only way to save Sharisha from a slow death is – quite literally – to blow her up.

As in *Wish*, the rational explanation provided by scientists is demonstrably inadequate and while tragedy and farce intermingle, even the death of the whale is ultimately seen, like that of *Wish*, in a primarily anthropocentric light. Explaining to the mayor that he is only trying to ensure a quick death, the scientist is mindful that the scene could quickly escalate into a diplomatic incident:

> The politicians from the national legislature are more concerned about South Africa's image in the international community. 'They will accuse us of savagery and barbarism,' says a member of the parliament. 'The markets will react negatively. The rand will go down.' 'The rand will go down in any case,' says a sceptic. 'Someone farts in Bolivia and the rand comes tumbling down.' This brings about another round of guffaws, which the member of parliament interprets to be at his expense. He leaves in a huff, his entourage in tow.
>
> (224–25)

The ending of Mda's novel – comic and plaintive by turns – confirms that the Whale Caller's love for the whale has been both sexual and spiritual; mind and body are emphatically one. Nor is Saluni's attitude towards Sharisha as dismissive as she would have it appear: she recognises in the whale a genuine rival for her lover's affections, even 'mooning' the whale as the best insult she can think of since verbally expressed antagonism isn't possible in this case. What the novel shares with *Wish* and *Bear*, then, aside from its affirmation of sensual relations between humans and animals, is an attempted bridging of the Cartesian gulf between body and spirit, human emotion and animal emotion. Life and love, for both animal and human, is depicted in terms of the unity of mind and body in a fully realised if fictionally rendered demonstration of the embodied nature of being espoused by Elizabeth Costello in Coetzee's seminal texts.

If Moby Dick cannot escape the symbolic freight conferred upon him both by his author and a century and a half of critical commentary, this is because

> [t]he narrative, form and thematic [of Melville's novel] are all driven by the question: What do whales mean? Critical replies to this have concentrated upon reading Cetaceans as a screen for the projection of human meanings, [and] attended only incidentally to what else they might mean, or how they might mean otherwise – that is, the ways in which whales trouble or escape human representation.
>
> (P. Armstrong 2008: 101)

The quest for Moby Dick in Melville's novel, along with the critical quest for that novel's meaning, have tended to erase whales as effectively as their bodies are 'rendered' on the *Pequod* and other (both real and fictional) commercial whaling boats. And while Melville certainly raises the question of the agency of his fictional whale – a question that also troubles accounts of encounters with his real-life counterpart – Moby Dick still tends to be read either as the general symbol of a malign universe or as an embedded commentary on American politics in the 1840s (P. Armstrong 2008: 101).

Like *Moby-Dick*, *The Whale Caller* is concerned with contemporary – in this case, South African – politics, but none of its three principal characters, nor their novelistic interactions, can be considered symbolic of these. Meanwhile, Mda's substitution of the romance for the quest genre has further ramifications. For example, the Whale Caller is quick to reject the comparison made between his practices and those of the 'shark callers' of New Ireland when he realises that the object of this alternative exercise is to lure sharks – considered as prey – to their deaths (11–12). Killing whales for consumption, he believes, is 'tantamount to cannibalism' (12). He also dismisses comparison with the other whale caller employed by the local tourist board, whom he considers to be no more than a 'showman' (12) – making the novel's tragic ending, with its accompanying vow of penitence, more poignant still.

In *Wish* and *Bear*, the animal protagonists are depicted as being able to communicate directly with their human lovers, and both exercise a degree of agency. In *The Whale Caller*, on the other hand, bodily contact is all but impossible, even though both other members of the love triangle fervently believe in Sharisha's ability to respond. Response, as Jacques Derrida has memorably explored in such essays as 'The animal that therefore I am', has traditionally been denied to animals, despite their obvious capacity to return the human gaze, which raises the potentially unsettling question, not of how *we* see animals, but of how they see *us*. Thus, while there is no consensual sex between animal and human in *The Whale Caller*, as there is in *Wish* and – inconclusively – in *Bear*, there is the suggestion that the human subjectivity of Mda's unnamed protagonist is constituted by his wished-for response by a member of another species, and that this subjectivity is radically altered, even profoundly unravelled, by her death. This inversion of the 'normal' process of human subjectification is echoed in the practice of whale watching. Saluni is undone by Sharisha's steady gaze, which the Whale Caller experiences by contrast as sexual ecstasy. And perhaps most tellingly, the tourists wait patiently for the whales' solicited appearance in order to reify their own witnessing presence at that spot. What all three novels suggest, then, is that the strongest of human emotions – love – is not and cannot be confined to our own species. Thus, while animals may remain a mystery to us, and while our relations with them certainly demand re-thinking, such challenges can only be undertaken once we acknowledge our fundamental need for emotional attachment to other animals, and to the animals that we (therefore) are ourselves.

Conclusion

In a letter to his South African counterpart William Plomer, the British writer J.R. Ackerley admits that he makes no distinction between humans and animals, stating further that 'if the word "human" had never been invented we might all be a great deal happier than we are' (Parker 1989: 406). In the half-century since Ackerley first wrote those words, we have become increasingly aware of human rights and their manifold abuses. But we have made significantly less progress towards the realisation, not so much that rights need to be extended to other species, but that the fundamental distinction between the human and the animal needs to be re-thought. Another way of saying this might be that since the rights of humans and animals are inextricably interwoven, the righting of wrongs in relation to all living creatures, as well as to the extra-human environment, cannot be accomplished as long as we continue to treat these issues as discrete. While rights remain an important safeguard, most post-colonial writers have chosen to address the question of these wrongs, less through legal or rationalistic frameworks than in imaginative writing that is both finely attuned to the injustices attached to the racism–speciesism nexus and consistently attentive to the emotional lives of animals and our relationship to animals – lives and relationships in which our instinctive empathy with animals is neither scornfully dismissed nor systematically suppressed.

Notes

1 An earlier version of this section of the discussion appeared in the editorial, *Interventions* 9.1(2007): 1–11.
2 In 2008 Spain's parliament became the first to begin the process of granting 'human rights' status to Great Apes, which include chimpanzees, gorillas, bonobos and orang-utans.
3 Since JJ's parents are deaf, his own 'first language' is 'sign'. *Wish* also raises comparable questions to those raised by philosopher Peter Singer in relation to *essential* human qualities. If spoken language is one attribute which differentiates us from animals, what of those humans who cannot speak?

Similarly, it seems worth asking to what extent certain categories of humans, as well as animals, are already *spoken for*. Gayatri Spivak's influential formulation of the problem of colonised voices in 'Can the Subaltern Speak?' makes a convincing case for the ways in which self-expression for the colonised is circumscribed by the very processes of conquest and colonisation themselves (Spivak 1988). Colonised animals and ecosystems share this subaltern positioning, but they are even more inhibited by the lack of any vocal communication that humans are generally prepared to recognise as intelligible – a problem all the more acute when the animals in question are seen in other respects as being proximate to ourselves. The Great Apes are usually the first to come into this category. Monkeys and apes have always troubled the human/animal divide, so it is not surprising that they have been used regularly in fiction as vehicles for the critique of human societies and have been imaginatively accorded speech in order to do so. However, incidences of this long-standing European tradition are relatively rare in postcolonial texts, which is not surprising either given the equally established association of monkeys and apes with colonialist forms of racist vilification (see the Introduction to this part of the book).

Two literary works – both written by Europeans – which critically reflect on these problems, are Pierre Boulle's 1965 science fiction classic *Monkey Planet* (originally published in 1963 in French as *La planète des singes*) and Jenny Diski's 1994 novel *Monkey's Uncle. Monkey Planet* vividly imagines a reversal of human/ape dominance in order to explore the linked processes of racial determinism and colonisation, especially in relation to the problems of racial positioning and subaltern speech. On Monkey Planet, it is the non-human apes that are civilised and socially organised, while humans are little more than degenerate animals, running wild in the forest and mercilessly hunted by the militaristic gorillas – themselves positioned in a subaltern relationship to the intellectually superior chimpanzees and orang-utans – for their sport.

On Monkey Planet (which ironically turns out to be our own), humans become objects of the same violence and scientific curiosity that have been routinely visited on earth by humans on animals in general and, until recently, on monkeys and apes in particular, with the various scientific experiments inflicted upon them offering a further reminder of those historically performed on subject peoples under colonial rule. To the regime's scientists (chimpanzees), humans lack coherent speech and have only limited intelligence; even attempts to learn 'their' language are dismissed as mere imitation, and rebellious human behaviour is conveniently taken as further evidence of innate savagery in accordance with the regime's set beliefs.

It would be difficult to find a clearer illustration of the problems confronting subaltern individuals, be they human or animals, in attempting to 'speak' to a dominant culture. Boulle's work graphically demonstrates the powerful ways in which dominant attitudes and practices become both self-perpetuating and self-serving, precluding the possibility of recognising alternative forms of intelligence and self-expression. Such forms come under scrutiny in *Monkey's Uncle*, which draws inventively on Lewis Carroll's work to offer a transformative 'looking-glass' entry into another world. As in *Monkey Planet* (and, indeed, as in Carroll's 'Alice' tales), this world stands our own on its head, asking us to reconsider what is 'sane' and 'normal', and making a mockery of the usual rules by which decisions around 'sanity' and 'normality' are made.

At the beginning of *Monkey's Uncle*, protagonist Charlotte Fitzroy, who has suffered a nervous breakdown that seems to run in the family – depression had previously accounted for her nineteenth-century ancestor, Robert FitzRoy – falls down her own version of a psychological rabbit-hole and meets Jenny, her phantasmagorical orang-utan guide. It is Jenny, a 'situational' rather than a 'blood' descendant, who will lead Charlotte away from the brink of madness; and it is situation, rather than inheritance or bloodlines, that matters most – or so Diski's novel suggests – in the contemporary world. Charlotte is consequently able to identify more readily with Jenny, a fantasy orang-utan in the zoo, than with such established figures as Freud, Marx and Darwin; and it is Jenny who acts as Charlotte's teacher, even if the wisdom she offers is transmitted through human registers – for animals, however sympathetically they are represented in literature, can never be made to represent themselves.

While much of the conversation between Charlotte and Jenny in the novel is comically rendered, it has a serious underlay. Charlotte's attempts to probe the possible causes of her breakdown lead her to revisit fundamental questions about genes and inheritance, ancestors and descendants, and the very nature and purpose of life. But once subjected to cross-species scrutiny, these questions are relativised; as Jenny humorously points out, to a sloth it is the rest of the world that is moving too fast. In its own idiosyncratic way, *Monkey's Uncle* suggests that human-animal encounters may lead to 'the disorienting recognition of vast possibilities beyond the parameters of what we usually think of as "normal"' (Sax 2009: 167). Animal fables and fantasies, in this sense, are far more than critical exposures of the human will to dominate; they also remind us that human apprehensions of existence are not those of the majority of planetary life. Thus, whether such works are written in colonial/postcolonial contexts or not, they contribute to decolonising our present by opening up new ways of understanding others that are not skewed in self-interest or bound to dominant narratives of the past. Some of the material in the latter part of this note previously appeared in modified form in Robert Cribb, Helen Gilbert and Helen Tiffin, *Wild Man from Borneo*, Honolulu: University of Hawai'i Press, 2014.

4 Although JJ's sexual encounter with Wish is not an instance of same-sex desire, the perversity that is attributed to it also hints at the policing of the 'normal' and the 'natural' that is a principal target for queer theory and its correlate, queer ecology. Queer ecology – or at least the field that explicitly identifies as such – is a more recent phenomenon than postcolonial queer studies, which has been around for a decade and more now, drawing on and extending the insights of seminal queer theorists operating at least a decade before that (Hawley *et al.* 2001; Gopinath 2005; Puar 2008). Despite the adjective-noun combination, queer ecology is better seen as an ecologically oriented branch of queer theory than as a 'queering' of ecology; and like all queer theory, it is fundamentally 'at odds with the normal, the legitimate, and the dominant' (Halperin 1997: 62) – with the self-authorising practices and structures of an obdurately 'heteronormative' world.

A breakthrough volume is the eponymous *Queer Ecologies: Sex, Nature, Politics, Desire* (2010), co-edited by the Canadian scholars Catriona Mortimer-Sandilands and Bruce Erickson. In their wide-ranging introduction, the co-editors use Ang Lee's 2006 movie *Brokeback Mountain* to stage a dialogue between queer and ecological politics that reveals 'the powerful ways in which understandings of nature inform discourses of sexuality, and also the ways in which understandings of sex inform discourses of nature; they are linked, in fact, through a strong evolutionary narrative that pits the perverse, the polluted, and the degenerate against the fit, the healthy, and the natural' (2010: 2–3). Queer theory, seen this way, registers an all-out attack on the ideological hijacking of the 'natural'. Heavily influenced by the biopolitical theories of Foucault and driven by a strongly materialist and constructivist view of 'nature', queer ecology aims to subvert the heteronormative organisation of sexual politics under the sign of the 'natural' while working towards more inclusive understandings (e.g. via the polymorphous figure of the 'queer animal') of the sexual politics of the natural world. This leads, at one level, to the extension of biopolitics into zoopolitics – a move queer ecology shares with the higher-visibility field of animal studies (Shukin 2009; Wolfe 2013) – and, at another, to the mapping of certain kinds of *desire* onto certain kinds of *places*: a critical cartography that challenges the labelling of places as 'wholesome' or 'degenerate' according to heteronormative codes of sexual conduct and exchange.

Queer ecology's relationship with postcolonialism is problematic. Most of the contributors to *Queer Ecologies*, even as they attack heteronormative social relations, tend to uphold the normative value of North American experiences of wilderness and landscape, though the co-editors freely admit that 'cross-cultural, transnational, and postcolonial investigations [in the field] are only just beginning', and that these have the potential to challenge the 'cultural specificity of dominant Western ideas of sex and space' as well as to further highlight 'the fragility [...] of the articulations of [...] bodies and natures' that are the primary subjects of their own text (2010: 21). In those postcolonial approaches that do exist (e.g. Cruz-Malavé and Manalansan 2002; Spurlin 2006), queer ecology is as much about disrupting *ethnic* as *sexual* norms, and about critically analysing the relationship between these. Queer ecology, in this last context, looks to interrogate the power relations surrounding exotic constructions of the ethnic other, whose sexual attractiveness is a function of his/her ability to meet dominant cultural expectations of ethnic 'authenticity' and to fulfil the fantasy criteria of white male western desire (Huggan 2001).

A writer whose work resonates with these themes is the Japanese Canadian novelist and poet Hiromi Goto. Much of Goto's work, in the words of the critic Wendy Gay Pearson, constitutes a 'poetic and polemical intervention into the embodied effects of discourses of racialization and sexualization, of their combination in orientalism, and of the hermeneutics of citizenship within the Canadian public sphere' (2007: 75–76). A key strategy is Goto's invocation of the *monstrous*. Goto's fiction and poetry is populated by 'monstrous' figures of different kinds who are constructed as such by the dominant society; these 'monsters' are threatening to the body politic in part because they represent an alternative to it, a different (queer) way of thinking about the ways in which the normal, the natural, and eventually the human itself are defined (Pearson 2007: 79; see also Toffoletti 2004).

Goto's 'monsters' *are* different: in her 2001 novel, *The Kappa Child*, a Japanese Canadian girl finds herself mysteriously pregnant by a kappa, a curious spirit-creature that blesses all those, however eccentric or excluded, who believe in it; while in the title story of her 2004 short-story collection *Hopeful Monsters*, another pregnancy yields another 'anomalous' child born, as was its mother before it, with what the doctor euphemistically calls a 'caudal appendage' – a tail (2004: 148). A simple operation would remove the anomaly, but the mother decides that the tail will stay, recognising that she herself has 'been an amputee her whole life, without knowing it' (2004: 160); and that the best home for the baby is with the lesbian couple she had previously met in parenting classes, who are understandably shocked by her assumptions about their own 'abnormality' but provisionally agree to take in both child and mother (if not the white father, who likes 'Japanese girls' as long as they are stereotypically 'authentic') nonetheless (2004: 166–67; see also Pearson 2007: 81).

'Hopeful Monsters' takes its title from the American evolutionary biologist Stephen Jay Gould, whose filtered view is that 'radically beneficial adaptive traits' have the potential to create 'hopeful monsters' (Goto 2004: 135); and, as Pearson suggests in her useful gloss, Goto uses the apparently oxymoronic figure of the hopeful monster both to 'disrupt the iconicity of white maternity' and to reposition mother and child as co-producers of 'an alternative futurity in which monstrosity can be revalued and iconicity refused' (Pearson 2007: 81). This exemplary queer reading of the nuclear family reworks iconic versions of the (Canadian) national narrative within the framework of an ecological paradigm through which human-animal continuities are accepted and the heteronormative preconditions for 'natural' parenting are erased. At the same time, this paradigm is given a postcolonial dimension through the story's thinly veiled attack on a particular form of liberal racism, organised around orientalist notions of ethnic authenticity, in which white male protectionism (embodied here in the 'freak' child's conservative white father) loses its naturalising force.

5 Police records confirm a continuing use of animals as sexual objects, especially within farming communities where chickens, sheep, goats, horses, etc., continue to be accessible. Credible reports of the sale of young female orang-utans as sex-slaves continue to come from Malaysia and Indonesia.

6 For a comprehensive study of the significance of *Moby-Dick* for later writers and zoocriticism, see Armstrong 2008.

Postscript
After nature

Nature, says Raymond Williams, is one of the most complex words in the language, and ecocritics have had as much difficulty with it as everyone else (Williams 1983: 219; see also Buell 2005). Probably the most rigorous recent attempt to define the term has been that of the British eco-philosopher Kate Soper, who distinguishes between nature's three-fold deployment as a *metaphysical* concept through which 'humanity thinks its difference and specificity', a *realist* concept that refers to 'the structures, processes and causal powers that are constantly operative within the physical [environment]', and a *lay* or *surface* concept used in relation to 'ordinarily observable features of the world' (Soper, in Coupe 2000: 125). However, as she readily admits, these three concepts and the discourses deriving from them are rhetorically co-dependent. Conventional environmentalist valorisations of nature as being independent of human culture thus run up against the obvious obstacle that much of what passes for the 'natural world' is a product of human activity and, once this truism is accepted, the 'nature' one is seeking to promote and protect isn't 'natural' in any autonomous sense (124).[1]

This problem is compounded by the widespread perception that modernity, however defined, is 'post-natural' in the dialectical sense of losing human connection to the natural environment while simultaneously gaining a re-invigorated awareness that nature itself is continually re-formed. One version of this dilemma is that presented by Horkheimer and Adorno, much of whose work traces the historical process – consolidated by modernity – by which 'after *nature*', the mimetic relationship to nature that characterises what they call the 'pre-civilised period', becomes '*after* nature', the rational assertion of human beings over and against nature in what they call the 'historical phase' (Horkheimer and Adorno 1972: 180). For Adorno in particular, as for several other philosophers of modernity, alienation is the price human beings have paid for their increasing control and management of nature; the attempted recovery of a lost relationship to nature is thus a primary symptom of the historical phase, as articulated in those forms of 'repressed mimesis' (Adorno 1998: 162) by which the so-called return to nature is imaginatively captured in art. The mimetic faculty involves an emotional re-engagement with a universe increasingly subject to rational processes of abstraction and objectification; in this and other ways, Adorno can arguably be seen as an ecological thinker who, in showing how 'the progress of rationality turns into its opposite' (Gebauer and Wulf 1996: 292), suggests that the technologies developed and endorsed by modernity have the potential to emancipate, but also to eliminate, the world.

Another way of looking at Horkheimer and Adorno's 'historical phase' is through the 'end' or 'death' of nature thesis, which is generally couched in terms of the predominance of a new, *mechanical* order over an earlier, *organic* one, although – as in Horkheimer and Adorno – these two orders are by no means mutually exclusive, and any understanding of modernity must take account of the ways in which they are strategically enmeshed. Two influential versions of the end/death of nature thesis can be briefly examined here. The first belongs to the American environmental journalist Bill McKibben, who, in his recently re-issued 1989 book on global warming, *The End of Nature*, outlines that particular form of secular providentialism by which 'we [humans] are no longer able to think of ourselves as a species tossed about by larger forces – now we *are* those larger forces. Hurricanes and thunderstorms and tornadoes become not acts of God but acts of man' (McKibben 2006: xviii; emphasis his). Although McKibben's tone is self-consciously apocalyptic throughout, he still makes it clear that the end of nature is not the same thing as the end of the world; rather, it is to be understood both as a definitive loss of our comforting sense of the 'permanence of the natural environment' (7) and as an accompanying awareness that the realities of both conscious and unconscious human alteration (modern genetic engineering, climate change, etc.) have irreversibly transformed earlier ideas of nature as separate and eternal: 'The idea that nature – that *anything* – [can] be defined will soon be outdated. Because anything can be changed' (143).

For McKibben, the end of nature is synonymous with scientific methodologies for manipulating nature, with deliberate choices to bring about lasting changes to – for example – the genetic make-up of humans and other animals that 'exhibit a kind of power thought in the past to be divine' (66). This misplaced 'technocratic optimism' (Graham 2002: 8) is also the subject for the American feminist environmental historian Carolyn Merchant, whose seminal study *The Death of Nature* (1980) charts the transition from pre-modern images of the earth as a precariously balanced living organism to a modern 'mechanical order' in which the earth, now rendered fully exploitable for its resources, was seen – in a flagrant distortion of the available empirical evidence – to be inanimate and inert. Merchant sees the crucial break as having taken place in seventeenth-century Europe, with the rise of an experimental science that explicitly sought dominion over the natural world. The scientific revolution was one cause of the death of nature; the rise of industrial capitalism was another. And a third was colonial expansion, driven like capitalism itself by ideologies of possession, the global management of material assets, and the economically motivated conversion of human labour into natural resource. Bringing this history up to the present, Merchant sees the death of nature as lying behind the recent scientific advances of, e.g., contemporary biotechnology, which she reads as further evidence of the 'confluence of mechanical and commercial orders' (1992: 48) and of the technocratic view that nature, suitably retooled to match the latest global-corporate interests, is rendered inarticulate and inanimate even as 'dead' money is endowed with vital life (1992: 58).

A less negative view is that taken by Donna Haraway, who shares many of her fellow American historian of science's sworn ideological enemies – colonial racism, masculinist capitalism, and so on – but arguably parts company with her in her choice of ecological friends. Like Merchant's, Haraway's is a social constructivist view of science informed by overtly feminist principles, a view in which the social relations between nonhumans, as well as humans, are reified under the conditions of late capitalism, and life itself, in an ironically 'dyspeptic version of the technoscientific soap opera', is 'enterprised up' (Haraway 1997: 12). However, to a much greater extent than Merchant, Haraway sees the imaginative possibilities opened up by the implosion of nature and culture, as well as by the explosion of global technoscientific enterprise; in its unrivalled capacity to break down artificial boundaries between the subject and the object, the technical and the political, (post)modern technoscience, which Haraway sees as being characterised by its 'promiscuously fused and transgenic quality', may yet provide future models for a livable world (1997: 4, 270).

For Haraway, the recent discoveries of biotechnology, especially those associated with the Human Genome Project, afford the possibility of an exciting new 'cyborg vision' in which 'miscegenation between and among humans and nonhumans [will increasingly be] the norm' (121). 'The promise of the genome' (100) has the creative capacity to trouble genre as well as gender, suggesting that 'the great divide between Man and Nature [...] that founded the story of modernity', complete with its 'gendered corollary and colonial racial melodrama', may now have been definitively

breached (121). However, here as elsewhere, Haraway's posthuman utopianism is tempered by her awareness of the dangers of new biologically
oriented technologies, their potential to be enlisted in the service of fresh
forms of exploitation and domination in a scientifically recolonised
world. Hence her ambivalent reading of the cyborg (cybernetic organism) as a figure for *both* domination *and* resistance; and hence her later,
similarly ironic reading of OncoMouse, the world's first patented animal
and still probably its most memorable transgenic model, as both
boundary-transgressing cultural icon and encrypted 'civic sacrament' in a
'secularized salvation history' of western scientific progress and global-
corporate economic power (85). (After all, as Haraway admits, the
recent history of genetic patenting practices has been less suggestive of
the move towards a 'multicultural, democratic, biotechnological commons'
than of the ongoing investment of biotechnology in new forms of ecological imperialism defined in terms of transnational corporate biopower
(1997: 87; see also Kimball 1996).)

Whether nature is seen as being essentially at an end (McKibben,
Merchant) or as being eternally renewable (Haraway), 'post-natural' discourses simultaneously point to a crisis of *humanism* that, over at least
the last three decades, has had wide implications for understandings of
nature and the human across a wide spectrum of the sciences (particularly
biology, but also sociology and anthropology) and the arts. Ecocriticism
and postcolonialism have every reason to be suspicious, if not necessarily
dismissive, of humanism, which has been routinely attacked for practising a selective universalism that disguises specific race, class, gender and,
for that matter, species interests, and for providing an intellectual rationale
for the imperial civilising mission and other authoritarian regimes and
systems which, consciously or unconsciously, have abused humanity in
humanity's name (Chambers 2001; Davies 2007). ('It is almost impossible
to think', says Tony Davies ruefully, 'of a crime that has not been committed in the name of humanity; [and yet] the problem of humanism
remains an inescapable horizon within which all attempts to think about
the ways in which human beings have, do, might live together in and on
the world are contained' (2007: 131).)

Several of the most cogent recent critiques of humanism have been
gathered under the banner of the 'posthuman', like other 'posts' a slippery
concept which can either be seen as a radical departure from the main
idea that precedes it or as an ongoing interrogation of the terms on which
this idea has been historically conceived (Badmington 2000; Graham 2002;
Hayles 1999). While the posthuman is frequently reduced to popular
perceptions, alternately triumphal and terrifying, of the fusion of the
human with the intelligent machine, it is perhaps better understood as a

point of view characterised by the assumption that embodiment is an historical accident rather than a biological necessity; for if the body is looked upon as no more than an original prosthesis, then its extension or replacement with other prostheses becomes the 'continuation of a process that began before we were born' (Hayles 1999: 3).

For posthumanist ecocritics, the question of the animal is as important as the question of the machine, but the basic principle is the same: that of eroding ideological distinctions between the human and the non-human, often to the point of rendering the human inoperable as a foundational or explanatory category, or – what amounts to the same thing – showing the murderous arrogance with which human beings have taken ideas of the human to themselves, twisting them in their own individual interests or using them to justify their own immediate ends (Wolfe 2003: xi; see also Ehrenfeld 1981). Probably the most convincing of these critics to date has been Cary Wolfe, who in a series of closely argued books and journal articles has taken humanism to task for its anthropocentric prejudices and hierarchical presumptions, also seeing humanism's hidden hand in philosophies that are consciously egalitarian and anti-anthropocentric, such as those informing animal rights (Wolfe 1998, 2003, 2007). The question of rights, as has been suggested throughout this book, is a particularly tricky one to handle, underpinning as it does humanism's reactionary as well as revolutionary imperatives, and sometimes even shadowing the specifically *anti-* and *post*humanist initiatives of those, like Wolfe, who see humanism's historical reliance on increasingly discredited social/moral categories (the sovereign subject, the essentialist category of Man, etc.) as a sign that its ideological pre-eminence was already endangered before its days were officially done.

The problem with this view – and not just for Wolfe – is that the contemporary evidence suggests that humanism's days are far from over, and that the various anti- and posthumanisms currently rushing in to replace it are often given to 'secret[ing] a humanist rhetoric' (Soper 1995: 182) that 'betrays their hidden affinity with what they deny' (Davies 2007: 35). The point is well made in Martin Halliwell and Andy Mousley's *Critical Humanisms* (2004), when, in parrying Neil Badmington's claim that humanism is forever condemned 'to rewrite itself as posthumanism' (Badmington 2000: 9), the authors suggest that posthumanism might be similarly haunted by the humanist concerns it disavows (190). While most posthumanists would disagree with the conclusions Halliwell and Mousley reach, that the posthuman is but a 'particular kind of critical moment in the mutating but nevertheless identifiable discourse of human-ism' (190; see also Waldby 2000), it becomes more difficult to claim, as Iain Chambers does, that a combination of poststructuralist philosophy and postcolonial cultural criticism has left the western humanist inheritance in tatters, with its fundamental assurances (the sovereignty of the human subject, the transparency of its language, the truth of its rationalism) unsettled and its universalist pretensions undone (Chambers 2001: 2–3). For one thing, this overlooks the humanisms implicit, and sometimes explicit, in postcolonial criticism, from the 'revolutionary humanism' of Frantz Fanon to the 'civic humanism' of Stuart Hall, to that curious amalgam of Auerbachian humanism and Foucauldian anti-humanism that is the work of Edward Said (Gibson 1999; Halliwell and Mousley 2004; Huggan 2005). To be sure, these humanisms are all resolutely anti-Eurocentric, notably the 'new humanism' of Fanon which, in measuring Europe's atrocities against its achievements, concludes that 'if we want humanity to advance a step farther [...] we must invent and we must make new discoveries', since Europe has failed in its self-given mission to enlarge the human spirit, proving catastrophically incapable of producing the 'triumphant birth' of the 'new man' (Badmington 2000: 24, 26; see also Fanon 2005).[2] Indeed, postcolonial humanisms, on the whole, are theoretically post-*foundationalist* and historically post-*European*, acknowledging that the 'colonialist construction of Western civilisation as [a] beacon of enlightened humanity' (Halliwell and Mousley 2004: 9) has had devastating consequences, and that humanism's complicities with Empire have provided unwanted evidence of the inhumanity done to humanity in the name of Man (Davies 2007). However, they are not necessarily post-*humanist*, and the implications are – at least in the work of Fanon and Said, and their many postcolonial followers – that the historically necessary decolonisation of the 'human' leads not to a *post-* but a *pan-*humanism that opens up more generous understandings of the human defined in terms of cross-cultural solidarity and achievement rather than those more likely to seek shelter in comforting notions of cultural particularity and the privileges of birth. (Pan-humanism, interestingly enough, has also appeared on the ecocritical agenda, notably via the work of the American nature poet Gary Snyder, in which an ecological understanding of the complexities of the natural world requires a revitalised or, perhaps better, a re-extended form of humanism which, reaching out beyond the western boundaries of humanist philosophy, enthusiastically accommodates the non-human within humanistic thought (Snyder 1995; see also Huggan 2007b, Love 2003).)

While the continued critique of humanism is vitally important, this by no means implies a wholesale rejection of the human, as even the most ardent of posthumanists admit (Chambers 2001; Hayles 1999). However, to return now to Wolfe, there is a growing sense that academic researchers, both within and beyond the humanities, are confronting 'a social, technological and cultural context that is now in some inescapable sense posthuman, if not quite posthumanist' (Wolfe 2003: ix). Much of the recent high-profile work on animals, for example, has had the arguable effect, not just of probing the limits of the human, but of reconfirming the crisis of humanism in the academy at large (Wolfe 2003: x–xii; see also Daston and Mitman 2005, Wolfe 2007). The humanities will probably survive this latest, possibly exaggerated threat to their integrity. Whether they will adapt to it is another matter: the intriguing possibility of a posthumanist humanities remains moot. Whatever the case, the tension between pan-humanist and posthumanist approaches to academic research, one already inscribed within emergent fields like postcolonialism and ecocriticism, should prove to be a feature of contemporary English Studies – still the most common, if by no means the only, institutional receptacle for them – as it continues to struggle with its humanistic legacy for the foreseeable future to come.

This tension is also inscribed in two fairly recent postcolonial novels, Margaret Atwood's *Oryx and Crake* (2003) and Zadie Smith's *White Teeth* (2000), which critically engage with a variety of 'post-natural' themes and posthuman possibilities. Each of these novels can be briefly dealt with in turn here before, in bringing them together, this study draws finally to its close. Several of Atwood's early works, e.g. *The Edible Woman* (1969) and, perhaps especially, *Surfacing* (1972), had been explicitly concerned to break down masculinist/colonialist attitudes to nature attached to what the Australian ecofeminist Val Plumwood calls a 'hyper-separation of humans from nature and other animals': one that creates a 'polarized understanding in which the human and the non-human spheres correspond to two quite different substrates or orders of being in the world' (Plumwood 2003: 55). In a satirical twist perhaps more character-istic of her later novels, *Oryx and Crake* adapts this transformative process to a millenarian context in which the new chosen race (the Children of Crake, named after their egomaniacal creator) must fight for space with other genetically modified creatures and a handful of desperate human remnants in a radically altered 'post-natural' world. More reminiscent of *The Handmaid's Tale* than *Surfacing*, and closer in spirit to H.G. Wells's prescient anti-vivisectionist fable *The Island of Dr. Moreau* than to either of these, *Oryx and Crake* offers a grotesque – simultaneously ridicu-lous and terrifying – perspective on Haraway's promissory cyborg universe in which virtually everything has been crossed with virtually everything else and absolutely everything is for sale (Haraway 1991, 1997). Atwood's main satirical targets are familiar enough – genetic engineering and/as eugenics, virtual reality and/as pornography, the new technologies and/as alternative creationism – and all are linked, directly or indirectly, to her

overarching topic of the exploitative aspects of twenty-first-century corporate biopower (Foucault 1970, 1977; see also Haraway 1991).[3] At the
centre of it all are the twin figures of Crake, a latter-day Moreau, and his
equally belated humanist counterpart Jimmy – alias Snowman, 'an illusion
of a white man, here today, gone tomorrow' (Atwood 2003: 232) – whose
failed attempt to check his former friend's eliminationist ambitions to
create a new posthuman race has left him stranded in a ruined half-world
where, lethally infected with the virus Crake has bequeathed him, he is
left with no other choice than, like one of Beckett's doomed postmodern
survivalists, to go on (318, 376).

This blasted world is the paradoxical consequence of Crake's eco-
philosophy, a violent form of techno-ecological utopianism through which
he looks to steer 'the nature of nature in a direction more beneficial to those
hitherto taken' (305), and to salvage the wrecked post-Enlightenment
ideal of perfectibility by reducing life to a controlled experiment in which,
sooner or later, all recognisable traces of human error and weakness will
be gone. Like Bacon's New Atlantis, Crake's brave new world is a triumph of scientific administration and surveillance in which scientists
alone possess the secret of nature, entrusting to themselves the future of
the earth (Merchant 1980: 180–81). Much of Atwood's satire depends, in
fact, on a less-than-subtle reworking of Bacon's model for the era of
global corporate capitalism: the company geneticist Crake is the scientist-
as-magus, charged with the task of creating new organisms and species,
while his aptly named Paradice Project – itself a 'transgenic' cross of
organic and mechanical utopias – riskily deploys the latest scientific technologies in order to re-assert human dominion over nature (Merchant
1980: 185). The visible results of this warped eugenicist fantasy are the
Children of Crake, ironically hybrid products of the latest form of technological purism, whose natural innocence has been artificially created
and whose non-competitive, sexually and nutritionally healthy habits
fulfil the seemingly impossible possibility of driving destructive (racist,
hierarchical, territorial) instincts once and for all out of the 'ancient
primate brain' (Atwood 2003: 316). These ironies are then compounded
by the text's competing eco-fundamentalisms, with Crake's most ardent
foes being those anti-corporate eco-warriors who, like Jimmy's legendary mother, prove more than capable of killing (or being killed) in the
name of the lives they fanatically protect (185–87).

Atwood's satirical targets are drawn from both ends of the political
spectrum, with familiar sideswipes being taken at media-driven compassion
fatigue ('"There aren't any sides as such", [said Crake]. "Let's change
channels," [said Jimmy]' (185)), and at those faux-radical forms of retro-
activism that are most likely to be practised by 'severe-looking baggy-boobed

women [and] spindly members of marginal, earnest religious groups, in T-shirts with smiley-faced angels flying with birds or Jesus holding hands with a peasant or God is Green on the front' (186). Some targets, however, are more deserving than others, as is the cynical perception that, since power is ubiquitous and ubiquitously abused, everything ends up by becoming 'much like itself' (264). The most obvious alternative to this pervasive culture of cynicism in the text is its scandalised treatment of global sex trafficking, as relayed through the story of Oryx, a young Asian girl sold off by impoverished parents and later shipped to America, where, initially designated as Crake's plaything, she eventually becomes Jimmy's ill-fated lover-muse and hand-picked subject of his emergent moral outrage and residual liberal-humanist distress: '"Did they rape you," [Jimmy asks]. She would never tell him. "It wasn't real sex, was it?" he asked. "In the movies. It was only acting. Wasn't it?" [...] "But Jimmy, you should know [said Oryx]. All sex is real"' (150). While both Crake's and Jimmy's exotic/erotic fantasies are consistently ironised throughout the text, the irony does not extend to the sex trade itself, whose all-too-human victims confront the limits of the naturalised 'post-realism' that is Crake's aesthetic element, and that provides the twisted justification for his decision to re-create the world in his own image even as the real world is effectively destroyed. The fate of Oryx also suggests that the text is not entirely disabused of the various 'retro' ideologies (liberal humanism, socialist feminism, New Age environmentalism) it mocks; nor are the figures (notably Jimmy and his mother) in whom these ideologies are invested entirely deluded in their sympathies even if they are mistaken in their methods or foolish in their choice of friends. In this sense, perhaps, Atwood's novel emerges by default as a feminist, an environmentalist and, not least, a humanist text: one which, in acknowledging the continuing realities of female/environmental/human subjection, examines some of the ways in which age-old practices of physical domination and oppression are now being revisited on what social theorists have increasingly taken to describing as a 'post-bodied and post-human' modern world (Featherstone and Burrows 1996: 2; see also Graham 2002, Hayles 1999).

Published three years earlier than *Oryx and Crake* and expertly timed to coincide with the new millennium, Zadie Smith's *White Teeth* also takes satirical aim at fanaticism and zealotry of all stripes, taking in the documented 'holocausts' of animal rights and the fabricated 'apocalypses' of Seventh Day Adventism, and all in the overriding context of a 'great immigrant experiment' (Smith 2000: 281) in which opportunities for postcolonial and/or postsecular conviviality have repeatedly been squandered in the face of lingering colonial hierarchies and persistent racial contempt (281–22, 53–54; see also Gilroy 2004).[4] Like its most obvious literary precursor, Salman Rushdie's *The Satanic Verses* (1988), *White Teeth* is at once an apology for cultural 'mongrelization' (Rushdie 1991: 394) and a spirited attack on its implacable opposite, cultural purism, offering an exhaustive Rushdiean medley of self-deconstructing immigrant legends: the chameleonic figure of the migrant; the imagined panacea of self-renewal; the ever-present burden of the past.

However, if the promises and illusions of Islam remain very much at the centre of Rushdie's novel, their space in Smith's has largely been usurped by the secular history of the *genome*, that 'holy grail of modern biological research' through which popular scientific images of human perfectibility are played out (Graham 2002: 117; see also Hubbard and Wald 1999). *White Teeth*, in this sense, is *The Satanic Verses* for the age of the Human Genome Project – if also a cautionary tale, improbably prophetic in its intensity, for an age in which competing religious (fundamentalist) as well as secular (civilisationist) extremisms have since converged in the nightmarish collision courses of 9/11, 7/7 and Iraq. Elaine Graham's succinct itemisation of the discursive properties of the gene perfectly maps the satirical co-ordinates of Smith's novel:

> Within the discourse of the Human Genome Project and throughout contemporary molecular biology the gene occupies a number of discursive spaces simultaneously. It is a thing of nature and the very essence of life. For a biochemist it is the catalyst for the formation of essential proteins. In the bio-informatics systems that record the genes' sequences, it is a string of binary data that encodes its own particular molecular 'signature'. In sociobiological discourse, it is the icon of destiny; and for the biotechnological corporations that stand to profit from the patenting and marketing of genetic information for medical research purposes, it is a highly lucrative commodity. The gene is [both] a potent object of desire [and] a convenient element that comes to stand vicariously for the complex mixture of environment, sociability, natural selection and biology which separates 'human' from 'almost-human'. The gene, and by association the Human Genome Project, thereby comes to *represent* what it means to be human, [allowing DNA to play] a decisive role in negotiating the mixture of curiosity and anxiety engendered by a blurring of the boundaries between 'us' and 'them'.
>
> (24)

These discourses come together, in Smith's novel, in the figure of the brilliant geneticist Marcus Chalfen, a satirical perversion of the liberal improver, whose biomedical research on transgenic animals accords with his 'firm belief in the perfectibility of all life' (Smith 2000: 269). Chalfen believes the underlying purpose of his research to be the elimination of the random; as the press release accompanying his latest work announces, 'The FutureMouse [*aka* OncoMouse: Haraway 1997] holds out the tantalizing promise of a new phase in human history where we are not victims of the random but instead directors and arbitrators of our own fate' (370). Needless to say, the events of the novel prove otherwise, unfolding as they do through a succession of biological accidents and historical contingencies, and featuring a catalogue of dysfunctional families and thrown-together characters whose shifting alliances and friendships defy the laws of genetic predictability (even the central friendship of the novel, that between Archibald Jones and Samad Iqbal, is an unlikely product of the arbitrary exigencies of war). The novel, in this sense, provides a comic exercise in the cultural confusions, but also the social normalcy, of hybridity; similarly, it finds nothing special about those who consider themselves to be special, rejoices in the blunders of would-be heroism, and uses the tangle of history – mostly colonial history – to repeatedly disprove the 'inevitable consequences' of nature's laws (249; see also Young 1995). The novel's various modulations of celebratory hybridity – the mixed-race child (Irie), the cyborg dyad (Archie/Samad) – provide the grounds for Smith's wide-ranging satire on both genetic *determinism* (as an historical explanation for human characteristics and behaviour) and genetic *determination* (as a future rationale for human improvement and the racialised modelling of ideal type). They also give the lie to those ideological 'geneticisation' processes that either falsely equate human genetics with human biology or, equally erroneously, assume a metonymic relationship between the gene and the sum-total of human life (Graham 2002: 121–22).

At the same time, as with Atwood, there is a profoundly human, even humanist, backlash to Smith's criticism of the ideological implications of genetics as the scientific study of hybridity, dedicated to the controlled production of experimental posthuman hybrids of its own (Graham 2002; Haraway 1997). Also like Atwood, Smith seems to see the figure of the corporate geneticist as a postmodern Moreau, the 'author of life as patentable code' (Haraway 1997: 97) and dispensable commodity, presiding over the 'nature of no nature, where nature and culture are [scientifically] spliced together and enterprised up' (85). Thus, while the art of 'materialized refiguration' (64) that finds perhaps its most refined technological expression in genetic splicing offers further proof of the permeable boundary between human beings, machines and animals, it also provides a sobering reminder that what Haraway calls 'the scramble for the control of genes', with all its ethical implications, is one of *the* global-capitalist battles of the present day (57). At the centre of the battle is the figure of the transgenic mouse, as much cultural metaphor as scientific model, and Haraway's privileged pint-sized symbol for the monumental 'tussles over meanings, purposes, violations, and origins' that characterise the new posthuman/post-natural sphere (85). In *White Teeth*, accordingly, the FutureMouse project is made to bear a symbolic weight its cyborg protagonist cannot possibly carry; freighted with both the promises and the threats inscribed within the ambivalent figure of the posthuman (Graham 2002), the mouse eventually does what its natural instincts tell it to: it escapes (Smith 2000: 462). In this gleefully ironic version of the return to nature, the instinctive need to survive trumps the redemptive promise of the genome, while a further moral to the tale might be that the natural – animal or human – triumphantly re-emerges at the point where it seems already to have been discredited, in a putatively 'post-natural' world.

Smith's larger point here seems to be that the 'roots' versus 'routes' debate, in both its religious and its secular forms, is essentially unsolvable; what matters more is human beings' enduring capacity to escape repetition while exerting some degree of local agency over the global conditions in which their society is transformed (140, 168). This emphasis on the human, and on social change, remains characteristic of the post-colonial novel at a time when ideas of the human are increasingly being challenged, and where the place of human beings within a broader, eco-logical network of relations is now widely registered if not always ade-quately informed. Whether that makes up-to-the-minute novels like *Oryx and Crake* or *White Teeth* paradoxically out of date is another matter. Certainly, postcolonial writers like Atwood and Smith, along with other writers in this book, perfectly understand the ecological dictum that human liberation will never be fully achieved without radically challenging the historical conditions under which human societies have constructed themselves in relation to other societies, *both* human *and* non-human, and in the process have built barriers between themselves and the 'others' they have effectively created as a means of defining their own identities and defending their social norms (Plumwood 2003; Wolfe 2003). A 'rights-based environmental ethic' (Regan 1983: 363) invites a more inclusive view, but it too has its problems, all the more so at a moment when rights abuses are themselves being abused by those with global power (Chow 2002; Newman 2007). Rights discourses, as this book has sug-gested, are as likely to impede as to improve broad-based understandings of the liberationist projects of postcolonialism, ecocriticism and zoocri-ticism. While a move beyond rights may yet provide the step that both projects need to save themselves from the worst excesses of the human, what is probably most needed is not the capacity to think beyond the human, but the courage to imagine new ways in which human and non-human societies, understood as being ecologically connected, can be creatively transformed.

Notes

1 Buell's glossary entry for 'nature' in *The Future of Environmental Criticism* repeats Williams and Soper (see above) but also adds Cicero's pioneering distinction between 'first' (primordial) and 'second' (created) nature – a distinction drawn upon, if often to be rejected, by a large number of interested parties ever since. As Buell suggests, the first/second nature distinction has come under fire for overlooking the production of *all* nature, but it still lurks behind such recent formulations as 'third nature', in which nature is technologically reproduced. On 'third nature', see Wark 1994; also Wilson 1992.

2 For a recent discussion of the 'new humanism', see Homi Bhabha's foreword to the 2004 re-issue of *The Wretched of the Earth*. For Bhabha, Fanon's 'new humanism' is not only located within the context of emerging 1960s decolonisation movements but also contains useful lessons for our contemporary globalised world. More specifically, the 'new humanism' instantiates the 'search for human agency in the midst of the agony of oppression' (xxxvi) – a struggle that continues in the face of today's 'neoliberal technocratic elitism' (xi), and one that issues a salutary reminder that contemporary global capitalism has impeded the full flourishing of human potential that Fanon saw as the condition of a decolonised world.

3 'Biopower', a term usually attributed to the French historian Michel Foucault, refers to the totality of techniques for the social control of the human body, as manifest in 'disciplinary regimes of medical government' (Nadesan 2008: 93) and, more recently, in technological forms of 'genetic governance' like GM and the identification of 'genetic risk' (Bunton and Petersen 2005). Biopower, and the specific 'biopolitical' strategies attached to it, maintain but also manipulate connections between the perceived 'health of the population and the economic and political security of the state' (Nadesan 2008: 93). Biopower, in this sense, is a potentially dangerous form of social surveillance, and is frequently manipulated in corporate interests that trade on the ideologically motivated distinction between those considered to be 'healthy' and those feared as being 'health risks'.

4 The term 'postsecular', like its equally elusive sister terms the 'postcolonial' and the 'postmodern', is perhaps best seen as enacting what Kwame Anthony Appiah (1997) calls a 'space-clearing gesture' through which the distancing prefix implicitly challenges the root word ('colonial', 'modern', 'secular') to which it remains, nonetheless, inextricably bound. However, while postsecularism might seem to imply an automatic antagonism towards all things secular, its closest antonym is not secularism but *fundamentalism* and, in this sense, it challenges both the extremes of dogmatic religion and the equally dangerous intransigence of the so-called 'secular mind' (King 2009). Certainly, this view of the postsecular accords well with Smith's text, which maintains

both a healthy (postmodern?) scepticism towards legitimating narratives and a deep (postcolonial?) distaste for the racism/sexism/speciesism that is perpetrated in their name. 'Conviviality' – in Paul Gilroy's generous sense of the term, supported by Smith – offers an antidote to the destructiveness of fundamentalist race-logic while maintaining its own (postsecular?) suspicion towards the blandishments of western liberal-pluralist thought.

Annotated bibliography

Bibliographies of this kind are necessarily selective, and to some at least these choices will come across, if not as random, then as skewed towards contemporary works. We make no apologies for this: postcolonial ecocriticism is a relatively new field, albeit not so new that there aren't already a few established classics: Alfred Crosby's *Ecological Imperialism* comes to mind here or, a decade later, the work of another environmental historian, Richard Grove. There are clearly leaders in the field as well, many of them operating at least in part outside of western contexts: these include such inspirational writer-activists as Ken Saro-Wiwa, Wangari Maathai, Vandana Shiva and Arundhati Roy. Postcolonial ecocriticism is a multidisciplinary field, and the list below goes at least some way towards recognising this, featuring both single- and multi-authored volumes of literary criticism and theory, environmental history and philosophy, and conservation biology, along with numerous virtually unclassifiable crossover works. Some of these works fall more readily into the related fields of animal studies and zoocriticism than they do into the field of ecocriticism; but as we have been suggesting throughout this book, the boundaries between genres are in many ways as porous as those between humans and animals themselves. Likewise the boundaries between methods, with 'postcolonial' serving more as a leaky shelter – if still a shelter – than as a methodologically watertight umbrella term. However it is defined, postcolonial ecocriticism is a *growing* field, and its shape and scope will no doubt change as it develops; not its priorities, though, which join together a wide variety of ongoing environmental and social struggles within the overarching context of an incompletely decolonised world.

Adams, William M. and Martin Mulligan, eds. *Decolonizing Nature: Strategies for Conservation in a Post-Colonial Era*. London: Earthscan, 2003.

Varied collection of essays by academics and conservation practitioners; makes for equally interesting reading alongside Grove's *Green Imperialism* (see below) for critical insights into the colonial legacies of conservation and those new forms of colonisation that operate under the rubric of 'conservation' today. Contributors to the volume are *critical* of conservation in so far as it reinforces 'the ongoing colonisation of the natural world by the market' (79), but also *committed* to conservation as a practically oriented but also deeply ethical engagement with the changing relations between people, the natural environment, and wildlife. What is needed today, the editors argue, is a more *inclusive* discourse about nature that involves the active participation of formerly colonised peoples, and a more *dynamic* discourse that takes full account of 'complex global sociopolitical change' (2). The contributors offer mixed views as to whether this is possible. Some, like the British geographer Bill Adams, argue that while conservationists today have by no means freed themselves from the colonial mindset, they are still capable of managing the transition to a postcolonial era; others, like the Australian Aboriginal activist-academic Marcia Langton, are more sceptical, seeing national and international environmental regulation as limiting opportunities for Australian Aborigines and other indigenous peoples to practise their customary rights. Perhaps unsurprisingly, the essays offer markedly different views of what conservation entails in different sets of social and historical circumstances; and as Hector Magome and James Murombedzi argue in their chapter, the decolonisation of nature at one level may inadvertently cause its re-colonisation at another, e.g. as a result of yawning discrepancies between local conservationist initiatives and global bureaucratic controls (131). What is clear from all the essays, however, is that conservation today – while considerably more diverse and democratic than it once was – remains linked to centralised planning and development exercises that often override the wishes and interests of local people. The 'decolonisation of nature' therefore remains very much a work in progress – as is decolonisation itself.

Armstrong, Philip. *What Animals Mean in the Fiction of Modernity*. London: Routledge, 2008.

Seminal work of zoocriticism, clearly influenced by postcolonialism but not determined by it, and implicitly challenging its fixation on empire as the conceptual and material lynchpin for thinking about the modern world. Focuses instead on the fictional representation of animals under three aspects: 'the relationship between human-animal narratives and the social practices and conditions from which they emerge; the evidence of exchanges between human and non-human forms of agency; and the documentation of shifts in emotional and affective engagements between humans and other animals' (2). Begins with the Ur-texts of Swift (*Gulliver's Travels*) and Defoe (*Robinson Crusoe*), both read – with different results – as 'parables of modernity' (32) and as illustrations of an unstable shift in human-animal relations during the eighteenth century; then proceeds, via other foundational human-animal encounter narratives (*Frankenstein*, *The Island of Dr. Moreau*, *Moby-Dick*), to a broader analysis of twentieth and twenty-first century fiction that takes in the modernist 'therio-primitivism' (142) of Lawrence and Hemingway, the postmodern eco-apocalypticism of Atwood and Findley, and the postmodern-cum-postcolonial anti-captivity narratives of Martel, Coetzee and Høeg. As Armstrong suggests, certain continuities are maintained throughout: the forcible enlisting of the animal to define the human; the coded interaction between both in establishing and interrogating the basis for

240 Annotated bibliography

modernity; and the disruptive use of parody and satire, both to underline human frailties and to set up the imaginative parameters for new, potentially trans-species understandings of the self. WAM possibly overstates the case in claiming that 'the relationship between human and non-human life [would become] the defining labour of modernity' (49); but its salutary insistence that animals are far more than mere projection screens for human needs and interests, alongside its equally valid recognition that literature continues to play a valuable role in thinking beyond the human, has been influential for postcolonial zoocriticism – not least for the original and second editions of this book.

Bartosch, Roman. *Environmentality: Ecocriticism and the Event of Postcolonial Fiction*. Amsterdam: Rodopi, 2013.

Useful alternative to prevalent materialist approaches to postcolonial ecocriticism. Mounts an eloquent if at times over-elaborate defence of literature and literary studies in terms of their capacity to reveal the aporias in ecocritical theory and practice, e.g. 'the tension between ecocentric and anthropocentric thinking, the problem of referring and adhering to science, and the problem of mimesis as a literary possibility for engaging with reality' (50). Insists, along with Derek Attridge, on the 'singularity' of literature; and, along with Hubert Zapf, on literature's emplacement within a broader 'cultural ecology' that links environmental to representational crisis, opening up new ways of understanding and experiencing otherness in which 'reading postcolonial texts ecocritically [...] becomes an ethical act that constitutes itself through the qualities of literature and not by an application of moral concepts to a text' (81). However, the salutary emphasis on what Attridge calls the 'literary event' doesn't make for particularly interesting readings, with Bartosch taking refuge in dated formalist vocabulary in his analysis of, among others, Amitav Ghosh's *Hungry Tide* (see also Mukherjee below). Bartosch's hermeneutic focus also drastically underplays the power differentials in the texts he analyses, begging the question of what might make them 'postcolonial' in the first place other than the obvious cultural differences they inscribe.

Beinart, William and Lotte Hughes. *Environment and Empire*. Oxford and New York: Oxford University Press, 2007.

Even-handed, suitably wide-ranging account of the transverse relations between environment and empire, arranged around a series of loosely connected environmental themes in British imperial history, e.g. Caribbean plantation slavery, the Canadian fur trade, the exploitation of India's forests, and the colonial origins of oil extraction in the Middle East. Resists Marxist approaches to environmental history, e.g. Jason Moore's 'world-ecology', while insisting as Moore does that imperial modes of expropriation and governance work *through*, rather just *upon*, nature; also largely avoids postcolonial theory, preferring instead to use 'post-colonial' as a hyphenated historical term. Particularly interesting on conservationist themes, bringing out the double-edged function of imperial/colonial conservation in protecting local environments – if not necessarily the people who live there – while furthering metropolitan commercial concerns. Values the know-how of indigenous peoples, whose anti-colonial resistance struggles have often had environmentalist motives, while recognising that continuing battles over the ownership and management of natural resources in the postcolonial era do not preclude indigenous assertions of 'the right to exploit resources, often on an industrial scale' (351). Indicates the ambivalent role of environmental history in postcolonial ecocriticism, which uses history to complicate the generalities of environmental determinism, but still arguably isn't as attentive as it might be to the ecological intricacies of historical change.

Caminero-Santangelo, Byron. *Different Shades of Green: African Literature, Environmental Justice, and Political Ecology.* Charlottesville, VA: University of Virginia Press, 2014.

Groundbreaking book on literature and environment in a continent shaped by 'global political and economic forces [as well as] the long shadow of colonial development' (1). Reads African literature in English within a variety of local and regional contexts while re-affirming its contribution to the global environmental justice movement. Part of the general 'ecological turn' in postcolonial ecocriticism (see the Preface to this volume), *DSG* insists on the value of a cross-disciplinary political ecological approach that takes account of the global social and political inequalities that drive environmental change. However, it also insists on what the author calls 'postcolonial regional particularism', gauging the extent to which social and environmental change, which operates across multiple scales, emphasises significant differences within the continent while also challenging those 'imperial universalizing discourses' that create a falsely unitary view of African nature – and Africa itself (9). Similarly questions homogenising western views of what counts or not as 'environmentalism' and 'environmental writing', going beyond the obvious examples of Maathai and Saro-Wiwa (see below) to show the range of ways in which contemporary African writers have brought attention to the environmental changes 'wrought by colonial ideology and policy [as well as to] the benefits of [...] indigenous environmental practice and epistemology' (38). Rightly refuses to sentimentalise the latter, though still tends to subscribe to the potentially misleading assumptions that govern distinctions between global North and South (see Guha and Martinez-Alier below). Produces interesting 'contrapuntal' readings of culturally diverse African writers, but pays insufficient attention to the *linguistic* plurality that belongs to this diversity, raising the question of whether English remains the privileged *lingua franca* of African ecocriticism – and the further question of whose interests it then serves.

Carrigan, Anthony. *Postcolonial Tourism: Literature, Culture, Environment.* London: Routledge, 2011.

Important environmentally oriented study of the world's largest industry. Densely written at times, but meticulous and scholarly. Determinedly cross-disciplinary, but stakes a particular claim for the value of imaginative literature – and the imagination itself – in contributing to current tourism-related debates on sustainable development and responsible consumption. Literary examples are drawn primarily from the Caribbean and Pacific Island regions, with Sri Lanka functioning as a counter-example towards the end. Looks at the negative representations surrounding such apparently intractable problems as 'environmental appropriation and dispossession, cultural commoditization, and sexual consumption' (xv), but also at the more positive ways in which postcolonial writers shape alternative futures, not just for their own communities but for the global tourist industries themselves. Complicates simplistic homologies between mass tourism and colonialism while recognising that progressive tourism models, e.g. community-based tourism and 'pro-poor tourism', tend to be held back by a neoliberal economic climate characterised by renewed or continuing patterns of exploitation and by 'asymmetrical economic flows' (4, 19). Advocates a leftist 'eco-materialist' approach (see also Mukherjee below) that is attentive to aesthetic as well as political concerns, and to the symbiotic relationship between these. Practising what it preaches, also offers close readings that demonstrate both the transformative power of storytelling and the various formal strategies used to critique destructive colonial legacies and to open up 'indigenized' alternatives in which local customs are promoted and non-exploitative practices preferred.

Crosby, Alfred W. *Ecological Imperialism: The Biological Expansion of Europe, 900-1900*. Cambridge: Cambridge University Press, 2009 [1986].

Now into its tenth printing, *EI* is probably the single most influential work for postcolonial ecocriticism, even if contemporary practitioners might not share its derivative view of (former) settler colonies as 'Neo-Europes', or its geo-deterministic stance on the biological expansion of Europe into the New World. Crosby's main thesis is that the mass exodus of Europeans to the 'Neo-European' lands during the nineteenth century owed significantly to biogeographical factors, and that a particular form of imperialism – ecological imperialism – would prove just as effective in displacing/replacing those lands' indigenous peoples as the more traditional forms of imperial conquest and occupation that were deployed, both in the New World and elsewhere. *EI* traces the long history of ecological imperialism, from the gradual introduction of European crops and livestock to the rapid spread of European diseases to which indigenous peoples had little in-built defence. European settler-invaders, Crosby suggests, were attracted to lands that were distant from their own but had similar climates, and although they would also succeed in creating 'Neo-European' societies in the tropics, 'the prerequisites [for this were] stiff' (141). Technological superiority alone is not enough to explain the flourishing of white European settlers in the 'Neo-Europes'; rather, these settlers took advantage of favourable biogeographical circumstances and conditions to develop forms of agriculture that were already familiar to them, even if the local flora and fauna and – not least – the local people were emphatically not. Meanwhile, imported species – both domestic and feral – thrived and, along with deadly pathogens, helped provide an overwhelming advantage to European invaders, whose viral settlement of the 'Neo-Europes' took place in biogeographical conditions marked by conspicuously uneven exchange (216). While some of *EI*'s vocabulary is out of date, possibly even offensive, to postcolonialists, its ecological emphasis turns out to have been well ahead of its time. It remains a major reference point for contemporary biopolitical work on, e.g., 'native' versus 'invader' species, while its long-historical approach has been further extended in recent postcolonial incursions into debates on global climate change.

Curtin, Deane. *Environmental Ethics for a Postcolonial World*. Lanham, MD: Rowman & Littlefield, 2005.

General-purpose book by one of America's leading environmental philosophers. Sees contemporary environmental problems as stemming in part from a failure of moral imagination and looks for ways of redressing this, e.g. 'ethical community development based on the democratic reconciliation of people with place' (xii). Issues addressed include the population crisis, cross-cultural conflict over place, indigenous attitudes to environment, and food security. Argues somewhat idealistically for the idea of 'ecological community', i.e. that co-inhabitants of the earth are part of a single community, and that the social, environmental and economic standards of justice applied to this community are intertwined (7). A similarly schematic view is that of globalisation as 'a form of neocolonialism' (18) based on self-serving First World attempts to 'develop' the Third World. Clearly influenced by Gandhian communalist thought, *EE* takes a largely *culturalist* approach to colonialism as 'an attack on one's identity', consequently seeing anti-colonial resistance as 'a matter of reclaiming one's identity and the power to define oneself' (45). Also takes an *ecological* approach: 'Colonialism has always depended on exploitation of the ecological diversity of traditional agriculture to produce commodities that are sold back to the third world on credit provided by the first world' (59). Underscored – as in Curtin's other work – by a globalist view of 'ecological citizenship' (196) based on communitarian principles and a cross-culturally sensitive extension of individual moral concerns.

DeLoughrey, Elizabeth and George B. Handley, eds. *Postcolonial Ecologies: Literatures of the Environment*. Oxford and New York: Oxford University Press, 2011.

Perhaps the best example to date of the 'ecological turn' in postcolonial ecocriticism (see the Preface to this volume), *PE* is a state-of-the-art collection by a strong international cast of contributors. Thematically and geographically diverse, though there is a possible over-emphasis on the Caribbean and a political inclination – drawn in part from political ecology – towards the global South. An excellent introduction by the editors focuses on (1) the ecological interdependencies of place and space, and (2) the political implications of these in the historical contexts of colonialism and the continuing inequalities that attach to globalisation, especially if not exclusively in the global South. Insists on what the editors call 'the alterity of both history and nature' (4) – the irreducibility of the natural world to human interests and frames of human time. Concentrates nonetheless on the historical relationship between literature, landscape and colonisation; on the historical embeddedness of ecocriticism within 'race, class, gender, and colonial inequities' (9); and on the alternative understandings of ecological resilience and sustainability that might help counteract an ongoing history of ecological imperialism in which 'biotic and political ecologies are materially and imaginatively intertwined' (13).

Griffiths, Tom and Libby Robin, eds. *Ecology and Empire: Environmental History of Settler Societies.* Edinburgh: Keele University Press, 1997.

Wide-ranging collection featuring a number of high-profile contributors: Thomas Dunlap, Tim Flannery, David Lowenthal, John MacKenzie – and the editors themselves. Taking its cue from Alfred Crosby (see Crosby above), argues that ecology and empire 'forged a historical relationship of great power [which] radically changed human and natural history across the globe' (1). Indicates environmental historians' reluctance to use the term 'postcolonial' (see Beinart and Hughes above), but shares postcolonialism's transnational reach and its critical take on the different ways in which imperialisms of both past and present are imbricated with the ecosystems within which they operate and which they themselves transform. In a number of the essays, ecology is seen as a 'science of empire' (63) pressed into the service of 'developing' the colonies while rationalising the acclimatisation of European imports and neglecting the economic and ecological potential of indigenous species and practices (73). Takes a largely 'settler' perspective, seen within the context of what Dunlap calls 'an Anglo world' (76) in which the original colonies of settlement, even after political independence, 'retained their ties to Britain [...] and built and maintained networks among themselves' (76). Dunlap's model of an 'Anglo world' is contestable, based as it is on the colonial notion of 'a common language and core culture' (84), raising the difficult question as to whether settler-oriented approaches to ecology and empire risk reinforcing the metropolitan, 'neo-centric' thinking they are seeking to contest (226). Some alternatives are given to this model – as Michael Williams reminds us, not all 'imperial designs of one group over another have to be "western" or equated with "colonialism"' (170) – but the focus on what Donald Meinig calls 'settler empires', particularly those of Australia and South Africa, is limiting even as it claims to be internally differentiated and internationally diverse.

Grove, Richard H. *Green Imperialism: Colonial Expansion, Tropical Island Edens and the Origins of Environmentalism, 1600-1800.* Cambridge: Cambridge University Press, 1995.

Along with *Ecological Imperialism* (see Crosby above), *GI* is a foundational work for postcolonial ecocriticism, even if – as is customary with imperial environmental history – the term 'postcolonial' is conspicuous by its absence, and postcolonial theories and methods are peripheral (if not necessarily irrelevant) to the author's main concerns. A meticulously researched historical work, *GI* succeeds in giving the lie to 'presentist' views of environmental concern and conservationist intervention, demonstrating 'the central significance of the colonial experience in the formation of western environmental attitudes and critiques' (3). Focuses on tropical islands – especially but by no means exclusively those of the Caribbean – as laboratories for colonial conservationist experiments, challenging the 'hypothesis of a purely destructive environmental imperialism' (7), but also admitting that much of the thinking of the early colonial conservationists was 'contradictory and confused' (12). Grove's main argument is that many of the ideas that are central to western environmentalism today were first developed at the peripheries of an expanding European system – a system in which scientific methods and fantastical theories commingled, and islands in particular came to stand in metaphorically for the ecological limits of a newly 'discovered' world. Ecological pressures, Grove suggests, were more keenly felt at 'the colonial periphery' (61), though he attempts to distance himself from the 'core-periphery' dichotomies of world-systems theory, recently given an ecological slant in the work of Jason Moore (see Beinart and Hughes above). These pressures gave rise to conservationist initiatives that were not necessarily 'western' in design or 'European' in origin – an important insight which chimes with postcolonial ecocriticism's more globally distributed, culturally polycentric approach. Nor is it safe to assume that indigenous knowledge of the environment was blithely dismissed in the colonies; often it was assiduously incorporated into new evaluations of nature that recognised the potentially damaging effects of European economic activity, and that acknowledged the value of long-term environmental security for the effective management of the colonial state (3, 480). Grove's work acts as a valuable corrective to the widespread view that modern environmentalism is 'exclusively a product of European and North American predicaments and philosophies' (486), though it paradoxically retains a European focus that refracts the core back through the periphery – a methodological aporia it arguably shares with 'first-wave' postcolonial theory (see the Introduction to this book).

Guha, Ramachandra and Joan Martinez-Alier. *Varieties of Environmentalism: Essays North and South.* London: Earthscan, 1997.

Draws on the authors' combined strengths in environmental history (Guha) and ecological economics (Martinez-Alier) to produce 'a work of comparative history, an account and analysis over time of [those] varieties of environmentalism [they hold to be] characteristic of the modern world' (viii). The operative word is 'varieties', Guha and Martinez-Alier's main aim being to distinguish between the post-materialist ('full-stomach') environmentalisms of the First World and the survival-oriented ('empty-belly') environmentalisms of the Third (xxi). These latter are often social justice-based, involving lengthy and sometimes bloody struggles over diminishing natural resources that are subsumed under the catchy label, 'the environmentalism of the poor' (5). The environmentalisms of the South, Guha and Martinez-Alier suggest, rely more than their Northern counterparts on traditional modes of direct-action protest and organisation, although they also admit that the contrast between Third World militancy and First World litigation needs qualifying – as was the case when the book was written and is even more the case today. Similarly, *VE*'s distinction between First and Third Worlds, or even between global North and South, now comes across as slightly dated, overlooking the fact that in today's global economy both the resources and – just as crucially – the language of 'growth' and 'development' have been hijacked by transnational corporations and roving cosmopolitan elites. Still, Guha and Martinez-Alier have been influential in setting the tone for more recent work by e.g. Carrigan, DeLoughrey and Nixon, that marries their neo-Marxist socio-economic analysis to a more consciously cross-cultural approach. These authors take a more explicitly anti-colonial perspective than do Guha and Martinez-Alier, though the former's bracing attack on the 'green imperialism' of the western wilderness ethic is a notable exception, while the latter's analysis of 'biopiracy' (see also Shiva below) points to a latter-day instance of neoliberal biocolonialism in which global corporate profit flies in the face of local property rights.

Kete, Kathleen, ed. *A Cultural History of Animals in the Age of Empire.* Oxford: Berg, 2011.

Part of a six-volume series which outlines the changing function of animals in human society and culture throughout history, *ACH* brings together seven informative essays exploring the cultural role played by animals in the long nineteenth century (1800–1920), a time of significant imperial expansion and rapid industrial change. As Kete's useful introduction suggests, a correlation can be traced during this period between the exercise of imperial power and the assertion of 'empire over the animal', while animals were caught up in changing, often contradictory, definitions of the post-Enlightenment self (2). Domination of animals thus lay side by side with kindness towards animals, with both coming together in what Kete calls the 'phantasmagoria' of nineteenth-century pet keeping, 'a fantasy relationship of human and animal most visible in the trope of the animal as child' (15). Attention is given in the volume to the contemporaneous representation of animals in literature and the visual arts; to the strategic 'animalization' of humans; and to the instrumental uses of animals for entertainment, educational and scientific purposes within a broad imperial context in which changing views of the human-animal relationship mirrored both European imperial triumphalism and growing fears over the limits and legitimacy of imperial control.

Maathai, Wangari. *Unbowed: One Woman's Story*, London: Arrow Books, 2008.

Conventional battler's memoir by the charismatic Nobel Prize-winning Kenyan environmentalist, founder of the Green Belt Movement and – along with the late Ken Saro-Wiwa (see below) – best-known contemporary black African social and environmental campaigner on the global stage. Begins by colourfully describing the ecology of the colonial African world in terms accessible to a lay international readership; goes on to offer an environmental explanation of the Mau Mau rebellion in terms of the British denial of customary Kikuyu rights to shelter and space (62). Echoes Saro-Wiwa in seeing decolonisation as a three-way struggle – as much ethnicity-based as nation-driven – for 'land, freedom and self-governance' in which the fundamental principles of social and environmental justice are invoked (63). Adopts a curiously uncritical approach to the US (where Maathai went to college in the early 1960s), though admits to parallels between social and environmental divisions in Kenya, routinely blamed at the time on colonialism, and those in America, which were just as automatically connected to the country's slave-holding past (87). Concentrates after that on the post-Independence period in Kenya, where Maathai would quickly make her name, not just for her grassroots environmentalist work but also for her women's rights activism, going on to become an inspirational ecofeminist figure and a celebrity figurehead for freedom and democracy (hence her popularity in the First World) and the environmentalism of the poor (hence her popularity in the Third).

MacKenzie, John M. *The Empire of Nature: Hunting, Conservation and British Imperialism*. Manchester: Manchester University Press, 2008 [1988].

Part of the excellent MUP series 'Studies in Imperialism', also edited by MacKenzie, *EON* draws on a wide range of nineteenth- and early twentieth-century colonial hunting practices to 'illuminate the nature of imperial power when exercised in the relationship between humans and the natural world' (ix). As MacKenzie remarks in the Introduction, 'the colonial frontier was also a hunting frontier' (7), and hunting was intricately bound up in the symbolic and material practices of Empire. Comparing nineteenth-century hunting practices in southern, Central and East Africa with their colonial counterparts under the Raj, MacKenzie demonstrates how hunting, which operated on both continents as a powerful mode of 'symbolic governance of the environment' as well as a lucrative means of extending trade relations with local peoples, sutured the ideology of imperial expansion to the exploitation of wild game (117). *EON* also shows how later preservationist and conservationist moves to protect wild animals in Africa and South Asia were connected to the desire – whether tacit or explicit – to shore up elite privilege. This connection is traced, not just to the colonial history of conservation (see also Grove above), but also to the more recent creation of national parks for international tourism, with modern-day safari tourism representing an alternative, more environmentally friendly but no less sybaritic form of the colonial hunt (309).

Miller, John. *Empire and the Animal Body: Violence, Identity and Ecology in Victorian Adventure Fiction*. London: Anthem Press, 2012.

A lively study of human-animal relations in Victorian adventure fiction, where 'the polarity of human and animal is both central to imperial mythologies and a point at which they collapse' (3), *EAB* explicitly situates itself at the interface of animal studies, postcolonial studies and ecocriticism, but is alert to the tensions within and between these, not least the perhaps inevitable persistence of anthropocentrism and the 'rival claims [of] ecosystem preservation [and] individual animal rights' (17). Sees human interaction with non-human animals as integral to the adventure hero's engagement with far-flung 'foreign' regions, and violence towards those animals as 'inscribed in narrative expectations of the form' (31). Makes an interesting companion text to MacKenzie's more historical *Empire of Nature* (see MacKenzie above), e.g. in its analysis of the relationship between imperial masculinities and hunting cultures, or in its charting of the connections between nineteenth-century imperial conquest, the commodification of animal bodies, and the natural-historical practices of collection and classification, with these latter being aimed at the consolidation of a 'natural' imperial order that was implicitly questioned, just as the violence underwriting scientific knowledge of animal behaviour was simultaneously displayed and denounced (96). Similarly, representations of animals in Victorian adventure tales by Ballantyne, Henty and others turned out to be riven by anxieties around e.g. resemblances between humans and the Great Apes that provided unwanted reminders of humanity's 'bestial inheritance' (169); constructing what Miller aptly calls 'an ambivalent human subjectivity that fail[ed] to marshal its own savagery', such tales would offer surprisingly sophisticated post-Darwinian examples of the fundamental uncertainty of the species divide (183).

Mukherjee, Upamanyu Pablo. *Postcolonial Environments: Nature, Culture and the Contemporary Indian Novel in English*. London: Palgrave Macmillan, 2010.

Probably the clearest and most consistent example so far of a committed 'eco-materialist' approach, drawing on the Marxist strands of both postcolonialism and ecocriticism. Contemporary neoliberalism, rather than historical colonialism, appears to be the main target, with an emphasis on the Indian subcontinent though it is implied that similar conditions obtain in 'Africa, Latin America and much of the rest of the world' (5). Might be faulted for adopting a somewhat deterministic approach to the literature it analyses, but also insists on 'literary singularity' (see Bartosch above) and the specificity of Indian cultural forms (12). Perhaps the dominant concept throughout is 'unevenness', which Mukherjee sees in aesthetic as well as political-economic terms in the novels he discusses. Chapters on Roy, Ghosh, Sinha and Joshi examine carefully historicised facets of this 'aesthetics of uneven development' (81) – 'uneven style' (Roy), 'cyclonic form' (Ghosh), mixed 'archaic' and contemporary registers (Sinha and Joshi) – all of which invite us to consider 'the novel's own historical unfolding as a differential cultural form' (186). The back-and-forth movement between uneven development and uneven form produces supple readings of the primary texts, though to what extent these are representative of the contemporary Indian English novel, let alone of the novel in general, remains a moot point.

Nixon, Rob. *Slow Violence and the Environmentalism of the Poor*. Cambridge, MA: Harvard University Press, 2011.

Award-winning eco-activist study, forcefully and elegantly written, and strongly geared towards environmental injustice and the environmentalism of the poor in the global South (see Guha and Martinez-Alier above). Claims dissident inspiration from Said, Carson and Guha and brings their respective disciplines together: literary studies, science writing, social and environmental history. *SV* campaigns passionately for a transnational approach to environmental issues and problems informed by global social and environmental justice movements; it also argues more polemically against the 'parochialism' and 'transcendentalism' Nixon sees in certain, deep ecology-inspired strands of American ecocritical thought. Focuses on environmental forms of 'slow violence', e.g. climate change and toxic drift, that are potentially catastrophic in their effects but are difficult to pin down, thereby 'hinder[ing] our efforts to mobilize and act decisively' (2). Documents heroic resistance to globally manufactured forms of ecological imperialism by recent and contemporary Third World writer-activists (e.g. Maathai, Roy, Saro-Wiwa) and indigenous environmentalist groups. Persuasively shows how writing itself constitutes a form of activism, albeit in necessary dialogue with other activisms, citing the work of both First and Third World public intellectuals whose spirited engagement with 'transnational questions arising from the borderlands between empire, neoliberalism, environmentalism, and social justice' (31) is clearly informed by worldly and planetary concerns. Provides an excellent array of case studies, mostly taken from the global South.

Roos, Bonnie and Alex Hunt, eds. *Postcolonial Green: Environmental Politics and World Narratives*. Charlottesville: University of Virginia Press, 2010.

Takes a consciously global approach to environmental issues, seeing 'globalism' as primarily a latter-day form of 'colonialism based upon economic and cultural imperialism' (3), thereby justifying postcolonial methods of analysis. Focuses, on the one hand, on social and environmental justice in the contexts of local and global exploitation and impoverishment and, on the other, on 'world narrative' – a somewhat under-theorised term that opens up postcolonial analysis to, for example, the diverse literatures and cultures of the United States. The chapters themselves cover a wide range of issues and locations, with some of the most interesting material coming from outside the usual postcolonial circuits: Pavel Cenkl's piece on the tensions between western-scientific and indigenous ways of knowing in the Arctic, for instance, or Gang Yue's on the 'green orientalism' that continues to surround postcolonial and/or post-socialist images of 'eco-Tibet'. Pablo Mukherjee's opening chapter on Arundhati Roy sets the tone for a materialist approach and the best essays in the volume maintain this, though the broader role of creative writing in addressing, and itself contributing to, social and environmental issues isn't really taken up again until Ursula Heise's excellent overview at the end.

Roy, Arundhati. *The Algebra of Infinite Justice*. London: Flamingo, 2002.

Coruscating set of essays from India's premier Anglophone writer-activist (though, in typically forthright fashion, Roy dismisses the 'double-barrelled appellation [writer-activist as an] awful professional label' that has been foisted upon her just because she happens to 'take sides' (175)). The essays skewer hypocrisy and fanaticism of all kinds, both secular and religious, with particular animus being directed at the excesses of 'Corporate Globalization', characteristically capitalised, which Roy sees as working in cahoots with a power-hungry postcolonial Indian state. The two lead-off essays, published at least twice before, have become classics of a certain, non-institutional kind of oppositional postcolonial ecocriticism: emotionally overwrought, personally invested rather than ideologically committed, and deeply attuned to the social and ecological injustices that feed off one another in the overarching context of a neoliberal world order orchestrated – or so Roy sees it – by the United States. Roy's stylistic mannerisms can grate, but her work remains rhetorically powerful, with most of the essays pitting themselves ferociously against (state) neocolonialism and (global) neoliberalism while claiming some degree of sympathetic identification with the environmentalism of the poor (see Guha and Martinez-Alier above; also Shiva below). Roy has been criticised – not least in this book – for using her celebrity status to speak on others' behalf, but this criticism can only be carried so far, and the essays are mainly aimed at her cosmopolitan peers, both within and outside India, as a way of mobilising dissent.

Saro-Wiwa, Ken. *A Month and a Day: A Detention Diary*. London: Penguin, 1995.

Posthumously published memoir of the legendary Nigerian writer-activist, who was eventually executed in late 1995 after serving two prison terms on trumped up charges for a murder he did not commit. Along with *Genocide in Nigeria* (1992), *AMD* gives testament to Saro-Wiwa's life-long struggle on behalf of an Ogoni people caught, with catastrophic consequences, between predatory global petro-capitalism and a kleptocratic Nigerian state. Saro-Wiwa has been an enormously influential figure for postcolonial ecocriticism (see also Maathai above), not least because he came almost single-handedly to embody an ethnic-minority struggle for environmental justice and human rights. In *AMD*, Saro-Wiwa identifies the primary context for this struggle as one of 'internal coloni-alism' (18), but lurking in the background is the further context of British colo-nialism, one enduring effect of which has been 'to shatter Ogoni society and inflict on us a backwardness from which we are [still] trying to escape' (72). Founder of the globally recognised Movement for the Survival of the Ogoni People (MOSOP), Saro-Wiwa is generally seen today as an inspirational political leader, but he mainly saw himself as an aspiring 'intellectual man of action', a late-twentieth-century version of *l'écrivain engagé* (81). Notwithstanding, far more attention has been given to the activist than to the writer, though recent postcolonial ecocritical work has gone some way towards redressing this (see, for example, Caminero-Santangelo, Nixon, and the first edition of this book).

Shiva, Vandana. *Staying Alive: Women, Ecology and Development*. London: Zed Books, 2002 [1988].

Classic early work of ecofeminism and counter-developmental resistance, in line with Guha and Martinez-Alier's work on the environmentalism of the poor but giving it an added gender dimension (see Guha and Martinez-Alier above). Associates the dominant (neoliberal) development model with violence against both nature and 'women who depend on nature for drawing sustenance for themselves, their families, [and] their societies' (xvi). Sees Third World women – and rural Indian women in particular – as being at the forefront of an alternative grassroots movement to conserve forests, lands and waters and to protect nature as 'the living force that supports life' (xvii). Combines Shiva's own scientific background (she is a trained physicist) with a Hindu-derived 'feminine principle' that challenges the reductionist and universalising tendencies of 'patriarchal' science, which she somewhat intemperately sees as an instrument of colonialism and a 'social and political project of modern western man' (21). Champions the cause of traditional thought and 'ethno-science' (33) as having the capacity to maintain ecological health and the 'dialectical unity' of living systems, which Shiva counter-poses – via Hindu cosmology – to the Cartesian view of nature as 'environment' and 'resource' (40). Tends rather blithely to blame the 'arrogance of the west' (44) and to overlook conspicuous inequalities within the Hindu 'ecological' worldview; also lapses at times into a root-and-branch rejection of development *per se*. Highlights the Chipko movement as a paradigmatic example of a non-violent social/environmental struggle based on the 'feminine principle'. Likewise challenges 'masculinist' models of food production (e.g. the green revolution) and water management (e.g. big dams: see also Roy above), putting its faith instead in those Third World women whose 'privileged access to survival expertise' (224) qualifies them, more than anyone, to lead the recovery of an ecologically damaged earth.

Shukin, Nicole. *Animal Capital: Rendering Life in Biopolitical Times*. Minneapolis: University of Minnesota Press, 2009.

A suitably challenging addition to the University of Minnesota Press 'Posthumanities' series, *AC* looks at the ways in which animals – and the general signifier that stands in for them, 'the animal' – operate as 'a hinge allowing powerful discourses to flip or vacillate between literal and figurative economies of sense' (5). Animal *signs*, Shukin suggests, cannot and must not be separated from animal *bodies*; indeed, it is the exploitability of the latter that allows us to understand how animals function as a form of capital within the complex networks of biopower that regulate social life (8). Shukin's main argument, in fact, is that the discourses and technologies of biopower are made most visible at the species boundary, where human biopolitics and its animal equivalent, zoopolitics, converge. *AC* provides a wide variety of examples that highlight the mutual instrumentality of animal signs and animal bodies, ranging from the iconic trafficking of beaver pelts in colonial Canada – a kind of primal scene that recalls founding national narratives without acknowledging the violence, both material and symbolic, that accompanied them (4) – to the contemporary moral panics surrounding so-called 'zoonotic' diseases (e.g. 'Asian' bird flu) that jump from animal to human bodies, mapping racial anxieties and phobias onto 'entangled ethnic-animal flesh' (46). While not necessarily adopting a postcolonial approach, *AC* amply illustrates the destructive co-workings of racism and speciesism in colonial and neocolonial networks of commodity production where animal alterity is routinely fetishised (225), and an endlessly recycled global capitalism finds new and inventive ways of extending its 'biopolitical management of life' (230).

Wright, Laura. *"Wilderness into Civilized Shapes": Reading the Postcolonial Environment*. Athens GA: University of Georgia Press, 2010.

Open-ended approach to some of the environmental concerns explored in postcolonial 'fictional representations that are neither works of science nor philosophy' (1). Belongs to the early 'second wave' of critical works – the first edition of *Postcolonial Ecocriticism* among them – that bemoan the dearth of postcolonial scholarship on the environment, an assertion that might have been true at the time but would hardly be valid now. Provides competent, if somewhat theory-shy, readings of what have since become canonical postcolonial 'eco-texts' – Martel's *Life of Pi*, Coetzee's *Disgrace*, Mda's *The Heart of Redness* (see also Armstrong above) – but also ranges these alongside lesser known works or those that deserve more consideration in terms of postcolonial/environmental theory, e.g. Hulme's *The Bone People* or Ngũgĩ's *Petals of Blood*. Both of these latter are seen to some extent from an ecofeminist perspective that either links 'environmental devastation to symbolic prostitution' (Ngũgĩ) or asserts women's role as 'environmental caretakers' in the invention of a new national mythology (Hulme) (33, 159). Ecofeminism, in fact, provides the plural methodological grounding for Wright's analysis, which is otherwise largely content to stay on a thematic level and rarely probes beneath the surface of the text. Accordingly, the most impressive chapter is the one that explicitly announces itself as an exploration of postcolonial ecofeminism – partly because it departs from both postcolonial and ecofeminist orthodoxies, revising 'precolonial, colonial and postcolonial environmental mythology to place women at the forefront of positive social and environmental change' (130).

Works cited

Achebe, Chinua (1988) 'An Image of Africa: Racism in Conrad's *Heart of Darkness*', Robert Kimbrough (ed.) (3rd edn), *Heart of Darkness: An Authoritative Text, Background and Sources Criticism*, New York and London: Norton, 251–61.

——(1975) 'The Novelist as Teacher', in *Morning Yet on Creation Day*, New York: Anchor Press, 67–73.

——(1958) *Things Fall Apart*, London: Heinemann.

Adams, Carol J. (1990) *The Sexual Politics of Meat: A Feminist-Vegetarian Critical Theory*, New York: Continuum.

Adorno, Theodor (1998) *Aesthetic Theory*, Minneapolis: University of Minnesota Press.

——(1978) *Minima Moralia: Reflections from Damaged Life* (trans. E.F.N. Jephcott), London: Verso.

Aidoo, Ama Ata (2001) *Changes: A Love Story*, New York: The Feminist Press.

Allen, Chadwick (2002) *Blood Narrative: Indigenous Identities in American Indian and Maori Literary and Activist Texts*, Durham, NC: Duke University Press.

Alpers, Paul (1996) *What is Pastoral?* Chicago: University of Chicago Press.

Anand, Divya (2008) 'Words on Water: Nature and Agency in Amitav Ghosh's *The Hungry Tide*', *Concentric: Literary and Cultural Studies* 34, 1, 21–44.

Anderson, Virginia De John (2004) *Creatures of Empire: How Domestic Animals Transformed Early America*, New York: Oxford University Press.

Appadurai, Arjun (1996) *Modernity at Large: Cultural Dimensions of Globalization*, Minneapolis: University of Minnesota Press.

Appiah, Kwame Anthony (1998) 'Preface', in Abdul Rasheed Na'Allah (ed.) *Ogoni's Agonies: Ken Saro-Wiwa and the Crisis in Nigeria*, Trenton, NJ: Africa World Press, xix–xxi.

——(1997) 'Is the "Post-" in "Postcolonial" the "Post-" in "Postmodern"?' In Anne McClintock, Aamir Mufti and Ella Shohat (eds) *Dangerous Liaisons: Gender, Nation, and Postcolonial Perspectives*, Minneapolis: University of Minnesota Press, 420–44.

Apter, Andrew (1998) 'Death and the King's Henchmen: Ken Saro-Wiwa and the Political Ecology of Citizenship in Nigeria', in Abdul Rasheed Na'Allah (ed.)

Ogoni's Agonies: Ken Saro-Wiwa and the Crisis in Nigeria, Trenton, NJ: Africa World Press, 121–60.

Arens, William (1998) 'Rethinking Anthropology', in Francis Barker *et al.* (eds) *Cannibalism and the Colonial World*, Cambridge: Cambridge University Press, 39–62.

——(1979) *The Man-Eating Myth: Anthropology and Anthropophagy*, New York: Oxford University Press.

Armbruster, Karla and Kathleen R. Wallace (eds) (2001) *Beyond Nature Writing: Expanding the Boundaries of Ecocriticism*, Charlottesville: University of Virginia Press.

Armstrong, Philip (2008) *What Animals Mean in the Fiction of Modernity*, London: Routledge.

Armstrong, Susan and Richard G. Botzler (eds) (2003) *The Animal Ethics Reader*, London: Routledge.

Ashcroft, Bill, Gareth Griffiths and Helen Tiffin (1989) *The Empire Writes Back: Theory and Practice in Post-Colonial Literatures*, London: Routledge.

Attridge, Derek (2004a) *J.M. Coetzee and the Ethics of Reading*, Chicago and London: University of Chicago Press.

——(2004b) *The Singularity of Literature*, London: Routledge.

Attwood, Bain (ed.) (1996) *In the Age of Mabo: History, Aborigines and Australia*, St Leonards, Allen & Unwin.

Atwood, Margaret (2003) *Oryx and Crake*, Toronto: McClelland & Stewart.

——(1972) *Surfacing*, Toronto: McClelland & Stewart.

——(1969) *The Edible Woman*, Toronto: McClelland & Stewart.

Badmington, Neil (ed.) (2000) *Posthumanism*, Houndmills: Palgrave.

Bahri, Deepika (1994) 'Disembodying the Corpus: Postcolonial Pathology in Tsitsi Dangarembga's *Nervous Conditions*', *Postmodern Culture*, online source: http://muse.jhu.edu/journals/postmodern_culture/v005/5.1bahri.html, accessed February 17, 2014.

Baker, Steve (2001) *Picturing the Beast: Animals, Identity and Representation*, Urbana, Ill.: University of Illinois Press.

——(2000) *The Postmodern Animal*, London: Reaktion.

Balme, Christopher B. (1999) *Decolonizing the Stage: Theatrical Syncretism and Post-Colonial Drama*, Oxford: Clarendon Press.

Barber, Karin (1995) 'Money, Self-Realization, and the Person in Yoruba Texts', in J. Guyer (ed.) *Money Matters: Instability, Values, and Social Payments in the Modern History of African Communities*, Portsmouth, NH: Heinemann, 205–24.

Barclay, Robert (2002) *Meļaļ*, Honolulu: University of Hawai'i Press.

Barkawi, Tarak and Mark Laffey (2006) 'The Postcolonial Moment in Security Studies', *Review of International Studies* 32, 2, 329–352.

Barker, Clare (2012) *Postcolonial Fiction and Disability: Exceptional Children, Metaphor and Materiality*, London: Palgrave Macmillan.

Barker, Clare and Stuart Murray (2010) 'Disabling Postcolonialism: Disability Cultures and Democratic Criticism', *Journal of Literary and Cultural Disability Studies* 4, 3, 219–236.

Barker, Francis, Peter Hulme and Margaret Iversen (eds) (1998) *Cannibalism and the Colonial World*, New York: Cambridge University Press.

Barnard, Rita (2004) 'J.M. Coetzee's *Disgrace* and the South African Pastoral', *Contemporary Literature* 44, 2, 199–224.

——(2002) 'Coetzee's Country Ways', *Interventions* 4, 3, 384–94.

Bate, Jonathan (2000) *The Song of the Earth*, London: Picador.

——(1991) *Romantic Ecology: Wordsworth and the Environmental Tradition*, London: Routledge.

Beck, Ulrich (2009) *World at Risk*, Cambridge: Polity Press.

Benitez-Rojo, Antonio (1992) *The Repeating Island: The Caribbean and the Postmodern Perspective* (trans. James Maraniss), Durham, NC: Duke University Press.

Bennett, Bruce (1991) 'An Ecological Vision – Judith Wright', in B. Bennett (ed.) *An Australian Compass: Essays on Place and Direction in Australian Literature*, Fremantle: Fremantle Arts Centre Press, 158–75.

Best, Steve (2009) 'The Rise of Critical Animal Studies: Putting Theory into Action and Animal Liberation into Higher Education', *State of Nature*, online source: www.stateofnature.org/?p=5903, accessed February 22, 2014.

Bhabha, Homi (2004) 'Foreword', in Frantz Fanon, *The Wretched of the Earth* (trans. R. Philcox), New York: Grove Press, vii–xli.

——(1994) *The Location of Culture*, London: Routledge.

Black, Jan Knippers (1999) *Development in Theory and Practice: Paradigms and Paradoxes*, Boulder, CO: Westview Press.

Blair, Ruth (2007) '"Transported Landscapes": Reflections on Empire and Environment in the Pacific', in Helen Tiffin (ed.) *Five Emus to the King of Siam: Environment and Empire*, Amsterdam: Rodopi, 85–111.

Blond, Phillip (ed.) (1998) *Post-Secular Philosophy: Between Philosophy and Theology*, London: Routledge.

Boal, Augusto (1988) *Theatre of the Oppressed*, London: Pluto Press.

Bongie, Christopher (1998) *Islands and Exiles: The Creole Identities of Post/Colonial Literature*, Stanford: Stanford University Press.

Boulle, Pierre (1965) *Monkey Planet*, Harmondsworth: Penguin.

Brady, Emily (2014) 'Aesthetic Value, Ethics and Climate Change', *Environmental Values* 23, 551–70.

Brathwaite, Edward Kamau (2002) *Magical Realism*, 2 vols., New York and Kingston: Savacou North.

——(1997) 'MR', *Annals of Scholarship* 12, 1/2, 1–28.

——(1987) *X/Self*, New York: Oxford University Press.

——(1982) *Sun Poem*, New York: Oxford University Press.

——(1977) *Mother Poem*, New York: Oxford University Press.

Brennan, Timothy (2004), 'From Development to Globalization: Postcolonial Studies and Globalization Theory', in Neil Lazarus (ed.) *The Cambridge Companion to Postcolonial Literary Studies*, Cambridge: Cambridge University Press, 120–38.

——(1997) *At Home in the World: Cosmopolitanism Now*, Minneapolis: University of Minnesota Press.

Brewster, Anne (2010) 'Indigenous Sovereignty and the Crisis of Whiteness in Alexis Wright's *Carpentaria*', *Australian Literary Studies* 25, 4, 98–100.

——(1994) 'Oodgeroo: Orator, Poet, Storyteller', *Australian Literary Studies* 16, 4, 93–104.

Britton, S. (1980) 'The Spatial Organisation of Tourism in a Neo-Colonial Economy: A Fiji Case Study', *Pacific Viewpoint* 21, 2, 144–65.

Brodber, Erna (1998) *Myal*, London and Port of Spain: New Beacon.

Brohman, John (1996) 'New Directions in Tourism for Third World Development', *Annals of Tourism Research* 23, 1, 48–70.

Brophy, Sarah (2002) 'Angels in Antigua: Diasporic Melancholy in Jamaica Kincaid's *My Brother*', *PMLA* 117, 2, 265–77.

Brouillette, Sarah (2007) *Postcolonial Writers in the Global Literary Marketplace*, Basingstoke: Palgrave Macmillan.

Bruner, Edward W. (2005) *Culture on Tour: Ethnographies of Tourism*, Chicago: University of Chicago Press.

Bryant, Raymond (1998) 'Power, knowledge and political ecology in the Third World', *Progress in Physical Geography* 22, 79–94.

Brydon, Diana (1998) *Timothy Findley*, New York: Twayne.

Buckle, Tony (1995) 'Land Relations and Social Dynamics: Reflections on Contemporary Land Issues in South Africa, with Particular Reference to the Eastern Cape', in Anthony Lemon (ed.) *The Geography of Change in South Africa*, Chichester: Wiley, 65–84.

Buell, Frederick (2003) *From Apocalypse to Way of Life: Environmental Crisis in the American Century*, New York: Routledge.

Buell, Lawrence (2005) *The Future of Environmental Criticism: Environmental Crisis and Literary Imagination*, Oxford: Blackwell.

——(2001) *Writing for an Endangered World: Literature, Culture, and Environment in the U.S. and Beyond*, Cambridge, MA: Harvard University Press.

——(1995) *The Environmental Imagination: Thoreau, Nature Writing, and the Formation of American Culture*, Cambridge, MA: Harvard University Press.

Bunton, Robin and Alan Petersen (eds) (2005) *Genetic Governance: Health, Risks and Ethics in a Biotech Era*, New York: Routledge.

Calarco, Matthew (2002) 'On the Borders of Language and Death: Derrida and the Question of the Animal', *Angelaki* 7, 2, 17–25.

Caminero-Santangelo, Byron and Garth Myers (eds) (2011) *Environment at the Margins: Literary and Environmental Studies in Africa*, Columbus, OH: Ohio University Press.

Campbell, Mary Baine (1988) *The Witness and the Other World: Exotic European Travel Writing, 400–1600*, Ithaca, NY: Cornell University Press.

Carrigan, Anthony (2011) 'Review of Graham Huggan and Helen Tiffin, *Post-colonial Ecocriticsm: Literature, Animals, Environment*', *Journal of Postcolonial Writing* 47, 3, 352–353.

Carrigan, Anthony (forthcoming, 2015) 'Towards a Postcolonial Disaster Studies', in Elizabeth DeLoughrey, Jill Didur and Anthony Carrigan (eds) *Global*

Ecologies and the Environmental Humanities: Postcolonial Approaches, London: Routledge.

——(2008) 'Representations of Tourism in Postcolonial Island Literatures', Unpublished PhD thesis, University of Leeds.

Carter, Paul (1987) *The Road to Botany Bay: An Essay in Spatial History*, London: Faber.

Caruth, Cathy (ed.) (1995) *Trauma: Explorations in Memory*, Baltimore, MD: Johns Hopkins University Press.

Casteel, Sarah Phillips (2007) *Second Arrivals: Landscape and Belonging in Contemporary Writing from the Americas*, Charlottesville, VA: University of Virginia Press.

——(2004) 'New World Pastoral: The Caribbean Garden and Emplacement in Gisèle Pineau and Shani Mootoo', *Interventions* 5, 1, 12–28.

Chakrabarty, Dipesh (2012) 'Postcolonial Studies and the Challenge of Climate Change', *New Literary History* 43, 1, 1–18.

——(2009) 'The Climate of History: Four Theses', *Critical Inquiry* 35, 192–222.

Chamberlin, J. Edward (2003) *If This Is Your Land, Where Are Your Stories? Finding Common Ground*, Toronto: Knopf Canada.

Chambers, Iain (2001) *Culture after Humanism: History, Culture, Subjectivity*, London: Routledge.

Chatterjee, Partha (1986) *Nationalist Thought and the Postcolonial World: A Derivative Discourse?*, Minneapolis, MN: University of Minnesota Press.

Cheah, Pheng (2004) *Spectral Nationality: Passages of Freedom from Kant to Postcolonial Literatures of Liberation*, New York: Columbia University Press.

Chow, Rey (2002) *The Protestant Ethic and the Spirit of Capitalism*, New York: Columbia University Press.

Christie, Sarah, Geoffrey Hutchings and Don MacLennan (1980) *Perspectives on South African Fiction*, Johannesburg: A.D. Donker Ltd.

Cilano, Cara and Elizabeth DeLoughrey (2007) 'Against Authenticity: Global Knowledges and Postcolonial Ecocriticism', *Interdisciplinary Studies in Literature and Environment* 14, 1, 71–86.

Clark, Timothy (2010) 'Some Climate Change Ironies: Deconstruction, Environmental Politics and the Closure of Ecocriticism', *Oxford Literary Review* 32, 1, 131–149.

Clarke, William C. (1990) 'Learning from the Past: Knowledge and Sustainable Development', *The Contemporary Pacific* 2, 2, 233–53.

Clay, Edward and Ola Stokke (eds) (2000) *Food Aid and Human Security*, London: Frank Cass.

Clingman, Stephen (1986) *The Novels of Nadine Gordimer: History from the Inside*, London: Allen and Unwin.

Cloete, Elsie (2007) 'Tigers, Humans and Animots', *Journal of Literary Studies*, 23, 3, 314–22.

Coetzee, J.M. (2003) *Elizabeth Costello*, London: Secker and Warburg.

—— (2000) [1999] *Disgrace*, London: Vintage.

—— (1999) *The Lives of Animals*, London: Vintage.

——(1998) [1983] *Life & Times of Michael K*, London: Vintage.

——(1995) 'Meat Country', *Granta* 52, 42–52.

——(1990) *Age of Iron*, New York: Random House.

——(1988) *White Writing: On the Culture of Letters in South Africa*, New Haven, CT: Yale University Press.

——(1986) *Foe*, Johannesburg: Ravan Press.

Collett, Anne (ed.) (1998) *Span* 46: Special Issue: 'Gardening in the Colonies' (April).

Commoner, Barry (1972) *The Closing Circle: Nature, Man, and Technology*, New York: Knopf.

Conrad Joseph, (1963) [1901] *Heart of Darkness*, New York: Norton.

Coupe, Laurence (ed.) (2000) *The Green Studies Reader: From Romanticism to Ecocriticism*, London: Routledge.

Cribb, Robert (2007) 'Conservation in Colonial Indonesia', *Interventions* 9, 1, 49–61.

Cribb, Robert and Li Narangoa (2004) 'Dynamics of Land and Identity in Pacific Asia: Reflections on Attachment to Land', *The International Journal of the Humanities* 1, 1093–1102.

Crist, Eileen (2007) 'Beyond the Climate Crisis: A Critique of Climate Change Discourse', *Telos* 141, 29–55.

Crosby, Alfred W. (1986) *Ecological Imperialism: The Biological Expansion of Europe, 900–1900*, Cambridge: Cambridge University Press.

——(1973) *The Columbian Exchange: Biological and Cultural Consequences of 1492*, Westport, CT: Greenwood Press.

Cruz-Malavé, Arnaldo and Martin Manalansan (eds) (2002) *Queer Globalizations: Citizenship and the Afterlife of Colonialism*, New York: New York University Press.

Curnow, Allen (1982) *Selected Poems*, Auckland: Penguin.

Curtin, Deane (2005) *Environmental Ethics for a Postcolonial World*, Lanham, MD: Rowman & Littlefield.

——(1999) *Chinnagounder's Challenge: The Question of Ecological Citizenship*, Bloomington, IN: Indiana University Press.

Dangarembga, Tsitsi (1988) *Nervous Conditions*, Seattle: The Seal Press.

Danielsson, Bengt and Marie-Thérèse Danielsson (1986) *Poisoned Reign: French Nuclear Colonialism in the Pacific*, Ringwood, VIC: Penguin.

Darian-Smith, Kate, Liz Gunner and Sarah Nuttall (eds) (1996) *Text, Theory, Space: Land, Literature, and History in South Africa and Australia*, London: Routledge.

Dash, Michael (1998) *The Other America: Caribbean Literature in a New World Context*, Charlottesville: Virginia University Press.

Daston, Lorraine and Gregg Mitman (eds) (2005) *Thinking with Animals: New Perspectives in Anthropomorphism*, New York: Columbia University Press.

Davidson, Basil (1984) 'The Bible and the Gun', *Africa: A Voyage of Discovery with Basil Davidson*, Chicago: Home Vision.

Davidson, Jim (1977) 'Interview: Kath Walker', *Meanjin* 36, 4, 428–41.

Davies, Tony (2007) *Humanism*, London: Routledge.

Davis, Jack (1984) *Kullark (Home)/The Dreamers*, Sydney: Currency Press.

Davis, Lennard (ed.) (1996) *The Disability Studies Reader*, New York: Routledge.

Davis, Mike (1999) *Ecology of Fear: Los Angeles and the Imagination of Disaster*, New York: Vintage.

Deepak, Anne C. (2013) 'A Postcolonial Feminist Social Work Perspective on Global Food Security', *Affilia*, online source: http://aff.sagepub.com/content/early/2013/12/27/0886109913516456.abstract, accessed February 17, 2014.

Defoe, Daniel (1972) [1719] *Robinson Crusoe*, Oxford: Oxford University Press.

DeLoughrey, Elizabeth (2009) *Routes and Roots: Navigating Caribbean and Pacific Island Literatures*, Honolulu: University of Hawai'i Press.

——(2007a) 'Quantum Landscapes: A "Ventriloquism of Spirit"', *Interventions* 9, 1, 62–82.

——(2007b) *Roots and Routes: Navigating Caribbean and Pacific Island Literatures*, Honolulu: University of Hawai'i Press.

——(1999) 'The Spiral Temporality of Patricia Grace's *Potiki*', *Ariel* 30, 1, 59–83.

DeLoughrey, Elizabeth, Renee Gosson and George Handley (eds) (2005) *Caribbean Literature and the Environment: Between Nature and Culture*, Charlottesville, VA: University of Virginia Press.

DeLoughrey, Elizabeth and George B. Handley (eds) (2011) *Postcolonial Ecologies: Literatures of the Environment*, New York: Oxford University Press.

De Rivero, Oswaldo (2001) *The Myth of Development: The Non-Viable Economies of the Twenty-First Century*, London: Zed Books.

Derrida, Jacques (2002) 'The Animal that Therefore I Am (More to Follow)' (trans. David Wills), *Critical Inquiry* 28, 2, 369–418.

Desai, Anita (2000) [1999] *Fasting, Feasting*, New York: Vintage.

Devlin-Glass, Frances (2008) 'A Politics of the Dreamtime: Destructive and Regenerative Rainbows in Alexis Wright's *Carpentaria*', *Australian Literary Studies* 23, 4, 392–407.

Diamond, David (2007) *Theatre for Living: The Art and Science of Community-Based Dialogue*, Victoria, BC: Trafford Publishing.

Dibblin, Jane (1988) *Day of Two Suns: US Nuclear Testing and the Pacific Islanders*, London: Virago.

Diski, Jenny (1994) *Monkey's Uncle*, London: Weidenfeld and Nicolson.

Dobson, Andrew (1995) *Green Political Thought*, London: Routledge.

Dodds, Susan (1998) 'Justice and Indigenous Land Rights', *Inquiry* 41, 2, 187–205.

Donnell, Alison (1995) 'She Ties Her Tongue: The Problems of Cultural Paralysis in Postcolonial Criticism', *Ariel* 26, 1, 101–16.

Doyle, Laura (1996) 'The Racial Sublime', in Alan J. Richardson and Sonia Hofkosh (eds) *Romanticism, Race, and Imperial Culture, 1780–1834*, Bloomington, IN: Indiana University Press, 15–39.

Eagleton, Terry (2005) *Holy Terror*, Oxford: Oxford University Press.

Eco, Umberto (2006) *On Literature*, New York: Mariner Books.

Ehrenfeld, David W. (1981) *The Arrogance of Humanism*, New York: Oxford University Press.

Ehrlich, Paul (1968) *The Population Bomb*, Cutchogue, NY: Buccaneer Books.

Elder, Glen, Jennifer Wolch and Jody Emel (1998) '*Le Pratique Sauvage*: Race, Place and the Human–Animal Divide', in Jennifer Wolch and Jody Emel (eds)

Animal Geographies: Place, Politics and Identity in the Nature-Culture Borderlands, London: Verso, 72–90.

Emel, Jody and Jennifer Wolch (1998) 'Witnessing the Animal Moment', in *Animal Geographies: Place, Politics and Identity in the Nature-Culture Borderlands*, London: Verso, 1–26.

Empson, William (1966) [1935] *Some Versions of Pastoral*, Harmondsworth: Penguin.

Engel, Marian (1976) *Bear*, Toronto: McClelland & Stewart.

Escobar, Arturo (1995) *Encountering Development: The Making and Unmaking of the Third World*, Princeton, NJ: Princeton University Press.

Esteva, Gustavo (1997), 'Development', in Wolfgang Sachs (ed.) *The Development Dictionary*, London: Zed Books, 6–25.

Ettin, Andrew V. (1984) *Literature and the Pastoral*, New Haven, CT: Yale University Press.

Fanon, Frantz (2005) [1963] *The Wretched of the Earth* (trans. R. Philcox), New York: Grove Press.

Featherstone, Mike and Roger Burrows (eds) (1996) *Cyberspace/Cyberbodies/Cyberpunk: Cultures of Technological Embodiment*, London: Routledge.

Fennell, David (1999) *Ecotourism: An Introduction*, New York: Routledge.

Ferguson, Moira (1994) *Jamaica Kincaid: Where the Land Meets the Body*, Charlottesville, VA: University of Virginia Press.

Ferrier, Carole (2008) '"Disappearing Memory" and the Colonial Present in Recent Indigenous Women's Writing', *JASAL* 8, 37–55.

Fiddes, Nick (1992) *Meat: A Natural Symbol*, London: Routledge.

Filewod, Alan (1992) 'Averting the Colonial Gaze: Notes on Watching Native Theater', in Per Brask and William Morgan (eds) *Aboriginal Voices: Amerindian, Inuit and Sami Theatre*, Baltimore, MD: Johns Hopkins University Press.

Findley, Timothy (1985) *Not Wanted on the Voyage*, London: Macmillan.

Fischer, David (1992) *Stopping the Spread of Nuclear Weapons: The Past and its Prospects*, London: Routledge.

Fischer, Steven Roger (2002) *A History of the Pacific Islands*, London: Palgrave.

Fisher, William F. (ed.) (1995) *Toward Sustainable Development? Struggling Over the Narmada River*, New York: M.E. Sharpe.

Flannery, Tim (2005) *The Weather Makers: Our Changing Climate and What It Means for Life on Earth*, London: Penguin.

Forbes, Curdella (2012) *Ghosts*, Leeds: Peepal Tree Press.

Forster, E.M. (1924) *A Passage to India*, New York: Harcourt, Brace and Company.

Foucault, Michel (1977) *Discipline and Punish: the Birth of the Prison*, London: Penguin.

——(1970) *The Order of Things: An Archaeology of the Human Sciences*, New York: Pantheon.

Franzen, Jonathan (2010) *Freedom*, New York: Farrar, Straus and Giroux.

Freeman, Carol (2005) 'Is This Picture Worth a Thousand Words? An Analysis of Harry Burrell's Photo of a Thylacine with a Chicken', *Australian Zoology* 33, 1, 1–16.

Fuchs, Miriam (1994) 'Reading Toward the Indigenous Pacific: Patricia Grace's *Potiki*, a Case Study', *Boundary 2* 21, 1, 165–84.

Fudge, Erica (2008) *Pets*, Stocksfield, UK: Acumen.

——(2002) *Animal*, London: Reaktion.

Gadgil, Madhav and Ramachandra Guha (eds) (1995) *Ecology and Equity: The Use and Abuse of Nature in Contemporary India*, London: Routledge.

Galdikas, Biruté (1980) 'Living with Orangutans', *National Geographic* 157, 6, 830–53.

Garrard, Greg (2004) *Ecocriticism*, London: Routledge.

——(2000) 'Radical Pastoral?' in Laurence Coupe (ed.) *The Green Studies Reader: From Romanticism to Ecocriticism*, London: Routledge, 182–86.

Gauch, Suzanne (2002) 'A Small Place: Some Perspectives on the Ordinary', *Callaloo* 25, 3, 910–19.

Gebauer, Gunter and Christoph Wulf (1996) *Mimesis: Culture-Art-Society*, Berkeley, CA: University of California Press.

Gelder, Ken and Jane M. Jacobs (1998) *Uncanny Australia: Sacredness and Identity in a Postcolonial Nation*, Melbourne: Melbourne University Press.

George, Rosemary (1999) *The Politics of Home: Postcolonial Relocation and Twentieth-Century Fiction*, Berkeley, CA: University of California Press.

Ghai, Anita (2002) 'Disability in the Indian Context: Post-Colonial Perspectives', in Mairian Corker and Tom Shakespeare (eds) *Disability/Postmodernity: Embodying Disability Theory*, London: Continuum, 88–100.

Ghosh, Amitav (2004) *The Hungry Tide*, London: HarperCollins.

Gibson, Nigel (1999) *Rethinking Fanon: The Continuing Dialogue*, London: Humanity Books.

Gifford, Terry (1999) *Pastoral*, London: Routledge.

Gilbert, Helen (1998) *Sightlines: Race, Gender, and Nation in Contemporary Australian Theatre*, Ann Arbor, MI: University of Michigan Press.

Gilbert, Helen and Jacqueline Lo (2007) *Performance and Cosmopolitics: Cross-Cultural Transactions in Australasia*, Houndmills: Palgrave.

Gilbert, Helen and Joanne Tompkins (1996) *Post-Colonial Drama: Theory, Practice, Politics*, London: Routledge.

Gilroy, Paul (2004) *After Empire: Melancholia or Convivial Culture?* London: Routledge.

Glissant, Edouard (1989) *Caribbean Discourse* (trans. J. Michael Dash), Charlottesville, VA: University of Virginia Press.

Glotfelty, Cheryll and Harold Fromm (eds) (1996) *The Ecocriticism Reader: Landmarks in Literary Ecology*, Athens, GA: University of Georgia Press.

Goldie, Terry (1989) *Fear and Temptation: The Image of the Indigene in Australian, Canadian and New Zealand Literatures*, Kingston, ON: McGill-Queen's University Press.

Goldsworthy, Peter (1995) *Wish*, Sydney: Angus & Robertson.

Goodall, Jane (1971) *In the Shadow of Man*, Boston, MA: Houghton Mifflin.

Gopinath, Gayatri (2005) *Impossible Desires: Queer Diasporas and South Asian Public Cultures*, Durham, NC: Duke University Press.

Gorak, Irene (1991) 'Libertine Pastoral: Nadine Gordimer's *The Conservationist*', *Novel* 24, 3, 241–56.

Gordimer, Nadine (1977) [1974] *The Conservationist*, London: Penguin.

Goto, Hiromi (2004) *Hopeful Monsters: Stories*, Vancouver: Arsenal Pulp Press.

——(2001) *The Kappa Child*, Calgary: Red Deer Press.

Gowdy, Barbara (1998) *The White Bone*, New York: Picador.

Grace, Patricia (1986) *Potiki*, Auckland, NZ: Penguin.

Graham, Elaine (2002) *Representations of the Post/Human: Monsters, Aliens and Others in Popular Culture*, New Brunswick, NJ: Rutgers University Press.

Greenspan, Brian (2001) 'Cannibals at the Core: Juicy Rumors and the Hollow Earth Chronotope in Ian Wedde's *Symmes Hole*', in Kristen Guest (ed.) *Eating Their Words: Cannibalism and the Boundaries of Cultural Identity*, Albany: State University of New York Press, 149–65.

Griffiths, Tom (2000) 'Travelling in Deep Time: La Longue Durée in Australian History', online source: www.australianhumanitiesreview.org/archive/Issue-June-2000/griffiths4.html, accessed January 13, 2014.

——(1999) 'Legend and Lament', review essay, *The Australian's Review of Books*, 11–13 (March).

——(1997) *Hunters and Collectors: The Antiquarian Imagination in Australia*, Cambridge: Cambridge University Press.

Griffiths, Tom and Libby Robin (1998) *Ecology and Empire: The Environmental History of Settler Societies*, Seattle, WA: University of Washington Press.

Grove, Richard (1995) *Green Imperialism: Colonial Expansion, Tropical Island Edens and the Origins of Environmentalism, 1600–1860*, Cambridge: Cambridge University Press.

Guha, Ramachandra (2000) *The Unquiet Woods: Ecological Change and Peasant Resistance in the Himalayas*, Berkeley, CA: University of California Press.

Guha, Ramachandra and Joan Martinez-Alier (1997) *Varieties of Environmentalism: Essays North and South*, London: Earthscan.

Gunew, Sneja (2000) 'Introduction: Multicultural Translations of Food, Bodies, Language', *Journal of Intercultural Studies* 21, 3, 227–237.

Hage, Ghassan (2003) *Against Paranoid Nationalism: Searching for Hope in a Shrinking Society*, Annandale, NSW: Pluto Press.

——(2000) *White Nation: Fantasies of White Supremacy in a Multicultural Society*, London: Routledge.

Hall, C. Michael and Hazel Tucker (eds) (2004) *Tourism and Postcolonialism: Contested Discourses, Identities and Representations*, London: Routledge.

Hall, Ruth and Lungisile Ntsebeza (eds) (2007) *The Land Question in South Africa: The Challenge of Transformation and Redistribution*, Cape Town: Human Sciences Research Council Press.

Halliwell, Martin and Andy Mousley (eds) (2004) *Critical Humanisms: Humanist/Anti-Humanist Dialogues*, Edinburgh: Edinburgh University Press.

Halperin, David (1997) *Saint Foucault: Towards a Gay Hagiography*, Oxford: Oxford University Press.

Hannerz, Ulf (1996) *Transnational Connections: Culture, People, Places*, London: Routledge.

Haraway, Donna (2003) *The Haraway Reader*, New York: Routledge.

——(1997) *Modest Witness @ Second Millennium: FemaleMan Meets OncoMouse: Feminism and Technoscience*, New York: Routledge.

——(1991) *Simians, Cyborgs, and Women: The Reinvention of Nature*, New York: Routledge.

Harris, Cole (2002) *Making Native Space: Colonialism, Resistance, and Reserves in British Columbia*, Vancouver, BC: UBC Press.

Harris, Wilson (1987) *The Infinite Rehearsal*, London: Faber & Faber.

Harvey, David (2005) *The New Imperialism*. (2nd edition), New York: Oxford University Press.

——(1997) *Justice, Nature and the Geography of Difference*, Oxford: Blackwell.

Hau'ofa, Epeli (2000) 'Epilogue: Pasts to Remember', in Robert Borowsky (ed.) *Remembrance of Pacifics Past: An Invitation to Remake History*, Honolulu: University of Hawai'i Press, 453–71.

——(1998) 'The Ocean in Us', *The Contemporary Pacific* 10, 2, 392–410.

——(1993) 'Our Sea of Islands', in E. Waddell, V. Naidu and E. Hau'ofa (eds), *A New Oceania: Rediscovering Our Sea of Islands*, Suva: University of the South Pacific.

Havinden, Michael and David Meredith (1996) *Colonialism and Development: Britain and its Tropical Colonies, 1850–1960*, London: Routledge.

Hawley, John C. (ed.) (2001) *Post-Colonial, Queer: Theoretical Intersections*, Albany, NY: State University of New York Press.

Hayles, N. Katherine (1999) *How We Became Posthuman: Virtual Bodies in Cybernetics, Literature, and Informatics*, Chicago: University of Chicago Press.

Head, Dominic (1998) 'The (Im)possibility of Ecocriticism', in Richard Kerridge and Neil Sammells (eds) *Writing the Environment: Ecocriticism and Literature*, London: Zed Books, 27–39.

Heidegger, Martin (1971) 'Building Dwelling Thinking', in Albert Hofstadter (ed.) *Poetry, Language, Thought*, New York: Harper & Row, 149–50.

Heise, Ursula (2008) *Sense of Place and Sense of Planet: The Environmental Imagination of the Global*, New York: Oxford University Press.

——(2006) 'The Hitchhiker's Guide to Ecocriticism', *PMLA* 121, 2, 503–16.

Hereniko, Vilsoni (2001) 'David and Goliath: A Response to "The Oceanic Imaginary"', *The Contemporary Pacific* 13, 1, 163–68.

Highway, Tomson (2005) *Ernestine Shuswap Gets Her Trout*, Vancouver: Talonbooks.

——(1988) *The Rez Sisters*, Saskatoon, SK: Fifth House.

Hodge, Bob and Vijay Mishra (1991) *Dark Side of the Dream: Australian Literature and the Postcolonial Mind*, Sydney: Allen & Unwin.

Holst-Petersen, Kirsten (1984) 'First Things First: Problems of a Feminist Approach to African Literature', *Kunapipi* 6, 3, 35–47.

Hoogvelt, Ankie (1997) *Globalization and the Postcolonial World: The New Political Economy of Development*, Houndmills: Palgrave.

Hooper, Glenn (ed.) (2005) *Landscape and Empire, 1770–2000*, Farnham: Ashgate.

Horkheimer, Max and Theodor Adorno (1972) *Dialectic of Enlightenment: Cultural Memory in the Present*, New York: Herder & Herder.

Hubbard, Ruth and Elijah Wald (1999) *Exploding the Gene Myth: How Genetic Information is Produced and Manipulated by Scientists, Physicians, Employers, Insurance Companies, Educators, and Law Enforcers*, Boston: Beacon Press.

Huggan, Graham (forthcoming, 2015) 'Australian Literature, Risk, and the Global Climate Challenge', *Lit: Literature Interpretation Theory*.

——(2007a) *Australian Literature: Postcolonialism, Racism, Transnationalism*, Oxford: Oxford University Press, 161–80.

——(2007b) 'Postcolonialism, Ecocriticism and the Animal in Canadian Fiction', in Fiona Becket and Terry Gifford (eds) *Culture, Creativity and Environment: New Environmentalist Criticism*, Amsterdam: Rodopi, 161–80.

——(2005) '(Not) Reading *Orientalism*', *Research in African Literatures* 36, 3, 124–31.

——(2004) '"Greening" Postcolonialism: Ecocritical Perspectives', *Modern Fiction Studies* 50, 3, 701–33.

——(2001) *The Postcolonial Exotic: Marketing the Margins*, London: Routledge.

——(1994) 'Echoes from Elsewhere: Gordimer's Short Fiction as Social Critique', *Research in African Literatures* 25, 1, 61–74.

Huggan, Graham and Helen Tiffin (eds) (2007) 'Green Postcolonialism', special issue of *Interventions* 9, 1.

Huggan, Graham and Stephen Watson (eds) (1996) *Critical Perspectives on J.M. Coetzee*, Houndmills: Macmillan.

Hulme, Mike (2009) *Why We Disagree about Climate Change: Understanding Controversy, Inaction and Opportunity*, Cambridge: Cambridge University Press.

Hulme, Peter (1998) 'Introduction: The Cannibal Scene', in Francis Barker, Peter Hulme and Margaret Iversen (eds) *Cannibalism and the Colonial World*, Cambridge: Cambridge University Press, 1–38.

Hyde, Lewis (1998) *Trickster Makes This World: Mischief, Myth, and Art*, New York: Farrar, Straus & Giroux.

Ihimaera, Witi (1987) *The Whale Rider*, Auckland, NZ: Heinemann.

Indyk, Ivor (1993) 'Pastoral and Priority: The Aboriginal in Australian Pastoral', *New Literary History* 24, 4, 837–55.

Ingold, Tim (2011) *Being Alive: Essays on Movement, Knowledge and Description*, London: Routledge.

Ishtar, Zohl de (1994) *Daughters of the Pacific*, Melbourne: Spinifex Press.

Jenkins, Lee (2007) 'New World/NewWord Style', *Contemporary Literature* 48, 1, 165–171.

Kane, Paul (2004) 'Woful Shepherds: Anti-Pastoral in Australian Poetry', in Judith Ryan and Chris Wallace-Crabbe (eds) *Imagining Australia: Literature and Culture in the New New World*, Cambridge, MA: Harvard University Press, 269–85.

Kelman, Ilan and J.C. Gaillard (2010) 'Embedding Climate Change Adaptation within Disaster Risk Reduction', in R. Shaw *et al.*, *Climate Change Adaptation and Disaster Risk Reduction: Issues and Challenges. Community, Environment and Disaster Risk Management* 4, 2, Bingley: Emerald Books, 23–46.

Keown, Michelle (2007) *Pacific Islands Writing: The Postcolonial Literatures of Aotearoa/New Zealand and Oceania*, Oxford: Oxford University Press.

——(2005) *Postcolonial Pacific Writing*, London: Routledge.

Kilgour, Maggie (1998) 'The Function of Cannibalism at the Present Time', in *Cannibalism and the Colonial World*, Cambridge: Cambridge University Press, 238–59.

——(1990) *From Communion to Cannibalism: Anatomy of Metaphors of Incorporation*, Princeton, NJ: Princeton University Press.

Kimball, Andrew (1996) 'Biocolonization', in J. Mander and E. Goldsmith (eds) *The Case Against the Global Economy*, San Francisco; Sierra Club Books.

Kincaid, Jamaica (1999) *My Garden (Book)*, New York: Farrar, Straus & Giroux.

——(1988) *A Small Place*, New York: Farrar, Straus & Giroux.

King, Jane (2002) 'A Small Place Writes Back', *Callaloo* 25, 3, 885–909.

King, Mike (2009) *Postsecularism*, London: Routledge.

King, Thomas (1993) *Green Grass, Running Water*, New York: Houghton Mifflin.

Knox-Shaw, Peter (1996) 'Dusklands: A Metaphysics of Violence', in Graham Huggan and Stephen Watson (eds) *Critical Perspectives on J.M. Coetzee*, Houndmills: Macmillan, 107–19.

Koenigsberger, Kurt (2007) *The Novel and the Menagerie: Totality, Englishness, and Empire*, Columbus, OH: Ohio State University Press.

Krech, Shepard III (2000) *The Ecological Indian: Myth and History*, New York: Norton.

Lang-Peralta, Linda (ed.) (2006) *Jamaica Kincaid and Caribbean Double Crossings*, Newark, DE: University of Delaware Press.

Larrain, Jorge (1989) *Theories of Development: Capitalism, Colonialism and Dependency*, Cambridge: Polity Press.

Latour, Bruno (2004) *Politics of Nature: How to Bring the Sciences into Democracy* (trans. Catherine Porter), Cambridge, Mass: Harvard University Press.

Lazarus, Neil (2006) 'Postcolonial Studies after the Invasion of Iraq', *New Formations* 59, 10–22.

——(1999) *Nationalism and Cultural Practice in the Postcolonial World*, Cambridge: Cambridge University Press.

Lazarus, Neil and Crystal Bartolovich (eds) (2002) *Marxism, Modernity, and Postcolonial Studies*, London: Routledge.

Lee, Ang, dir. (2006) *Brokeback Mountain*, Los Angeles, CA: Paramount Pictures.

Levin, Jonathan (2002) 'Beyond Nature? Recent Work in Ecocriticism', *Contemporary Literature* 43, 1, 171–86.

Lewis, Krishna Ray (1995) '*The Infinite Rehearsal* and Pastoral Revision', *Callaloo* 18, 1, 83–92.

Litfin, Karen (2000) 'Environment, Wealth, and Authority: Global Climate Change and Emerging Modes of Legitimation', *International Studies Review* 2, 2, 119–148.

Loomba, Ania (1994) 'Overworlding the Third World', in Patrick Williams and Laura Chrisman (eds) *Colonial Discourse and Post-Colonial Theory: A Reader*, New York: Columbia University Press, 305–23.

Lousley, Cheryl (2004) '"Hosanna da, our home on natives' land": Environmental Justice and Democracy in Thomas King's *Green Grass, Running Water*', *Essays in Canadian Writing*, 81 (Winter), 17–29.

Love, Glenn (2003) *Practical Ecocriticism*, Charlottesville, VA: University of Virginia Press.

Macaskill, Brian (1990) 'Interrupting the Hegemonic: Textual Critique and Mythological Recuperation from the White Margins of South African Writing', *Novel* 23, 2, 156–81.

MacCannell, Dean (1992) *Empty Meeting Grounds: The Tourist Papers*, London: Routledge.

MacKenzie, John M. (1988) *The Empire of Nature: Hunting, Conservation and British Imperialism*, Manchester: Manchester University Press.

Manne, Robert (2004) 'Sending Them Home: Refugees and the New Politics of Indifference', *Quarterly Essay* 13, 1–95.

Mannur, Anita (2009) *Culinary Fictions: Food in South Asian Diasporic Cultures*, Philadelphia, PA: Temple University Press.

Mares, Peter (2001) *Borderline*, Sydney: University of New South Wales Press.

Martel, Yann (2001) *Life of Pi*, Toronto: Random House.

Marzec, Robert P. (2007) *An Ecological Postcolonial Study of Literature: From Daniel Defoe to Salman Rushde*, New York: Palgrave MacMillan.

Marx, Leo (1964) *The Machine in the Garden: Technology and the Pastoral Ideal in America*, New York: Oxford University Press.

Maslin, Mark (2008) *Global Warming: A Very Short Introduction*, Oxford: Oxford University Press.

Masson, Jeffrey Moussaieff (2003) *The Pig Who Sang to the Moon: The Emotional World of Farm Animals*, New York: Ballantine Books.

Mazel, David (1996a) 'American Literary Environmentalism as Domestic Orientalism', *ISLE* 3, 2, 37–45.

——(1996b) 'American Literary Enviromentalism as Domestic Orientalism', in Cheryll Glotfelty and Harold Fromm (eds) The Ecocriticism Reader, Athens, GA: University of Georgia Press, 137–146.

McCully, Patrick (1996) *Silenced Rivers: The Ecology and Politics of Large Dams*, London: Zed Books.

McKay, Robert (2003) 'Animal Ethics in the Fiction of J M Coetzee', *The Literary Representation of Pro-Animal Thought: Readings in Contemporary Fiction*, Unpublished PhD: The University of Sheffield.

McKibben, Bill (2006) *The End of Nature*, New York: Random House.

McSweeney, Joyelle (2005) 'Poetics, Revelations, and Catastrophes: An Interview with Kamau Brathwaite', online source: www.raintaxi.com/online/2005fall/brathwaite.shtml, accessed January 13, 2014.

Mda, Zakes (2005) *The Whale Caller*, Harmondsworth: Penguin.

——(1998) 'Current Trends in Theatre for Development in South Africa', in Derek Attridge and Rosemary Jolly (eds) *Writing South Africa: Literature, Apartheid, and Democracy, 1970–1995*, Cambridge: Cambridge University Press, 257–64.

Meeker, Joseph (1972) *The Comedy of Survival: Studies in Literary Ecology,* New York: Charles Scribner's.

Melville, Herman (2002) [1851] *Moby-Dick,* New York: Norton.

——(1972) [1846] *Typee,* Harmondsworth: Penguin.

Merchant, Carolyn (1995) *Earthcare: Women and the Environment,* London: Routledge.

——(1992) *Radical Ecology: The Search for a Livable World,* New York: Routledge.

——(1980) *The Death of Nature: Women, Ecology, and the Scientific Revolution,* London: HarperCollins.

Mies, Maria and Vandana Shiva (1993) *Ecofeminism,* London: Zed Books.

Mintz, Sidney W. (1986) *Sweetness and Power: The Place of Sugar in Modern History,* New York: Penguin.

Mitchell, W.J.T. (1998) *The Last Dinosaur Book,* Chicago: University of Chicago Press.

Mittee, Ledum (1999) 'Oil, Arms and Terror: The Ogoni Experience', *Interventions* 1, 3, 430–38.

Mongia, Padmini (1997) 'The Making and Marketing of Arundhati Roy', India: Fifty Years After Conference: University of Barcelona, Spain.

Montaigne, Michel de (1958) [1580] 'Of Cannibals', *Montaigne: Essays* (trans. J. M. Cohen), Harmondsworth: Penguin, 105–18.

Montgomery, Georgina M. and Linda Kalof (eds) (2012) *Making Animal Meaning,* Lansing, MI: Michigan State University Press.

Mortimer-Sandilands, Catriona and Bruce Erickson (eds) (2010) *Queer Ecologies: Sex, Nature, Politics, Desire,* Bloomington, IN: Indiana University Press.

Morton, Timothy (2013) *Hyperobjects: Philosophy and Ecology after the End of the World,* Minneapolis, MN: University of Minnesota Press.

——(2007) *Ecology without Nature: Rethinking Environmental Aesthetics,* Cambridge, MA: Harvard University Press.

Morton, Timothy (2013) *Hyperobjects: Philosophy and Ecology after the End of the World,* Minneapolis, MN: University of Minnesota Press.

Mount, Dana and Susie O'Brien (2013) 'Postcolonialism and the Environment', in Graham Huggan (ed.) *The Oxford Handbook of Postcolonial Studies,* Oxford: Oxford University Press, 521–539.

Mowforth, Martin and Ian Munt (1998) *Tourism and Sustainability: Development and New Tourism in the Third World,* London: Routledge.

Mukherjee, Pablo (2011) '"Tomorrow There Will Be More of Us": Toxic Postcoloniality in *Animal's People*', in Elizabeth DeLoughrey and George B. Handley (eds) *Postcolonial Ecologies: Literatures of the Environment,* New York: Oxford University Press, 216–235.

——(2010) *Postcolonial Environments: Nature, Culture and the Indian Novel in English,* Houndmills: Palgrave Macmillan.

——(2006) 'Surfing the Second Waves: Amitav Ghosh's Tide Country', *New Formations* 59, 144–57.

Murphy, Patrick (2000) *Farther Afield in the Study of Nature-Oriented Literature,* Charlottesville, VA: University of Virginia Press.

Na'Allah, Abdul Rasheed (ed.) (1998) *Ogoni's Agonies: Ken Saro-Wiwa and the Crisis in Nigeria,* Trenton, NJ: Africa World Press.

Nadesan, Majia Holmer (2008) *Governmentality, Biopower, and Everyday Life*, New York: Routledge.

Naipaul, V.S. (1988) *The Enigma of Arrival*, New York: Vintage.

——(1974) *Miguel Street*, London: Heinemann.

——(1962) *Middle Passage: Impressions of Five Societies, British, French and Dutch, in the West Indies and South America*, London: André Deutsch.

Najita, Susan Y. (2006) *Decolonizing Cultures in the Pacific: Reading History and Trauma in Contemporary Fiction*, London: Routledge.

Narain, Sunita and Anil Agarwal (1991) *Global Warming in an Unequal World: A Case of Environmental Colonialism*, Delhi: Centre for Science and Environment.

Newell, Peter and Matthew Paterson (2010) *Climate Capitalism: Global Warming and the Transformation of the Global Economy*, Cambridge: Cambridge University Press.

Newman, Judith (2007) *Fictions of America: Narratives of Global Empire*, London: Routledge.

——(1988) *Nadine Gordimer*, Manchester: Manchester University Press.

Ngugi wa Thiong'o (1986) *Decolonising the Mind: The Politics of Language in African Literature*, London: James Currey.

Niblett, Michael (2014) 'Time and Tidalectics Wait for No Nam: Catastrophe and Creativity in the Work of Kamau Brathwaite', *Moving Worlds: A Journal of Transcultural Writings* 14, 2, 108–26.

Nichols, Molly (2011) 'Review of Graham Huggan and Helen Tiffin, *Postcolonial Ecocriticism: Literature, Animals, Environment*', *Critical Quarterly* 53, 1, 100–105.

Nixon, Rob (2011) *Slow Violence and the Environmentalism of the Poor*, Cambridge, MA: Harvard University Press.

——(2005) 'Environmentalism and Postcolonialism', in Ania Loomba, Suvir Kaul, Matti Bunzl, Antoinette Burton and Jed Esty (eds) *Postcolonial Studies and Beyond*, Durham, NC: Duke University Press, 233–51.

——(1992) *London Calling: V.S. Naipaul, Postcolonial Mandarin*, Oxford: Oxford University Press.

Nolan, Maggie (1998) 'The Absent Aborigine', *Antipodes* 12, 1, 7–13.

Noonuccal, Oodgeroo (Kath Walker) (1994) 'Speeches', in Kathie Cochrane (ed.) *Oodgeroo*, St Lucia, QLD: University of Queensland Press, 187–229.

——(1970) *My People*, Milton, QLD: Jacaranda Press.

O'Brien, Susie (2009) 'Review of Graham Huggan and Helen Tiffin, *Postcolonial Ecocriticism: Literature, Animals, Environment*', *Postcolonial Text*, online source: http://www.postcolonial.org/index.php/pct/article/download/1239/1034, accessed February 22, 2014.

——(2007) '"Back to the World": Reading Ecocriticism in a Postcolonial Context', in H. Tiffin (ed.) *Five Emus to the King of Siam: Environment and Empire*, Amsterdam: Rodopi, 177–99.

——(2001) 'Articulating a World of Difference: Ecocriticism, Postcolonialism and Globalization', *Canadian Literature* 170/171, 140–58.

Omvedt, Gail (1999) 'An Open Letter to Arundhati Roy', The Friends of the River Narmada, 21 June 2004, online source: www.narmada.org/debates/gail/gail.open.letter.html.

Orwell, George (1989) [1945] *Animal Farm*, Harmondsworth: Penguin.

Overton, John and Regina Scheyvens (eds) (1999) *Strategies for Sustainable Development: Experiences from the Pacific*, London: Zed Books.

Paddle, Robert (2000) *The Last Tasmanian Tiger: The History and Extinction of the Thylacine*, Cambridge: Cambridge University Press.

Parker, Peter (1989) *Ackerley: A Life of J.R. Ackerley*. London: Constable.

Parry, Benita (2004) *Postcolonial Studies: A Materialist Critique*, London: Routledge.

——(1996) 'Speech and Silence in the Fictions of J.M. Coetzee', in Graham Huggan and Stephen Watson (eds) *Critical Perspectives on J.M. Coetzee*, Houndmills: Macmillan, 37–65.

Patterson, Annabel (1987) *Pastoral and Ideology: From Virgil to Valéry*, Berkeley, CA: University of California Press.

Pearson, Wendy Gay (2007) '"Whatever That Is": Hiromi Goto's Body Politics', *SCL/ÉLC* 32, 2, 75–92.

Peet, Richard, Paul Robbins and Michael Watts (eds) (2010) *Global Political Ecology*, London: Routledge.

Pepper, David (1993) *Eco-Socialism: From Deep Ecology to Social Justice*, London: Routledge.

Perrett, Roy W. (1998) 'Indigenous Rights and Environmental Justice', *Environmental Ethics* 20, 4, 377–91.

Plumwood, Val (2003) 'Decolonizing Relationships with Nature', in William H. Adams and Martin Mulligan (eds) *Decolonizing Nature: Strategies for Conservation in a Post-Colonial Era*, London: Earthscan, 51–78.

——(2001) *Environmental Culture: The Ecological Crisis of Reason*, London: Routledge.

Poe, Edgar Allan (1999) [1838] *Narrative of Arthur Gordon Pym*, New York: Penguin.

Poon, Angelia (2006) 'In a Transnational World: Exploring Gendered Subjectivity, Mobility, and Consumption in Anita Desai's *Fasting, Feasting*', *Ariel* 37, 2/3, 33–48.

Porter, Dennis (1991) *Haunted Journeys: Desire and Transgression in European Travel Writing*, Princeton, NJ: Princeton University Press.

Povinelli, Elizabeth (2002) *The Cunning of Recognition: Indigenous Alterities and the Making of Australian Multiculturalism*, Durham, NC: Duke University Press.

Prentice, Chris (2005) 'Riding the Whale? Postcolonialism and Globalization in *Whale Rider*', in Clara Wilson and Janet Wilson (eds) *Global Fissions, Postcolonial Fusions*, Amsterdam: Rodopi: 247–67.

Puar, Jasbir (2008) *Terrorist Assemblages: Homonationalism in Queer Times*, Durham, NC: Duke University Press.

Quayson, Ato (2007) *Aesthetic Nervousness: Disability and the Crisis of Representation*, New York: Columbia University Press.

——(1998) 'For Ken Saro-Wiwa: African Postcolonial Relations Through a Prism of Tragedy', in Abdul Rasheed Na'Allah (ed.) *Ogoni's Agonies: Ken Saro-Wiwa and the Crisis in Nigeria*, 57–80.

Radin, Paul (1956) *The Trickster: A Study in American Indian Mythology*, London: Routledge & Kegan Paul.

Raglon, Rebecca and Marian Scholtmeijer (2007) '"Animals are not Believers in Ecology": Mapping Critical Differences between Environmental and Animal Advocacy Literatures', *Interdisciplinary Studies in Literature and Environment* 14, 2, 123–39.

Rahnema, Majid and Victoria Bawtree (eds) (1997) *The Post-Development Reader*, London: Zed Books.

Randeria, Shalini (2007) 'Global Designs and Local Lifeworlds: Colonial Legacies of Conservation, Disenfranchisement and Environmental Governance in Post-Colonial India', *Interventions* 9, 1, 12–30.

Ratcliffe, Greg and Gerry Turcotte (eds) (2001) *Compr(om)ising Post/Colonialism(s): Challenging Narratives and Practices*, Sydney: Dangaroo.

Read, Peter (2000) *Belonging: Australians, Place and Aboriginal Ownership*, Cambridge: Cambridge University Press.

Regan, Tom (1983) *The Case for Animal Rights*, Berkeley, CA: University of California Press.

Reynolds, Henry (2004) 'Introduction', in Katherine Thomson, *Wonderlands*, Sydney: Currency Press, ix–x.

Rich, Paul (1984) 'Apartheid and the Decline of Civilization Idea: An Essay on Nadine Gordimer's *July's People* and J.M. Coetzee's *Waiting for the Barbarians*', *Research in African Literatures* 15, 3, 365–93.

Rigby, Kate (2013a) 'Confronting Catastrophe in a Warming World', in Louise Westling (ed.) *The Cambridge Companion to Literature and Environment*, Cambridge: Cambridge University Press, 212–225.

——(2013b) 'The Poetics of Decolonisation: Reading *Carpentaria* in a Feminist Ecocritical Frame', in G. Gaard, S. Estok and S. Oppermann (eds) *International Perspectives in Feminist Ecocriticism*, London: Routledge, 120–136.

——(2004) 'Earth, World, Text: On the (Im)possibility of Ecopoeisis', *New Literary History* 35, 3, 427–42.

Robbins, Paul (2011) *Political Ecology: A Critical Introduction*, Oxford: Wiley-Blackwell.

Robie, David (1989) *Blood on Their Banner: Nationalist Struggles in the South Pacific*, London: Zed Books.

Robin, Libby (2008) 'The Eco-humanities as literature: a new genre?' *Australian Literary Studies* 23, 3, 290–304.

Rollin, Bernard (2000) 'Scientific Ideology, Anthropomorphism, Anecdote, and Ethics', *New Ideas in Psychology* 13, 109–18.

Roos, Bonnie and Alex Hunt (eds) (2010) *Postcolonial Green: Environmental Politics and World Narratives*, Charlottesville, VA: University of Virginia Press.

Rose, Deborah Bird (1996) *Nourishing Terrains: Australian Aboriginal Views of Landscape and Wilderness*, Canberra, ACT: Australian Heritage Commission.

Ross, Andrew (1991) *Strange Weather: Culture, Science, and Technology in the Age of Limits*, New York: Verso.

Rowell, Andrew (1996) *Green Backlash: Global Subversion of the Environmental Movement*, London: Routledge.

Rowell, Andrew, James Marriott and Lorne Stockman (2005) *The Next Gulf: London, Washington and Oil Conflict in Nigeria*, London: Constable & Robertson.

Roy, Arundhati (2002) *The Algebra of Infinite Justice*, London: HarperCollins.

——(1999) *The Cost of Living*, London: HarperCollins.

——(1997) *The God of Small Things*, London: HarperCollins.

Rushdie, Salman (1991) *Imaginary Homelands: Essays 1981–1991*, London: Granta.

——(1988) *The Satanic Verses*, London: Viking.

Ryan, Allan J. (1999) *The Trickster Shift: Humour and Irony in Contemporary Native Art*, Vancouver: UBC Press.

Ryel, R. and T. Grasse (1991) 'Marketing Ecotourism: Attracting the Elusive Ecotourist', in T. Whelan (ed.) *Nature Tourism: Managing for the Environment*, Washington, DC: Island Press, 164–86.

Sachs, Wolfgang (ed.) (1997) *The Development Dictionary: A Guide to Knowledge as Power*, London: Zed Books.

Said, Edward (1993) *Culture and Imperialism*, London: Vintage.

——(1983) *The World, the Text, and the Critic*, Cambridge, MA: Harvard University Press.

——(1978) *Orientalism*, New York: Vintage.

Sanders, Mark (2002) 'Disgrace', *Interventions* 4, 3, 395–404.

Saro-Wiwa, Ken (1998) 'We Will Defend Our Oil With Our Blood', in Abdul Rasheed Na'Allah (ed.) *Ogoni's Agonies: Ken Saro-Wiwa and the Crisis in Nigeria*, Trenton, NJ: Africa World Press, 343–59.

——(1995) *A Month and a Day & Letters*, Banbury, Oxford: Ayebia Clarke Publishing Ltd.

——(1992) *Genocide in Nigeria: The Ogoni Tragedy*, Port Harcourt: Saros International.

——(1989) *On a Darkling Plain: An Account of the Nigerian Civil War*, Port Harcourt: Saros International.

Saunders, Kriemild (ed.) (2002) *Feminist Post-Development Thought: Rethinking Modernity, Post-Colonialism and Representation*, London: Zed Books.

Sax, Boria (2009) 'Who Patrols the Human-Animal Divide?' *Minnesota Review* 73/4, 165–70.

Scholtmeijer, Marian (1993) *Animal Victims in Modern Fiction: From Sanctity to Sacrifice*, Toronto: University of Toronto Press.

Schulze-Engler, Frank (1998) 'Civil Critiques: Satire and the Politics of Democratic Transition in Ken Saro-Wiwa's Novels', in Abdul Rasheed Na'Allah (ed.) *Ogoni's Agonies: Ken Saro-Wiwa and the Crisis in Nigeria*, Trenton, NJ: Africa World Press, 285–307.

Scott, Helen (2002) '"Dem Tief, Dem a Dam Tief": Jamaica Kincaid's Literature of Protest', *Callaloo* 25, 3, 977–89.

Selvon, Samuel (1975) *Moses Ascending*, London: Davis-Poynter.

Sen, Amartya (2000) [1999] *Development as Freedom*, New York: Anchor.

Shakespeare, William (2000) [1611] *The Tempest*, Cambridge: Cambridge University Press.

Sharrad, Paul (2003) *Albert Wendt and Pacific Literature: Circling the Void*, Manchester: Manchester University Press.

Sherry, Mark (2007) '(Post)colonising Disability', *Wagadu* 4, online source, http://appweb.cortland.edu/ojs/index.php/Wagadu/article/viewArticle/323/610, accessed February 11, 2014.

Shiva, Vandana (2011) [1999] *Biopiracy: The Plunder of Nature and Knowledge*, Delhi: Natraj Publishers.

——(ed.) (2007) *Manifestos on the Future of Food and Seed*, New York: South End Press.

——(1997) *Biopiracy: the Plunder of Nature and Knowledge*, New York: South End Press.

——(1991) *The Violence of the Green Revolution: Third World Agriculture, Ecology and Politics*, London: Zed Books.

——(1988) *Staying Alive: Women, Ecology and Development*, London: Zed Books.

Shoemaker, Adam (1994) 'Performance for the People', *Australian Literary Studies* 16, 4, 164–77.

Shriver, Lionel (1994) *Game Control*, New York: HarperCollins.

Shukin, Nicole (2009) *Animal Capital: Rendering Life in Biopolitical Times*, Minneapolis, MN: University of Minnesota Press.

Siebert, Charles (2008) 'Family Ties: The Elephants of Sambura', *National Geographic Magazine* (September).

——(2006) 'An Elephant Crackup?', *The New York Times Magazine*, 8 Oct.

Simmons, Diane (1994) *Jamaica Kincaid*, New York: Twayne.

Singer, Peter (1990) *Animal Liberation*, London: Cape.

Singh, Satyajit (1995) 'Introduction', in Jean Drèze, Meera Samson and Satyajit Singh (eds) *The Dam & The Nation: Displacement and Resettlement in the Narmada Valley*, Delhi: Oxford University Press, 1–25.

Sinha, Indra (2007) *Animal's People*, London: Simon and Schuster.

Slaughter, Joseph (2008) *Human Rights, Inc.: The World Novel, Narrative Form, and International Law*, New York: Fordham University Press.

Slemon, Stephen (1992) 'Bones of Contention: Post-Colonialism and the "Cannibal Question"', in Anthony Purdy (ed.), *Literature and the Body*, Amsterdam: Rodopi, 163–78.

——(1988) 'Magic Realism as Post-Colonial Discourse', *Canadian Literature* 116, 9–24.

Smith, Dale (2001) *What the Orangutan Told Alice: A Rain Forest Adventure*, Nevada City, CA: Deer Creek Publishing.

Smith, Zadie (2000) *White Teeth*, London: Faber & Faber.

Snyder, Gary (1995) *A Place in Space: Ethics, Aesthetics, and Watersheds*, Washington, DC: Counterpoint.

Soper, Kate (1995) *What is Nature? Culture, Politics and the Non-human*, Oxford: Blackwell.

Soyinka, Wole (1996) *The Open Sore of a Continent: A Personal Narrative of the Nigerian Crisis*, Oxford: Oxford University Press.

Spiegel, Marjorie (1988) *The Dreaded Comparison: Human and Animal Slavery*, New York: Mirror.

Spivak, Gayatri C. (2003) *Death of a Discipline (The Wellek Lectures)*, New York: Columbia University Press.

——(1999) *A Critique of Postcolonial Reason: Toward a History of the Vanishing Present*, Cambridge, MA: Harvard University Press.

——(1988) 'Can the Subaltern Speak?' in Cary Nelson and Lawrence Grossberg (eds) *Marxism and the Interpretation of Culture*, Chicago: University of Illinois Press, 271–313.

——(1987) *In Other Worlds: Essays in Cultural Politics*, London: Methuen.

Spurlin, William J. (2006) *Imperialism within the Margins: Queer Representation and the Politics of Culture in Southern Africa*, New York: Palgrave.

Spybey, Tony (1996) [1992] *Social Change, Development and Dependency: Modernity, Colonialism and the Development of the West*, Cambridge: Polity Press.

Stow, Randolph (1981) [1979] *Visitants*, London: Picador.

Subramani (2001) 'The Oceanic Imaginary', *The Contemporary Pacific* 13, 1, 149–62.

Sugars, Cynthia (ed.) (2004) *Unhomely States: Theorizing English-Canadian Postcolonialism*, Peterborough, ON: Broadview Press.

Suleri, Sara (1992) *The Rhetoric of English India*, Chicago: University of Chicago Press.

Szasz, Andrew (1994) *Ecopopulism: Toxic Waste and the Movement for Environmental Justice*, Minneapolis, MN: University of Minnesota Press.

Thomas, Keith (1984) *Man and the Natural World: Changing Attitudes in England 1500–1800*, Harmondsworth: Penguin.

Thomson, Katherine (2004) *Wonderlands*, Sydney: Currency Press.

Tiffin, Helen (ed.) (2007a) *Five Emus to the King of Siam: Environment and Empire*, Amsterdam: Rodopi.

——(2007b) 'Pigs, People and Pigoons', in Laurence Simmons and Philip Armstrong (eds) *Knowing Animals*, Boston: Brill, 244–65.

——(2001) 'Unjust Relations: Post-Colonialism and the Species Boundary', in Gary Ratcliffe and Gerry Turcotte (eds) *Compr(om)ising Post/colonialism(s)*, Sydney: Dangaroo Press, 30–41.

——(1995) '"Under the Kiff Kiff Laughter": Stereotype and Subversion in *Moses Ascending* and *Moses Migrating*', in Susheila Nasta and Anna Rutherford (eds) *Tiger's Triumph: Celebrating Samuel Selvon*, Sydney: Dangaroo Press 130–39.

Todorov, Tzvetan (1984) *The Conquest of America: The Question of the Other*, New York: Harper & Row.

Toffoletti, Kim (2004) 'Catastrophic Subjects: Feminism, the Posthuman, and Difference', *third-space* 3, 2, 36 pars., online source: www.thirdspace.ca/articles/3_2_toffol letti.htm, accessed February 12, 2014.

Tomlinson, John (1999) *Globalization and Culture*, Cambridge: Polity Press.

Tompkins, Joanne (2006) *Unsettling Space: Contestations in Contemporary Australian Theatre*, Houndmills: Palgrave.

Trexler, Adam and Adeline Johns-Putra (2011) 'Climate change in literature and literary criticism', *Wiley Interdisciplinary Review: Climate Change* 2, 2, 185–200.

Trigger, David and Gareth Griffiths (eds) (2004) *Disputed Territories: Land, Culture and Identity in Settler Societies*, Hong Kong: Hong Kong University Press.

Twain, Mark (1970) [1905] *King Leopold's Soliloquy*, New York: International Publishers.

Vadde, Aarthi (2011) 'Cross-Pollination: Ecocriticism, Zoocriticism, Post-colonialism', *Contemporary Literature* 52, 3, 565–573.

Van Fossen, Anthony (2005) *South Pacific Futures: Oceania Toward 2010*, Brisbane: The Foundation for Development Corporation.

Viswanathan, Gauri (1990) *Masks of Conquest: Literary Studies and British Rule in India*, London: Faber & Faber.

Vital, Anthony (2008) 'Toward an African Ecocriticism: Postcolonialism, Ecology and *Life & Times of Michael K*', *Research in African Literatures* 39, 1, 87–106.

Voss, A.E. (1977) 'A Generic Approach to the South African Novel in English', *UCT Studies in English* 7, 110–21.

Walcott, Derek (1998) *What the Twilight Says: Essays*, London: Faber & Faber.

Waldau, Paul (2013) *Animal Studies; An Introduction*, New York: Oxford University Press.

Waldby, Catherine (2000) *The Visible Human Project: Informatic Bodies and Posthuman Medicine*, London: Routledge.

Walker, Shirley (1991) *Flame and Shadow: A Study of Judith Wright's Poetry*, St Lucia, QLD: University of Queensland Press.

Ward, Herbert (1910) *A Voice from the Congo: Comprising Stories, Anecdotes and Descriptive Notes*, London: Heinemann.

Wark, McKenzie (1994) 'Third Nature', *Cultural Studies* 8, 1, 115–32.

Warren, Karen and Nisvan Erkal (eds) (1997) *Women, Culture, Nature*, Bloomington, IN: Indiana University Press.

Wasserman, Renata (1984), 'Re-inventing the New World: Cooper and Alencar', *Comparative Literature* 36, 2, 130–45.

Waters, Anita M. (2006) *Planning the Past: Heritage Tourism and Post-Colonial Politics at Port Royal*, Lanham, MD: Lexington Books.

Watts, Michael (1994) 'Oil as Money: The Devil's Excrement and the Spectacle of Black Gold', in S. Corbridge, R. Martin and N. Thrift (eds) *Money, Power and Space*, Oxford: Blackwell, 406–45.

Webster, Steven (1998) *Patrons of Maori Culture: Power, Theory, and Ideology in the Maori Renaissance*, Dunedin, NZ: University of Otago Press.

Wedde, Ian (1986) *Symmes Hole*, Auckland, NZ: Penguin.

Wegerif, Marc, Bev Russell and Irma Grundling (2005) *Still Searching for Security: The Reality of Farm Dweller Evictions in South Africa*, Johannesburg: Social Surveys and Polokwane North: Nkuzi Development Association.

Weil, Kari (2010) 'A Report on the Animal Turn', *differences* 21, 2, 1–23.

Wendt, Albert (1999a) *The Best of Albert Wendt's Short Stories*, Auckland: Random House.

——(1999b) *Flying-Fox in a Freedom Tree and Other Stories*, Auckland: Longman Paul.

——(1992) *Black Rainbow*, Auckland: Penguin.

——(1983) 'Towards a New Oceania', in Guy Amirthanayagam (ed.) *Writers in East–West Encounter*, London: Methuen, 202–15.

——(1977) *Pouliuli*, Auckland: Penguin.

Wenzel, Jennifer (2011) 'Forest Fictions and Ecological Crises: Reading the Politics of Survival in Mahasweta Devi's "Dhowli"', in Elizabeth DeLoughrey and George B. Handley (eds) *Postcolonial Ecologies: Literatures of the Environment*, New York: Oxford University Press, 136–155.

——(2000) 'The Pastoral Promise and the Political Imperative: The Plaasroman Tradition in an Era of Land Reform', *Modern Fiction Studies* 46, 1, 90–113.

White, Patrick (1997) [1976] *A Fringe of Leaves*, London: Vintage.

Wicomb, Zoe (2000) 'Translation and Coetzee's *Disgrace*', *Journal of Literary Studies* 18, 3/4. 209–33.

Williams, Mark (1990) *Leaving the Highway: Six Contemporary New Zealand Novelists*, Auckland: Auckland University Press.

Williams, Raymond (1985) *Keywords: A Vocabulary of Culture and Society*, New York: Oxford University Press.

——(1983) [1958] *Culture and Society: 1780–1950*, New York: Columbia University Press.

——(1973) *The Country and the City*, London: Chatto & Windus.

Williams, Robyn (2001) *2007: A True Story, Waiting to Happen*, Sydney: Hodder.

Wilson, Alexander (1992) *The Culture of Nature: North American Landscape from Disney to the Exxon Valdez*, Oxford: Blackwell.

Wilson, Rob and Wimal Dissanayake (eds) (1996) *Global/Local: Cultural Production and the Transnational Imaginary*, Durham, NC: Duke University Press.

Winter, T. (2007) *Post-Conflict Heritage, Postcolonial Tourism: Tourism, Politics and Development at Angkor*, London: Routledge.

Wiwa, Ken (2000) *In the Shadow of a Saint*, London: Doubleday.

Wolf, Naomi (1991) *The Beauty Myth: How Images of Beauty are Used Against Women*, New York: Anchor-Doubleday.

Wolfe, Cary (2013) *Before the Law: Humans and Other Animals in a Biopolitical Frame*, Chicago: University of Chicago Press.

——(2007) *Animal Rites: American Culture, the Discourse of Species, and Posthumanist Theory*, Chicago: University of Chicago Press.

——(ed.) (2003) *Zoontologies: The Question of the Animal*, Minneapolis, MN: University of Minnesota Press.

——(1998) 'Old Orders for New: Ecology, Animal Rights, and the Poverty of Humanism', *Diacritics* 28, 2, 21–40.

Worster, Donald (1994) [1977] *Nature's Economy: A History of Ecological Ideas* (2nd edn), Cambridge: Cambridge University Press.

Wright, Alexis (2013) *The Swan Book*, Artarmon, NSW: Giramondo.

——(2011) 'Deep Weather', *Meanjin* 70, 2, 70–83.

——(2007) *Carpentaria*, Artarmon, NSW: Giramondo.

Wright, Derek (1992) 'Black Earth, White Myth: Coetzee's Michael K', *Modern Fiction Studies* 38, 2, 435–44.

Wright, Judith (1996) *A Human Pattern: Selected Poems*, Watsons Bay, NSW: Imprint Books.

Wright, Laura (2010) *"Wilderness into Civilized Shapes": Reading the Postcolonial Environment*, Athens, GA: University of Georgia Press.

——(1991) *Born of the Conquerors*, Canberra, ACT: Aboriginal Studies Press.

——(1975) *Because I Was Invited*, Melbourne: Oxford University Press.

Young, Robert (2003) *Postcolonialism: A Very Short Introduction*, Oxford: Oxford University Press.

——(2001) *Postcolonialism: An Historical Introduction*, Oxford: Blackwell.

——(1999) '"Dangerous and Wrong": Shell, Intervention and the Politics of Transnational Companies', *Interventions* 1, 3, 439–64.

——(1995) *Colonial Desire: Hybridity in Theory, Culture and Race*, London: Routledge.

Zamora, Lois Parkinson and Wendy B. Faris (1995) *Magical Realism: Theory, History, Community*, Durham, NC: Duke University Press.

Zoellner, Robert (1973) *The Salt-Sea Mastodon: A Reading of Moby-Dick*, Berkeley, CA: University of California Press.

Index

green cultural studies, and
ecocriticism 25n6
Green Grass, Running Water (King)
21, 183–86, 196–97
green imperialism 246
Green Imperialism (Grove) 238,
244–45
green postcolonialism 23n2
'Green Revolution' 4
Grove, Richard 3, 147n8, 203, 238,
244–45
Guha, Ramachandra 1–2, 22n1,
245–46, 248, 250
Guiana 126
guilt: liberal 75; postcolonial 95n14;
white Australian 102, 107–9
Gulliver's Travels (Swift) 239

Handley, George B. 243
The Handmaid's Tale (Atwood) 230
Haraway, Donna 22, 226–27, 234–35
Harris, Wilson 96–97n21
Hastings, Governor Warren 165
haunting 146n2
Hau'ofa, Epeli 19, 55, 61
Hawaiki 65–66
Heart of Darkness (Conrad) 21,
159–62, 164–67, 172, 186
The Heart of Redness (Mda) 252
hegemonic centrism 4–5
Heidegger, Martin 122
Heise, Ursula 81, 2n8, 93n11, 96n17,
249
Hemingway, Ernest 239
Himalayas, peasant revolt of 1970s
in 1
Hindu thought 250–51
historical phase (Horkheimer and
Adorno) 203–4, 224–25
history: alterity of 243; imaginative
transformation of 133, 141
Hodge, Bob 147–48n11
hollow earth theory 62–63
home, Aboriginal words for 138
homo oeconomicus 65
Hopeful Monsters (Goto) 222n4
Hughes, Lotte 240
Hulme, Keri 252
human-animal communication *see*
communication, inter-species

human/animal divide: changing views
of 239, 246; Coetzee and Derrida
on 197; difference and similarity in
172; encounters across 221n3;
foundational texts of 180; in *The
Hungry Tide* 206–7; in literature
21, 166–68, 247; masculinist/
colonialist attitudes to 230;
materialist understanding of 12;
monkeys and apes in 219n3; and
posthumanism 228; and power
169–70; questioning vii, 186,
218–19
human-animal hybrids 181–82, 209, 226
humanism: and ecological sentiment
104; in *Oryx and Crake* 232; as
rationale of imperialism 22;
suspicion of 227–28; in *White
Teeth* 234; *see also* new humanism
humanities: and ecology 16; and
posthumanism 229–30
humanity: abused in humanity's name
227; denial of 145
human/nature divide 6, 122, 224–25
humanocentrism *see*
anthropocentrism
Human Rights, Inc. (Slaughter) 25n8
humans: category of 18, 26n8; as part
of animal being 183
human supremacy *see*
anthropocentrism
humility, ironical 99
The Hungry Tide (Ghosh) 21–22,
185, 190–91, 202–8, 240
Hunt, Alex 249
hunting 10–11, 162–64, 247
hybridity, celebratory 234
hyena 189
hyperobjects 80, 95n16

Ibo people 162, 166
ideology: bourgeois 99; of empire and
genre 15; pastoral 100, 119; of
possession 135; white-settler 119
*If This Is Your Land, Where Are
Your Stories?* (Chamberlin) 136
Ihimaera, Witi 19, 58, 65–67
'An Image of Africa' (Achebe) 159
imagination: moral 243; sympathetic
212

imperialism: and classification of
nature 248; creolised history of
87–88; and development 32;
Euro-100; globalisation as 25n4;
and humanism 229; and hunting
164, 247; new 91n4; and
postcolonialism 2–3, 11, 22n1;
power to narrate under 182; and
the sublime 147n7; writing of
wrongs of 21–22; *see also*
ecological imperialism
independence, of Pacific Islands 56
India: conservation pressure on 205;
forestry in 240; importance of
dams to 48; Narmada Valley
Development Project 48–49;
nuclear bomb testing 51–52;
partition of 203; postcolonial
development in 1–2; privatisation
of energy sources in 48; Roy's
critique of state 249
Indians, American *see* Native
Americans
indigeneity: meaning of 137; theories
of 6
indigenous core 74
indigenous cultures: crisis of 54–55;
erasure of 184; European views of
5, 7; relation to modernity 59, 111;
self-monitoring of 35
indigenous justice 104
indigenous knowledge 245, 249
indigenous land: appropriation of 3;
title to 136–37, 139–40, 142, 144
indigenous literature 137
indigenous peoples: displacement of
13, 18, 69, 102, 137; and
environmental values 142, 148n13,
239, 241, 243
indigenous theatre/performance 20,
137–39, 144–45
Indonesia: Dutch environmental
legislation in 204; nature reserves
in 154
industrialisation 1
inequalities, human 18
infinite rehearsal 87, 96–97n21
Ingold, Tim 96n18
inheritance 115
instrumentalism 104

interconnectedness: ecological
141–42; global 78, 82; human and
animal 126; settler and indigenous
103, 139; of social and
environmental struggle 92n6;
uneven 131
'Interfaces' (Wright) 108
International Monetary Fund (IMF) 31
International Year for the World's
Indigenous People 40
Iron Triangle 49, 51
irony, and pastoral 101, 136
irreducibility, fiction of 152
Ishtar, Zohl de 58–59
The Island of Dr. Moreau (Wells)
230, 239
island paradises 127

Johnson, Lyndon 30
Jumbo 170, 179n9
justice, environmental and social 3,
20, 35, 68, 131, 248–49

The Kappa Child (Goto) 222n4
Kenya 246–47
Kete, Kathleen 246
Kincaid, Jamaica 19, 71, 75, 78–79,
127
King, Thomas 21, 183–85, 196
King Leopold's Soliloquy (Twain)
159
kinships, atrophied 66
knowledge/knowledge-systems,
alternative 20, 66, 85; *see also*
indigenous knowledge
Krech, Shepard 148n13
Kullark (Davis) 138–39

Laffey, Mark 157n4
'Lament for Passenger Pigeons'
(Wright) 108
land: Aboriginal title to *see*
indigenous land, title to; colonial
ideologies of 137, 187; connection
with labour 131; cultural attitudes
to 20, 119–20; empty 184; nativist
and developmentalist
understandings of 71–72; poetic
reading of 111; protection of
commons 73–74; in refugee theatre

144; resisting colonisation 114, 116;
settler attachment to 98, 102–3,
106, 108, 121
landlords 100, 119
land reform 146n4
landscape: carceral 122; Caribbean
132–33; in Naipaul 128–30; silent
114–15; uncanny 138
Langton, Marcia 239
language: of animals 168, 170–71,
174–75; in Coetzee 125; of
development 246; in *Heart of
Darkness* 161; indigenous 173; loss
of 137, 140; Māori 74; in *Monkey
Planet* 220n3; scientific 95n17; sign
209–10, 219n3; teaching 187; and
understanding 15; *see also* English
language
Lawrence, D. H. 239
Lazarus, Neil 22n1
Lee, Ang 221n4
Leopold II, King of Belgium 159,
178n1, 178n4
libertinism 118–19
Life of Pi (Martel) 21, 189–93, 201–2,
201n3, 252
linguistic cognition 198, 201
literary criticism: Bartosch on 240;
language of 95n17; as political 36;
and racism/speciesism 166; and
tourism 70–71
literary genres, animal-specific 156
literary singularity 248
literary tourism 95n14
literature/postcolonial literature ix–x,
12–14, 16–17, 20, 84, 86, 121;
animal abuse in 21–22; and
development 35; leading role in
humanities 16–17; nature in 13; in
postcolonial ecocriticism ix–x, 12,
14, 25n6; pursuit of justice 20,
23n2; *see also* writing
The Lives of Animals (Coetzee) 21,
172, 177, 197–99, 201, 212
'Living With The Weather' (Bate)
95n16
Lo, Jacqueline 148n14
local: construction of the
69–70, 92–93n10; fetishisation
of 65

The Location of Culture (Bhabha)
185
London Calling (Nixon) 134
Lowenthal, David 244
luxury conservation 117

Maathai, Wangari 238, 246–47, 249
Mabo ruling 147n10
machines, intelligent 227
MacKenzie, John 162–65, 244, 247
magic realism 83–84, 86–87
Magome, Hector 239
Maharashtra 48
man-eaters 205–6
Māori/Māori Renaissance 65, 71–72,
74, 93n13, 137, 142
market, sustainability of 34
Marshall Islands 56, 59–61
Martel, Yann 21, 189, 191, 193,
201–2, 239, 252
Marx, Karl 179n8
Marxism: and Caribbean pastoral
128; and environmentalism 22n1;
and postcolonial studies 2, 14, 91n4
Marzec, Robert 92n8
MAS (mainstream animal studies)
xn1
masculinism 251
Masson, Jeffrey Moussaieff 178–79n8
materialism, and ecological balance
108
materials and ideas, relationship
between 6–8
matriarchy 164, 171
Mau Mau rebellion 246
McKay, Robert 197–98
Mda, Zakes 21, 138, 147n9, 213,
215–16, 252
meat 194; *see also* carnivory
mechanical order 225–26
Meinig, Donald 244
Meḻaḻ (Barclay) 58, 60–62
Melville, Herman 62–63, 186, 200,
215, 217
memory: folk 133; personal 60;
scholarly interest in 212; *see also*
cultural memory; elephant memory
mercantilism 82, 87
metaphorisation 94n13
metonymic shift 77